# BRIDGING THE STRAIT

## Taiwan, China, and the Prospects for Reunification

# STUDIES ON CONTEMPORARY TAIWAN

The Studies on Contemporary Taiwan Series features academic works by Chinese scholars from Taiwan on the island's key political, economic, social, and cultural issues. The works for the series were selected from outstanding doctoral research produced by Taiwanese scholars while pursuing degrees at overseas universities.

In what ways does the China reunification issue affect Taiwan? How has increased democratization affected policymaking in Taiwan? What are the prospects for further democratization in Taiwan? The authors, having studied abroad, bring a unique international perspective to these and other critical questions surrounding their own nation's development and future prospects.

The books in this series also have benefited from the review and input of distinguished members of the international community of Taiwan scholars, who have helped the authors and editors to refine and develop the research for publication.

# BRIDGING THE STRAIT

## Taiwan, China, and the Prospects for Reunification

Hsin-hsing Wu

HONG KONG
OXFORD UNIVERSITY PRESS
OXFORD NEW YORK
1994

Oxford University Press

Oxford   New York   Toronto
Delhi   Bombay   Calcutta   Madras   Karachi
Kuala Lumpur   Singapore   Hong Kong   Tokyo
Nairobi   Dar es Salaam   Cape Town
Melbourne   Auckland   Madrid

and associated companies in
Berlin   Ibadan

Oxford is a trade mark of Oxford University Press

First published 1994

© Oxford University Press 1994

The 'Studies on Contemporary Taiwan' series is published in
cooperation with Sinorama Magazine, Taipei, Taiwan,
Republic of China

British Library Cataloguing in Publication Data
available

Library of Congress Cataloging-in-Publication Data
Wu, Hsin-hsing, 1953–
Bridging the Strait : Taiwan, China, and the prospects for
reunification / Hsin-hsing Wu.
p.   cm. — (Studies on contemporary Taiwan)
Includes bibliographical references and index.
ISBN 0-19-585765-8 : $29.00
1. Taiwan—Politics and government—1988–   2. China—Politics and
government—1976–   3. Chinese reunification question, 1949–
I. Title.   II. Series.
IN PROCESS
951.05'8—dc20   93-42311
CIP

ISBN 0-19-585765-8

Printed in Hong Kong
Published by Oxford University Press (Hong Kong) Ltd
18/F Warwick House, Taikoo Place, 979 King's Road, Quarry Bay, Hong Kong

*To My Parents Wu Teh-jun and Chen Li-chiao*

# Preface

CHINA has been divided for forty-four years. The Republic of China (ROC) on Taiwan and the People's Republic of China (PRC) on the mainland refuse to recognize each other and each government officially proclaims itself as the sole representative of the whole Chinese nation in the international community. The two governments also claim each other's territory as their own. This constitutes the so-called 'two China issue'. In the past decade, however, the situation has been changing, albeit slowly at first. The PRC has launched its 'peaceful offensives', a series of proposals for negotiating with the ROC starting in 1979 and Taipei finally made an initial positive move in 1987, allowing Taiwan Chinese to contact their mainland compatriots for humanitarian, national interest and commercial reasons.

This book focuses on the attitudes and policies of the so-called 'two Chinas' toward each other from 1979 to June 1992 and the connection between the ROC's domestic political development and the resolution of the two China issue. Six main variables, specifically the economic and political systems of the PRC and the ROC, Taiwan's politics, and the Taiwan Independence Movement, have been selected as indicators to help analyze and predict the evolution of the two China issue.

This book suggests that the gradual increase of transactions and communications between the two Chinas since 1987 should contribute to the 'normalization' of relations between the two Chinas. Nevertheless, these transactions and communications are not expected to lead to the political reunification of the two Chinas in the foreseeable future due to four main obstacles: the PRC's intention to localize and isolate the ROC internationally; the PRC's refusal to exclude the use of military force against the ROC; the difference between the two Chinas' living standards and political philosophies; and the Taiwan Independence Movement.

This book also finds that current domestic political trends in the ROC suggest that the ROC is gradually steering away from the course of reunification. The Taiwan Chinese may not press for independence if the ruling Kuomintang fulfills its promise concerning political reform and is able to break through Taiwan's international isolation. Finally, this book forecasts that the PRC might eventually reach a tacit understanding and agree to co-exist with the ROC in the international community of nations in the short term while retaining the hope of reunification with the ROC in the longer term.

It is difficult to express sufficiently my gratitude for the warm encouragement, understanding and help which I have received while writing this book. It is due to the support of so many people that I have enjoyed piecing together some of the thousands of bits of information into what I hope is a meaningful contribution to the scholarship on this important issue.

Special thanks go to Professor Leslie T. Holmes, Head of the Department of Political Science, University of Melbourne, Australia. I am deeply indebted to his assistance, direction and advice during my research in Australia. I am also grateful to Professor C. L. Chiou, Department of Government, University of Queensland, and Professor I. F. H. Wilson, Department of Political Science, Australia National University, for their critical views and comments.

I am grateful to Dr. Yu-ming Shaw, a former spokesperson of the Government of the Republic of China, and Mrs. Alice Yu Sun, Publisher of Taipei's Commercial Times, for their encouragement. And I would like to thank Ms. Wei-yu Liu, Assistant of the Institute of Social Science Studies, National Cheng-Kung University, for her conscientious reading of the manuscript before it was submitted to the publisher.

Hsin-hsing Wu
Tainan, Taiwan
Republic of China

# Contents

# List of Tables

# List of Appendices

# Abbreviations

Concerning the Republic of China:
  DPP: Democratic Progressive Party
  KMT: Kuomintang
  ROC: Republic of China
  TAPPS: Tang-Wai Association of Public Policy Studies

Concerning the People's Republic of China:
  CCP: Chinese Communist Party
  CPPCC: Chinese People's Political Consultative Conference
  NPC: National People's Congress
  PRC: People's Republic of China
  SAR: Special Administrative Region

# Note on Romanization and Terminology

IN 1978, the State Council of the People's Republic of China announced that it had decided to use the Chinese phonetic alphabet, called 'Pinyin', to standardize the romanization of the names of people and places in China. The change went into effect on 1 January 1979. Hence the old spelling system (Wade-Giles)—including spellings such as Mao Tse-tung or Teng Hsiao-ping—was changed.

Nevertheless, romanization of Chinese names and terms in this book is determined by context. Discussions involving the affairs of the People's Republic of China use the new Pinyin system, which is officially accepted by the Beijing Government; discussions involving the affairs of the Republic of China use the old Wade-Giles system, which is accepted by the Taipei Government.

Due to the politically sensitive issues of recognition and governmental legitimacy, this book uses a neutral approach in data collection, reference selection and terminology. Overtly politically biased terms are avoided. 'The People's Republic of China' (PRC) is used instead of 'Red China' or 'Communist China' and 'The Republic of China' (ROC) instead of 'Free China' or 'Chinese Taipei'.

While using the official respective titles to name the two Chinas, this book (for convenient reasons, such as avoidance of name repetition) periodically refers to the PRC as 'mainland China', 'the mainland' or 'Beijing' and the ROC as 'Island China', 'Taiwan' or 'Taipei'.

# Introduction

IT has been more than four decades since political control of the Chinese mainland changed hands from the Republic of China (ROC) to the People's Republic of China (PRC); however, the rivalry, struggle and mutual suspicion between these two rival governments has not diminished with time. Each side claims that they represent the whole Chinese nation, territory and population. On one side, the ROC on Taiwan has continuously—at least in official pronouncements—maintained that they would recover the mainland, and on the other, the PRC on the mainland has consistently wanted to reunify Taiwan with the mainland. Four principal factors need to be noted when analyzing this situation.

(1) Common Heritage. Both Chinas share the same cultural and historical tradition. From the past history of dynastic cycles, they believe that China must be reunited after a certain period of time. Neither side dares to bear the historical indictment of abandoning part of China's territory. As Deng Xiaoping said explicitly, 'historians will write better of those people who have strived and worked hard for the glorious task of reunification'.[1] In a similar vein, according to Dr. Yu-ming Shaw, a former spokesperson of the ROC Government, has also said that 'since ancient times, the notion of one unified China has been deeply embedded in the minds of all Chinese. . . . Under the burden of Chinese history neither the ROC nor the PRC could dare to deviate from the one-China concept and still claim legitimacy as a Chinese entity'.[2] These statements reveal the two Chinas share a common heritage about the tradition of a unified China.

(2) Common Revolutionary Goals. Both the Kuomintang (KMT) and the Chinese Communist Party (CCP) regard themselves as revolutionary parties. The former proclaims itself to be 'revolutionary democratic party',[3] while the latter espouses belief in a theory of uninterrupted revolution. When the founding father of the ROC, Dr. Sun Yat-sen (1866–1925), died in the early stages of the Republic, he pointed out to his people in his last will and testament that the purpose of the 1911 revolution—of rejuvenating the Chinese nation—had not yet been fulfilled: 'our comrades must still continue to strive to their utmost' to attain this cherished goal.[4]

According to Professor Wang Gungwu, these words could be interpreted differently at various times: in the 1920s, the words were a clarion call to fight against the warlords, while during the 1930s to early 1940s, the clause meant to construct a New China and to fight against the Japanese.[5] Nowadays, the term 'revolution' means the reunification of the two Chinas so that a unified China can attain 'a position of freedom and equality among the family of nations'.[6]

For its part, the ROC has been trying to introduce a political system based on Dr. Sun's 'Three Principles of the People' back to the mainland. Until this goal is achieved, the revolution is indeed considered far from complete.[7] To the PRC, the task of reunification with Taiwan has become an symbol of China's full independence. Deng Xiaoping has indicated that when the two sides of the Taiwan Strait have reached agreement about reunification, 'it will be officially announced. But foreign interference in reunification absolutely will not be permitted, because it would only indicate that China has not won complete independence'.[8]

(3) Conflict Between Ideologies. The ROC to a considerable extent is a capitalist system, while the PRC advocates communism. Guidelines for both Chinese governments regard their doctrines as policies that can serve as a beacon to lead the Chinese people into a promising future. In the CCP's eyes, capitalism implies a state of criminal exploitation, corruption, and despair devoid of social justice and equality. The moribund social system of capitalism therefore must be eradicated by violent measures and replaced by socialism. Being disciples of Marx and Lenin, Beijing's leaders undoubtedly regard the ROC as a remnant of capitalism and would do anything to get rid of it and reunify Taiwan under communism. The PRC's leader, Deng Xiaoping, has even said that 'Communist China can never learn from or import the capitalist system'.[9]

After forty years, since the end of armed conflict in 1949 the ROC's achievements, especially in the economic sphere, have earned international acclaim. According to the Marxist theory of determinism, those countries that are highly industrialized and rich can more readily evolve into a communist society than low income, under-developed or developing countries.[10] If the theory is correct, the ROC would become a socialist society before the PRC as the ROC is more advanced industrially. The Government of the ROC insists that

implementing their ideology results in the preferable alternative and hope that their example 'serves to prod the PRC to
change and reform' its system; thus the ROC claim they are
the hope of the whole Chinese people.[11]

(4) *Realpolitik*. The author believes that the current situation
between the PRC and the ROC is the continuation of the civil
war of forty-three years ago by different means, in which both
the KMT and the CCP fought not only for political power, but
also for cultural and political legitimacy. So far these sources
of contention have not been resolved and are the underlying
principal obstacles to the resolution of the China issue. Since
1979, a new phase in the relationship of the two Chinas has
begun with the PRC launching a series of diplomatic initiatives aimed at bringing about a negotiated reunification with
the ROC (the 'Peaceful Offensive'). At the same time, the PRC
has threatened to use military force should the ROC continue
to refuse to enter into negotiations. Notwithstanding this threat,
a more relaxed atmosphere prevails, which can be ascribed
to the following factors.

After forty years, both Beijing and Taipei have recognized
the political reality that one cannot deny the existence of the
other; meanwhile, on both sides, people are weary of hearing
about perpetual civil conflict. Past experience and the present
situation have clearly domonstrated that the declared policy
of 'Recovery of the Mainland' on the part of the ROC and
'Liberating Taiwan by Force' by the PRC are unrealistic. There
appears to be a mutual recognition on the part of both Chinas
that the time has come to solve their differences on a rational and practical basis.

The climate of *detente* in the global arena since the 1970s
and the collapse of Communism in Eastern Europe and the
USSR have had a direct impact on the relations of the two
Chinas. The United States of America (USA) has contributed
to the relaxation of relations between the two Chinas. Although
the USA has constantly denied any involvement in the China
issue, its policies have effected some moderation and acted
as a buffer on the two Chinas' behaviour and relations.

In order to carry out its grandiose 'four modernizations' in
agriculture, industry, national defence and science and technology, Beijing needs a peaceful environment to concentrate
on implementing the necessary programmes and on managing the internal problems which ensued from pursuing the

'open door' policy. In short, the situation since 1979 in the Taiwan Strait is that 'tensions are at an all-time low' or at least in comparison to the last forty years.[12]

The change of leadership in both Chinas since the mid-1970s has also contributed to the relaxation of relations across the Taiwan Strait. When the two bitter opponents Chiang Kai-shek and Mao Zedong died in 1975 and 1976 respectively, that part of the antagonism between the two Chinas which was derived from these two leaders ended. The new leaders in both Chinas were more pragmatic in handling the two Chinas' relations, being more concerned with economic development than with the struggle of ideologies.

Since 1986, internal developments in Taiwan have impacted positively on the relationship between Beijing and Taipei. The ROC Government has lifted martial law, which had stood 37 years, and allowed its people to visit their relatives on the mainland. In the meantime, Taipei also has permitted mainland Chinese to come to Taiwan on a case-by-case basis for family reunions and looking after their sick relatives. Trade relations between the two Chinas have been rapidly expanding. Cultural and academic exchanges have also been launched. The net result of these developments is that the Taiwan Chinese have been struck with the so-called 'Mainland China Fever'.

On 20 May 1990, ROC President Lee Teng-hui in his inaugural address declared that if the PRC can recognize the overall world trend and the common hope of all Chinese, implement political democracy and a free enterprise economic system, renounce the use of military force in the Taiwan Strait and not interfere with the ROC's development of foreign relations on the basis of a one-China policy, the ROC would be willing, on a basis of equality, to establish channels of communication, and encourage free academic, cultural, economic, trade, scientific, and technological exchanges, with the PRC in order to lay a foundation of mutual respect, peace, and prosperity. President Lee said that 'we hope then, when objective conditions are suitable, we will be able to discuss our national reunification, based on the common will of the Chinese people on both sides of the Taiwan Straits'.[13] All of these developments would certainly increase the possibility of a peaceful reunification of China.

In the meantime, the political situation in Taiwan has changed dramatically since 1986. Opposition parties have been allowed to form and press censorship has also been lifted. The ruling KMT can no longer monopolize the formulation of the ROC's mainland China policy thanks to the irreversible trend of democratization in Taiwan. Some members of the main opposition party, the Democratic Progressive Party (DPP), even suggest that the possibility of declaring Taiwan's independence and a permanent separation of Taiwan from the China mainland is not impossible. This stance is in direct opposition to the current position of long standing of the two Chinas: that there is only one China, and Taiwan is a part of China. In the 1986 election for the Legislative Yuan in the ROC, the new party gained 23 per cent of the votes and proclaimed their victory as a fledgling party. More recently, the new party won 31.83 per cent of the votes cast in the 1992 election. Thus the DPP and its policies will play an important role in the evolution of a resolution of the two China issue, and the development of the relations between the two sides will become more unpredictable.

## Purpose of the Study

From the above, the nature of the two China issue began to change after 1979. The relationship between the two Chinas has changed from one characterized by hostility to *rapprochement*. The means to resolve this issue have also changed from declared intentions to use force to actual peaceful means, and the approach to solving this issue involves not only the notion of reunification but also independence as the question of whether Taiwan should reunify with the mainland or declare its independence has become a topic of intense debate within the ROC.

Two main questions need to be addressed. Is the *rapprochement* between the two Chinas to continue in the future and eventually lead to a peaceful resolution of the two China issue? Contributing factors to peaceful resolution must be considered. A corollary issue is if peaceful reunification is not the final result, then why? The other critical question is what are the implications for and impact on the two China issue of the ROC's domestic political development? The crux of the issue is whether the political transformation within the ROC will steer Taiwan away from reunification?

So far, numerous publications and seminars have analyzed Beijing's new policy towards Taiwan since 1979. However, few books exist which systematically examine the emerging political situation in Taiwan, especially the linkage between Taiwan's political development and the resolution of the China issue. Since the two China issue is one that needs both the PRC and ROC to solve, merely overemphasizing Beijing's viewpoints and neglecting Taiwan's in this regard might distort the nature of the issue itself and certainly would not assist in resolving the problem. Therefore, a study on the two China issue from the perspective of the ROC becomes necessary. Through this book the author hopes to provide another approach for those who are interested in Chinese affairs to gain a better understanding and a broader appreciation of the issue, and perhaps eventually contribute to the resolution of the two China issue.

As discussed above, 1979 marked the watershed in the two Chinas' relations. *Rapprochement* and peace replaced hostility. 1986 was also an important year, for both the ROC's domestic political development, and the course of the two China issue. In 1991, Taipei sent a non-official delegation to the PRC to meet Beijing's leaders, the first of its kind since 1949. On 16 July 1992, the ROC enacted the 'Special Regulations on the Legal Relations between the People of Taiwan and the Mainland'. From Taipei's perspective, this law has legalized and institutionalized the exchanges that occurred between the two Chinas since 1987. This legislation reveals Taipei's intention to normalize relations between the two Chinas. Therefore, this book will focus on two principal areas.

1.   The attitude and policies of the PRC and the ROC toward each other from 1979 to June 1992;

2.   The course of the ROC's domestic political development from 1979 to June 1992 and implications for the two China issue.

## Integration Theory and the Two China Issue

Approaches to the study of international politics inevitably reflect, at least to some extent, the background and preferences of analysts. The theoretical framework selected for this analysis is the integration theory of international relations,[14] because, in contrast to other theoretical approaches, the main thrust of theory, emphasizing peaceful means to political unification, more closely approximates the relations across the Taiwan Straits since 1979, that is, integration of Taiwan and the mainland through peaceful rather than coercive means.

Three different schools in the theory of integration have been categorized by Ernst B. Haas as follows: federalism, communications, and neo-functionalism.[15] In this book, some concepts of integration advanced by Karl W. Deutsch, representing the communications school, and Ernst B. Haas, from the school of neo-functionalism, are employed as the analytical framework because their theories are useful to understand the process of the two Chinas' integration.

Communications theorists, such as Karl W. Deutsch, Roger Cobb, Charles Elder, and Donald J. Puchala, have used transaction flows as one set of variables to assess the level of integration in Europe.[16] They have hypothesized that the study of quantitative densities of transactions is the first step towards estimating the degree to which people are connected with each other. Simply speaking, they gathered data on a large number of what they consider integrative indicators, including mail flows, trade, tourism, and telephone calls, as the basis to measure and compare the process of integration. The theory of this school's suggests that an intensive pattern of communication between countries will result in a closer community among these countries if loads and capabilities to manage these increased transaction flows remain balanced. In the case of the two Chinas, the transaction flows, such as the contacts, trade, and investment between the two Chinas can be monitored as a set of variables to assess the level of integration between Taiwan and the mainland.

Deutsch states that the main tasks of integration are to maintain peace among national units; to attain greater multipurpose capabilities of a community of nations (this can be indicated at least roughly by a community's total gross national product (GNP), per-capita GNP, and the scope and diversity of a community's current undertakings); to accomplish some specific tasks within the community (e.g. the growth of jointly shared functions, institutions, and resources within the community); to provide a new self-image and role identity (this can be measured, for example, by the frequency of use of common symbols and by relevant aggregate data on the actual behaviour of the community members).[17] He also suggests examining four background conditions as the criteria for testing the success or failure of regional integration: (1) mutual relevance of the national units to one another; (2) compatibility of values and some actual shared rewards among the units; (3) mutual responsiveness among the national units; and (4) some degree of general common identity or loyalty among governments within that community.[18]

Deutsch sets forth two concepts of what he describes as a 'security community' as the main goal of integration: an amalgamated security community, in which the integrated political units have not only preserved peace in the community but also formed a single unit with a common government (for example, the United States today); and a pluralistic security community, in which separate governments retain legal independence and the main aim of integration is for community peace (for example, the United States-Canada and Norway-Sweden today). Deutsch and his collaborators found twelve essential conditions necessary to achieve an amalgamated security community:[19]

1. Mutual compatibility of the main values relevant for political behaviour;
2. A distinctive and attractive way of life;
3. Expectations of stronger and rewarding economic ties or shared rewards;
4. A marked increase in the political and administrative capabilities of at least some of the participating units;
5. Superior economic growth of at least some participating units (as compared to neighboring territories outside the area of prospective integration);
6. Some substantial unbroken links of social communication across the mutual boundaries of the territories to be integrated, and across the barriers of some of the major social strata within them;
7. A broadening of the political elite within at least some political units, and for the emerging larger community as a whole;
8. Relatively high geographic and social mobility of persons, at least among the politically relevant strata;
9. Multiplicity of the scope of the flow of mutual communications and transactions;
10. Some overall compensation of rewards in the flows

of communications and transactions among the units to be integrated;

11.   A significant frequency of some interchange in group roles (such as being in a majority or a minority, a benefactor or a beneficiary, an initiator or a respondent) among the political units;

12.   Considerable mutual predictability of behaviour.

Deutsch states that pluralistic security communities are easier to establish and to maintain than amalgamated security communities and hence often are a more effective means to keep the peace among their members. He suggests that three major conditions must first be fulfilled for the creation of a pluralistic security community:[20]

1.   Compatibility of major political values among regional actors;

2.   Mutual predictability of political, economic, and social behaviour of units to be integrated;

3.   Capacity of the governments and politically relevant strata of the participating countries to respond to one another's messages, needs, and actions quickly, adequately, and without resort to violence.

Deutsch argues that the process of integration often begins around a 'core area consisting of one or a few political units which are stronger, more highly developed, and in some significant respects more advanced and attractive than the rest'.[21] The government and political elites of such potential core areas often act as active leaders and unifiers for the emerging integrated political systems (England played such a role in the integration of the British Isles). Subsequently, integration would proceed in three stages:

1.   The stage of leadership by intellectuals, during which intellectuals (even a minority of intellectuals) are the main proponents of an integration movement;

2.   The stage of great politicians, during which more and more interest groups begin to swing behind the movement. Mutually rewarding and political compromises are worked out among the integrative units;

3.   The stage of mass movements or large-scale elite politics, during which the integration movement has become a consensus among the people and political unification becomes intensely practical.[22]

Nevertheless, Deutsch regarded the process of integration as a 'learning process' in which integrative activities are likely to move forward and then retreat in a manner somewhat resembling a learning curve. In order to maintain the rising slope of the learning curve and eventually achieve political unification, the relevant elites and governments need to promote the appeal of integration to the general population. For example, individuals or groups should be told or promised that new or greater 'rights and liberties' will be a result of integration, which in turn would bring more political, social, and/or economic 'equality' and a more rewarding 'way of life'. This could take the form of a promise of prosperity and material well-being.[23]

Ernst B. Haas, Philippe C. Schmitter, Leon N. Lindberg, Joseph S. Nye and others advocate the neo-functionalist approach to analyzing intergration.[24] This school stresses 'the instrumental motives of actors; it looks for the adaptability of elites in line with specialization of roles;' it takes 'self-interest for granted and relies on it for delineating actor perceptions'. In addition, neo-functionalists rely on the primacy of 'incremental decision-making over grand designs and purposive behavior because decision-makers stumble from one set of decisions into the next as a result of not having been able to foresee many of the implications and consequences of earlier decisions'.[25] Haas, in his work *The Uniting of Europe*, postulates that actors' decisions to proceed with integration, or to oppose it, depend upon their expectations of gain or loss within the unit to be integrated. He assumes that integration proceeds as a result of the support of relevant elites or vested interest groups of countries for essentially pragmatic rather than altruistic reasons. Elites having expectations of gain from integrative activities are likely to seek out similarly minded elites across national frontiers.[26]

Similar to David Mitrany's doctrine of 'ramification', Haas also advances the concept of 'spill-over' to explain the increasing momentum of integrative activities. He refers to 'spill-over' as 'the expansive logic of sector integration', and suggests: 'If actors, on the basis of their interest-inspired perceptions, desire to adapt integrative lessons learned in one context to a new situation, the lesson will be generalized'.[27] Examining the European integration movement in the 1960s, Haas concluded that there was a considerable degree of 'spill-over'. For example, objectives, such as a common external tariff, uniform rules of competition, a freer market for foreign labor, and a community agricultural policy, have gradually 'come close to voiding the power of the national state in all realms other than defence, education, and foreign policy'.[28]

'Political leadership' is another important concept within Haas's integration theory. He argues that the integrative interest based merely upon pragmatic considerations—for example, expectations of economic gain or improving technical functions such as telecommunications and postal services— is 'ephemeral' unless such an integrative process is supported by a political commitment on the part of statesmen. Haas therefore writes:

> as in the case of purely economic criteria, however, it is most doubtful that the demonstration of the (integration) process proves anything with respect to its causes. Integration is the result of specific decisions made by governments acting in conjunction with politically relevant, organized groups. Unless it is suggested that these actors deliberately seek to improve communication, Deutsch's concepts do not contribute directly to the study and projection of motives and expectations responsible for decisions to integrate.[29]

This desire to understand motivation of actors explains why the neo-functionalists stress analysis and observation of actors' perceptions and behaviour toward integration. Haas believes that data on transactions alone is not a valid indicator of the integrative process unless the data is 'reinterpreted in terms of actor perceptions'.[30] Therefore, the *sine qua non* for successful international integration, Haas argues, is the commitment of major political elites and governmental leaders. Ronald Inglehart states in this connection that strong political leaders are a most important factor in determining the role that a country will play in efforts toward political integration.[31]

In addition, the neo-functionalists broach the concept of 'externalization' of integration. Haas has found that external factors can promote regional integration if it is in the interests of a third party. However, external factors may have a reverse effect if this contrary result is in a third party's interests.[32] For example, in the case of the West Indies Federation (1958–1962), which failed, the external actor, Britain, was unwilling to develop an internal elite unit in support of the

Federation.[33] As Joseph S. Nye hypothesizes, 'the further integration proceeds, the more likely third parties will be to react to it, either in support or with hostility'.[34]

Haas has pointed out the similarities and differences between both the communications and neo-functionalist approaches. As regards similarities, both approaches

> share a commitment to a certain number of independent variables considered of great salience: regional transactions and the gains or losses associated with them by actors; verbal and symbolic communications between crucial elites; mutual expectations of elites; mutual responsiveness between elites; and the adequacy of institutions to handle the transactional and communicational load.

Turning now to differences, the communications approach considers 'all types of transactions equally salient and therefore measures whatever the statistics permit to be measured; neo-functionalists, however, argue that welfare-related and foreign or defence policy issues are most salient for actors.' Haas writes that neo-functionalists

> prefer to observe bargaining styles and strategies as their basic data rather than to stress the volume and rate of transactions or the ebb and flow of public opinion. Moreover, they prefer to study cases of organizational growth or decay rather than the aggregate data preferred by the advocates of the communications approach.

Haas says that 'generality' and 'systemic character' are the communications approach's strength, while the strength of the neo-functional approach is its 'closeness to the actors'[35] involved in the process.

In summary, although the two foregoing schools differ in emphasis of importance of variables some common ground between them still exists. Both approaches implicitly hold that the process of amalgamation will be long and slow, despite Haas' suggestion that the elite's transfer of loyalty to new institutions proceeds more quickly than the developing community ties between the masses of people. They both all agree on the condition of successful integration, that is, peaceful change and a voluntary merging of political entities. The mechanisms described by these two approaches are gradual yet become more pervasive, that is, first contact arising from simple issues which expands; this is the spill-over or ramification effect.

Both schools treat integration as a process in which the elites and the masses gradually redefine their beliefs and attitudes during contact between political entities, rather than a condition in which a consensus and shared homogeneous values have already been achieved. They both emphasize the role that the elites play during the process of integration because they believe that 'it is the elites who initiate amalgamation, not the masses'.[36] Both approaches also share the view that adequate institutions are necessary to handle the increased transactional and communicational load between national units. All of these concepts mentioned above can be used as the indicators to observe the progress of the two Chinas towards integration.

Nevertheless, the beginnings of integration theory are rooted in the analysis of the European Community during the 1950s. Therefore, most concepts of and techniques employed in integration are mainly derived from European society, 'the modern pluralistic-industrial democratic polity'.[37] Whether the analytical framework derived from European experience is applicable to integration in the third world remains inconclusive although some neo-functionalists, such as Joseph S. Nye[38] and Bruce M. Russett,[39] have already applied this framework to analyze other parts of the world and referred to the so-called 'non-Western' experiences of integration. Haas 'would have little hesitation in applying the technique of analysis here used to the study of integration under NATO, the Scandinavian setting, the organization for European Economic Co-operation, or Canadian-United States relations' but 'would hesitate to claim validity for it in the study of regional political integration in Latin America, the Middle East, or South-East Asia'.[40] Haas's comments reflect the fact that integration theory formulated from European experience may not necessarily be universally applicable to the study of every regional integration throughout the world since various regions and the countries within them have different specific tasks to complete before attaining the desired state of integration.

Integration theory is usually concerned with entities coming together to form an integrated new unit for the first time. In this sense, the reader might question whether or not it is applicable to the two China issue, since this situation involves two units that were once unified. One can argue, however, that integration theory most certainly is of relevance, for the following reasons. Regardless of the policies followed by Beijing or Taipei, and whatever the formal status of the PRC and the ROC in international law, most analysts in practice treat the PRC and the ROC as separate entities. In fact, they have now existed as separate units for four decades—a not inconsiderable period, especially in view of the huge transformations that have occurred both within each of them and in the world at large since 1949. Elements of general integration theory have been selected which are appropriate to a better understanding of the particular relationship between the PRC and the ROC. In so far as the nature of the integration theory relative to the two China issue *per se* is still unproven, this book will mainly deal with the actual reality of the two China issue rather than the integration theory.

Following this very cursory overview of the integration approach, the author would argue that many of the concepts and definitions of integration can be utilized as an analytical device for a better understanding of the two China issue. The two Chinas' situation can be summarized as follows.

The integration of the two sides of the Taiwan Strait is a process involving the two contending Chinas, both holding mutually antagonistic claims that there is but one China and that only the ROC or the PRC can represent the sole Chinese government in the world community with its sovereignty and jurisdiction holding sway over the whole Chinese people and territories. Each government is trying to persuade its rival to shift loyalty, realization of expectations and authority over political activities towards itself so that the two individual Chinese political entities can be merged voluntarily to form a larger state. In this way, the two sides of the Taiwan Strait can resolve their conflict under the conditions of peaceful change over the long term.

## Organization of the Study

How do nations become integrated or disintegrated? What factors account for the varying levels of integration? Can we be predictive about the future? Can we determine the direction of integration in a given case? Perhaps one major difficulty in studying integration is the lack of agreement about the nature of the variables which the theoreticians attempt to study, explain or predict. Any success in answering these questions will depend on our ability to specify variables which affect integration.[41]

In this study, the author also confronts the same difficulty in choosing variables that will be useful to accurately depict and predict the nature and development of the two China issue. Nevertheless, the aforementioned models and concepts produced by Deutsch and Haas concerning the criteria for testing the success or failure of regional integration and analyzing the process of integration have provided a useful theoretical framework for examining the empirical data of the two Chinas' integration. The book selects six main variables, namely the economic and political systems of the PRC and the ROC, Taiwan's public opinion, transactions between the two Chinas, Taiwan's politics, and the Taiwan Independence Movement as the key points which are to be discussed in the following chapters.

Part I introduces Beijing's proposals and strategies and how Beijing managed the two China issue between 1979 and 1992. The introduction illustrates the background of the China issue, and outlines the direction of the research.

Chapter 1 introduces the PRC's strategies while Chapter 2 analyzes Beijing's unification proposals toward the ROC. The neo-functionalist approach and content analysis are used in Chapter 2 to analyze pronouncements and philosophy of Beijing's leaders, as reflected in relevant documents and newspaper reports. It also examines whether the PRC's policy toward the ROC corresponds with the principles of the theory of integration. Chapter 3 portrays some of the agencies and organizations set up by Beijing ostensibly to realize the quest for reunification of China.

Part II covers the responses of Taipei to the PRC's overtures, as well as the ROC's overall strategy *vis-à-vis* the PRC, and a series of counterproposals initiated by the ROC government. This part begins with a brief discussion of the political and economic situation on Taiwan in Chapter 4, while Chapter 5 discusses the responses of the ROC to Beijing's prosposals. In Chapter 6, the ROC's counterproposals for reunification of China are presented, while in Chapter 7, Taipei's underlying strategy is discussed. Chapter 8 catalogues Taipei's anti-united front organizations. Chapter 9 focuses on the recent relations between the two Chinas from 1987 up until the middle of 1992. Throughout Part II the analysis of newspapers and as well as magazines and case studies will be used to analyze the ROC's position and philosophy toward the issue.

Part III is devoted to an analysis of the prospects for further integration or disintegration of the relations between the two Chinas. Chapter 10 focuses on the viewpoints and attitudes of the general public in the ROC concerning the two China issue. It is believed that, as a result of the gradual transition to a democratic society in Taiwan, popular opinion to some extent exercises influence on the political elite that formulates the ROC's mainland policy.

Chapter 11 discusses the present relationship between the two Chinas using the communication and case-study approaches. It will use a number of data sources—trade volume, mail flow, cultural and sports exchanges, social mobilization and diplomatic activities—to analyze the two Chinas' relations and predict future evolution of these relations. The consequence of this evolution will influence the progress of the two Chinas' integration.

Chapter 12 discusses the analysis and development of the political situation and the recent political reforms in the ROC. Indices—including those reflecting constitutional durability, political legitimacy, governmental efficacy, and civil order—will be employed to examine the extent of national integration within the ROC on Taiwan and its implications for the resolution of the China issue.

Chapter 13 examines the opposition Democratic Progressive Party's (DPP) positions and attitudes toward the two China issue. This study, as the book title indicated, is primarily about reunification and not about independence; however, given the fact that the Taiwan Independence Movement, supported by the DPP, has influenced the content of the political debate over reform and reunification in the ROC, a brief discussion about this movement and its impact on the two China issue is essential.

Chapter 14 provides the conclusions of this book and the future prospects for resolution of the two China issue.

# Beijing's Proposals and Strategies

# Chapter 1

◼

## Beijing's Proposals Since 1979

UNLIKE the study of the rise of empires, which concentrates on the use of forceful territorial aggrandizement, the study of regional integration is to 'explain the tendency toward the voluntary creation of larger political units, each of which self-consciously eschews the use of force in the relations between the participating units and groups'.[1] The theory essentially hypothesizes that the process of integration involves the establishment of 'feelings of mutual amity, confidence, and identification' between the populations[2] of the polities concerned.

Since the People's Republic of China was founded in 1949, Beijing policy towards Taiwan can be roughly divided into the following three periods: (a) the period characterized by intermittent fighting (1949–58); (b) the cold war period (1959–78); (c) the period of detente (1979–present) which is the focus of this book.

During the first period, two small battles actually occurred in the Taiwan Strait. The PRC launched a successful assault on the minor offshore island of Tachen in January 1955. Subsequently, the PRC heavily bombarded Quemoy in August 1958 and seemed poised to take over Quemoy and Matzu, two small offshore islands near Fujian that remained in the hands of the Republic of China. Beijing, however, soon reduced its bombardment to a token shelling on odd numbered days of the calendar before finally ceasing altogether on 31 December 1978. Beijing's policy towards Taiwan in this period was to 'liberate Taiwan by force' or to 'wash Taiwan in blood'.

During the second period, the two Chinas shifted their struggle from actual fighting to the arenas of diplomacy and economics in the international community. Each side tried hard to blockade the other side's avenues to the outside world. A good example is the contest for membership and the right to represent China in the United Nations during the 1950's and 1960's. It was a war without bullets between the two Chinas.[3]

Since the late 1970s, the means of struggle have again changed as the 'peaceful reunification of Taiwan' has become the theme of Beijing's Taiwan policy. If these above-mentioned political slogans can be used as an indicator of the two Chinas' relations, we can generally conclude that the relations between the two sides of the Taiwan Strait over the years have improved rather than deteriorated.

As a result, some fundamental questions need to be answered. Why did the PRC decide to initiate a peaceful approach to court the ROC? Will this approach establish 'mutual amity, confidence, and identification' between the two Chinese states? What is the content of Beijing's new policy toward Taipei and its implication for the national integration of the Chinese? The author surveys and analyzes these questions in the following three chapters based on the following four main parts: (a) the PRC's proposals; (b) the factors involved in their formation; (c) the PRC's strategies toward the ROC; (d) the PRC's united front organizations and their purpose. This chapter presents Beijing's proposals since 1979.

## Three Links and Four Exchanges

On 1 January 1979 the PRC and the US established full diplomatic relations. At the same time, Beijing intensified its 'peaceful offensives' toward Taipei and adopted a 'Message to Compatriots in Taiwan' under the name of the Standing Committee of the Fifth National People's Congress.[4] These events were the prelude to new policies toward the ROC, and marked a new era in the relations between two Chinas.

In the message, Beijing stressed that the reunification of China is 'consonant with popular sentiment and the general trend of development' of relations between the two sides of the Taiwan Strait. The message suggests that the two Chinas should directly conduct 'three links' defined as transportation, postal services, and trade and 'four exchanges' in academic, cultural, sporting, and technological endeavours. Beijing also announced at the same time the cessation of shelling of the offshore islands still in the hands of the ROC to show its sincerity concerning the peaceful resolution of the China issue in another message.[5]

# The Nine-Point Proposal

On 30 September 1981, a new peaceful overture of the PRC offered more generous terms. Ye Jianying, the Chairman of the Standing Committee of the PRC's National People's Congress, issued the following 'Nine-Point' proposal:[6]

1. In order to bring an end to the unfortunate separation of the Chinese nation as early as possible, we propose that the Communist Party and the Kuomintang Party hold talks on a reciprocal basis, to co-operate for the third time to accomplish the great cause of national reunification.

2. We propose that the two sides of the [Taiwan] Strait make arrangements to facilitate reunions and visits by relatives and tourists as well as academic, cultural and sports exchanges, and reach an agreement thereupon.

3. After the country is reunified, Taiwan can enjoy a high degree of autonomy as a special administrative region (SAR) and it can retain its armed forces. The Central Government will not interfere with local affairs on Taiwan.

4. Taiwan's current socio-economic system will remain unchanged, so will its way of life and its economic and cultural relations with foreign countries. There will be no encroachment on the proprietary rights and lawful right of inheritance over private property, houses, land and enterprises, or on foreign investments.

5. People in authority and representative personages of various circles in Taiwan may take up posts of leadership in national political bodies and participate in running the state.

6. When Taiwan's local finance is in difficulty, the Central Government may subsidize it as is fit for the circumstances.

7. Taiwan Chinese who wish to come and settle on the mainland will be guaranteed that proper arrangements will be made for them, that there will be no discrimination against them, and that they will have freedom of entry and exit.

8. Taiwan's industrialists and businesses are welcome to invest and engage in various economic undertakings on the mainland, and their legal rights, interests and profits are guaranteed.

9. The reunification of the motherland is the responsibility of all Chinese. We sincerely welcome Taiwan Chinese of all circles to make proposals and suggestions regarding affairs of state through various channels and in various ways.

In order to demonstrate its sincerity and resolve, the National People's Congress (NPC) of the PRC formally adopted the 'Special Administrative Region' (SAR) provision in the PRC's new Constitution which was passed by the Fifth NPC conference in December 1982.[7] Article 31 of the Constitution stipulated that 'the state may establish special administrative regions when necessary. The systems to be instituted in special administrative regions shall be prescribed by law enacted by the National People's Congress in the light of specific conditions'.[8]

## The Six-Point Proposal

On 26 June 1983, at a meeting with Winston L. Y. Yang, a Chinese-American scholar, Deng Xiaoping, then the Chairman of the Central Military Commission of the Chinese Communist Party (CCP) as well as the *de facto* leader of the PRC, put forward another proposal for the peaceful reunification of China outlining political parameters for a reunified Taiwan:[9]

> 1. Taiwan will become a SAR after the reunification and may retain its independent nature and practise a system different from that of the mainland;
> 2. Taiwan may exercise independent jurisdiction and the right of final judgment need not reside in Beijing;
> 3. Taiwan may also keep its own armed forces, so long as they do not constitute a threat to the mainland;
> 4. The mainland will station neither troops nor administrative personnel in Taiwan;
> 5. Taiwan's political party, government, and armed forces will all be administered by Taiwan itself;
> 6. Seats in the Central Government will be reserved for Taiwan.

In the meantime, Deng Xiaoping said autonomy has its limits, thus 'complete autonomy' is simply out of the qestion. 'Complete autonomy' would mean 'two Chinas,' not one unified China. He stressed that the social system on Taiwan would be allowed to be different from that on the mainland, but only the PRC is entitled to represent China in the international arena.[10]

# The Proposal of 'One Country, Two Systems'

A clearer and more concrete policy regarding the peaceful reunification of China was embodied and put forward under the concept of 'one country, two systems' on 26 September 1984 when the PRC and the British Government initialled a joint declaration on the retrocession of Hong Kong, that is, the British transfer of authority over this colony to the PRC in 1997.

According to Beijing, the concept of 'one country, two systems' did not begin with Hong Kong, but with the issue of Taiwan. Although the Nine-Point statement by Ye Jianying did not use the term 'one country, two systems,' in fact, that in so many words was what it was.[11] Therefore, when the Hong Kong issue of the return of came up in 1982, the PRC decided to apply the concept to Hong Kong to test its feasibility. Deng Xiaoping has stated clearly that the resolution of the Hong Kong question would directly influence the settlement of the Taiwan issue.[12] The PRC 'seemed honestly to believe that the Hong Kong experience was equally applicable to Taiwan and, by applying it, they could unify the motherland and make China rich, strong, and glorious again'.[13]

Under the policy of 'one country, two systems,' the PRC will allow Hong Kong to become a SAR as authorized by Article 31 of its Constitution, after resuming sovereignty over Hong Kong. Hong Kong after 1997 is to enjoy a high degree of autonomy with its foreign and military affairs being ultimately controlled by the Beijing central government. The Hong Kong SAR will be vested with executive, legislative and independent judicial power, including that of final adjudication. The Hong Kong SAR is to be administered by Hong Kong people and its social and economic systems are to remain unchanged after 1997. Hong Kong's position as an international financial center is not to be altered. The Hong Kong SAR will remain financially independent from the PRC and Beijing will not levy taxes on the Hong Kong SAR. Under the name of 'Hong Kong, China,' the Hong Kong SAR may maintain and develop its economic and cultural ties with other nations and membership within international organizations. Hong Kong is to retain the right to issue travel documents necessary for exit from and entry into Hong Kong. Finally, the PRC, in the joint declaration, promised that after it assumes rule over Hong Kong in 1997, the colony will remain capitalist for 50 years.[14]

Based on the Hong Kong formula, Deng Xiaoping said in 1984 that Beijing's plan for Taiwan is essentially the same but even more generous than the terms for Hong Kong. For example, Taiwan may retain its military force after the reunification of China. He went on to stress that 'our actions will follow our words, and we will never play tricks' on Taiwan.[15]

The above-mentioned four proposals constitute the main framework of Beijing's new policy toward Taipei since 1979. During this period, we find that the PRC's policy toward the ROC became increasingly more favourable towards Taipei. In the following pages, the author discusses how these proposals were formed.

## The Formulation of Beijing's Policy

Li Jiaquan, the deputy director and researcher of the Taiwan Research Institute of the Chinese Academy of Social Sciences, has divided the development of mainland China's policy since 1979 towards Taiwan into three stages, in terms of different proposals that Beijing has put forward.[16] This division is accepted here, with the caveat that the author uses four stages to include the period since Li produced his analysis. These stages are as follows: (a) late 1978 to mid-1981; (b) mid-1981 to 1983; (c) 1984–1985; (d) 1986 to the present. This periodization can help us to understand clearly the causality between Beijing's policy formation and related factors.

## The First Stage: Late 1978 to mid-1981

1979 was a watershed in both the PRC's domestic policy and the relations between Taipei and Beijing. After ten turbulent years of Cultural Revolution, the Chinese on the mainland, including leader Deng Xiaoping, weary of the political manoeuvering, violence, and destruction which characterized that upheaval, wished to reconstruct mainland China 'through seeking truth from facts'.[17] In the meantime, the PRC had completed normalization of diplomatic relations with the US, and hoped to speed up reunification with Taiwan. A stalemate marked by no communications had existed for 30 years and some innovation was needed to break this stalemate. Against this background, the PRC leadership, at the Third Plenary Session of the 11th Central Committee of the CCP held in December 1978, finally decided to make 'the peaceful reunification of the motherland a strategic policy'.[18]

Beijing's main motivation at this stage seems to have been to exploit the perceived loss of morale in Taipei after the US, the most important supporter of Taipei, had severed official ties with the ROC. The PRC eventually wanted 'to call on Taipei to surrender'.[19] The PRC also intended to use this peaceful approach to unification to gain leverage over the US concerning future arms sales to the ROC. Beijing believed and still believes that a peaceful resolution of the China issue would create a situation where Washington had no excuse to sell arms to Taipei.[20] The PRC also thought that the 'peaceful offensive' would put the ROC into a difficult dilemma. If Taipei decided to contact Beijing, it would alarm Taiwan Chinese who might worry about a 'sellout' of Taiwan by the KMT.[21]

In fact, internal politics in Taiwan have been 'delicate and confrontational at times, and any move by the government to negotiate with the PRC regarding Taiwan's future would immediately trigger mass opposition',[22] and disturb that island's stability. If the ROC refused to talk with Beijing, this refusal would put Taipei on the defensive and allow it to be criticized as intransigent. 'In either event, Beijing stands to gain'.[23] Thomas J. Bellows' analysis has concluded that the purpose of Beijing's peaceful policy toward Taiwan has been to try to wear down the psychological defenses of the people, particularly the great majority on Taiwan who have never known communism personally or directly participated in the anti-communist struggle. He elaborated on this notion, saying that the PRC's strategy has been trying to sow discord between the indigenous Taiwanese Chinese and the mainlanders in Taiwan. This policy also offered the PRC a pretext to resort to military means if the ROC turned down Beijing's suggestions.[24]

Although the intent of Beijing's proposals can be interpreted in many ways, integration theory may produce a useful means of analysis. Karl W. Deutsch has stated that early in the course of the integrative process, 'a psychological "no-war" community often also develops. War among the prospective partners comes to be considered as illegitimate; serious preparation for it no longer commands popular support'.[25] The PRC's 'no-war' strategy toward the ROC at a minimum reduces the tension between the two sides of the Taiwan Strait. It also gives the two Chinese states more latitude to solve their problems.

During his trip to the US in January 1979, Deng Xiaoping, in the capacity of Vice Premier of the State Council of the PRC, told American congressmen that 'we [will] no more use the term "liberate Taiwan". We will respect the reality and Taiwan's present system as long as Taiwan can return to the motherland. . . . We will expedite our pace to reunify Taiwan with the motherland'.[26] Deng and others would soon spell out generally what Taiwan could expect after reunification.

On 28 February 1979, Liao Chengzhi, the PRC official then in charge of Overseas Chinese relations, indicated that the resolution of the two China issue would not 'injure our Taiwan compatriots' welfare, change their way of life, or downgrade their living standard'.[27] In October 1979, Deng told Watanabi Saiki, publisher of Asahi Shinbun of Japan, words to the effect that the PRC did not have too many demands of Taiwan, 'we only ask Taiwan to abolish its official title "Republic of China" and to lower its national flag.' Deng in this conversation also offered a number of conditions for Taiwan to consider—including retaining their social system and life style, and enjoying autonomous status after Taiwan rejoined the mainland. Deng went so far as to intimate that Taiwan could maintain its armed forces and that the PRC would continue to recognize Taiwan as a 'local government'.[28]

In May 1980, Deng proposed even more generous terms to Taiwan before his Japanese guest Yashi Kazuo, Board Director of Japan's National Policy Research Institute. He said that, apart from maintaining its own life style, living standards, and social system, Taiwan would also be able to retain its relations with foreign nations on an unofficial basis, maintain its autonomy and keep its army. Moreover, he allowed for the possibility that Taiwan would be administered by Taiwan Chinese after reunification.[29]

During the first stage, the PRC 'has shown remarkable innovation and initiative'[30] to encourage the ROC to talk about reunification. The formulation of Beijing's policy toward Taipei, especially the conditions put forward, was gradually built on each previous proposal. On 30 September 1981, Beijing's peaceful offensive reached a climax when Marshal Ye Jianying broached his 'Nine-Point Proposal'.

## The Second Stage: Mid-1981 to 1983

If the 'Message to Taiwan Compatriots' issued on 1 January 1979 marked the starting point of Beijing's new policy toward Taiwan, then the statement of the Nine-Point Proposal represented an important change in the direction of this policy. Comparing the two documents, three important differences have been evident. The message's mention of principles has developed into concrete negotiation terms in the Nine-Point Proposal. Although the message put forward the idea of 'three links and four exchanges', this was not a concrete proposal but merely a statement of principle designed to sound out Taiwan's views. The Nine-Point Proposal, however detailed conditions necessary to settle the reunification issue. A second difference was that in the Nine-Point Proposal Beijing for the first time suggested that in any talks between the CCP and the KMT, both parties would be on an equal footing.[31] In the message Beijing regarded itself as the central government and Taipei as one of its 'local governments'.[32] The third area of progress is that the Nine-Point Proposal not only consolidates the previous conditions that were put forward by the PRC between 1979 to mid-1981, it further expands those conditions to apply to general areas of endeavour ranging from national feelings to the politics, society, economy and life styles of the Taiwan Chinese.

Aside from facilitating reunification with Taiwan, Beijing's Nine-Point Proposal also has another main purpose, specifically to demonstrate its commitment to a peaceful resolution of the two China issue to the USA. The PRC was disturbed when President Reagan entered the White House because of Reagan's pro-Taipei position. Reagan had said that if he was elected, he would make the American Institute in Taiwan (AIT) an official liaison office and also would renew arms sales to the ROC.[33] Beijing's strategy paid off and neutralized Reagan's position on Chinese affairs. He accepted Beijing's statements that the PRC would commit itself to a peaceful approach to resolve the China issue. Evidence of this acceptance can be found in the Communique of 17 August 1982 drawn up between the US and the PRC. In the document Washington stated that:

> The United States Government understands and appreciates the Chinese policy of striving for a peaceful resolution of the Taiwan question as indicated in China's Message to Compatriots in Taiwan issued on 1 January 1979 and the Nine-Point Proposal put forward by China on 30 September 1981. The new situation which has emerged with regard to the Taiwan question also provides favorable conditions for the settlement of United States-China differences over United States arms sales to Taiwan. Having in mind the foregoing statements of both sides, the United States Government states that it does not seek to carry out a long-term policy of arms sales to Taiwan.[34]

Further evidence of the rewards to China of a peaceful strategy was found in the US's explanation of the communique. John H. Holdridge, Assistant Secretary for East Asian and Pacific Affairs of the State Department, said that if the PRC maintained a peaceful approach to the Taiwan question, this 'will permit gradual reduction' of arms sales to Taiwan.[35]

The Nine-Point Proposal was not the end of Beijing's innovations in formulating its Taiwan policy. At the opening ceremony of the 12th Party Congress of the CCP in September 1982, Deng Xiaoping openly declared that the realization of national reunification of the motherland would be one of the PRC's three main tasks in the 1980s. The other two tasks are the achievement of socialist modernization and the anti-hegemonist struggle to maintain world peace.[36]

On 4 June 1983, Deng Yingchao, Chairman of the National Committee of the Chinese People's Political Consultative Conference, said 'we respect history and reality. The CCP and the KMT can supervise each other for the foreseeable future, peacefully coexist, and mutually co-operate after reunification'. She said that 'Taiwan as a SAR can retain its economic system, and that the capitalist and the socialist systems can complement and support each other'.[37]

On 18 June 1983, again in order to encourage Taipei to initiate contact, Deng Xiaoping told the participants who attended the Seminar on Science and Technology Policy in Beijing that if the ROC decided to negotiate with the PRC, it would be on an equal basis. Such negotiations would not be between the central government (Beijing) and the local government (Taipei) but a negotiation between the two political parties.[38] On 26 June 1983, Deng Xiaoping put forward his 'Six-Point Proposal'. This document included new terms such as Taiwan being allowed to exercise independent jurisdiction and the PRC not stationing troops in Taiwan after reunification, as added inducements to Taipei.

## The Third Stage: 1984–1985

As we have seen, Beijing, in order to minimize Taiwan's suspicion about its sincerity for peaceful reunification of the motherland, has repeatedly improved its terms toward Taipei since 1979. Beijing's initiatives have yielded rewards in the international community. However, the 'generosity' of its policy toward Taiwan has also alarmed Taiwanese Chinese, who feel Beijing's offerings should be treated with caution. The ROC on its part is wary about the PRC proposals because of past experience of ostensible cooperation between the KMT and CCP during the Republican period. On the other hand, the PRC may propose more generous conditions in the future. Therefore, the best policy for the ROC would seem to be to wait and see. Perhaps the ROC might be convinced if the PRC actually demonstrated sincerity and reliability over its proposals. Thus, the retrocession of Hong Kong becomes a test case. The PRC decided to apply the concept of 'one country, two systems' to the colony, and hopes that the absorbing of the Hong Kong can serve as a model of reunification with the ROC and persuade Taipei to start discussions.[39]

In October 1984, Deng Xiaoping used the phrase 'one country, two systems' for the first time before a group of foreign guests and overseas Chinese from Hong Kong and Macao.[40] He also explained why the PRC had decided to adopt the peaceful approach to the transfer of the colony and the two China issue, saying that there are two ways to resolve the above two situations: peaceful and non-peaceful. The non-peaceful way was deemed inappropriate because the 'reluctant acquiescence of the Hong Kong people and the British people would result in chaos'. Deng indicated that 'even if armed conflict would not result, Hong Kong would become a depressed, insalubrious region, not something we look forward to'.[41] Therefore, Beijing thinks that a peaceful approach through the 'one country, two systems' policy is reasonable and at the same time acceptable to both the Hong Kong people and the British government.

As mentioned above, the PRC's 'one country, two systems' policy originated to deal with reunification with Taiwan, rather than Hong Kong, which is merely a testing ground for this policy. As James C. Hsiung points out, the reversion of Hong Kong to the PRC in 1997 has brought serious risks to Beijing 'from the standpoint of its ultimate Taiwan scheme. However, it also has enabled Beijing to demonstrate the feasibility of its "one country, two systems" policy if the model retrocession of Hong Kong succeeds'.[42]

After the signature of the 'Joint Declaration' between the PRC and the British Government at the end of 1984, Beijing's policy toward Taipei centered on promoting its 'one country, two systems' policy. In 1987, when the Portugese Government agreed to employ the 'one country, two systems' formula to resolve the retrocession of Macao after 1999, Beijing's confidence about using this approach to resolve the two China issue was increased. Since this 'one country, two systems' model looms paramount, further examination of this policy is essential.

Based on the pronouncements of Beijing's leaders and academic works from the PRC, this policy's salient points can be summarized as follows:[43]

> 1. After China is reunified, people in the area presently controlled by the PRC will follow the socialist system while people in Hong Kong and Taiwan (later on Macao is also included) will continue their capitalist ways of life. Hong Kong will remain a capitalist system for 50 years after the PRC resumes the exercise of its sovereignty in 1997. As to the questions of when and how Taiwan will change from its existing system to the socialist system after reunification, this will be decided by history. At the end of this century, the PRC's economy in terms of GNP will be quadrupled, while by 2021 the PRC will enter the median ranks of developed countries and the expansion of the PRC's economy will attain the level of advanced countries by 2049. By that time, a unified China will be all socialist because the living standards of the Mainland, Taiwan, and Hong Kong will all be roughly the same level and the latter two would then have no excuse not to follow the Mainland's system. Hong Kong and Taiwan's stability and prosperity will promote the development of mainland China's economy.

2. Under the 'one country, two systems' principle, Beijing will be the undisputed central government, thus would dictate national defence and foreign policy. Taiwan could be provided with more generous terms than Hong Kong which at present means Taipei would maintain the right to retain its army, party and political systems after reunification. The army, however, must be put under the unified command of the People's Liberation Army. In the capacity of 'local government', Taiwan and Hong Kong can maintain and develop their official or unofficial ties with other countries and international organizations under the title of 'Taiwan, China' or 'Taipei, China' and 'Hong Kong, China' and the like. It should be noted that the 'local government's' authority is granted by the central government, and is not an inalienable right.

3. PRC scholars argue that the rationale of the 'one country, two systems' policy is rooted in peaceful coexistence, which corresponds with the ideology of Marxism and the dialectical materialistic conception of history. They argue that, in terms of the theories of Marxism, capitalism and socialism do in fact co-exist in the world arena. Since the world can have two different social systems why, can't a country? Hence the 'one country, two systems' policy does not contravene Marxist tenets. Other scholars argue that conditions of history, politics, and geography rather than ideology determine relations between countries. Therefore, the unification of a country is determined by the factors of ethnicity, culture, language, customs, and habits, and not fashioned by the rhetoric of ideology. Since systems based on capitalism and socialism can peacefully coexist in the international arena for a long time, so, too, could two systems within one country. In the Chinese case, capitalism and socialism could complement and support each other for the greater good of the country.

4. Beijing stresses that the 'one country, two systems' policy is not a measure of expediency or a fraudulent scheme. It has originated from the PRC's developing experience and is not to be changed. Meanwhile, the 'one country, two systems' concept not only satisfies the fundamental principles espoused by the PRC, for example, that there is only one China and that the PRC is the sole representative of the whole Chinese people; but also allows a flexible approach to handling the China issue, that is, it provides a solution to the co-existence of the capitalist and communist systems within China. The Chinese mainland can be a socialist system while Hong Kong, Taiwan and Macao remain capitalist. The

latter three would in theory not influence the basic nature of the PRC's system but complement it.

5. The 'one country, two systems' concept is a major initiative of paramount leader of Deng Xiaoping. The political structure and the independent foreign policy strategy of the PRC constituted under the rubric of 'one country, two systems' are to become the basic features of Chinese-style socialism in the 21th century. The 'one country, two systems' policy is not only a strategic policy to be applied to settle the two China issue but can also serve as a model for resolving international disputes as well.

After PRC President Li Xiannian put forward another proposal that Taiwan can also 'keep its existing intelligence-gathering system' after reunification,[44] the PRC had 'finally exhausted its options and reached a stage where new policies on Taiwan will not be forthcoming for a while'.[45] Although Beijing has seemed to be no longer as vigorous in issuing proposals for integration of the two Chinas, the situation has not been static. In fact, the PRC's peaceful approach has gradually influenced Taiwan's perception of and policy making toward mainland China, despite Taipei's official position of maintaining the 'Three Nos' policy, that is, no compromise, no negotiation, and no contact with the PRC, and the continued unenthusiastic official response toward Beijing's proposals.

Since 1986, in order to adjust itself to external changes such as further isolation from the international community and the pressure of Beijing's vigorous peaceful overtures, as well as increasing demands for democratization within Taiwan, the ROC Government has launched a number of new initiatives to help itself weather these political uncertainties.

One of these new initiatives involves Taipei's reassessment of its Mainland China policy. Since this reassessment, the two Chinas' relations have evolved into a fourth stage spanning 1986 to the present. Compared with the first three stages, the relations between the two Chinas during this period is more dynamic and interactive. Because of this fundamental difference, the fourth stage is discussed in Chapter 9. The next chapter examines Beijing's strategies toward Taiwan.

# Chapter 2

## Beijing's Strategies Toward Taipei

ON the basis of the content of Beijing's documents, speeches of leaders, and policy pronouncements since 1979, the PRC's strategies toward the ROC have been categorized into five approaches: an appeal to nationalism; fulfilling historical mission; an appeal to relatives and friends; united front endeavours; and promoting economic reforms. In the meantime, the PRC has maintained two immutable and non-negotiable principle in its Taiwan policy: (a) insisting on its sovereign position as the sole representative of all Chinese people in the world; and (b) not excluding the use of force to settle the China issue. These approaches and principles together constitute the PRC's 'carrot and stick' strategy toward the ROC which has been employed since 1979.

## 1. The Appeal to Nationalism

In the words of John Stuart Mill, 'the strongest cause for the feeling of nationality. . . is identity of political antecedents; the possession of a national history, and consequent community of recollections; collective pride and humiliation, pleasure and regret, connected with the same incidents in the past'.[1] In the Chinese case, nationality identity is not a serious problem. Both Taiwan and the mainland are populated mainly by Han people. They identify with the same cultural antecedents and possess the same history. Although the two Chinas have been separated for more than forty years, the two Chinese Governments both abide by the principle of Chinese nationalism and stress national homogeneity. They always remind their people of this common heritage through their education and cultural programs.

Of course, the PRC realizes this fact. The 'Message to Taiwan Compatriots' in 1979 refers to Chinese national feelings, pride, and traditions:

> The Chinese nation is a great nation. It accounts for almost a quarter of the world's population and has a long history and brilliant culture, and its outstanding contributions to world civilization and human progress are universally recognized. . . . The Chinese nation has great vitality and cohesion. Throughout its history, foreign invasions and internal strife have failed to split our nation permanently. . . . Every Chinese, in Taiwan or on the Mainland, has a compelling responsibility for the survival, growth and prosperity of the Chinese nation. . . . If we do not quickly set about ending this disunity so that our motherland is reunified at an early date, how can we answer our ancestors and explain to our descendants?[2]

Similiar rhetoric can also be found in other writings.[3] Huan Xiang, at the time the Vice President of the Chinese Academy of Social Sciences, had argued that to the mainland Chinese, the Taiwan question is a highly sensitive issue. He said that 'past experience shows that no one should miscalculate in any way the strong sentiment of the Chinese nation, which went through untold tribulations in a hundred vicissitudinous years'.[4] Zhao Quansheng listed four main reasons why the PRC insists on reunifying Taiwan, with nationalism ranked first.[5]

The PRC not only uses nationalism as a strategy to persuade Taiwan to reunify with the mainland, but also criticizes and challenges Taipei's proclamation as the legitimate heir to Dr. Sun Yat-sen's legacy and Chinese culture. In the minds of Chinese people, Dr. Sun stands as the legitimate successor of Chinese culture and political orthodoxy. The ROC regards Sun as the father of the country and employs his work *The Three Principles of the People* (Nationalism, Democracy, and the People's Livelihood) as the blueprint of the ROC's political development while Beijing does not. Nevertheless, the PRC praises Sun as a patriotic hero and a 'predecessor of revolution'.[6] There is an important message in Dr. Sun's work regarding nationalism. He said that

> The Chinese people . . . have no national spirit. . . . We are in fact but a sheet of loose sand. We are the poorest and weakest state in the world, occupying the lowest position in international affairs. . . . Our position now is extremely perilous. . . . If China perishes, she will perish at the hands of the Great Powers. . . . If we want to resist might we must

espouse nationalism and in the first instance attain our own
unity, then we can consider others and help the weaker,
smaller peoples to unite in a common struggle against the
oppressors.[7]

In fact, the Century of Humiliation is a painful experience
to all Chinese. It explains why Mao Zedong happily announced
that 'the Chinese people have stood up!' on 1 October 1949,
the day of the foundation of the PRC.[8] The PRC has always proclaimed that it has realized Dr. Sun's ideas and rebuilt China
into a 'prosperous, democratic and strong country'. Its intentions, according to Herbert S. Yee, are clearly on the one hand
to 'undermine the Kuomintang's claim to be the vanguard of
Sun's political and social ideals and boost the CCP's legitimacy in ruling China'[9] and on the other hand to demonstrate
'the mutual heritage of the KMT and the CCP'.[10] In April 1981,
when the KMT rejected the PRC's 'three links and four exchanges'
proposal at the 12th KMT Party Congress, Beijing immediately denounced the ROC and criticized Taipei. 'While pay-
ing lip service to the "Three People's Principles" laid down
by Dr. Sun Yat-sen, the Kuomintang authorities have long
since betrayed these principles—nationalism, democracy and
people's livelihood, depending externally on foreign powers
and oppressing the people at home'.[11]

## 2. Fulfilling the Historical Mission

Scholars in the field of international relations have been
attempting to analyze how and why foreign policy decisions
are made. They argue that each country's foreign policy is
made by human beings who are influenced by international,
domestic, and bureaucratic factors as well as idiosyncratic,
cybernetic, and cognitive elements. At least four decision-
making models have been developed and widely used by
scholars to analyze the process of decision-making since the
1950s, and these emphasize different factors and elements in
the process. These models are: (a) the rational actor model;
(b) the bureaucratic politics model; (c) the domestic politics
model; (d) the idiosyncratic, cognitive, and cybernetic model.[12]
Examining all of these models is beyond the scope of this
study but the lastly named model is employed here as it

emphasizes the analysis of leaders' psychological attitudes as being central to policy formation. Since the elite leadership of the PRC is possibly the most crucial level of policy formation, this model should provide clearer insight into the reunification policy of the PRC.

In reviewing the PRC's proposals, it can be found that almost every innovation or new initiative on Taiwan is put forward or at least approved by Deng Xiaoping—the most powerful leader in the PRC since 1978. Deng's power is derived from the Chinese political tradition of respect for seniority and elders, and the nature of authoritarian communist rule. Another very important factor is Deng's control of the People's Liberation Army since 1979. In fact, Deng has retired from all of his government posts, but the last two he vacated were the chairmanship of the Military Commission of the CCP Central Committee and of the Central Military Commission of the PRC in 1990. Although other leaders such as Hu Yaobang, Zhao Ziyang, Deng Yingchao, and Li Xiannian, have also played a role in the decision-making process, their prestige and power have paled in comparison with those of Deng Xiaoping.

Since Deng is the principal decision-maker in formulating the PRC's policy toward the ROC, to understand his psychology, perceptions, and values concerning the China issue becomes essential. Richard C. Snyder has emphasized the importance of the individual's motivation 'as a major determinant of the decision-making process' because individuals usually 'speak on behalf of states and rationalize their policy actions'.[13] Besides, the idiosyncratic model also assumes that the personal characteristics of decision makers can make a difference in policy outcomes.

In Chinese culture and tradition, there are three ways to attain immortality in one's life: to attain virtue, to achieve distinction, and to leave worthy writings to posterity. Therefore, any individual who can accomplish any one of these three things will be regarded as a 'great man' in Chinese history. The psychological attitude of Deng and other leaders of the PRC concerning the resolution of the China issue are influenced by this tradition. It also explains to some extent why these leaders always connect the resolution of the China issue to history and view 'the reunification of the motherland' as 'the sacred mission that history has handed to our generation'.[14] Deng has spoken candidly in this regard. He told

Winston L. Y. Yang, a Chinese-American scholar, that the reason why he wants to see reunification is because

> We are to accomplish the cause left unaccomplished by our predecessors. If the Chiangs and all those who have devoted themselves to the cause of reunifying China can accomplish this cause, they will find themselves better recorded in history. Of course, it will take time to achieve the peaceful reunification. But it is not true to say that no one is anxious about this. People like us in old age hope that our national reunification will be realized at an earlier date.[15]

Deng here not only reveals his own concern about becoming a great personage in Chinese history, but also tries to persuade Chiang Ching-kuo to join him in this aspiration, thereby achieving historical distinction as well. If Deng could reunify China his prestige would surpass that of Mao Zedong and his name would be recorded in Chinese history as another national hero. If this observation is valid no wonder Beijing has pushed so hard for reunification since 1979.

The PRC's leaders understand quite well the benefits of appealing to history and nationalism as these are perhaps the areas with the most factors in common between the two Chinas. Beijing reckons that using these two appeals as an excuse for reunifying China is reasonable and justifiable.

John K. Fairbank has analyzed the two China issue and its relationship to Chinese culture and history. He writes that

> Peking and Taipei agree on 'One China' because China began as a culture island and spread outward, civilizing the uncouth and incorporating all Chinese in a single civilization; and for two thousand years the unity of this Chinese realm has meant peace; its disunity, war. Reinforced by history, China's national-culturalism today is monolithic, whereas European nationalisms are mere political subdivisions within European culture. After a century of humiliation, China's claims to sovereignty express this resurgent unity, and 'Two Chinas' is an utter blasphemy.[16]

It seems to the author that perhaps this sense of historical mission and the psychological attitude of striving for immortality through achievement are the main motivations for Beijing leaders to resolve the China issue at an early date.

According to Richard Solomon, Mao Zedong told Henry Kissinger in 1973 that the PRC-USA can improve relations 'without [Taiwan] for the time being. Let it come after 100 years.' Deng Xiaoping echoed this view in 1978 when he stated publicly in Japan that Taiwan's status 'will inevitably be resolved—if not in ten years then in 100 years; if not in 100 years, then in 1000 years'. However, at the beginning of the 1980s, Deng suddenly changed the thrust of his rhetoric and said the 'reunification of the motherland' is one of the three main tasks of the PRC during the 1980s. Solomon's analysis is that Deng has a feeling that 'Taiwan's reunification with the PRC could only become more difficult with the passage of time'. Deng is getting old, he himself 'no doubt wished to make progress on an issue of great emotional and nationalistic significance to the Chinese'.[17]

Another member of the old guard, Chen Yun, a former Politburo member and the principal figure of the conservative faction in the PRC, also expressed the same viewpoints in 1986 and said that:

> although we have rows between the two sides of the Taiwan Straits, Chiang Ching-kuo and ourselves both still adhere to the one China principle and oppose the position of independence for Taiwan. As Taiwan's elders, however, are gradually passing away, I doubt whether their young successors would continue to follow this principle. Therefore, we'd better plan early and reunify Taiwan as soon as possible during the rest of our limited life-spans.[18]

Apparently, Beijing's Taiwan policy reflects the mentality of ageing leaders. Whether this motivation can help to resolve the two China issue remains to be seen, especially after Deng and his peers all disappear from the political stage.

## 3. An Appeal to Relatives and Friends

The PRC's leaders have a tendency to emphasize their common background or experience with the ROC leaders. They have endeavoured to employ an emotional dimension, through friends, schoolmates, colleagues, or relatives who are in the ROC to gain access to Taipei's power center and influence Taipei's mainland China policy. For example, Liao Chengzhi, the PRC official in charge of Overseas Chinese relations, wrote an open and warm letter in 1982 to the ROC President Chiang

Ching-kuo, offering to come to Taiwan to initiate 'peace talks'. Liao is the son of Liao Zhongkai, one of the founders of the KMT. His letter reviewed his long relationship with Chiang. Actually, their friendship dates back to their boyhood and they also studied together in the Soviet Union. In the letter, he made a strong emotional appeal to Chiang:[19]

> Dear Brother Ching-kuo:
> It is unfortunate that we haven't heard from each other for so many years. Recently I was told that you are somewhat indisposed and this has caused me much concern . . . I sincerely hope that you will take good care of yourself. . . . Since you are presiding over the administration of Taiwan, you have unshirkable responsibility for the realization of a third [CCP and KMT] cooperation. It would be easier to talk the matter over at a time when leaders on both sides were once schoolmates and close friends who know one another well . . .
> I recently read one of your writings in which you expressed 'fervent hopes that my father's soul would be able to return to the homeland and be reunited with our forefathers.' I was overwhelmed with emotion when I read this. . . . After reunification, [the remains of] your father should be moved back and buried in the native soil . . . in fulfillment of your filial wishes . . .
> The longing for old friends grows with age. If it is convenient for you, I would pack and set out for a visit to Taipei to seek enlightenment from our elders. Through all the disasters the brotherhood has remained; a smile at meeting, and enmity is banished.

Another example of an approach to relatives and friends is the former general-secretary of the CCP Hu Yaobang's sentimental appeal to Chiang in his speech at the 70th anniversary of the 1911 Revolution on 10 October 1981. Hu said that 'does Mr. Chiang Ching-kuo not love his natal land? Doesn't he want to have Mr. Chiang Kai-shek's remains moved back and buried in the cemetery of the Chiang family in Fenghua?' Hu used that occasion to openly invite Chiang and 13 other high ranking ROC officials to visit mainland China, including Madame Chiang Kai-shek and Mr. Chiang Wei-kuo (Chiang Ching-kuo's stepbrother).[20]

Before 1979, the PRC accused both Chiang Kai-shek and Chiang Ching-kuo of committing 'atrocities' against the Taiwanese people and betraying the Chinese people, as puppets of

American imperialists. The two Chiangs, however, suddenly became national heroes after 1979 because of their steadfast adherence to the 'One China' principle. Since then Beijing characterized them as major contributors to China's unity, and Chiang Kai-shek as a hero during the period of Anti-Japanese War (World War II).[21] Hence, Chiang's hometown in Fenghua, Zhejiang Province, has become a famous summer resort, and since the renovated home of Chiang's family has been 'opened to the public, visitors have swarmed in'.[22]

Beijing has placed hopes on Chiang and the other KMT old guard because it believes that their affection for their ancestral homes on the mainland can be used to draw them into negotiations on reunification. Beijing is attempting to utilize the political power of these ruling mainlanders through this approach to speed the pace of reunification and prevent Taiwan .from drifting into '*de facto* independence'.[23] However, time seems to be against this approach as most of the old guard of both sides of the Taiwan Strait will pass away within the next five to ten years and has already lost much of its power.

# 4. United Front Work

Mao Zedong proclaimed that the united front is one of the three 'magic weapons' of the CCP's revolution in defeating its enemies, the other two being Party building and armed struggle.[24] He asserted that the fundamental principle of the united front is to maintain independence and the initiative, to assume leadership, to ally with the left, to attract the middle and to attack the right, to combine united front tactics with armed struggles, and to exploit the contradictions among others.[25] In short, the essence of the united front has been to 'unite with the secondary enemies while attacking the major ones'.[26] The composition of the united front has not been constant, it can be changed at any time in terms of the need of the mission and the objectives of revolution.[27]

According to Mao, the early history of united front of the CCP has developed in three different stages: the First Great Revolution from 1924 to 1927; the War of Agrarian Revolution from 1927 to 1937; and the War of Resistance Against Japan (World War II). During the first two stages, the CCP's united front was mainly formed by the proletariat and the peasantry, the main supporters of the CCP, and the national bourgeoisie or big bourgeoisie considered to be the secondary enemies of the CCP; imperialism and the feudal warlords of the Chinese were regarded at the main enemies of the CCP. The united front during the third stage was formed by the proletariat and the peasantry once again as the main supporters of the CCP, and the national bourgeoisie, the KMT and the CCP. The KMT at that time was viewed as the secondary enemy of the CCP. This array of forces stood against Japan's invasion of China. Japan now was the main enemy.[28] After 1949, the work of the united front of the CCP had two purposes: 'internally, to unify Taiwan with the mainland; and internationally, to form coalition of the Third World and the Second World against the two superpowers'.[29]

In 1979, Ulanhu, then Director of the United Front Work Department of the Central Committee of the CCP, announced at a national conference on united front work that 'in the new period China's united front should be called the revolutionary patriotic united front. It is a broad union of socialist labourers and all patriots'.[30] According to Ulanhu, the 'revolutionary and patriotic united front' is formed on the one hand by socialist workers, peasants and intellectuals and all other patriots who support socialism as its political basis within the PRC (the main proponents of the PRC), and on the other hand has included those Chinese who reside in Taiwan, Hong Kong, Macao and overseas. The common denominator takes support for the reunification of China as its political basis. This group of Chinese residing outside the PRC are the PRC's secondary enemies, as their ideology is different from that of mainland China. Ulanhu stresses that so long as these Chinese who reside abroad love the PRC and support its course of reunification, they all should be united. Yen Mingfu, the head of the CCP United Front Work Department, elaborated on this saying that under the banner of the unity of the Chinese nation, 'we will unite and co-operate with all those who favour reunification of the motherland, regardless of their class origin, party affiliation, political orientation or beliefs'.[31]

Based on the broad parameters of the 'revolutionary and patriotic united front' of the PRC cited above, we can conclude that any Chinese, no matter where he or she lives, even though he or she 'does not support socialism',[32] so long as he or she advocates Beijing's reunification policy, he or she would still be a 'patriot' and would be regarded as part of the united front by the PRC. Beijing's officials do not mention who are the main enemies of its united front, but we may conclude that they would be those who do not support, or even oppose, the PRC's reunification task. If so, the KMT and the Democratic Progressive Party (DPP) could be at present the two major enemies of the PRC's united front. In terms of Beijing's own logic, however, this is not quite correct. In fact, the KMT also advocates reunification. Are they still to be regarded enemies of the PRC's united front? The final criterion on whether the members of the two parties are 'patriots' or not, is 'to love the motherland, to love the CCP, and to love the PRC'.[33] If they are not patriots as defined above, then they are the main enemies of the PRC's united front.

This strategy has a four-fold purposes: to expand the united front alliance as widely as possible to serve Beijing's purpose; to identify potential enemies and isolate the main enemy; to split the unity of the main enemy; and to convert the ideology of Taiwanese Chinese to that of the PRC and to enlist their support of Beijing's reunification course and in this way undermine the ROC because Taipei does not endorse the PRC's reunification conditions. The writings of mainland Chinese scholar Xu Xianzhang support this analysis. He proclaims that at least ninety-nine percent of the Chinese population can be included under Beijing's new united front.[34] In other words, only one percent of the population is regarded as the PRC's main enemy. Who then is Beijing's main enemy? Peng Zhen, then Chairman of the NPC, answered this question explicitly. He said that those who 'with ulterior motives have been supporting, overtly or covertly, the "movement for the independence of Taiwan"' and those who have been 'engaged in activities for "two Chinas" or "one China, one Taiwan" in a deliberate attempt to obstruct and undermine the cause' of reunification under the government of the PRC are the main enemy of Beijing's united front.[35]

From past experience, the 'united front' efforts serve as the CCP's 'carrot' and the threat of 'armed struggle' as its stick, which together with 'Party building', that is, to strengthen the internal organization and structure of the CCP, constitute the 'magic weapons' of the CCP to resolve all difficulties. In order to unite Taiwanese and mainland Chinese, Beijing has put forward many incentives to enlist the Taiwanese people's support. Policies offering increasing concessions to Taiwanese Chinese regarding living, sightseeing, investing in the mainland, and other areas have been successively formulated since 1979. Has Beijing's united front strategy paid off? How has the KMT countered this strategy? These issues are to be examined in the following chapters. Meanwhile, Chapter Three further discusses the question of how the PRC carries out its united front works toward the ROC. Before doing that, the author will continue to analyze Beijing's other strategy—the economic reforms.

## 5. Economic Development

According to World Bank statistics, in 1979, the PRC's GNP per capita was US$260, placing it 102nd on a list of 124 countries.[36] Deng Xiaoping has admitted this poverty by saying that 'we belong to the category of poor countries in this world'.[37] He told the leaders of the PRC that 'we should ponder the question: what have we really done for the people?'[38] At the same time, Deng seems to have understood that if the PRC remains in poverty, the appeal of reunification with Taiwan would be less convincing and ultimately unsuccessful. He therefore pledges that the PRC will match Taiwan's thriving economy in the future.[39] Deng has sketched the goals regarding the PRC's economic development as follows:

> On the whole, our goals are not too ambitious. We will give ourselves 20 years—that is, from 1981 to the end of the century—to quadruple our GNP and achieve comparative prosperity, with an annual per capita GNP of US$800 to US$1,000. Then we will take that figure as a new starting point and try to quadruple it again, so as to reach a per capita GNP of US$4,000 in another 50 years. What does this mean? It means that by the middle of the next century we hope to reach the level of the moderately developed countries. . . . By reaching that goal, . . . we will demonstrate to mankind that socialism is the only solution and that it is superior to capitalism.[40]

In early 1985, a research project called 'China at 2000' was completed by a panel of experts and scholars in the PRC. Wang Huijiong, Research Fellow of the State Council Technological and Economic Research Centre, outlined the results of this project and said that by the year 2000, the PRC 'will attain or surpass the goal of "meeting the basic needs" in living standards set for the developing countries'. He said that by the year 2000, the mainland Chinese will be able to enjoy a better life. 'Durable consumer goods such as TV sets, cassette recorders, refrigerators and washing machines will be popular in cities and towns.'[41]

Due to the limitations of the author's scope of research, this book does not examine the details of the PRC's economic development programs since 1979.[42] It is necessary to briefly analyze, however, the political implications of the PRC's economic reforms for the resolution of the China issue. This strategy in essence involves a 'stick and carrot' approach. On the one hand, the PRC's economic development is to gradually improve the living standards and conditions of the mainland Chinese people, which is an essential factor to attract the Taiwan Chinese to reunification under the aegis of the PRC. The PRC's economic development is to keep the mainland open to the outside world's capital and technology which enhances the prospects for integration—starting with economic contact—between the two Chinas, because the ROC, like many other Western countries, can also provide capital and other wherewithal to the mainland. Furthermore, when the PRC concentrates on economic construction, the possibility of resorting to military means to resolve the China issue in the short term is less likely because the PRC 'needs a peaceful environment' to proceed with its modernization program.[43]

However, the economic development of the PRC in the long term could also generate an adverse situation for the ROC. As Beijing will become more wealthy in the future when—and if—Beijing quadruples its annual GNP to US$1,000 billion by the year 2000,[44] Deng Xiaoping has pointed out 'if we allocate 1 per cent of [US$1,000 billion] to national defence, that means $10 billion; 5 per cent means $50 billion. With $10 billion we could accomplish a lot of things, and it would be easy to upgrade our military equipment'.[45] A more powerful PRC in terms of military strength would certainly become more difficult for the ROC to resist if Beijing decided to use force against Taiwan regardless of the cost. A more powerful PRC could also be a threat to the Western world if the future leaders of the PRC so wish.

In 1985, Hu Yaobang, then Secretary General of the CCP, told Lu Keng, publisher of a Hong Kong-based magazine *Pai-Hsing*, that the PRC at this stage 'would not use force against Taiwan because of a lack of military strength'. However, he said that Beijing might use force against Taiwan 'in the future five or ten years because at that time the PRC may have sufficient military capability to conquer Taiwan' if Taipei still refused to negotiate with Beijing.[46]

The above comments by Beijing's leaders have, to some extent, revealed the connection between the PRC's economic development and Beijing's strategy to resolve the China issue. Whether Beijing can successfully achieve its ambitious goals of economic development remains to be seen. This strategy combines both courting the Taiwanese Chinese (the 'carrot') and enhancing the PRC's capability and power to take over Taiwan by force (the 'stick').

## One China Principle

There are some cardinal principles that Beijing has not retreated from in any solution of the two China issue proposed since 1949. It has consistently maintained the positions[47] that

1. The PRC is the sole legitimate government representing the Chinese people.
2. Taiwan is a province of China, and an inalienable part of China's territory. The liberation of Taiwan by the Chinese people is an internal affair of China which brooks no foreign intervention.
3. The so-called theory that the status of Taiwan is as yet unsettled is unacceptable.
4. Any two-China policy or a one-China, one-Taiwan policy or any similar policy is unacceptable.
5. The so-called Taiwan Independence Movement is unacceptable.

The first two positions reflect Beijing's attitude toward its legitimacy, sovereignty, and independence, while the last three are designed to prevent Taipei abandoning reunification and obtaining assistance from other countries to establish its independence.

With these points in mind, the PRC's policy toward the ROC

since 1949 has contained an element of egoism. For example, Beijing always proclaims that it is the 'central government' and Taipei is the 'local authority or government'; that the mainland constitutes the 'main body of China' and the PRC is the 'motherland' of all Chinese around the world, and other such pronouncements. Beijing's ideas comes from 'a tradition of Chinese suzerain authority over semi-autonomous terri- tories'[48] since ancient times, which explains to some extent why the leaders of the PRC have designed the 'one country, two systems' policy, agreeing to give Taiwan, Hong Kong, and Macao some residual political power as well as maintaining some degree of autonomy. As Chiu Hung-dah has argued, the PRC's policy toward the ROC is 'to give . . . the power of gov- erning, but no concession on sovereignty'.[49]

It is because of these principles that the PRC has constantly and consistently challenged the ROC's legitimacy and sover- eignty in the international arena since 1949. We may say that legitimacy and sovereignty in fact are the two central factors of the two China issue. The most obvious strategy that Beijing uses to exert pressure on Taipei is to isolate the ROC in the international community because the PRC's leaders hope that such 'isolation will cause a split'[50] within the ROC and dis- solve Taiwan's unity. The PRC not only attempts to persuade other countries to sever diplomatic ties with the ROC (the number of countries that still recognize the ROC has been reduced from a peak of 68 in 1969 to 29 as of March 1993)[51] it also tries to obstruct other countries who wish to maintain unofficial ties with Taipei.

In March 1982, Beijing sent a note to the foreign diplomatic missions in the PRC to request the countries concerned not to permit the ROC to establish 'commercial offices, informa- tion offices or liaison offices for scientific-technological ex- changes' in their countries and not to establish similiar offices in Taiwan.[52] In July 1983, Beijing again issued a statement which requested other countries not to permit 'any organs of the Taiwan authorities to perform "consular functions"', to issue visas, or to establish 'any organ in Taiwan to perform such functions'.[53]

Beijing's strategy on the diplomatic front is to establish the perception and understanding that the ROC is the PRC's local government. Therefore, any country that wants to have ties with Taipei should obtain permission either tacitly or explicitly from Beijing in advance; otherwise, the PRC may take retaliatory action against the country concerned. The case of the sale of submarines from Amsterdam to Taipei may serve as an example.[54] Over the years, the PRC has modified its 'exclusion' policy and agreed to coexist with Taipei in some international organizations such as the International Olympic Committee and the Asian Development Bank, on the condition that Taipei can not use its official name—the Republic of China—and national flag and emblem, instead using the name of 'Taipei, China' or 'Chinese, Taipei' to participate in these organizations. In a sense the PRC is trying to make the ROC one of Beijing's local governments by default and to prevent the name of 'the Republic of China' from appearing in the international community so that the claim that there is only one China—the People's Republic of China—can be sustained. Is the PRC's strategy conductive to the resolution of the two China issue or having exactly the opposite effect? What is Taipei's response? These questions are to be discussed in Chapters Five, Six, Seven and Eleven.

## Military Threat

PRC scholars Li Shenzhi, Vice President of the Academy of Social Sciences in Beijing, and Zi Zongyun, Deputy Director of the Institute of North America, the Chinese Academy of Social Sciences in Beijing, have come to two conclusions about Beijing's Taiwan policy: Taiwan must be reunited with the mainland, and the PRC would make every effort to achieve reunification by peaceful means. They explain why a peaceful resolution to reeunification is in the PRC's interests:[55]

(1)   Beijing does not want to hurt national feelings;
(2)   Beijing needs a peaceful environment to implement the four modernizations;
(3)   The use of force would hamper Beijing's relations with Western countries, especially the USA;
(4)   Beijing wants to avoid creating a trigger-happy impression internationally;
(5)   Psychologically, a peaceful settlement would be a more generally acceptable resolution of the issue;
(6)   The use of force would ruin Taiwan's economy, which would run contrary to the PRC's interest.

Although the PRC 'prefers' peaceful resolution of the China problem, it also announces that 'it will never promise to renounce using force against Taiwan under any circumstance. If all of the avenues toward the peaceful resolution of the issue were blocked, and when Beijing is cornered without any other options, the PRC will keep the right to resort to non-peaceful means'.[56] Under what kind of circumstances will Beijing resort to force against Taiwan? According to speeches by the PRC's leaders and other related materials published since the 1970s, Beijing has set five circumstances under which force would be is used:[57]

(1)   An indefinite refusal by Taiwan to enter into negotiations;
(2)   An attempt by the Soviet Union or other countries to interfere in the ROC's affairs and the resolution of the China issue;
(3)   An attempt by Taipei to develop nuclear arms;
(4)   Proclamation of Taiwan as an independent nation;
(5)   Revolution and chaos occuring within Taiwan.

During the 1970s, the PRC placed more emphasis on the circumstances of (2), (3), and (4) due to that period's prevailing situation. The ROC had been confronted with the worst setback in its diplomatic relations when the PRC replaced it as the representative of China in the United Nations in 1971. At this point in time, the US, Taipei's main supporter, began to contact the PRC, which further weakened the ROC's international position. In this situation, both the PRC and the US were worried 'that the ROC might start to ally with the USSR', and would be 'driven to develop nuclear weapons or to declare its independence'.[58] All of these actions would be contrary to the PRC's interests. In order to prevent Taipei from taking any such action, Beijing therefore issued threats to use force. During the 1980s, the PRC has shifted to emphasize the circumstances of (1), (4), and (5) as conditions under which force would be used. The PRC was worried that the post-Chiang KMT 'will be a pluralistic organ torn by intense power struggles, thus rendering the Kuomintang less powerful and affecting Taiwan's political stability'.[59] Therefore, if revolution or chaos was to occur, or if someone thought 'that the time for proclaiming Taiwan's independence is ripe and openly pushes for Taiwanese independence under external influence', the PRC would unhesitatingly use force against Taiwan.[60]

On 17 April 1988, the ROC's Democratic Progressive Party (DPP) passed a resolution during the Provisional Meeting of its Second Party Congress and proclaimed that the DPP would advocate Taiwan's independence under the following four conditions:[61]

(1)   if the KMT unilaterally embarked on talks with the CCP;
(2)   if the KMT betrayed the Taiwanese people's interests;
(3)   if the PRC forcefully reunified Taiwan;
(4)   if the KMT does not sincerely attempt to bring about genuine democracy.

The 'April 17 Resolution' completely dashed Beijing's hopes that the DPP would not openly support the concept of independence. It also revealed that Taiwan's degree of democratization as indicated by the tolerance of freedom of speech had proceeded beyond the PRC's estimate. Besides, Beijing's original strategy 'of using the KMT to check the idea and expansion of Taiwanese independence within Taiwan has proved useless'.[62] Whether Beijing decides to focus on the use of force to deter the possible declaration of Taiwanese independence deserves close attention.

The PRC's intentions in threatening the use of force are obvious. It wants to hold sway over the resolution of the two China issue and wishes to keep all policy options open. Meanwhile, the PRC, through this threat, can 'constrain Taipei's behavior' as well as its 'freedom of action',[63] press Taipei to start talks with Beijing, and block progress toward Taiwan's independence.[64] On 10 May 1985, Hu Yaobang said that the PRC cannot promise not to use force to resolve the two China problem; otherwise, Taipei would be 'free from worries and sleep in peace' and would never want to start talks with the PRC.[65]

Beijing's strategy seems to be to keep the threat of force alive as a trump card in solving the two China question and prevent the issue getting out of the PRC's control. Can this strategy succeed or produce exactly the opposite effect? Could the PRC successfully use force to achieve its goal if those circumstances outlined earlier were to prevail? These questions are to be further examined in Chapter Seven.

# Chapter 3

■

## United Front Organizations

THE organizational structure of the PRC's united front toward the ROC is shown in Table 3-1. The organization of the PRC's united front is quite large and widespread within the PRC. Beijing's leaders have repeatedly emphasized the importance of the united front work in realizing the objective of reunification. Xi Zhongxun, a former Politburo member of the CCP, said at the 1986 United Front Works Conference of the CCP that 'every party member must contribute to the united front work because it is the CCP's good tradition and a policy that does matter concerning the motherland's future developments'.[1]

Table 3-1 shows that the whole organizational structure of the PRC's united front work is led directly and indirectly by the Political Bureau of the CCP. Within the CCP the 'Leading Group for Taiwan Work' is the principal decision-making body formulating Beijing's policy and the united front work toward the ROC. Before 1987, Liao Chengzhi (the former political bureau member who died in 1983) was in charge of this group; he was succeeded by Deng Yingchao, the widow of Zhou Enlai as well as a former politburo member and the Chairman of the Chinese People's Political Consultative Conference, who in turn was followed by Yang Shangkun, former President of the PRC and the Permanent Vice Chairman of the CCP Central Committee Military Commission as well as the Vice Chairman of the Central Military Commission of the PRC. Since 1993, the newly elected PRC President Jiang Zemin has replaced Yang as the head of this office. Jiang is also the General Secretary of the CCP and the Chairman of the CCP Central Committee Military Commission as well as the Chairman of the Central Military Commission of the PRC.

From this list, it seems that Taiwan united front work is to some extent a high priority for the PRC. As of July 1993, the other leading members of this group include Qian Qichen a politburo member, a vice premier, and the former Minister of

Foreign Affairs of the PRC; Wang Zhaoguo, head of the Taiwan Affairs Office in the State Council and of the Central Office of Taiwan Affairs within the CCP; in addition, Wang is also head of the CCP's United Front Work Department and the Vice Chairman of the CPPCC Eighth National Committee; Jia Chunwang, Minister of State Security in the State Council; Xiong Guangkai, Assistant to the Chief of General Staff of the PLA; and Wang Daohan, President of the Association for Relations Across the Strait.[2] The fact that this group does not include any economic or trade specialists strongly indicates that Beijing still regards relations between the two Chinas primarily political in nature rather than economic, which require special attention.[3]

In November 1990, Wang Zhaoguo, the former Governor of Fujian province, replaced Ding Guangen as the Head of the Office in charge of Taiwan in the State Council. In June 1991, Wang again replaced Yang Side as the Director of the CCP Central Office for Taiwan Affairs.[4] Within this group, the Central Office for Taiwan Affairs handles the day-to-day operations of the Taiwan united front and leaves the final decision-making to Jiang Zemin or Deng Xiaoping. In addition, each province, city, county, and autonomous region in the PRC also has similiar groups and offices to implement executive orders.

The CCP's 'United Front Work Department' was headed by Yan Mingfu prior to 24 June 1989 and is presently headed by Wang Zhaoguo. It is perhaps the oldest united front agency of the CCP, and has branch offices in every province, city, county, and autonomous region. This Department serves as the coordinator of the PRC's united front efforts of the related government and non-government agencies and associations.[5]

The 'Leading Group for Solidifying Taiwan Compatriots and Dependents Affairs' is headed by Wang Feng, a member of the Central Advisory Commission of the CCP.[6] The working objective of this group focuses on those Taiwanese and their dependents as well as those former KMT military and government personnel who still reside in the mainland. These people were purged and punished during the Cultural Revolution because of their past connections with the KMT. Since 1979, in order to rectify policy errors, the PRC has repeatedly issued a number of instructions to the appropriate government agencies to look after the welfare of these people more carefully.[7]

Hence, it may be said that past connections with the ROC have become beneficial for these people.

Within the PRC Government, at least seven agencies so far are known to participate in the united front efforts. Liao Hui heads the Overseas Chinese Affairs Office and is responsible for the management of united front activities for the overseas Chinese within and outside the PRC.[8] The main task of this office is to encourage the overseas Chinese, including the Taiwanese Chinese, to support Beijing's reunification policy and the 'four modernization programmes'.[9] Lu Ping is the director of the Hong Kong and Macao Affairs Office.[10] This office was founded in 1983 when Beijing decided to resolve the issue of the retrocession of Hong Kong and Macao and is mainly responsible for Hong Kong and Macao affairs. Given Hong Kong's importance and role as a pivot between the two Chinas, this office can influence Beijing's united front efforts toward Taiwan; thus, it is a cabinet level unit within the PRC's State Council.

The Taiwan Affairs Office, coming into existence in July 1988, is headed by Ding Guangen, Vice Minister of the State Planning Commission of the State Council. This office is ranked within the PRC's State Council as a cabinet ministry level unit.[11] In November 1990, Wang Zhaoguo replaced Ding as the new head of this office.

The foundation of this office has further shown Beijing's concern to achieve an early resolution of the two China issue and indicates that it is stepping up its united front work toward Taiwan. Since Taipei modified its mainland China policy in 1987 and allowed Taiwanese Chinese to visit their relatives as well as trade with the mainland, Beijing has felt the need to establish a new agency to handle the gradually expanding ties between both Chinas.

In addition, there are two offices in charge of Hong Kong, Macao, and Taiwan affairs under the rubric of the Ministry of Foreign Affairs. The functions and workings of these two offices, however, are different from the previous two offices responsible for Taiwan, Hong Kong and Macao. These offices mainly monitor international affairs and issues that concern Taiwan, Hong Kong and Macao.

The Bureau for Taiwan Trade Affairs was established within the Ministry of Foreign Economic Relations and Trade in the early 1980s.[12] The function of this office is mainly to oversee the economic and trade relations between the two Chinas.

Moreover, it also plays the role as a watchdog to monitor and control the commercial relationship between the two sides of the Taiwan Strait.[13]

In order to manage the new situation of increased ties that has developed since 1987 between the PRC and ROC, Beijing has decided to reinforce Hong Kong's role as a bridge for promoting better relations between the two Chinas. In 1988, the PRC established a new organizational unit called the Taiwan Affairs Department within the Hong Kong Branch Office of Xinhua News Agency, the *de facto* PRC representative in Hong Kong. This department is nominally headed by Zhou Nan, the director of Xinhua in Hong Kong, but in fact comprises officials from various government agencies including trade, culture, sport, and intelligence, as well as the united front.[14]

The Overseas Chinese Affairs Committee of the NPC is led by Ye Fei, Central Committee member of the CCP, and Vice Chairman of the Standing Committee of the NPC, and is also a part of the PRC's united front system toward overseas Chinese.[15] Perhaps the Chinese People's Political Consultative Conference (CPPCC) is the PRC's biggest united front work organization with 2,800 offices and 350,000 employees located throughout the mainland.[16] The CPPCC plays the role of a bridge, connecting the CCP and those 'democratic parties, groups, and non-party democratic people within Mainland China. The main task of the CPPCC at this stage is to make every effort to solidify and develop the PRC's patriotic united front'.[17] For example, if a Chinese from Taiwan visits his or her relatives in the countryside, the cadres of the CPPCC and the United Front Department in that area will show up and look after his or her interests and offer the necessary services to the 'Taiwan Compatriot'.[18]

The United Front Work Department of the CCP instructs local cadres in the principles of treating the visitors to the mainland from Taiwan.

> Not only should you receive the Taiwan Compatriots warmly, you also need to introduce and propagate to the Taiwan Compatriots through vivid and active ways the promising situation of every front's work of our country. You should let them see the agricultural and industrial productions of our hinterland especially the continuous improvement of our science and technology industries. By so doing, it can help to strengthen the Taiwan Compatriots' confidence in

> trusting the motherland as well as to aspire to unify with the motherland. Meanwhile, you should not only let them see the positive side of our advanced development, but also need to let them understand our negative side so that they can realize our difficulties and backwardness.[19]

The CPPCC, in order to cope with the new situation of expanded relations between the PRC and ROC, reorganized a Committee for Reunification of the Motherland in August 1988.[20] The previous titles of this institution were the Working Group for Reunification of the Motherland formed in September 1983, and the Group for Propaganda Toward Taiwan established in 1979.[21] Qian Weichang, a member of the CPPCC National Committee, is the head of this association. He has said that the reorganization of this association within the CPPCC is in the hope that it can expedite the reunification task more quickly.[22]

There are nine so-called 'democratic parties' in the PRC as indicated in Table 3-1. The name of each party's chairman is indicated after the party name.[23] Some of these parties have their local organizations in different areas of mainland China. They receive subsidies from the CCP regularly and cooperate with the CCP to carry out the united front work towards Taiwan. They are, however, merely symbols of the PRC's claim to be a democratic and multi-party system and are not viable opposition parties so that their influence in the CCP's decision-making process is marginal.

Turning to the ostensibly non-official mass organizations, the All-China Federation of Returned Overseas Chinese was formed in October 1956 and has been led by Zhuang Yanlin since 1989. According to Beijing, the basic policy and task of this federation is to protect the interests of the returned overseas Chinese and their dependents. The federation will 'fly high the banner of patriotism, and unite all of the returned overseas Chinese, their dependents, and the overseas Chinese to devote themselves to the prosperity, flourishing, and reunification of the motherland'.[24]

The All-China Federation of Taiwan Compatriots was founded on 27 December 1981. One of the main functions of this institution is to promote the welfare of 29,000 Taiwanese and their families still living on the mainland. The purpose of this organization also is to exalt patriotism, to unite the Taiwanese Chinese both within and outside of Taiwan, and to promote

**Table 3-1:** Organizational Structure of the PRC's United Front Efforts

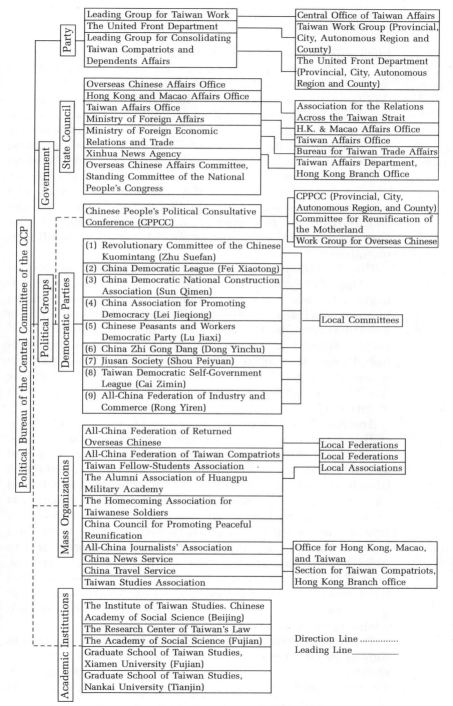

*Source*: Compiled by the author on the basis of relevant materials.

friendship among the Taiwanese Chinese so that it can speed up the achievement of 'the great task of reunification of the motherland'.[25] According to its constitution, the mission of this federation is to assist the Taiwanese Chinese to understand the PRC's Taiwan policy and the current situation in the PRC; to communicate to the Taiwanese Chinese's wishes and proposals to the Beijing Government; to actively promote economic, cultural, academic, and sporting exchanges between the two sides of the Taiwan Strait; to assist those Taiwan Chinese who have returned the mainland for various and sundry purposes such as to worship ancestors, visit relatives and tourism; and to cooperate and coordinate with the relevant agencies of the PRC to accomplish the above-mentioned objectives.[26]

This federation issues its own publication called *Taishin Magazine* (The Voice of the Taiwanese), and has organized many activities in the past ranging from academic seminars to summer camps for overseas Taiwanese Chinese.[27] Zhang Kehui has been the President of this institution since 1991.[28] He is a returned Taiwanese Chinese. This federation has established many local offices all over the mainland and perhaps is one of the most active and influential groups in executing the PRC's united front work towards the Taiwanese Chinese at this stage.

Another related group is the Taiwan Fellow-Students Association, started in November 1981 and including scholars, experts, and students who have studied in Taiwan or abroad and returned to the mainland. In addition to maintaining friendship with and helping to resolve difficulties of returned Taiwan students, the other main tasks of this Association is to implement the PRC's four modernization programmes; to promote academic exchanges between mainland China and Taiwan, Hong Kong, Macao, and overseas Chinese; and to press forward the 'great task of reunification of the motherland'.[29] In recent years, this association has held seminars on the current situation in Taiwan and the two China issue. 'Many pro-Taipei scholars who reside abroad are also invited and attend these seminars'.[30]

The Alumni Association of Huangpu Military Academy was formed in June 1984. According to its constitution, this association's purposes are 'to glorify the spirit of Huangpu; to maintain friendship among erstwhile schoolmates; to promote the reunification of the motherland; and to increase China's prosperity'.[31] Anyone who has studied or received training courses in this military academy residing either in the mainland or in Taiwan regardless of whether they studied before or after 1949 are all eligible to become a member of this association. This membership policy enables it to expand the alliance of united front within and outside of the PRC.

Huangpu is the cradle of both Chinas' military leadership. Its alumni are ubiquitous in the PRC, the ROC, and amongst the overseas Chinese. In both Chinas, alumni of Huangpu have considerable influence, as most of them hold high-ranking posts in the army and other government agencies. This Association is mainly aimed at those alumni who reside in Taiwan and overseas. This strategy has alarmed the ROC and led Taipei to form its own parallel organization, the Alumni Association of Military Academies of the ROC, in July 1988 to counter Beijing's united front offensives in this direction.[32] This PRC association is currently headed by Ho Jinru and has issued its own magazine called *Huangpu* since June 1988.

The Homecoming Association for Taiwanese Soldiers is also a united front group founded on 19 October 1988. There are about 1,375 native-Taiwanese soldiers drafted to fight the communists who were left behind after the PRC took over the mainland in 1949. They have contended that it is their legal right to return to Taiwan and to visit their relatives in Taiwan and have also stated that the KMT has the moral obligation to look after their well-being. Receiving redress on these issues is the principal purpose of this association. Members of this group also strive to 'promote contacts between the two sides of the Taiwan Strait for reunification of the motherland'.[33]

Another united front organization is the China Council for Promoting Peaceful Reunification. Formed on 22 September 1988, it is a grand alliance, backed by the PRC's CPPCC, of people from all walks of life. This association has 8 presidents, 48 standing directors, 189 directors, and 24 advisors. Almost all PRC VIPs and celebrities who are not members of the CCP have been invited to join this group. The importance of this association is therefore obvious. According to this association's constitution, the main purpose of this group is to unite people from all walks of life both within and outside the mainland, to promote person-to-person contacts and exchanges between the two sides of the Taiwan Strait and ultimately to realize the peaceful reunification of China.[34] This association publishes a magazine named *The Reunification Forum*.

The All-China Journalists' Association and China News Service are the two main units in the PRC that conduct united front efforts directed at Taiwan's journalists. Since the ROC allowed its journalists to directly cover news stories in the mainland starting in May 1989, Taiwan's press corps have flocked to the mainland to report news. In fact, the Bureau for Hong Kong, Macao, and Taiwan within the All-China Journalists' Association is actually managing the united front operations. Staffs of this unit are ordered to render any necessary assistance to Taiwan's journalists. Mu Dongping, the present deputy director of this office, is the one who is in charge of affairs related to Taiwan's press. Mu's father, Mu Qing, currently is the Director of the PRC's Xinhua News Agency.[35]

Since Taipei began to permit people residing in Taiwan to visit relatives living on the mainland in November 1987, the Section for Taiwan Compatriots within the Hong Kong branch office of the PRC's China Travel Service has been created for handling the business of Taiwan people's travels to and within the mainland.[36]

To respond to Taipei's request for non-official exchanges between the two Chinas, Beijing, in December 1991, has established the Association for the Relations Across the Straits as a counterpart organization to Taipei's Straits Exchanges Foundation (SEF). Nominally this association is non-official; in fact, it is directed and administered by the State Council's Taiwan Affairs Office. Wang Daohan, the former city mayor of Shanghai, is in charge of the PRC organization. According to Wang, this association, although non-official, strives to promote the direct 'three links', (postal services, transportation, trade) between Taiwan and the mainland 'under the orders of the State Council and the Communist Party to realize the peaceful reunification task on the basis of "one country, two systems"'.[37]

In addition to forming the above-mentioned institutions, Beijing has also begun to enhance its Taiwan studies research and academic programmes since 1987. Generally speaking, the PRC's Taiwan research has been quite weak; therefore, the PRC usually can not clearly understand the developments and changes of the ROC's politics, which has 'always led Beijing to make inadequate policy decisions regarding Taiwan'.[38] In January 1987, a mainland scholar wrote an article in which he urged Beijing to establish the field of 'Taiwanology', to strengthen the study of Taiwan and overcome the difficulties obstructing Beijing's efforts toward Taiwan 'caused by the hiatus of theory and practice'.[39] In order to better understand the ROC, the Institute of Taiwan Studies of the Social Sciences Academy in Beijing set up a study group and visited Hong Kong at the end of 1987 in the hope that such a field trip would enable those researchers directly involved to more clearly understand the ROC's political, economic, and social systems, which to some extent are similar to those of Hong Kong. The perception of this institute's researchers of the KMT 'still stay in the old days when the KMT was corrupt and inept'.[40]

By June 1989, there were five main institutions in the PRC that engaged in Taiwan studies:

(1)   The Institute of Taiwan Studies, in the Chinese Academy of Social Sciences in Beijing. This unit, with about 50 researchers, was founded in September 1984. It published its first issue of *Taiwan Studies Quarterly* in March 1988, covering topics including Taiwan's foreign relations, politics and, law, including society and economic developments. This Institute is the biggest and most influential academic unit in the PRC within the field of Taiwan studies. It also serves as a think-tank for Beijing's Taiwan policy-making.[41]

(2)   The Research Center of Taiwan's Law in Fuzhou, Fujian province, established in December 1988, analyzes the ROC's legal and customs systems. This center is led by Cheng Xu, Chairman of the Standing Committee of the Fujian Provincial 7th People's Congress, and is attached to the provincial people's congress. The main purpose of this Center is to solve the legal problems that have inevitably cropped up due to increasing trade and investment contacts between the two sides of the Taiwan Strait.[42]

(3)   The Social Sciences Academy, also in Fuzhou, also keeps an eye on Taiwan affairs because of its geographical convenience being located near Taiwan and close to considerable Taiwanese investment.

(4)   Both Xiamen University in Fujian and Nankai University in Tianjin have established a graduate programme of Taiwan

studies. Xiamen University has also published a journal, *Taiwan Research Quarterly*, since 1983.[43]

In a similar vein, since 16 August 1988, several 'Taiwan Studies Associations' have been founded in Beijing, Shanghai and Guangzhou, comprising most of the PRC's professional Taiwan watchers. Obviously, the foundation of these Associations are not only designed for closer cooperation of the mainland's Taiwan researchers in each city but also for forming an academic united front aimed at the ROC.

The foregoing description and analysis reveal that the PRC's united front network toward Taiwan is enormous and virtually ubiquitous within the PRC, and comprises the PRC's party, army, and government, academic circles, and the general public as well. Obviously, the function and mission of some of these organizations and agencies overlap. When Beijing devotes so many resources into its Taiwan united front work, it is understandable that Taipei is very concerned and feels threatened by Beijing's activities.

Beijing not only implements its united front endeavours within the mainland, it also instructs its diplomats, students, and citizens who travel abroad to carry out united front efforts directed at Taiwanese Chinese. In an 'Internal Document' entitled 'A Note For Citizens Going Abroad' issued by the Liaison Office of the People's Government of Guangdong Province in 1985, people are instructed

> 1. to have friendly relations with Taiwan's officers, students, and compatriots; to make every effort to persuade them to side with us and expand the patriotic united front. Before going abroad, you should make the necessary preparations in order to cope with the situations you encounter when you meet Taiwan's people overseas.
>
> 2. to fly high the banner of patriotism and to easily carry out the united front work. In your conversation with people from Taiwan, you should stress our Party's Taiwan policy and tell them that the reunification of the motherland is the common responsibility of all Chinese including the Taiwan compatriots. You should refute any idea of 'Two Chinas' and 'Independence for Taiwan' if Taiwan's people raise such a topic. . . You should actively and pragmatically introduce the current situation and the bright future of our country to your Taiwan friends . . .
>
> 3. to make yourself acquainted with Taiwan's people. You are allowed to attend academic exchanges and activities that

are organized by the people from Taiwan. You can also keep in touch with them. . . . However, you should be alert when you contact Taiwan's people. You should report in time to your team leader or cadres in our embassies and consulates regarding the situations of Taiwanese communities and ask for further instructions.[44]

## Conclusion

The PRC's policy toward the ROC has evolved from actual sporadic fighting during the 1950s into a period of gradual adjustment towards a *modus vivendi* since the late 1970s. Beijing has put forward a number of proposals for solving the two China issue, which include appealing to the nostalgia of the old guard in Taiwan, nationalism and providing trade and investment incentives. It also encourages contacts and exchanges between partisans of the two Chinas, as well as visits to relatives and ancestral homes on the mainland, stressing their common heritage despite diverse social and political systems. All of these peaceful overtures have undoubtedly helped to stabilize the situation on both sides of the Taiwan Strait and led neither Beijing nor Taipei to see any virtue in fomenting the war hysteria on which both seemed to thrive at one time. The peaceful trend does presage a transition to a point where issues can eventually be settled by diplomacy rather than by force of arms.

Beijing has also intensified its Taiwan work by establishing a number of new agencies and institutions to expedite its united front efforts towards Taiwan in the hope of convincing all Chinese, especially the Taiwanese Chinese, to support its reunification course. Although the peaceful approach is Beijing's preference for settling the issue, Beijing so far has not promised not to use force against Taiwan as Taipei has requested, and calls Taipei its 'local government'—which contravenes the peaceful solution and equal footing principles.

From the perspective of integration theory, a 'peaceful approach' is the main prerequisite for beginning the amalgamation of different countries. This theory further posits that a 'spill-over' effect will occur if contacts start on simple issues which then will lead to further contacts involving complex issues. At this moment, non-political exchanges such as indirect trade and Taiwanese Chinese visiting their relatives in the mainland, have occurred between the two Chinas, which is a positive step toward the resolution of the two China problem. However, there are some policies and actions on the part of the PRC that might lead to the failure of integration rather than its success. These are: (a) early insistence on complete amalgamation; (b) early efforts to establish a monopoly of violence; and (c) outright military conquest'.[45]

Unfortunately, these three methods are more or less already incorporated in the PRC's policy for the resolution of the two China issue. Beijing insists on its proposed reunification course as the only way to integrate. It completely opposes other formulas which may offer more latitude for the two Chinas to amalgamate peacefully. Meanwhile, the threat of force also generates antipathy among the Taiwanese Chinese and will hinder the resolution of the China problem. In Chapters Five and Seven all of these factors will be examined in greater detail.

# Taipei's Responses, Proposals and Strategies

# Chapter 4

■

## The Republic of China on Taiwan

When Chiang Kai-shek withdrew to Taiwan in 1949, he proclaimed that one day soon he would 'counterattack and recover the mainland'.[1] He optimistically went on to say that during 'the first year in Taiwan we are going to make preparations for attacking the Communists; [during] the second year we will launch our attack; [in] the third year we shall make a clean sweep of the Communist bandits in the mainland; and in the fourth year we will recover our mainland'.[2]

Since then, forty-three years have passed. The Republic of China has not yet recovered the mainland, nor has the People's Republic of China liberated Taiwan. While the PRC has changed its policy toward the ROC since 1979, Taipei has also quietly modified its declaratory policy toward Beijing from 'counterattack and recover the mainland', mentioned above, to 'using thirty per cent military force and seventy per cent political force' to recover the mainland during the 1960s and 1970s and finally to 'reunification of China under the Three Principles of People' in the 1980s. These political slogans underscore the fact that the ROC's attitude and policy toward the PRC has become much less hostile with the passage of time.

Before continuing further, it is necessary to briefly review some background information about the position of neglected island China in the international community. This exercise provides a clearer perspective of the ROC today and its position and responses toward the PRC's peaceful overtures.

## A Brief History

The ROC was founded 1 January 1912, and was the first republic in Asia. However this fledgeling republic was plagued by trouble and 'suffered a series of civil wars and encroachments from foreign countries'.[3] In 1949, the ROC was defeated by the PRC (founded on 1 October 1949) and 'temporarily moved its government to Taiwan . . . and carried on the struggle against Communist tyranny and for a united, democratic China'.[4] Since then, the two Chinas have confronted each other. They refuse to officially recognize each other and each government proclaims itself as the sole representative of the whole Chinese people and nation in the international community. They also claim each other's territory, including many isles in the South China Sea, as their own. These conditions constitute the so-called 'two China issue'.

Taiwan, also known as Formosa, is an island off the southeastern coast of the Chinese mainland, separated from the mainland's Fujian province by the 130 to 200 kilometers width of the Taiwan Strait. Taiwan has an area of 35,873.1 square kilometers (13,850.7 square miles). The Penghu Pescadores and the two island groups of Quemoy and Matsu just off the Fujian coast are also ruled by the ROC. The ROC effectively controls an area of 36,179.1 square kilometers (13,968.8 square miles) in comparison to the PRC's size of about 9.6 million square kilometers (4 million square miles) which is about the same size as Holland, larger than Massachusetts and Connecticut combined,[5] and a little smaller than Tasmania.

There were only six million Taiwanese Chinese when President Chiang Kai-shek and his two million mainland followers arrived in Taiwan during the period from 1948 to 1950.[6] But by the end of 1991, Taiwan's population stood at about 20 million (the PRC's population is 1,150 million). Except for some 325,000 aborigines, the population is made up almost entirely of ethnic Chinese. Population density is 566 people per square kilometer, one of the highest figures in the world and five times greater than that of the PRC. The ROC on Taiwan has more people than Australia and New Zealand combined and nearly as many as Sweden, Norway, and Denmark combined. Taiwan and the Taiwanese Chinese are basically an extension of the Chinese mainland in terms of geographical structure as well as the culture, history, language, and ethnic composition of the inhabitants.

## Economic Condition

As Joseph Frankel has pointed out, the present-day ROC 'is not a continuation of the moribund nationalist regime which

lost out to the Communists on the mainland. . . . It is, however, economically thriving and apparently politically stable'.[7]
Indeed, the ROC has created a so-called 'economic miracle'
in the past four decades and together with South Korea,
Singapore, and Hong Kong has been called one of the 'four
little dragons' of Asia.[8] The appropriate statistical data about
the ROC's economic condition is provided in Table 4-1.

The ROC's economic development and social achievement
is among the top ranks of Asia countries, and the ROC's gross
national product (GNP) per capita in 1987 is almost fourteen
times that of the PRC. Moreover, Fredrick Chien, then Chairman
of the Council for Economic Planning and Development (the
ROC cabinet's economics think tank), predicted that by the
year 2000, the per capita GNP of the ROC will reach US$15,000
and the ROC will have assumed the role of a skill-intensive
industrial producer, a regional conference and financial centre, and an important computer software designing venue.[9]
For its part the PRC 'will attain or surpass the goal of "meeting the basic needs" in living standards set for the developing countries' by the year 2000[10] with per capita GNP around
US$800.[11] If so, the gap of living standards between the two
Chinas will be further enlarged by the year 2000.

In 1951, the per capita GNP of the ROC on Taiwan was a
mere US$100 with the international trade volume no more
than US$300 million. By 1990, the per capita GNP of the ROC
was US$7,997 with the international trade volume around
US$121.9 billion.[12] In other words, the per capita GNP of the
ROC during the past four decades has increased 50-fold while
the international trade volume has expanded 300-fold with an
annual average economic growth rate around 8 per cent.[13] 'By
1992, the ROC on Taiwan was the fourteenth largest trading
partner in the world and its GNP ranked twentieth, while its
per capita income exceeded US$10,000. Taiwan's foreign
exchange reserves rank second in the world, and it is the
world's seventh largest foreign aid donor'.[14] The surplus of
international trade has brought to Taiwan an affluent life style
with a much higher living standard than the PRC.

In early 1991, the ROC's foreign exchange reserve reached
around US$80 billion, the second largest in the world.[15] This
large foreign exchange reserve has meant that the ROC has no
need to borrow from abroad in the foreseeable future. According
to Chang Chi-cheng, then Director-General of the Central Bank,

# Table 4-1: STATISTICAL DATA: ROC on Taiwan June 1993

**POPULATION (end of Jan. 1989):**

| | |
|---|---|
| Taiwan area | 20,797,747 |
| Kinmen & Matsu | 50,617 |

**CRUDE BIRTH RATE (only Taiwan area):**

| | |
|---|---|
| 1989 | 15.72% |
| 1990 | 16.55% |
| 1991 | 15.71% |
| 1992 | 15.54% |

**LIFE EXPECTANCY (years):**

| | | |
|---|---|---|
| 1991 | Male | 71.83 |
| | Female | 77.15 |
| 1992 | Male | 71.92(p) |
| | Female | 77.23(p) |

**MEDICAL CONDITIONS (per 10,000 persons):**

| | |
|---|---|
| 1990 No. of health personnel: | 44.79 |
| No. of hospital beds: | 43.80 |
| 1991 No. of health personnel: | 47.15 |
| No. of hospital beds: | 45.14 |
| 1992 No. of health personnel: | 48.10(p) |
| No. of hospital beds: | 46.30 |

**LABOR FORCE:**

| | |
|---|---|
| Labor participation rate (%): | |
| 1989 | 60.12 |
| 1990 | 59.24 |
| 1991 | 59.11 |
| 1992 | 59.34 |

**UNEMPLOYMENT RATE (%):**

| | |
|---|---|
| 1989 | 1.57 |
| 1990 | 1.67 |
| 1991 | 1.51 |
| 1992 | 1.51 |

**ECONOMIC GROWTH RATE (%):**

| | |
|---|---|
| 1989 | 7.33 |
| 1990 | 5.02 |
| 1991 | 7.24 |
| 1992 | 6.06 |

**AMENITIES (end of 1992, per 100 homes):**

| | |
|---|---|
| Color TV sets | 99.30 |
| Refrigerators | 99.10 |
| Telephones | 96.10 |
| Washing machine | 90.30 |
| Air-conditioners | 58.00 |
| Motorcycles | — |
| Automobiles | 38.50 |

**EDUCATION (1991/92)**

| Schools | |
|---|---|
| Elementary | 2,509 |
| Junior High | 709 |
| Senior High | 186 |
| Vocational | 211 |
| College and University | 124 |
| Others | 3,080 |

| Students | |
|---|---|
| Elementary | 2,200.968 |
| Junior High | 1,179.028 |
| Senior High | 229,876 |
| Vocational | 500,721 |
| College and University | 653,162 |
| Others | 562,764 |

| | |
|---|---|
| Percentage of the population enrolled in schools: | 25.605 |
| Percentage of school children to school-aged children: | 99.79 |

**CHANGES IN PRICE INDICES:**

| Changes in Wholesale price index: | |
|---|---|
| 1989 | -0.38 |
| 1990 | -0.61 |
| 1991 | 0.17 |
| 1992 | -3.05 |

| Changes in consumer price index: | |
|---|---|
| 1989 | 4.40 |
| 1990 | 4.13 |
| 1991 | 3.62 |
| 1992 | 4.46 |

**GNP (at current prices, US$ million):**

| | |
|---|---|
| 1989 | 150,283 |
| 1990 | 160,913 |
| 1991 | 179,763 |
| 1992 | 210,886 |

**PER CAPITA GNP (US$):**

| | |
|---|---|
| 1989 | 7,512 |
| 1990 | 7,954 |
| 1991 | 8,788 |
| 1992 | 10,215 |

**FOREIGN TRADE (US$ MILLION):**

| Exports: | |
|---|---|
| 1989 | 66,304 |
| 1990 | 67,214 |
| 1991 | 76,178 |
| 1992 | 81,470 |

| Imports: | |
|---|---|
| 1989 | 52,265 |
| 1990 | 54,716 |
| 1991 | 62,861 |
| 1992 | 71,977 |

**TOURISM (persons):**

| Overseas Chinese & Foreign Visitors to Taiwan | |
|---|---|
| 1989 | 2,004,126 |
| 1990 | 1,934,084 |
| 1991 | 1,854,506 |
| 1992 | 1,873,327 |

| Chinese Tourists Going Abroad | |
|---|---|
| 1989 | 2,107,813 |
| 1990 | 2,942,316 |
| 1991 | 3,366,076 |
| 1992 | 4,214,734 |

**REMARKS:**
(p): preliminary

Source: Directorate General of Budget, Accounting & Statistics, Executive Yuan, Republic of China

the ROC's foreign debt in 1988 has dropped to only US$2 billion. He said that the ROC government will pay off this debt in advance and the ROC would soon become one of the few trading nations in the world that has no foreign debts'.[16]

Although the ROC has become more wealthy, Taipei has managed to achieve 'substantial' equality of income distribution. In 1953, the ratio between the incomes of households in the top 20 per cent income brackets and those in the bottom 20 per cent was 20.5 to one.[17] This ratio was reduced to between the range of 4.6:1 and 4.2:1 during the 1970s.[18] As Taiwan's economic changed from labor-intensive to capital intensive industries in the 1980s, the income gap ratio has widened from 4.33:1 in 1986 to 4.73:1 in July 1988.[19] The ruling Kuomintang (KMT) has been closely watching this development and has been trying to devise effective measures to prevent the gap from widening further.[20] The ROC's economic achievement in the past four decades is nothing short of remarkable. It has not only attained enormous economic growth but also substantial equality in the distribution of wealth. In fact, the Chinese on Taiwan at this moment have enjoyed the best living standards in Chinese history. This has led the ROC President Lee Teng-hui to say confidently that 'our economic growth rate now surpasses that of capitalist countries, and our distribution of wealth is more even than that of socialist countries'.[21]

## Political Situation

In 1981, Jurgen Domes labelled the ROC's political system as a 'development-oriented authoritarian system'.[22] According to Wilbur W. White, under the authoritarian political system 'the liberty of the individual in theory and in practice is entirely overshadowed by and subordinate to the authority of the state, and . . . governmental power is usually centered in a small, autocratic group of leaders'.[23] Roy C. Macridis has said that the essence of authoritarianism 'is absolute and unchallengeable power'. He gave three main conditions that give rise to authoritarian regimes: Firstly, a new nation-state requires unity and support from its people; it requires a period to consolidate and strengthen its leadership. When the new state perceives other states has as potentially hostile, under these circumstances the state has reason to use authoritarian means to quell dissent and ensure unity, to strengthen its control, and to develop institutions of command and support.[24]

Taiwan's situation more or less fulfills the above-mentioned three conditions. The transplanted KMT regime was completely new and strange to the Taiwan Chinese. The ROC faced not only the external threat from the PRC, but also encountered problems within Taiwan of friction between the mainland refugees and the Taiwan Chinese, especially after the unfortunate 'February 28 Incident' of 1947.[25] Therefore, it is perhaps not surprising that the ROC has used an authoritarian political system to govern Taiwan since 1945. In addition, the traditional Chinese penchant for an authoritarian political culture is also another reason. The ROC has evolved into an authoritarian political system, despite repeatedly pledging to institute 'democratic, constitutional politics.' Undeniably, the ROC's political system does not meet the Western world's standards of pluralism and liberalism; however, this system has contributed positively to the development of Taiwan in the past. As Ambrose Yeo-chi King has noted, the authoritarian political system has had a positive effect during the process of nation-building on Taiwan, especially in the early period. He elaborated, saying that the stability of politics and society in Taiwan under authoritarian rule has in fact created the prerequisite conditions for Taiwan's economic development, while economic development in turn has become the most important factor for the continued stability of Taiwan's politics and society.[26]

In 1986, the ROC began to relax its authoritarian policies. During September 1986, an opposition Democratic Progressive Party was formed in defiance of martial law. This newly founded party gained 23 per cent of the vote in the 1986 election expanding to 31.83 per cent and proclaimed victory as a new party gaining such a large share. In July 1987, martial law was lifted, 38 years after it came into force. Since then 'street protests, running at three a day, on issues ranging from pollution to independence have been coolly tolerated'.[27] In January 1988, Taiwan's 'Paper Ban', that is, the ban on starting newspapers was also lifted; since then, freedom of speech has genuinely come to the fore. Since 1988, street protests have averaged three a day. In February 1988, Dr. Ma Ying-jeou,

Deputy Secretary-General of the KMT, announced in the United States that the KMT would hand over the reins of government if it was unable to secure a majority vote in the next election.[28] Thus, some of the criteria used for measuring the degree of democratization of a country, such as freedom of speech, and the existence of multi-party systems, have been gradually emerging in Taiwan. All of these events and phenomena clearly indicate that democratization has developed step by step in the ROC, which 'enable the 20 million Taiwan Chinese to have the first genuine democratic political system in Chinese history'.[29]

## The Dilemma of the ROC

Unfortunately, in spite of its economic achievements, the ROC has continuously been isolated in the international community. Fewer and fewer countries have diplomatic ties with the ROC and recognize it as the sole representative of all China. This situation has left the ROC facing various dilemmas.

Externally, the 'one China' principle adhered to by both Taipei and Beijing has favored the PRC as a result of Taipei's diplomatic setbacks since the 1970s. The position of long standing held by both Chinas is that 'there is only one China, and Taiwan is a part of China'. When the ROC maintained full diplomatic relations with most other countries this principle could do no harm because the countries recognized Taipei as the 'one China' and therefore also recognized that 'Taiwan is a part of the ROC'. When the majority of countries shifted their recognition to Beijing, however, the 'one China' principle forced Taiwan into an unfavorable diplomatic position. Although the ROC still regards itself as the legitimate Chinese government, in reality this posture is weak and few countries accept it. The PRC understands this and frequently cites this 'one China fiction' so that it can prevent Taipei and other countries from deviating from the 'one China' course with the PRC as the one China.[30] This also explains why the PRC confidently maintains that the ROC will become one of its 'local governments after reunification; after all, Beijing seems genuinely to believe that Taipei is one of its 'local governments'.

The ROC can not retreat from this 'one China' position for a number of reasons. The 'self-pride' as well as a Confucian sense of political orthodoxy of the ROC ensures that it will not compromise with the PRC on this issue.[31] Retreat from this long held stance would mean the ROC's seeking another option such as the acceptance of two Chinas or a declaration of Taiwan independence which might upset the PRC and increase tension in the Taiwan Straits. Taiwan might undergo a period of transition and power struggle which would endanger the current leadership of the ROC government and the stability of Taiwan. In addition, most of Taiwan's Chinese are still attached to the mainland and do not want to cut ties between Taiwan and the Chinese mainland for pragmatic reasons such as family ties or business interests. Something that can be labelled a 'consciousness of a great China' that is, some Chinese people always believe that China was, is and always will be unified and a great civilization, makes many of Taiwan's Chinese believe that China should and will be reunited sometime in the future.

Insistence on the 'one China' principle, at least theoretically, maintains for the time being the integrity of China's territory and sovereignty without any argument over who is that 'China'. Taipei believes as long as it keeps the 'one China' position alive, the door will still be open for it to return to the mainland by the reunification of China according to Taipei's terms.[32]

Internally, Taipei's adherence to the 'one China' principle has brought confusion to its people and has become an issue disputed in Taiwan. Chinese in Taiwan have been taught that since ancient times China has always been a great country with a five-thousand-year history and huge territory as well as population, including both the mainland and Taiwan. In reality, however, as of mid-1992, today's ROC is located on a small island and only 29 countries recognize it as the sole representative of China. Hungdah Chiu, a professor of the School of Law of the University of Maryland, USA, has predicted that the ROC will be totally isolated diplomatically by the year 2000 if the 'one China' principle as currently espoused is still maintained by Taipei.[33]

An ironic combination of diplomacy and political reality have shaped the ROC into the image of talking like a giant but acting as a dwarf. This situation has become the ruling

KMT's Achilles heel and the root of discord in Taiwan, having generated debate within Taiwan between the pro-reunification (*Tong Pai*) and the pro-independence (*Du Pai*) groups. The tension inherent within this situation also reduces the confidence of Taiwanese about the island's future and hampers economic and political development in Taiwan. The KMT's urgent task at this stage is to convince its people that the maintenance of the 'one China' principle is for the public good and not just for some vested interest groups such as the old guard faction in Taiwan's parliament before 1992, and to prove that under the 'one China' principle the KMT can break out of its diplomatic isolation.

# Chapter 5

■

## The Responses of the ROC to PRC Proposals

IN 1979, when Beijing launched its 'peaceful offensive' and put forward the proposal of 'three communications and four exchanges' in the 'Message to Compatriots in Taiwan', ROC Premier Sun Yun-chuan instantly categorized this proposal as 'trickery and lies'.[1] When Ye Jiangying broached his 'Nine-Point Proposal' in 1981, Sun also rebuffed it adding that it was Beijing's intention to sow discord within Taiwan.[2] One of Taiwan's newspapers went so far as to label this proposal 'pure hokum—a united front pretense intended to deceive the democratic world and impress us'.[3] In a major speech in December 1983, the President of the ROC Chiang Ching-kuo responded to Deng Xiaoping's 'Six-Points' proposal by saying 'the endless united front tricks played by the Communist bandits are, to us, futile efforts that indicate they are at the end of their tether'.[4]

Regarding the PRC's 'one country, two systems' policy put forward in 1984, ROC Premier Yu Kuo-hua said that this policy is trying 'to delude the free world, to produce an illusion of "peaceful-coexistence" between the ROC and the Communist China. . . . If today we are not alert and naively discuss the so-called model, theory or system with the Communist bandits, it would only lead us to the limbo of self-destruction or to capitulate to the Communist bandits'.[5] In August 1988, Shen Chang-huan, former general-secretary to ROC President Lee Teng-hui, concluded that Beijing's Taiwan policy since 1979 was 'a plot that uses economic means to achieve political ends'. He reminded the Taiwanese Chinese to recognize Beijing's evil intention behind its 'smiling face', to be vigilant about Beijing's united front trick and to maintain an apprehensive consciousness as well as the consciousness of 'enemy and us'.[6] President Lee Teng-hui criticized Beijing's policy of 'one country-two systems' as a plot to downgrade the ROC's status to that of a local government under Beijing's authority. Lee went on to add that 'the Chinese Communists always repress us to come to its terms with force, therefore they will not renounce the use of force against us in the future.'[7]

From the above comments made by the leaders of the ROC we can sense the strong mistrust toward the PRC that exists in the ROC. This phenomenon can be ascribed to the following factors: (1) previous experience in dealing with the PRC; (2) Beijing has been proven to lack credibility and sincerity; (3) Beijing's proposals are unrealistic; and (4) political realities in the ROC.

## Past Experience

Beijing always refers to its two periods of cooperation with the KMT in the past: when Dr. Sun Yat-sen agreed to form a united front with the CCP and allowed individual CCP members to join the KMT in 1924; and when the KMT and the CCP cooperated during the War of Resistance Against Japan during the early stages of World War Two. The PRC therefore actively encourages the ROC to enter a third period of cooperation to resolve the two China issue.[8]

Due to the limitations of research as well as space, these two instances of cooperation between the two parties are not reviewed here. However, a brief discussion of the KMT's views towards these series of events is essential to understand why Taipei now still mistrusts Beijing and is not interested in a third-round of 'cooperation' with Beijing at this moment.

First of all, Taipei seems to regard these events not as examples of cooperation but incidents of 'the bitter struggle between the KMT and the CCP' for political power in the newly founded ROC.[9] Taipei maintains that in order to expand the influence of the newly established CCP (founded on 1 July 1921 in Shanghai), the CCP, at Moscow's inspiration, requested the formation of a united front with the KMT and to let individual CCP members join the KMT so that the two parties could fight together to accomplish China's national revolution.[10]

Taipei, however, accused the CCP of exploiting the first cooperative arrangement during the period from 1922–27 to mount a power struggle against the KMT. The accusations run as follows: the CCP continuously tried to split the KMT from within; intentionally distort public opinion against the KMT for the purpose of gaining grass roots support from the people, for example, plotting the Chungshan Frigate Incident, an attempt to kidnap Chiang Kai-shek in 1926; and produce negative public opinion of the anti-warlord Northern Expedition.[11] Taipei claimed that during the first period of cooperation, the CCP's armed forces grew and the CCP's membership also 'increased from 123 in 1922 to over 57,900 in April 1927. . . . The CCP clearly succeeded in their plot while the KMT suffered a tremendous loss in the national revolutionary movement.'[12]

The KMT accused the CCP of taking advantage of the second period of cooperation lasting from 1937–1945 to 'develop their armed forces and to enlarge their territorial control' which eventually led to a communist political subversion and open armed rebellion in the ROC after World War Two.[13] The Red Army, according to the PRC, expanded from 30,000 men in 1937 to 181,000 men in 1938 and then to 500,000 by the end of 1940. In the first half of 1945 the CCP's regular military force had reached 910,000 men accompanied by 2,200,000 militiamen. Finally, when Japan announced its surrender in September 1945, the CCP's regular armed forces had reached a total of 1,200,000 men.[14] In the meantime the territory and population under the CCP's control also increased from almost nothing in 1937 to over one million square kilometers (approximately 11 per cent of the land area of China) and 130 million people by September 1945.[15]

The KMT's viewpoint is that it is in part because the CCP exploited the KMT's goodwill during the two 'cooperations' (or united fronts) that the KMT was eventually ousted from the mainland. It is unfair to say, however, that the CCP is the sole cause of the KMT's loss of the Chinese mainland. There are in fact many other factors that led to the KMT's defeat in the mainland in the 1940s' civil war, most notably corruption and policy mistakes of the ROC government. Nevertheless, from the viewpoint of a zero-sum-game, it is clear that the KMT was the loser during these two periods of cooperation with the CCP. Therefore, unless the KMT can be persuaded that it will tangibly benefit, there is no possibility that the KMT in Taiwan at this moment would like to enter into a third round of cooperation with the CCP. As Thomas B. Gold points out, 'for the KMT, the term "united front" conjures up

only bitter memories culminating in defeat and humiliation. . . .
Calling on the KMT to give a third united front a try is a
doomed tactic'.[16]

## Lack of Credibility and Sincerity

Apart from its own past experience, Taipei also draws lessons
from the present and is not favourably impressed by the PRC's
record as a reliable neighbor. The case of Tibet may serve to
illustrate this point.

The PRC promised that the Tibetan people would 'have the
right of exercising national regional autonomy', and that the
PRC would not 'alter the existing political system in Tibet'
nor would change 'the established status, functions, and powers of the Dalai Lama' after concluding an agreement with Tibet
on 23 May 1951.[17] In this manner, Tibet was liberated peacefully by the Communists. Mao Zedong, however, was not sincere in the execution of this agreement. He merely wanted to
use this agreement to disguise his real intention of commu-
nizing Tibet. In an inner-party directive, Mao Zedong in April
1952 instructed his Working Committee in Tibet as follows:

> We must do our best and take proper steps to win over the
> Dalai Lama and the majority of his top echelon and to iso-
> late the handful of bad elements in order to achieve a grad-
> ual, bloodless transformation of the Tibetan economic and
> political system over a number of years. . . . For the time
> being, leave everything as it is, let this [present] situation
> continue, and do not take up these questions until our army
> is able to meet its own needs through production and wins
> the support of the masses a year or two from now.[18]

In 1959, Mao Zedong reckoned that the time was ripe and
sent the People's Liberation Army (PLA) into Tibet. Tibet was
conquered and occupied by the PRC and the Dalai Lama was
forced to take refuge in India. Tibet serves as a good lesson
to the ROC, and Taipei often reminds its people of the similarity between the conditions offered to Tibet in 1952 and
Beijing's proposals to Taiwan today.[19] Perhaps people might
counter, saying that it is unfair to compare Deng Xiaoping
with Mao because Deng seems to be more sincere than Mao.
From Taipei's viewpoint, however, both are communists and

there is no difference between them concerning the resolution of the China issue. They both intend to incorporate Taiwan into the PRC. While Mao in Taipei's view used the 'stick', Deng employs more of a 'carrot' strategy toward the ROC.

The contradictions within Beijing's Taiwan policy also reveals the PRC's unreliability and insincerity. Deng has said that the ROC can retain its military forces after reunification with the PRC. Beijing however, resolutely opposes any sale of military weapons to Taipei.[20] At this point, we might ask what is an army without arms? What will Taiwan do without arms if the Tibetan experience is repeated? The PRC also promises that Taiwan can maintain its current economic system and trade relations with other countries; it also asks those countries who have set up trade offices in Taiwan to shut them down. The PRC declaratory policy has prohibited Taiwan from establishing trade promotion centers or offices in other countries. We might wonder how Taiwan could have foreign trade without offices to promote it and to issue visas to the business people concerned? Beijing says that it will use peaceful means to realize reunification; however, it has repeatedly threatened to use military force against Taiwan. According to Winston L. Y. Yang, Beijing has made this threat no less than ninety times between 1979 and August 1988.[21] All of these instances explain why the ROC is so cautious about the PRC's peaceful gestures.

In fact, Taipei's suspicion of Beijing is not groundless. In April 1985 the General Office under the Central Committee of the CCP issued a 'confidential' internal document to its agencies and highlighted three main points regarding Beijing's efforts for the reunification of Taiwan:

> First, we should exploit the gradual liberalization situation of Taiwan's publication censorship. We should, through means of sending letters to editors of newspapers, or contributing articles to magazines, or donating money from overseas, sway Taiwan's Dangwai [people outside the KMT or opposition groups in Taiwan] opinion and guide this opinion gradually toward support for the idea of contact between Taiwan and the mainland. Further, we should try to influence the Dangwai opinion to support our proposals becoming debate issues within Taiwan's 'Legislative Yuan' [Congress]. By so doing, these proposals will create heavy pressure on the ruling KMT's decision-making concerning its mainland policy. Second, we should thoroughly understand each

*Dangwai* faction leader's thinking and position, and try through different kinds of channels to make friends with them . . . We should support them . . . so that they will not feel alone and isolated. . . If these leaders want to do business with us, we should give them special privileges and encourage them to do so . . Third, the conflict between the KMT and the *Dangwai* is becoming sharper and deeper day by day. We should grasp each opportunity, exploit each chance . . . to widen such a conflict within Taiwan. We should expand the general public's antagonism to the Kuomintang regime, and try to produce another "Kaohsiung Uprising" so as to create better conditions for Taiwan's revolution'.[22] (The Kaohsiung Uprising refers to a street demonstration in December 1979, the first of its kind since 1949. Many Taiwan dissidents were sentenced to long jail terms as a result. The Kaohsiung Uprising can be regarded as the beginning of Taiwan's democratic movement and their dissatisfaction with KMT rule.)

The above-mentioned instances have revealed the nature of Beijing's 'plot' against the KMT and the ROC and have also damaged the PRC's image as a reliable and sincere neighbor in the mind of most Taiwan Chinese. This document of the General Office has also revealed Beijing's misunderstanding of Taiwan's politics. Although the *Dangwai* (the forerunner of today's Democratic Progressive Party) opposed the KMT's government and its policies, their interests were not necessarily aligned with those of the CCP. After all, they agreed neither with the KMT nor the CCP regarding the future of Taiwan. In fact, this document might spur both the KMT and the *Dangwai* to foster a consensus regarding the PRC.[23] Professor C. L. Chiou has commented that it is understandable that the KMT would not accept Beijing's proposals due to the long struggle for power and ideological differences between the two parties. To most of the 20 million Taiwan Chinese, however, the PRC's serious lack of credibility is perhaps the main reason why they cannot accept Beijing's reunification policy.[24]

## Beijing's Proposals are Unrealistic

The first unrealistic aspect of Beijing's proposals, from Taipei's viewpoint, is the PRC's insistance that it is the 'central government' of China while the ROC is a 'local government'.[25] According to Beijing, two rationales explain this position:

> (1) In 1949, the Chinese people had overthrown the Chiang Kai-shek regime and established a government of their own choice. Therefore Taiwan should then have automatically come under jurisdiction of the Government of the PRC. The situation in China is that of a new government which is awarded all territories under the jurisdiction of an over-thrown government according to generally recognized principles of international law.[26]
> (2) Beijing has argued that since ancient times Taiwan has been an inalienable part of China. The countries who have established diplomatic ties with the PRC have formally recognized Beijing as the sole legitimate central government of China and, at least implicitly, Taiwan as part of China. According to this logic, Taiwan is Beijing's local government.[27]

Beijing's rationale on the surface seems plausible. Although the ROC had lost its civil war in the Chinese mainland, it still exists on Taiwan—a part of Chinese territory that the PRC cannot deny it. Therefore, China in effect is 'divided'[28] similiar to the two Koreas. The reality of the two China issue is that 'there is one nation with two contending regimes, who assert overlapping claims'.[29] Part of this reality is that these two Chinas 'have asserted legal identity with the previous national entity and have refused to recognize the *de jure* existence of their opposite numbers'.[30] The two Chinas both claim sole-representation status as the country's legitimate government and have made every effort to prevent third parties from recognizing the other side in the hope of buttressing its own 'identity and legitimacy while weakening that of the other side'.[31] The other important component in the two China issue is the extremely uneven division of population and territory, which has led to the PRC having 'enough political clout to prevent other nations from establishing diplomatic relations with both parties of the divided state'.[32] Thus the PRC has replaced the ROC in the United Nations dating back to 1971 and the countries recognizing the PRC outnumber those recognizing the ROC. This reality does not reflect the fact that, although Beijing has seats in most international organizations as sole representative of China, it still cannot act effectively for Taiwan and the Pescadores.[33] Therefore, the situation in China is that a new government (that of the PRC) emerged in the mainland in 1949 as a result of Chinese civil war, while the original Chinese government (that of the ROC) has not yet been overthrown and still exists on Taiwan.

People might argue that, since the ROC has lost its membership in the UN and a majority of countries have recognized the PRC as the sole representative of China, the ROC's international status is in question. The international status of a state is not necessarily tied to membership of the UN. Countries such as Switzerland, Monaco, Lichtenstein, and the two Koreas (before 1992) are not members of the UN but no one questions their national status.[34] Although only 30 states have maintained diplomatic relations with the ROC, Taipei's commercial and other semi-official and unofficial relations with other countries have still continued to increase. 'Clearly Taiwan was not being isolated from the international community'.[35]

An interesting perspective on the ROC's sovereignty is provided by reference to international law. According to Article 1 of the Montevideo Convention on Rights and Duties of States of 1933: 'The State as a person of international law should possess the following qualifications: (a) a permanent population; (b) a defined territory; (c) a government; and (d) the capability to enter into relations with other States'.[36]

The ROC possesses all of these attributes of a sovereign state.[37] The ROC Government has effectively governed the population of 20 million in the defined territorial area of Taiwan and the Pescadores (excluding mainland China) under the constitution drawn up in 1946 by the National Assembly. The ROC 'is thus a legally constituted government'.[38] Meanwhile, the ROC continues to exercise its sovereignty on Chinese soil. The changes in territory and population since 1949 'do not affect the continuity of its existence so long as its identity is preserved'.[39] As mentioned before, the ROC also has the capacity to enter into relations with other States. The number of countries that maintain diplomatic ties with Taipei is 'not large, but is comparable with the number of embassies in most small Third World countries'.[40]

Victor H. Li, in hearings before the Committee on Foreign Relations of the US Senate, testified that Taiwan is a 'de facto entity with international personality'.[41] James Crawford categorized Taiwan as one of the 'entities unrecognized as separate states' and as one of 'some special cases in the criteria for statehood'.[42] He argued that:

> although [Taiwan] is increasingly isolated from diplomatic intercourse, Taiwan continues to maintain strong informal and trade relations with many other states, and, in general, the status quo has remained unchanged . . . Taiwan is not a state, because it does not claim to be, and is not recognized as such: its status is that of a consolidated local *de facto* government in a civil war situation . . . [Taiwan] is a party to various conventions binding its own territory. Courts faced with specific issues concerning its status may treat it on a *de facto* basis as a well defined geographical, social, and political entity [with] . . . a Government which has undisputed control of the island. . . . Internationally the Government of Formosa is a well established *de facto* government, capable of committing the State to at least certain classes of transaction.[43]

The above discussions, at least to some extent, reflect some viewpoints that the ROC on Taiwan remains a legal and *de facto* Chinese government, which has no connection with the PRC. In fact neither Beijing nor Taipei 'physically represent all of the Chinese people, because neither today enjoys exclusive, unchallenged jurisdiction over all of the territories known to belong to that "one China" claimed by both regimes'.[44] The Chinese case clearly demonstrates that 'international law is inadequate in dealing with the international status of divided nations'.[45] The Chinese case also demonstrates that it is *realpolitik* that guides international law rather than the law guiding *realpolitik*. It was *realpolitik* which guided third parties' diplomatic recognition of the 'big China' (the PRC) instead of the 'small China' (the ROC) and hence created the special situation of the ROC in the world today.[46]

It seems that only by fulfilling four conditions could the issue of the 'unique international personality'[47] of the ROC as well as the sovereignty dispute between Beijing and Taipei over the 'one China' ever be solved: (a) the ROC renounces its claim over mainland China and becomes another Chinese government that only represents Taiwan and Pescadores (the two Chinas formula); (b) the Taiwanese Chinese abandon the old title of the 'ROC' and proclaim the founding of a new country on Taiwan and the Pescadores (the one China and one Taiwan formula). These two solutions both imply the cessation of relations between Taiwan and the Chinese mainland. The 'one China' and 'one Taiwan formula' simply indicates that Taiwan will become a brand new country, while the 'two China' solution stresses the continuation of the ROC with much less territory and a far smaller population; (c) the reunification of the two Chinas either through peaceful or non-peaceful means; (d) peaceful coexistence of both Beijing and Taipei who share together a 'one China' sovereignty internationally (essentially internationally the same as the Korean model). All of these will be further discussed in Chapter Ten.

The PRC's second rationale that Taiwan has been an inalienable part of China is also unsound. It is true that all of the countries who have established diplomatic relations with Beijing 'recognize' the PRC as the sole legitimate Chinese government. However they simultaneously refrain from recognizing Beijing's claim to sovereignty over Taiwan. They have used different phraseology such as 'taking note',[48] 'understanding',[49] 'acknowledging',[50] or 'fully understands and respects',[51] and so on, to 'circumscribe China's demand of "recognizing" its sovereignty over Taiwan'.[52] Some countries do not even bother to mention this point in their agreement with the PRC, such as Rwanda, the Federal Republic of Germany, and Libya.[53] There is also no evidence that these countries, apart from recognizing Beijing as the sole legitimate government of China, also recognize Beijing as the 'central government' of China and Taipei as its 'local government'. Therefore, there is no demonstrable connection between a country's recognition of the PRC and Beijing's rhetoric that Taipei is its 'local government'. That notwithstanding, it seems that the PRC is intentionally trying to take advantage of the ROC's 'one China' principle and the position that 'Taiwan is a part of China' since, due to the ROC's diplomatic isolation, Taipei finds it difficult to refute Beijing's claim to sovereignty over Taiwan.

However the above discussion clearly proves that Taiwan could refute Beijing's claim. No matter how seemingly persuasive its Taiwan policy may be, the PRC must understand that

> if the relegation of the ROC to the status of a 'local government' is unacceptable to Taipei, all the other offers by Peking would be immaterial. If by accepting Peking's terms Taiwan is reduced to a local government, subject to the authority of a 'central government' in Peking, it would not

mean much whether after reunification Taiwan is allowed to maintain its political and economic systems, or to maintain its constabulary force, or to be able to continue its trade relations abroad. Taiwan would simply lose its separate, independent existence that it enjoys today.[54]

If the ROC were to accept the PRC's offer today, then what would be the point of Taipei having pursued the task of national development, that is, to establish China as a free, democratic, and prosperous nation? Why should the ROC give up its economic and political achievements in Taiwan and subject itself to the rule of the PRC? Beijing must convince Taipei in this regard with realistic arguments offering tangible benefits to demonstrate that Taiwanese Chinese can have an even better life after reunification than they enjoy now rather than mere slogans such as 'rejuvenating the motherland' and 'all Chinese are looking for the reunification of China', otherwise, all of its endeavours will be in vain.

Taipei regards Beijing's proposals as 'too unreal and bizarre, raising more questions than are answered'.[55] For example, in the 'Nine-Point Proposal', Beijing promises that if Taiwan's local finances are in difficulty, the 'central government' may subsidize Taiwan as appropriate under the circumstances. This has been described 'as the joke of the century'.[56] As the economic disparity between the two Chinas has been described earlier in the chapter, no further discussion of this offer is needed here other than to mention again that the proposal reflects Beijing's ignorance about Taiwan and leads the Taiwan Chinese people to doubt Beijing's sincerity.

Beijing has promised in its proposals to allow the Taiwanese Chinese to maintain their own social, economic, political and military system after reunification. All the rights, privileges, and conditions, however, that Beijing has promised have already been enjoyed, to an even greater degree, under the ROC government on Taiwan as an independent nation. It borders on the ridiculous that Taipei and the Taiwanese Chinese need to get Beijing's permission to practice these rights and privileges. Why should they need another master?—'a new master who operates a failing system on the mainland'[57] in their eyes.

To use Hong Kong as a model for Taiwan's integration under the one country, two systems plan is also incorrect. An Zhiguo, the political editor of *Beijing Review*, has claimed that Hong Kong can serve as a model for Taiwan because in his opinion the two areas share the following common features: (1) both are parts of China's territory; (2) virtually all the residents in Taiwan are Chinese, 98 per cent of the 5.8 million people in Hong Kong are Chinese; (3) the majority of people in the two regions long for an early reunification of the country; and (4) both currently have a capitalist social system.[58] The first, second and fourth observations are obviously correct and need not be discussed but the third point is contentious. If Hong Kong and Taiwan both 'long for an early reunification' with the PRC, why is China still divided? Why has Hong Kong experienced a 'confidence crisis' with a rising tide of emigration during the past years?[59] Why does Taipei respond so coldly to Beijing's offers of reunification?

An's article also neglects to mention some important basic differences between Hong Kong and Taiwan, which makes the 'Hong Kong Model' inapplicable to Taiwan. According to some scholars,[60] Hong Kong is a colony and ruled by an alien government that lacks legitimacy, that is, it is unelected and unrepresentative of the Hong Kong people, while Taiwan is ruled by a Chinese government that has legitimacy. Hong Kong's return to China is the result of the expiration of a lease from the Chinese government to the British government, while Taiwan had already been returned to China from Japan in 1945 and is *de facto* governed by another Chinese government. Therefore, the Hong Kong issue is an international issue, while whether Taiwan would reunite with the mainland is principally a Chinese affair. Yet at the same time, Hong Kong is geographically contiguous to the mainland and is much more economically dependent on the PRC; for example, Hong Kong relies on the mainland to supply its daily water and food requirements. Finally, Hong Kong itself is virtually indefensible while Taiwan has always maintained armed forces sufficiently strong to deter Beijing from attacking.

Despite the fact that Taipei has never openly endorsed the 'one country, two systems' proposal, the ROC has always been interested in how this proposal would be implemented. James Soong, Secretary-General of the KMT, made a pertinent comment in an interview with Hong Kong's journalist Li Yi in March 1988. He said:

> We are always concerned and constantly keep our eyes closely on the developments of Hong Kong's situation. If

> Communist China, from the beginning [that is, after the signing of Sino-British Joint Declaration in 1984], genuinely does not intervene in Hong Kong's affairs and leaves the Hong Kong people alone in establishing their own democratic system, our people here might show interest [the PRC's 'one country, two systems']. Since Communist China [did not keep its promise to the Hong Kong people] and has already put its hands into Hong Kong affairs, we Taiwanese Chinese are driven to despair about 'one country, two systems.'[61]

Beyond the credibility gap, Taipei also can not accept Beijing's preconditions for implementing the 'one country, two systems' policy:[62] (1) the 'one China' or one country is the the PRC; (2) if the 'one country' principle is not accepted, then there would be no 'two systems'; (3) the 'two systems' are not equal, socialism is still dominant, while capitalism merely supplements socialism; (4) the so-called Special Administrative Region (SAR) is considered as a 'local government'; which may enjoy a high degree of autonomy but cannot contravene Beijing's constitution and policy; (5) how long the capitalist system can coexist with socialism within the context of 'one country' two systems' is ultimately decided by the PRC.

From Beijing's position, these preconditions are understandable because they represent the PRC's sovereignty and legitimacy over the 'one China'. As long as Beijing's national title, sovereignty, and legitimacy are preserved, other matters concerning the two China issue are all negotiable. All of these preconditions, however, are unacceptable to Taipei at this moment because they contravene the ROC's legitimacy and sovereignty. Therefore, whether this is the most 'scientific and creative policy design',[63] as one Beijing intellectual puts it, and could serve as a solution for the two China issue still remains to be seen. Nevertheless it can be argued that the proposal of 'one country, two systems' reveals to some extent Beijing's compromise with reality, and the PRC's tecit admission that its socialist system needs capitalism's assistance.[64]

Against this argument Taipei questioned how Beijing can 'justify the supremacy of socialism on the one hand and use capitalism as a means to win over their compatriots on the other?'[65] Taipei therefore offered a counterproposal to reunify China according to the formula of 'one country, one good system'.[66]

## Political Realities in Taiwan

When discussing the two China issue, the uneven distribution of population and territory between the two Chinas should not be overlooked. The ratio of population is 55:1, while the ratio of territory is approximately 265:1, both in favor of the mainland. This political reality has frequently reminded Taipei to look again before deciding to leap onto Beijing's reunification bandwagon. Yu-ming Shaw, then a spokesman of the ROC Government, has commented on this. He said, 'Faced with overwhelming pressures and shrewd tactics from the Chinese communists, the ROC enjoys little room for maneuver and an even smaller margin of error. Its weakness and alleged inflexibility stem not from a lack of effort but from its unique policy environment'.[67]

Raymond R. M. Tai, then director of the KMT's Culture Work Department, also made the same point. He said that if the ROC and the PRC 'were more or less equal, we could have negotiated'; however, 'if we sent one million people to the mainland, they would disappear. If they sent 10,000 people here, we would see them'.[68] All of these factors make Taipei appear indecisive in responding to Beijing's proposals. As Deutsch said, 'a crucial variable in responsiveness is capability' during the process of integration between countries.[69] If the ROC were to ignore its limited capability and responded favorably to the PRC's proposals, according to Russett's and Deutsch's theories, Taipei might quite possibly destroy, or at least undermine, its own functions and institutions during the request-response process of integration of the two Chinas.[70]

The ROC's domestic situation is another factor which has prevented Taipei from making any positive response to the PRC prior to 1986. Due to the fact that mainland-born Chinese have controlled the political institutions in Taiwan, and for historical reasons such as the 'February 28 Incident' of 1947, some Taiwan-born Chinese and some of the ruling mainlanders habour mutual suspicion over the ROC's mainland policy. The Taiwan-born Chinese wonder if Taiwan would be sold out if the rulers abandoned their present stubborn stance and make a deal with the Communists'[71] motivated by nostalgia and the consciousness of China's as a great nation. Antonio Chiang, publisher of a well-known magazine, *The*

*Journalist*, in Taipei, pointed out, we 'Taiwanese hate the [PRC's] proposal because they only appeal to the Kuomintang. They talk party to party. They think that reunification is only a family affair' between the KMT and the CCP.[72] Furthermore, some of the Taiwan-born Chinese, who comprise more than 80 per cent of Taiwan's 20 million population, consider that the ROC government 'is not truly representative of their wishes and interests, especially in its undue emphasis on Taiwan's reunification, which they see as a ploy by the KMT to monopolize political power. . . . Nor are they enthusiastic about China's unification, which they see as an impossible mission under KMT auspices, and a catastrophe if brought about by the Communists'.[73]

Against this background, any move by Taipei must be very cautious because 'internal politics in Taiwan are delicate and confrontational, and any move by the government to negotiate with the PRC regarding Taiwan's future would immediately trigger mass opposition'.[74] Such a move would also likely prompt a large scale capital outflow to other countries and intensify the confrontation between the Tong Pai and Du Pai factions, thus endangering Taiwan's political and social stability. James Soong has said that Beijing does not understand that a more pluralistic system is evolving in Taiwan adding that the KMT does not have a mandate from the Taiwanese people to negotiate with the PRC.[75]

James Soong's comments reveal the dilemma facing the KMT in Taiwan. In order to properly and effectively deal with the PRC, Taipei needs to obtain a mandate from the Taiwanese Chinese. Only through parliamentary reforms, including the complete re-election of its congress to replace those aged congressmen who were elected in the mainland four decades ago and are not qualified to represent the Taiwan Chinese, could such a mandate be given. By the end of 1991, all of these congressmen elected in the mainland were in fact forced to retire.

# Chapter 6

## Taipei's Proposals

The ROC's response toward the PRC's 'peaceful offensives' has been lukewarm. Perhaps Taipei's strategy was to continue the status quo as long as possible. 'Yet it is very difficult, if not impossible, for the weaker side to maintain the status quo if its stronger and aggressive opponent wants to change'.[1] Furthermore, Taipei's policy could be criticized as stubborn and inflexible, especially when Beijing has already offered so many 'reasonable conditions' for consideration. If the ROC could not offer any proposal to counter those of Beijing, some Taiwanese Chinese and overseas Chinese might think that the ROC has abandoned its aspirations to regain the mainland. This prospect might disappoint those who expect that China could be reunited someday and result in a loss of their support. Given this background Taipei felt compelled put forward serious proposals.

## Reunification of China Under the Three Principles

On 9 May 1980, Taipei first expressed its position toward the resolution of the China issue. The late Premier Sun Yun-chuan told a Japanese journalist during an interview that the reunification of China is the common wish of all Chinese people; however, he added, China must be reunited on the basis of freedom and democracy, not under the Chinese communists' totalitarian tyranny.[2] Therefore, 'freedom and democracy' could be considered Taipei's first condition for reunifying China.

In March 1981, the KMT, during its 11th Party Congress passed a resolution calling for 'Reunification of China Under the Three Principles of the People' as a formal counterproposal to Beijing's 'peaceful offensives'.[3] Since then, this resolution has become the ROC's criterion for action on reunification.

To most people the logic behind this resolution may seem hard to understand.[4] Why, for example, has the ROC adopted these 'Three Principles' as the premise for China's reunification? How can this policy be implemented? The author's interpretation of this policy, based on available documents, follows:

> 1. According to Dr. Sun Yat-sen, the Three Principles of the People are nationalism, democracy, and the people's well-being. He compared his Three Principles to those of the French Revolution—'Liberty, Equality, and Fraternity,' and President Abraham Lincoln's adage—'of the people, by the people, and for the people'.[5]
> 2. From Taipei's viewpoint, the task of building the 'New China' has not been completed, as Dr. Sun's Three Principles are not fully implemented. As well, Dr. Sun, who founded the ROC as a successor to the Ching Dynasty, legitimately represents the Chinese political and cultural systems. The ROC seems to believe that, because it is a direct successor to Dr. Sun, it therefore represents the Chinese orthodoxy tradition while the PRC's communism is a heresy which has destroyed Chinese culture, borne out by the events of the Cultural Revolution, and should be discarded.[6]
> 3. The ROC ascribes its 'economic miracle' to the practice of Dr. Sun's ideology, which has 'transformed [Taiwan] into the richest and freest province in 5,000 years of China's history.' Therefore the ROC believes that the Three Principles can serve as 'a blueprint for development and modernization of China'.[7] This success notwithstanding, the author would argue that the ROC's political development is merely in the beginning stages even during recent years and needs to be further perfected.

The policy of 'reunification of China under the Three Principles of the People' has the following three implications. It means that China should be reunified on the basis of freedom, democracy, prosperity, equality, and fraternity. A reunified China must be led by a government of the people, by the people, and for the people rather than a regime based on what essentially is a one-party dictatorship. It also means that China's reunification should be based on orthodox Chinese culture and tradition rather than on the heresy of Marxism-Leninism. Taipei believes that its anti-communist national policy 'is not a product of party and power struggles, but the key to national survival'.[8] Finally it means that China's reunification should be based on the successful model of Taiwan's developments and achievements[9] rather than on mainland's failing system—a reality admitted by no less a figure than Deng Xiaoping himself.[10] Taipei believes that if Beijing could accept its policy of 'reunification of China under the Three Principles', then the political, economic, social, and cultural gaps between the two Chinas would 'continue to narrow and the conditions for peaceful reunification can gradually mature'.[11]

In addition to this counterproposal, Taipei has put forward another three preconditions for the reunification of the two Chinas: (1) the PRC should abolish its insistence on the 'Four Cardinal Principles' manifested in the PRC's Constitution; (2) the PRC should cease its efforts to isolate the ROC in the international community; (3) the PRC should renounce its long-standing threat to use force against the ROC.[12]

## Why the Four Cardinal Principles are Irrelevant

On 30 March 1979, in order to regain the CCP's authority and clarify the PRC's ideological position after the Cultural Revolution, Deng Xiaoping gave a speech at a forum on the principles for the CCP's theoretical work and said that the PRC must uphold the following four cardinal principles:[13]
'1.   We must keep to the socialist road.
2.   We must uphold the people's democratic dictatorship.
3.   We must uphold the leadership of the Communist party.
4.   We must uphold Marxist-Leninism and Maoist thought.'

On 4 December 1982, these Four Principles were adopted by the Fifth National People's Congress (NPC) of the PRC at its Fifth Session and were written into the Preamble of the PRC's Constitution of 1982.[14] Principle 2 was amended at that time to read 'the people's democratic dictatorship'. Hence these Four Principles formally became the PRC's guiding principles and the CCP's platform of ideology and politics. However the PRC's Four Principles conflict with Taipei's ideological[15] and political system and this poses an important barrier to reunification.

Since these Four Principles have been enshrined in the PRC's Constitution, they may very well apply to Taiwan if the two Chinas were reunified under the formula of 'one country, two systems'. Although Beijing has said that the SAR can have its own legislation, it would be 'enacted by the National People's Congress' of the PRC.[16] Even if Taipei honestly believed that Beijing would keep its promise that 'the socialist system and socialist policies shall not be practiced'[17] in the SAR for a long period of time after the reunification, the PRC could break its promise right after reunification and modify its Constitution again (the Constitution promulgated in 1982 is the PRC's 4th Constitution). After all, Taiwan will lose any leverage against Beijing after reunification.

As well as a lack of trust in the PRC, several other reasons can explain why the ROC regards the Four Principles as irrelevant. Taipei ascribes the mainland's backward industrial status and poverty to the PRC's communist system,[18] which has failed not only on the Chinese mainland but also globally. Even a mainland scholar has suggested that communism is not 'an effective prescription to heal the mainland's economic and political problems'.[19] If communism is indeed ineffective, there is no reason for the PRC to uphold Marxist-Leninism and Mao Zedong's Thought as well as the socialist system as guiding principles for China's national construction.

Secondly, the people's democratic dictatorship has no clear role in Chinese reunification. According to Article 1 of the PRC constitution, the PRC is a 'socialist state under the people's democratic dictatorship led by the working class and based on the alliance of workers and peasants'. For the Taiwan Chinese, this cardinal principle causes great confusion. Are the PRC leaders considered working class and peasants? Obviously, they are not, instead forming a ruling class. That said, how does the 'people's democratic dictatorship' work? Will those members of the middle class who reside in the city be dictated to by workers and peasants? Most Taiwan Chinese are neither workers nor peasants. Will they be dictated to by these groups after reunification? The PRC does not answer these questions.

Why should the Chinese people uphold the leadership of the CCP—a party which has confessed that it has made many errors?[20] If China is forever under the rule of the CCP, how could there ever be a democratic political system in China? Furthermore, insistence on CCP leadership would deprive the KMT, the DPP, and other Chinese political parties of the right to govern China after reunification. Obviously one party rule by the CCP is unreasonable and unacceptable to the Taiwanese Chinese. In a democratic system the people should decide who shall lead them. If the CCP could prove its effective leadership the Chinese people would no doubt support a government led by the CCP. Otherwise the CCP should step down after the manner of Western democracies, and let other Chinese parties run China. In contrast, the KMT has never dared to say that it wants to monopolize political power or insisted on its leadership of Taiwan or of a reunified China. Therefore, if the PRC sincerely wishes to reunify China, it should take account of Taipei's suggestions. For example, Beijing can list these Four Principles in its party constitution, rather than in the nation's constitution where they are inappropriate.

## The Isolation of the ROC

The isolation of the ROC in the world community is perhaps the only area where Beijing has the upper hand over Taipei. Diplomatically, both Beijing and Taipei have in the past insisted on the 'one China, one seat' principle in international organizations. Thus, only one China will be represented on any organization and as more organizations award recognition to the PRC, the ROC thus loses representation in the international arena.

Isolation from the international community has created many difficulties for the ROC. First of all, it has reduced Taipei's authority within Taiwan and had caused 'the people to despise the government'.[21] Further, diplomatic isolation has created resentment within Taiwan, which has helped the momentum of support for Taiwan independence. Some dissidents have satirized the ROC's isolation by calling it 'the orphan of Asia', and have advocated independence so that Taiwan could rejoin the world community as a new nation.[22] Thirdly, the ROC's sovereignty over the 'one China' has also been challenged, due to its international isolation, decreasing the ROC's leverage if negotiation between the two Chinas begin.

Taipei has finally realized that if it can not survive in the world, it certainly could never reunify China according to its terms. If it loses its international status completely, how can it justify itself as a sovereign and independent state in the international arena and as a legal government domestically?

The threat of losing its international contacts was so great that by the early 1980s Taipei decided to be more flexible in handling its foreign relations. Evidence of this approach can be found in many cases, such as the ROC agreeing to use the name of 'Chinese, Taipei' to participate in the Olympic Games in 1984, 1988 and 1992. In April 1988, the ROC again agreed to sit in the same organization as the PRC at the annual meeting of the Asian Development Bank in Manila under the name of 'Taipei, China'. On 22 March 1988, Wei Yung, the late Chairman of the ROC Cabinet's Research, Development and Evaluation Commission, proposed the formula of 'Multiple Recognition' to temporarily resolve the two Chinas' dispute over the naming and seating in international organizations[23] (Chapter Ten will further discuss this issue). Taiwan's public opinion responded positively to this idea.[24] Beijing's response, however, was predictable. Beijing said that 'multiple recognition' would create the situation of 'two Chinas' or 'one China, one Taiwan' which in their eyes contravenes the 'one China' principle.[25]

It seems that the PRC believes that international isolation of the ROC will compel Taipei to submit to reunification on Beijing's terms. Isolation of Taiwan thus has constituted the 'stick' component of Beijing's 'stick and carrot' approach to policy toward the ROC since 1979. The PRC's intention to 'extinguish the title of "the Republic of China" from international societies' is understandable.[26] However, Beijing must realize that if it genuinely wishes to peacefully reunify with Taipei, it should try to find a feasible model to accommodate both Chinas within international organizations. By so doing, Beijing can not only earn the Taiwanese Chinese's friendship, but also demonstrate its sincerity to the ROC, which in turn would help to promote mutual understanding, and contribute to the eventual reunification of China. Last but not least, the improvement of the ROC's international status will reduce the pressure for Taiwanese independence, a situation that neither Chinese government wants to occur. According to President Nixon, one of the reasons why he sought reconciliation with the PRC in the late 1960s is that he did not want to leave the PRC 'forever outside the family of nations, there to nurture its fantasies, cherish its hates . . . to live in angry isolation'.[27] This thinking should also apply to relations between the PRC and the ROC.

## The Use of Force

Beijing's Taiwan policy since 1979 has been peaceful, but the policy as declared contains five conditions that will trigger the use of force by the PRC.

However, from Taipei's viewpoint, none of these conditions have been met at the moment. Trade, personal, and economic exchanges between the two Chinas, formally starting from 1987, are the best evidence of the ROC's intention to strengthen the two Chinas' relations. Besides, Taipei has stated that if Beijing promised to abolish its Four Principles, ceased its effects isolating Taiwan internationally and renounced the use of force against Taiwan, it would consider entering into talks with Beijing. Hence, when the time is right, negotiations between the two Chinas would become possible. Taipei has stated many times before 1991 that it would not ally with the USSR, due to its past negative experience with Moscow and ideological differences. At the end of 1991, the USSR ceased to exist.[28]

In the meantime, Taipei has also expressed clearly that it has no intention of developing nuclear weapons or of engaging in any activities related to the reprocessing of nuclear materials.[29] On the development of nuclear weaponry, Taipei points out that it would incur Beijing's preemptive attack and would be unforgivable and unthinkable for the ROC to use nuclear weapons on its compatriots on the mainland. As well, it would increase the ROC's financial burdens to develop such a weapon.[30]

Although the DPP has advocated Taiwan's independence, the official position of the ROC government is the 'one China' principle, thus Taiwan Chinese independence is unacceptable to the ruling KMT party.[31] Taiwan's politics have gradually become mature and institutionalized. This is best illustrated by the procedure for the succession of the presidency of the ROC without chaos, let alone revolution, in January 1988, when the late President Lee Teng-hui was immediately sworn in as the leader of the ROC after the death of Chiang Ching-kuo, following the provisions of the ROC constitution.

Beijing's five conditions under which it would use force do not presently exist in Taiwan. Why then does the PRC not abandon its threats to use force against Taiwan, which only produces tension across the Taiwan Straits and contributes nothing towards China's peaceful reunification? An editorial in Taipei's *China Times* pointed out that the Taiwanese Chinese would be glad to extend economic assistance to their mainland compatriots so that 'they can also enjoy modern life and rejuvenate the whole Chinese nation. . . . Before doing that, however, Peking must renounce the use of force against Taiwan. Otherwise we Taiwan Chinese would be agreeing to extend our financial aid to an enemy who constantly threatens to beat and kill us day after day'.[32]

Taipei's counterproposals reflect its own position and attitude toward the China issue. They imply the ROC's long-held belief that China should be reunified on the basis of traditional Chinese culture, ideology, and values. These counterproposals also demonstrate that the Taiwan Chinese do not trust Beijing's sincerity about resolving the China issue through peaceful means. Will the PRC take account of these proposals and make further concessions to the ROC? If so, what factors will bring about these concessions? If not, what barriers are there to further concessions? The next chapter will discuss these questions.

# Chapter 7

■

## Taipei's Strategies Toward Beijing

Is the ROC fighting a war without the possibility of victory? How can the ROC resist the 'peaceful offensives' from the PRC? In fact, the ROC has resisted so far and may have the chance to win, although victory would certainly not come easy.[1] Many factors are likely to contribute to Taipei's victory, such as the modernization of its economic and political systems. An effective army also contributes to Taiwan's stability and enhances Taipei's position in its struggle with Beijing. The author will discuss all of these dimensions in turn.

## Economic Dimension

The modernization of the economy has become Taipei's main strategy to counter Beijing's 'peaceful offensives'. In the early 1970s, Taipei decided to accelerate its economic development when confronted with a series of setbacks on the diplomatic front. Chiang Ching-kuo, then Premier of the ROC, said that 'so long as our economy continues to grow fast. . . . We will be able to meet any challenge from without and overcome any difficulty we may encounter in international politics so as to open up a bright future for our nation'.[2] The current situation of Taiwan has proved the foresight of Chiang's decision. Taiwan's continued prosperity has maintained domestic unity and stability during the current crises in Taiwan's international affairs, and at the same time has expanded economic relations with other nations. Economic development has become 'the best way to counter the threat of becoming isolated in the world. . . . The establishment of Nationalist China as a major trading nation is now also regarded as a means of preserving prestige and diminishing the credibility of Peking's claims to the island'.[3]

Taiwan's prosperity has also reduced the likelihood of its

people accepting communism. The 'economic miracle' has raised the Taiwan people's living standards, improved its democratic system and provided a measure of confidence. All this in Taipei's view demonstrates that its doctrines are superior to Beijing's. It puts the 'two China issue' on the table and lets all Chinese people, both domestically and abroad, judge for themselves. It also moderates the tense relations between the two Chinas and enables them to compete in promoting thier people's well-being. After all, the average person in the street is almost certainly more interested in their per capita income, the number and quality of cars, TVs, houses, and travelling opportunities than political ideologies.

The ROC's President Lee Teng-hui told the *Reader's Digest* magazine in October 1988 that 'what the ROC government can do is vigorously develop Taiwan as an example for a reunified China of the future'.[4] In fact Taiwan's economic achievements have caused Beijing to be concerned. For example, in August of 1979, Yu Qiuli, then a CCP Politburo member, acknowledged that 'in the peaceful competition between the mainland and Taiwan, the mainland had to declare itself the loser'. He admitted that 'the rapid development of the Taiwan economy and the standard of living on Taiwan is several times higher than that of any province on the mainland'.[5] The PRC scholar Ding Li also acknowledged that Taiwan's economic development can serve as a model for 'accelerating the completion of our country's socialist modernization programs'.[6]

Taiwan's economic achievements have also put pressure on the PRC's leaders and have prodded the PRC to engage in economic reforms. On 2 September 1986, Deng Xiaoping was interviewed by Mike Wallace from the Columbia Broadcasting System of the USA. Wallace asked Deng, 'Chairman Deng, you always say, "Seek truth from facts." And the facts are that Taiwan is prosperous, capitalist and doesn't want to reunify, this they say and their leaders say.' Deng answered that the difference of development between mainland and Taiwan is only temporary. . . . With the implementation of our existing policy, the growth rate [of the mainland] will not be slow and the gap [between the mainland and Taiwan] is being narrowed'.[7] Deng's comments revealed Beijing's intention to compete with Taipei on the economic front. Wallace's question also reminded Deng of how other countries judge the two Chinas. If the PRC cannot catch up with the ROC in economic development, its claim over Taiwan will be weaker. Taipei's strategy of shifting the two Chinas' struggle from military to economic competition is sound. If the PRC could not demonstrate the superiority of socialism, then socialism would not be welcomed in Taiwan, which accordingly would enhance Taipei's position in resisting Beijing. Furthermore, Taipei's economic strategy should benefit the mainland Chinese by spurring the government of the PRC to take measures to improve the lot of the people and make reunification more realistic in the future.

## Political Dimension

The modernization of politics is Taipei's second initiative to counter Beijing's 'peaceful offensives' (see Chapter 12 for a more detailed discussion). Professor Seymour M. Lipset has pointed out that 'democracy is related to the state of economic development. The more well-to-do a nation, the greater the chances that it will sustain democracy'.[8] He has also agreed that 'the stability of any given democracy depends not only on economic development but also upon the effectiveness and the legitimacy of its political system'.[9]

According to Professor Samuel P. Huntington, those aspects of modernization most relevant to politics can be broadly grouped into two catagories: social mobilization and economic development. The former refers to 'a change in the attitudes, values, and expectations of people from those associated with the traditional world to those common to the modern world'; while the latter refers to 'the growth in the total economic activity and output of a society. . . . Social mobilization involves changes in the aspirations of individuals, groups, and societies; economic development involves changes in their capabilities'.[10] He argued that 'political modernization involves assertion of the external sovereignty of the nation-state against transactional influences and of the internal sovereignty of the national government against local and regional powers. It means national integration and the centralization or accumulation of power in recognized national lawmaking institutions'.[11]

These theories have at least two consequences of relevance

to us. They suggest the close relationship between economic development and political democratization. The more one country's economy develops, the easier it is for that country to implement democracy. Also, when a country's economic development reaches some given level, the democratic consciousness of its people will also develop accordingly.[12] In addition, the stability of a country depends not only on economic development but also on political democratization, which eventually would become the main factor in maintaining a country's stability.

These theories also suggest methods for constructing strategies to counter Beijing's 'peaceful offensives'. The ROC seems to realize that, although the PRC's economy is still backward at this moment, the mainland would sooner or later improve its people's living standards and develop its economy if the PRC's policy of 'opening the door to the outside world and practising reform inside the mainland' remains in place for a long period of time. The effect of Taipei's economic strategy, thus, might decrease gradually over time. Taipei may need to initiate action on another front to challenge Beijing in order to maintain its leading position in the peaceful competition between the two Chinas. Moreover, people might criticize Taipei's position on the China issue as only representing the minority ruling class and vested interests such as the ageing mainland refugees, and not fully reflecting the Taiwanese Chinese view of the China issue.[13] Given the fact that the ROC's ageing parliamentarians, before 1991, have not had to face an election for 40 years, this criticism would be pertinent.

Political democratization in Taiwan can generate a four-pronged effect. It can reduce political disputes and conflicts and promote consensus and integration within Taiwan. A united Taiwan will leave no opportunity for Beijing to sow discord within Taiwan, and thus consolidate Taipei's position vis-à-vis Beijing. The experience of the ROC's political modernization might set an example for the PRC. The mainland Chinese people might ask the ruling CCP 'if the KMT can reform their political institutions why can we not?' Political modernization can improve the ROC's image in the world. As Professor John F. Copper has pointed out, 'Taiwan had to democratize quickly to tell the world that it was no longer an authoritarian dictatorship, and consequently, that it deserved to be consulted about its own future'.[14] If so, the democratization in Taiwan would be a positive response both to the PRC's threat and to the possibility of weakening confidence at home.[15] If Beijing were to follow Taipei's example and proceeded with political reform, then the ROC's goal of converting 'Communist China' from communism to a democratic system would become possible.

In short, Taipei's strategy toward Beijing are obvious. Taipei is trying 'to transplant its successful economic and political development models to the mainland'.[16] Meanwhile, the ROC also tries through this strategy to expand its latitude for action in countering the PRC. A competition in the economic and political arenas would not only benefit the general well-being of all Chinese people, but also make the reunification issue more meaningful. Taipei seems to believe that the timing of reunification 'depends more on the pace of reform on the mainland than on Taiwan. . . . The more time that is allowed to pass before any steps toward reunification take place, the more likely it will be that the matter is settled on terms favorable to Taiwan'.[17]

## Military Dimension

As Dean Acheson illustrated, during the last stages of World War Two, Switzerland possessed a well-trained army of 50 divisions which made the prospects of an invasion too costly for Germany to consider.[18] K. J. Holsti also said that small nations that 'are prepared to undertake a policy of "punitive resistance" may cause more powerful nations to leave them alone'.[19] The military preparedness of the ROC on Taiwan is intended to make the PRC's invasion of Taiwan too costly to consider and to undertake the necessary 'punitive resistance' against the PRC if Beijing triggers a war in the Taiwan Strait. Table 7-1 indicates the current military strength of the two Chinas.

Generally speaking, the ROC's force could 'currently put up a firm and sustained resistance against an invader by land, sea and air.'[20] However, this does not necessarily mean that the ROC can survive under an all-out attack by the PRC. John H. Holdridge, Assistant Secretary of State for East Asian and Pacific affairs, told the US's Senate Foreign Relations Committee in 1982 that from a 'practical military standpoint the "PRC could take Taiwan today with masses of men and material"... even though Taiwan has some technological advantages'.[21] Hence the key to whether Beijing will use force against Taipei or not lies in the cost Beijing is willing to pay for such a military action.

The reason Beijing refrains from using force against Taiwan as offered by scholars of the PRC[22] have been highlighted in Chapter 2.

Aside from these reasons, the ROC's military strength, the author would argue, is the dominant factor checking Beijing's use of force. Huan Kuocang, a mainland scholar who now resides in the US, said that 'the price for a non-peaceful settlement of the China issue, even a blockade of the Taiwan Strait, would be very costly to the PRC. Militarily, Taiwan possesses the retaliatory capability to bombard the coastal provinces of the mainland that comprise 40 per cent of the mainland's industrial productivity'.[23] Edmund Lee, another mainland visiting scholar to the US, also pointed out that 'an attack on Taiwan would ruin everything. And a war would destroy Chinese industry located in the coastal provinces— including Shanghai. ... Moreover, the primary concerns of the younger generation in the PRC are improving its poor living conditions and obtaining greater freedoms. These interests would not be served by war'.[24] Dick Wilson also indicated that the PRC will suffer heavy losses in a war across the Taiwan Strait.[25] In July 1985, an 'Internal Document' of the PRC, entitled 'All of the Party Members Should Implement the Taiwan Work: An Outline of Our Taiwan Policy and the Situation of Taiwan', issued by the Office for Taiwan Work of Fujian Province states that 'if we use force to against Taiwan, we would pay a high price which might hamper the progress of our four modernization programs and cause some international problems'.[26] In a word, an invasion of Taiwan would be costly for the PRC 'in not only military but also economic terms. Industrialization would be set back, access to Western technology and capital might be severed and China's image would suffer'.[27]

From the viewpoint of Taipei, the chance of 'a potential invasion by the mainland at this moment is low.' Frederick Chien, the ROC's former representative to the US and Chairman of the Council for Economic Planning and Development, made such a comment right after the Tienanmen Square Massacre on 4 June 1989. He went on to say that the US might come to rescue Taiwan by a variety of means, including selling of sophisticated weapons and providing satellite intelligence service to the ROC if the PRC were to use force against Taiwan.[28] Chien's comments were mainly based on the fact that the PRC has at this moment no real intention of invading Taiwan, due to the aforesaid considerations. He also expressed Taipei's confidence in its military strength.

According to Ray S. Cline's assessment, the ROC was ranked as the tenth leading military power in the world when the following formula is used: Equivalent units of combat capability = Manpower × Coefficient average (consisting of four elements: manpower quality, weapon effectiveness, infrastructure and logistic capability and organizational quality). The national will to resist an invader is also considered in Cline's assessment.[29] Cheng Wei-yuan, then the ROC's Defense Minister, was questioned in the Legislative Yuan on 10 April 1989 about Taiwan's capacity to repel an invasion from the mainland. He estimates the ROC could repel an invasion force numbering 2,000 jet fighters, 200 warships and a landing force of 20 divisions. He says that given Taiwan's size, only 300 fighters and five divisions could be sent in at any one time to a war zone on the island.[30] If the PRC did invade, however, it would run up against a formidable set of fortifications. According to Taiwan's military operational strategy for this contingency, codenamed 'Ku An' (solid peace), seven defence lines are to be drawn up, from the long-ranges missiles that make up the first defensive arc to Taiwan island's western highway system that is the last line of defence. The aim, according to a Taiwan newsmagazine, *The Journalist*, is to destroy any invasion force before it reaches Taiwan by using a combined air and sea defence, with missiles playing a critical role in the engagement.[31]

If Taipei's estimates are correct, the author would argue that the PRC might lose about one-third of its air and naval forces during an all-out war against Taiwan. This would create a significant problem for the PRC's defence strategy. Even if Taiwan's air and naval forces were totally destroyed, the PRC's forces would face another round of heavy casualties at the hands of the ROC's land forces waiting at Taiwan's beachhead for a decisive battle.

**Table 7-1:** Military Strength of the Two Chinas (1988)

| Countries | PRC | ROC |
|---|---|---|
| Population | 1,072,000,000 | 20,659,000 |
| Armed Forces Manpower | 3,200,000 | 405,000 |
| | | |
| Strategic Armed Forces: | | |
| Intercontinental Ballistic Missiles | 6 | 0 |
| Intermediate-range Ballistic Missiles | 60 | 0 |
| Medium-range Ballistic Missiles | 50 | 0 |
| Nuclear-fuelled Ballistic Missiles Submarines | 1 | 0 |
| | | |
| Army: | 2,300,000 persons | 270,000 persons |
| Infantry Divisions | 80 | 18 |
| Armoured Divisions | 10 | 2 |
| Field and Anti-Aircraft Divisions | 5–6 | 0 |
| Airborne Troops | 4 Divisions | 1 Brigade |
| Tank Groups | 0 | 4 |
| Surface-to-Air Missile Battalions | 0 | 5 |
| | | |
| Navy Manpower: | 300,000 | 35,500 |
| Submarines | 115 | 4 |
| Destroyers | 19 | 26 |
| Frigates | 34 | 10 |
| Patrol/Coastal Combatants | 850+ | 69 |
| | (235 missile craft) | (54 missile craft) |
| Mine Warfare | 128 | 8 |
| Amphibious | 76 | 27 |
| | | |
| Navy Air Force: | | |
| Bombers (10 H-6, 130 H-5) | 180 | 0 |
| Fighters (100 Q-5, 600 J-5/-6/-7) | 700 | 0 |
| | | |
| Marines Manpower | 4,500 | 30,000 |
| | | |
| Air Force Manpower: | 470,000 | 70,000 |
| Bombers | (H-5/-6) 420 | 0 |
| Ground-attack Fighters/Fighters | *4,500 | **400 |

\* Including 500 Q-5, 400 J-5, 3000 J-6/B/D/E, 250 J-7/J-7M, 30 J-8.
  (J-5 = MiG 17; J-6 = MiG 19; J-7 = MiG 21; J-8 = MiG 23).
\*\* Including 200 F-5E, 50 F-5F, 50 F-104G.

*Source*: *The Military Balance 1988–1989*, London: The International Institute for Strategic Studies, 1988, pp. 147–51 and 178–9.

During the Second World War the 'islands jumping' strategy of the US against the Japanese resulted in the US suffering heavy losses during its victories. For example, in order to mount an assault on several thousand Japanese troops occupying Kiska Island, a tiny island of the Aleutian Archipelago, the US, in August 1943, had mobilized battleships, cruisers, destroyers, minesweepers, and transports—with an invasion force of 34,000.[32] This case has shown that an offensive side may need many times the manpower of a defensive side in order to launch a successful invasion of an island. The improvement of firepower systems since World War Two would strengthen even further the defensive side's position.

Therefore, if the PRC intends to cross the Taiwan Strait to capture Taiwan, it needs to transport at least around 200–400 thousand soldiers. But, according to Parris H. Chang, the PRC's present naval force is backward and lacks the capability to conduct a large scale amphibious war. He said that it may take at least three years for the PRC to build ships with the necessary tonnage to transport around 100 thousand soldiers to Taiwan.[33] If Beijing were to launch efforts to overcome these logistical problems, this would alert Taipei, which would then have time to further strengthen Taiwan's defences and to consider other military options to counter the anticipated PRC invasion such as the development of nuclear and chemical weapons.

There is a wide difference of opinion in the ROC regarding the development of nuclear weapons. The PRC has possessed nuclear arms since 1964. Currently Taipei's policy is against nuclear weapons development. However, if the ROC's security came to a critical point, Taipei might change its non-nuclear arsenal policy. In fact the ROC has secretly proceeded with a nuclear programme since 1969. Under pressure from Washington however, the ROC has twice stopped work on a secret installation (once in 1977 and again in 1988) that could have been used to obtain the plutonium necessary to produce nuclear weapons.[34] Gary Milhollin, a former consultant to the US Defense Department on nuclear arms, said 'the establishment of a laboratory to extract plutonium would be an essential step of any effort by Taiwan to build a bomb or develop contingency plans for doing so. . . . If Taiwan could master the technology of plutonium extraction and build an extraction facility, it could shorten the time needed to make a bomb from years to months'.[35]

It has been said that the ROC's Chungshan Institute of Science and Technology, during the period between 1977 and 1982, through computer simulation[36] successfully exploded a nuclear device. If so, Taipei was, to some extent, already in possession of the technology of nuclear arms production as of the early 1980s. In fact, the ROC appeared to have planned such a program in 1988. The Sky Horse is 'a ballistic missile with a range of about 625 miles, so it can hit parts of the mainland'.[37] To the ROC, the possession 'of nuclear potential and gas warfare capability are thought to cancel the superiority in numbers and equipment of the People's Liberation Army'.[38] If Taipei did actually possess nuclear arms, it would enhance Taiwan's defense capability and deter a PRC invasion. The potential for nuclear war in the Taiwan Strait would also produce significant political repercussions that would benefit Taiwan's security. Countries such as Japan, US, and the ASEAN nations would be deeply concerned by a Taiwan Strait crisis and would seek to mediate between the two Chinas for a peaceful resolution of the two China issue.[39] Nevertheless, before Taipei can possess any kind of nuclear weapon, it would have to overcome two difficulties. It would have to persuade Washington to agree to its nuclear program, and it would have to prevent Beijing from making a pre-emptive attack on Taiwan's nuclear facilities.

There is no question that the possibility of Taiwan surviving a nuclear attack from Beijing is remote. The author would argue, however, that unless Beijing's decision-making is irrational, the chances of such a strike are small. This is because Beijing has a nuclear arms policy of no first-use against other countries. In addition, it would damage Beijing's image and cause outrage internationally were it to use nuclear weapons against a small non-nuclear country such as the ROC. Further, Taiwan after the nuclear strike would become a liability to Beijing. A devastated Taiwan does not serve Beijing's interests.

A more realistic scenario is if Beijing puts in place a blockade (or merely announces a blockade) of the Taiwan Strait and avoids confrontation with Taiwan's ground and air forces? Under the PRC's blockade, Taiwan's economic life-line, foreign trade, would be in danger. Foreign-flag shippers and oil tankers would cease stopping in Taiwan if such a blockade were effective. Psychologically, such a blockade would instill panic among the Taiwanese Chinese, destroy people's confidence in Taiwan's future, and create great economic and political difficulties for the Taipei government. If Beijing were to succeed with such a tactic, 'Taiwan [would be] captured intact, with virtually no blood shed on either side. If it fails, little is lost'.[40] This kind of scenario, the author would argue, is unrealistic from a political point of view. No matter what kind of non-peaceful means to which Beijing resorts, such as a blockade, a limited war, or an all-out war, to settle the China issue, the political impact would be the same. It would mean an end to the gradual improvement of relations between the two Chinas and a reintroduction of hostility into relations across the Taiwan Strait.

Facing the prospect of Beijing's overt hostility, the Taiwanese Chinese would immediately sever Taiwan's links (in areas as diverse as national feelings, economy, culture, and so on) with the mainland and declare Taiwan's independence. Hence, Beijing's goal of incorporation of Taiwan would be dashed. Beijing would taste a good deal of bitterness before gaining any benefit from such a hostile action towards Taiwan. In the face of Taiwan's announcement of independence, Beijing would have to respond. In the meantime, Taipei would try to break through Beijing's blockade. The situation in the Taiwan Strait would immediately escalate to the brink of a real war. If Beijing backed down from the blockade or did nothing in response to Taiwan's moves toward independence, this would be considered a sign of weakness and the PRC would lose face domestically and internationally. Therefore, it seems likely that Beijing would refrain from taking any non-peaceful steps to resolve the two China issue in the foreseeable future unless it has absolute confidence that it could win a war for the 'liberation of Taiwan'.

K. J. Holsti has said that 'those responsible for national security are rarely willing to rely merely upon the goodwill or professions of peaceful intent of other nations to ensure their own safety; as a consequence, they are likely to perceive few substitutes for the procurement, maintenance, and deployment of military forces'.[41] The ROC on Taiwan has continuously strived for military preparedness in the past four decades. Taipei has never regarded Beijing's peaceful gestures as a credible and reliable guarantee of Taiwan's security. Hau Pei-tsun, former Chief of the General Staff of the ROC and later premier, has said in 1989 that there is no so-called 'peaceful coexistence' but rather 'peaceful competition' between the two sides of the Taiwan Straits within a limited period of time and under the circumstances of a balance of military power. The time span for such peaceful competition might be three years, five years, eight years, or even 20 years, nobody can predict how long. Hau predicts two possible outcomes for such a 'peaceful competition'. He said that the mainland would gradually be democratized and liberalized and a potential war over the China issue would accordingly be ruled out, with the two sides of the Taiwan Strait eventually being led in the direction of reunification. If the mainland remains under totalitarian rule, however, a war over the China issue cannot be excluded. He concludes that there would be everlasting peace and stable peace between the two sides, and how long the situation characterized by peaceful competition can be maintained depends on whether the ROC possesses sufficient military strength to deter a mainland invasion.[42]

The ROC's defence expenditure was US$5,068 million (the PRC's was US$5,636 million) in 1987, the 21st highest in the world and the 8th highest in the Third World. In terms of per capita defence expenditure, the ROC's US$245 (the PRC figure was US$5) ranked 31st. In terms of GNP percentage, the defence expenditure of the ROC was 5.8 per cent (the PRC's was 2.6 per cent), ranking 26th. The ROC's defence expenditure in 1987 accounted for 40.7 per cent of that year's total government spending, second in percentage terms only to the United Arab Emirates.[43] In fiscal year 1993, the ROC's defence expenditure has reached US$10.9 billion (the PRC would be US$7.4 billion). All of these figures show that the ROC government and the Taiwanese Chinese have paid a costly price for their safety. Were the defence expenditures not so large, the author would argue, the ROC's economic development and the Taiwan people's social welfare would be even more advanced than it is today.

In the last ten years, the ROC has been spending millions of dollars on upgrading and improving Taiwan's weapons systems while defence manpower has been gradually reduced. Table 7-2 demonstrates that defence manpower in the ROC has been cut from 539,000 persons in 1979 to 360,000 in

**Table 7-2:** Defence Expenditure and Manpower of the ROC (1979–1992)

| Year | US$ Million* | GDP % | Manpower (Persons) |
|---|---|---|---|
| 1979 | 2,682 | 6.9% | 539,000 |
| 1980 | 3,194 | 8.0% | 438,200 |
| 1981 | 3,553 | 7.9% | 451,000 |
| 1982 | 3,100 | 7.8% | 464,000 |
| 1983 | 3,227 | 6.5% | 464,000 |
| 1984 | 3,684 | 6.7% | 484,000 |
| 1985 | 3,715 | 6.6% | 444,000 |
| 1986 | 4,256 | — | 424,000 |
| 1987 | 5,068 | — | 424,000 |
| 1988 | 6,700 | — | 405,500 |
| 1992 | 9,710 | — | 360,000 |

* The period between 1979–85 in US dollars at 1980 values; while after 1986 in current US dollars.

*Source*: Compiled from the 1983–84, 1984–85, 1985–86, 1986–87,1987–88, 1988–89 and 1992–93 annual issues of *The Military Balance*, London: The International Institute for Strategic Studies.

1992, while military spending has gradually increased from US$2,682 million in 1979 to US$9,710 million in 1992. Sophisticated weaponry in effect has been substituted for manpower.

From a variety of channels, especially from the US, the ROC's armour has increased from 775 tanks in 1979 to 1,364 tanks, including 309 M-48A5 main battle tanks and about 1,165 armoured infantry vehicles in 1992. There were only 300 armoured personnel carriers in 1979. The artillery arsenal has been increased from 850 guns and howitzers in 1979 to 1,200 (including 455 self-propelled artillery). The locally produced Kung Feng VI/III/IV multiple rocket launchers (MRL) were introduced into the army in the early 1980s. This has improved the firepower of land troops'. Anti-tank capabilities have mushroomed with the introduction of locally produced Kun Wu and TOW anti-tank guided weapons (ATGW). Defense against naval and air attack has been strengthened by the introduction of the Taiwan-made Hsiung Feng coastal defence surface-to-surface missiles (SSM) resembling the Israeli Gabriel and Ching Feng surface-to-surface/surface-to-air missiles (SAM), as well as the greatly expanded deployment of Nike Hercules, Improved HAWK, Chaparral and locally produced Tien Kung (Sky Bow) SAM.[44] Military experts claim the Tien Kung could replace the US-made Nike Hercules which has been deployed in Taiwan for years.[45] According to Taipei, its self-developed Tien Ma (Sky Horse) ballistic missile (the second generation of the Ching Feng missile) with a range of about 625 miles has approached the completion stage. It is believed that the US government is assisting Taipei to produce this missile in exchange for Taipei's promise not to develop nuclear arms.[46]

The ROC's air force has added 410 combat aircraft in the last decade. Emphasis has been placed on self-reliance in procurement with the main fighter, the F-5E, being produced in Taiwan on licence since the 1970s. Starting from 1983, Taipei has allotted US$1 billion for the development and production of the ROC's first Taiwan-built fighter plane with assistance from US contractors. In June 1989, this jet fighter, the IDF (Indigenous Defense Fighter) or Ching-kuo Fighter, successfully passed its flight test. The fighter, which is said to be similar to the US F16 and F20, will eventually be built to replace the nearly obsolete Lockheed F-104 and Northrop F-5E/F in the ROC Air Force. Taipei plans to build some 130 of these aircraft before 1996. The entire project is expected to cost around US$4 billion. Military sources in Taipei say the IDF is expected to give the ROC forces continued air superiority over the Taiwan Strait through the 1990s.[47] In the meantime, Taiwan successfully test-fired its first self-developed AAM Tien Chien (Sky Sword), which resembles the US-made Sidewinder, in April 1986. The IDF fighters will be equipped with the Tien Chien AAM and both will become the ROC's new air defence weapons.[48] Most recently, the ROC has been more active in procuring more advanced aircraft overseas. In September 1992, the US agreed to sell 150 F-16 A/B (MLU) fighter aircraft to Taiwan. Later that year, the French government also approved the sale of 60 Mirage 2000's to Taiwan. All of these new jet fighters are expected to be delivered before the year 2000, further strengthening Taiwan's military.

The ROC navy has also increased the number of its missile armed units, especially fast attack craft, in the past decade.

Weapons and equipment for anti-submarine warfare also have been procured and upgraded in recent years. In order to replace the old destroyer and frigate forces, 12 missile and anti-submarine warfare destroyers similar to the US Navy Perry-class FFG are under construction and are expected to go into service before the end of this century. In addition, the ROC has contracted to buy another six new guided-missile frigates from France to replace the old ones. All of these ships are to be the ROC's next generation of warships. The ROC has constantly strived to establish a submarine force. With the Dutch-built Hai Lung and Hai Hu (Zwaardvis) joining the ROC Navy in 1988 and 1989, Taiwan's submarine warfare capability has been significantly upgraded and improved.[49] According to Taipei, the quality of the two Dutch-made submarines has been proven in a 30-day-long underwater manoeuver in May 1989, and is better than any one of the PRC's traditional submarines. Taipei has claimed that its submarines could attack a number of the mainland's harbors including Qingdao, Shanghai, and Guangzhou if a war occurred in the Taiwan Strait.[50] On 3 June 1989, Premier Lee Huan revealed that the ROC has contracted with West Germany for the purchase of another 6 submarines for its naval force.[51] Although Berlin vetoed this deal in early 1993, Taipei has persisted in its efforts to buy state-of-the-art submarines. Taipei believes that if the ROC had 8 sophisticated submarines, it would be able to break through a sea blockade in the Taiwan Strait area, and could constitute a threat to the mainland's coastal harbors and cities.[52]

The ROC, in the past decade, has emphasized five key defence projects: (a) building next generation destroyers and frigates; (b) developing the IDF jet fighter; (c) modernizing the main battle tank force built around the M48A5 tank; (d) developing a variety of missiles; and (e) establishing its submarine fleet and enhancing its anti-submarine warfare capabilities. All of these programmes cost Taiwan taxpayers at least US$6 billion and should be completed no later than the year 2000. From these programmes Taiwan's defence strategy is very clear: to control the air; and the sea; and as a last resort, to fight war resisting invasion from the PRC's troops.

At this moment, Taipei has moved its major defence installations underground to eastern Taiwan's lofty Central Mountain Range area (Chia Shan Plan) to limit damage from any possible missile attack from the mainland (the defence systems in both Kinmen and Matzu have already gone underground).[53] Taipei has claimed that although the ROC armed forces are overwhelmingly outnumbered by those of the PRC, the ROC's 'high-quality weapons can be expected to offset any numerical disadvantage in a restricted theater of war like Taiwan'.[54] Although the ROC has planned and prepared its defence well, the PRC may still be able to capture Taiwan should war break out. Such a victory, however, would be very costly. If Beijing opts for non-peaceful settlement of the two China issue, it would be a catastrophe for Chinese on both sides of the Taiwan Strait.

## Three Nos Policy

If the modernization of its economic and political systems is Taipei's offensive strategy to counter Beijing's influence, then the so-called Three Nos Policy is the ROC's defensive strategy to check Beijing's aggressive united front tactics. This policy means that the ROC Government will not compromise with, not directly negotiate with, and not directly contact the PRC Government under any circumstances. People-to-people contact is acceptable. Taipei's rationale for this policy is that Beijing has not given up its ambition of annexing Taiwan. The 'peaceful offensives' since 1979, from Taipei's view, are merely propaganda aimed at creating disunity within Taiwan, allowing the PRC to take over Taiwan without bloodshed.[55] The PRC has retreated from its original tactics of non-peaceful means to peaceful but the original objective to annex Taiwan is unchanged. Given this situation, there is no reason for Taipei to compromise, negotiate, or initiate contact with its enemy.

The Three Nos Policy has many implications. Most importantly, it implies that Taipei will contend for sovereignty and legitimacy as the sole Chinese government. Taipei negotiating with Beijing would imply Taipei's indirect recognition of Beijing as another Chinese regime. Furthermore, from Beijing's view, Taipei is its local government, a position that the ROC cannot accept, therefore, Taipei's refusal to directly talk necessarily follows. Second, due to its comparatively weak position, caused by its smaller population and territory, and isolated international status, Taipei feels that it has no position of strength from which to conduct negotiations with Beijing. The ROC's late Premier Sun Yun-chuan has highlighted this by quoting President Kennedy 'the U.S. would never fear to negotiate but would never negotiate out of fear' and President Reagan 'America will negotiate only from a position of strength' and has said that 'the so-called "negotiation" proposal put forward by Communist China is in practice an intention to annex the ROC in Taiwan. . . . If the negotiations would break up, they would not exclude the use of force against Taiwan. According to the bitter lessons from history, we should never and will never be swindled again by the Communists'.[56] Last but not least, from Taipei's viewpoint, this policy serves to safeguard Taiwan's security and provide some leverage over Beijing.

General Hau Pei-tsun has defended the policy saying that the Three Nos Policy is an active and sound policy adding that it is because of the 'Three Nos' Policy that the PRC's Nine-Point and Six-point Proposals followed. He went on to say that 'only the one who has "strength" dares to say "no". In contrast, Communist China is going to practice "one country, two systems" in Hong Kong. Do the Hong Kong people dare to say no?'[57] General Hau's comments have explicitly indicated that the Three Nos Policy has induced Beijing to make further concessions to Taipei. The ROC's President Lee Teng-hui has compared the Three Nos Policy to Japanese swordsmanship. He said that 'when you cross swords with your antagonist, you must be patient and wait. It is useless for you to display too many small actions, only when you grasp the best opportunity and strike your antagonist instantly, can you therefore beat your antagonist once and for all'.[58] The Three Nos Policy, according to Taipei, is adjustable. Taipei has said that if the PRC agreed to accept Taipei's suggestions, that is, to stop trying to isolate the ROC and treat Taipei equally, renounce the use of force against Taiwan, and so on, Taipei might 'gradually alter its Three Nos Policy and further expand the contacts between the two sides of the Taiwan Strait'.[59]

# Chapter 8

■

## Taipei's Anti-United Front Organizations

The ROC has maintained a huge anti-united front network to counter the efforts of Beijing's united front organizations. This network has been enhanced, especially after the KMT's 13th Party Congress held in July 1988 (See Table 8-1). Each unit that is listed in the table is briefly described.

During the KMT's 13th Party Congress in 1988, Hsiao Chang-lo, Director of the Department of Mainland Operations, highlighted a draft of the KMT's future policy towards the mainland. This draft indicated the necessity of establishing a mainland work supervisory board under the KMT's Central Standing Committee and a mainland affairs workshop in the government to handle the issues related to the mainland.[1] In August 1988, the Workshop for Mainland Affairs was established within the ROC's Executive Yuan. A Guidance Group for Mainland Affairs has also been formed within the KMT to handle issues relating to the mainland.

The Workshop for Mainland Affairs was a cabinet-level task force headed by Vice-Premier Shih Chi-yang. Members included the ministers of the foreign affairs, finance, education, economic affairs, communications, the interior, national defence and justice ministries and directors-general from the government information office and national security bureau.[2] The main function of this unit was to coordinate and manage mainland affairs that concern the respective ministries. It was comprised of five sub-groups: culture, education, and journalism; economy, trade, and transportation; law, politics, and society; administration and policy research. The workshop held meetings once a month, with additional meetings being convened as necessary.[3] This workshop was the highest ranking government unit dealing with affairs between the two Chinas. In October 1990, this workshop was replaced by the Mainland Affairs Council (MAC).

Table 6-1. The Organizational Structure of the ROC's Anti-United Front Efforts

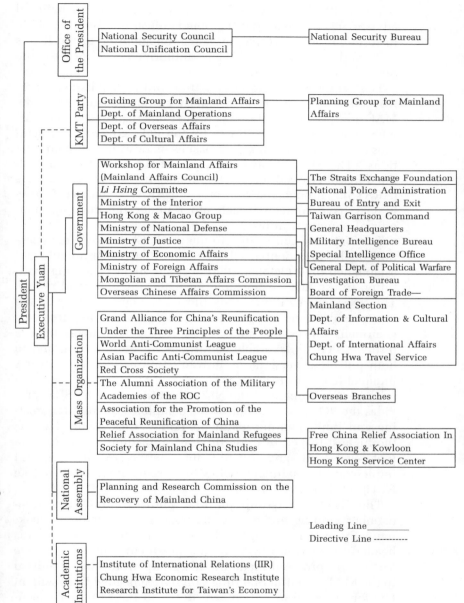

President

Executive Yuan

**Office of the President**
- National Security Council
- National Unification Council
— National Security Bureau

**KMT Party**
- Guiding Group for Mainland Affairs
- Dept. of Mainland Operations
- Dept. of Overseas Affairs
- Dept. of Cultural Affairs
— Planning Group for Mainland Affairs

**Government**
- Workshop for Mainland Affairs (Mainland Affairs Council)
- Li Hsing Committee
- Ministry of the Interior
- Hong Kong & Macao Group
- Ministry of National Defense
- Ministry of Justice
- Ministry of Economic Affairs
- Ministry of Foreign Affairs
- Mongolian and Tibetan Affairs Commission
- Overseas Chinese Affairs Commission

- The Straits Exchange Foundation
- National Police Administration
- Bureau of Entry and Exit
- Taiwan Garrison Command General Headquarters
- Military Intelligence Bureau
- Special Intelligence Office
- General Dept. of Political Warfare
- Investigation Bureau
- Board of Foreign Trade—
- Mainland Section
- Dept. of Information & Cultural Affairs
- Dept. of International Affairs
- Chung Hwa Travel Service

**Mass Organization**
- Grand Alliance for China's Reunification Under the Three Principles of the People
- World Anti-Communist League
- Asian Pacific Anti-Communist League
- Red Cross Society
- The Alumni Association of the Military Academies of the ROC
- Association for the Promotion of the Peaceful Reunification of China
- Relief Association for Mainland Refugees
- Society for Mainland China Studies

— Overseas Branches

- Free China Relief Association In Hong Kong & Kowloon
- Hong Kong Service Center

**National Assembly**
- Planning and Research Commission on the Recovery of Mainland China

**Academic Institutions**
- Institute of International Relations (IIR)
- Chung Hwa Economic Research Institute
- Research Institute for Taiwan's Economy

Leading Line _____
Directive Line -----------

*Source*: Compiled by the author on the basis of various materials.

Today, the MAC's overall function is to serve as national advisor, together with the National Unification Council (NUC), in formulating, coordinating, and implementing to the ROC's mainland policy. The MAC is authorized to supervise the Straits Exchange Foundation (SEF).[4]

The Straits Exchange Foundation (SEF), established on 21 November 1990, is an intermediary agency subsidized by the MAC and private grants. According to its regulations, the SEF, when commissioned to do so by the ROC government, manages technical and non-official issues in Taiwan-mainland relations.[5] The SEF acts as a surrogate of the MAC to deal with the PRC's Association for the Relations Across the Straits (ARATS). Through the SEF and the ARATS, the two Chinas in fact have contacted each other under the guise of non-official communication.

The National Unification Council (NUC), a provisional section of the Presidential Office of the ROC Government, was established on 7 October 1990. It is the highest ranking institution in the ROC responsible for managing mainland policy. The president of the ROC is the NUC's chairman, with the vice president and the premier serving as two of its three vice chairmen.[6] The establishment of the NUC demonstrates Taipei's resolve to create favorable conditions for reunification and to help put other versions of Taiwan's future, such as Taiwan's independence, to rest.

The establishment of the NUC, the MAC, and the SEF 'provides the ROC Government with a complete structure for creating and implementing mainland policy. Clearly, the NUC is the highest-placed of these three organizations, with the cabinet level MAC and the SEF formulating, researching, and implementing mainland policy under the framework it [the NUC] establishes'.[7]

The Guidance Group for Mainland Affairs: This nine-member guiding group was the most important policy-making body in formulating the KMT's mainland policy, and was headed by Ni Wen-ya, the former president of the Legislative Yuan. Any proposal made by this group would be submitted to the KMT's Central Standing Committee headed by President Lee for approval and then sent down to the MAC for execution.[8] According to this group's constitution, its tasks included: 'to discuss, design, research, and map out policy concerning the mainland; to research, discuss, and manage work related to the mainland ordered or delivered by the Chairman, that is, President Lee and the Central Standing Committee'.[9]

In July 1991, this Group was reorganized into two groups. For the purpose of enhancing the execution of Taipei's mainland policy, the Guidance Group's function has remained intact but the group members were reshuffled. Lee Huan, Premier of the ROC, has been in charge of this group. Within the Guidance Group, the Planning Group for Mainland Affairs has been established and headed by Hsu Shui-teh, Secretary-General of the KMT. Generally speaking, the Planning Group functions as a think-tank for the KMT in formulating mainland policy and as a secretariat for the Guidance Group.[10]

In the Kuomintang, there are three departments involved in the anti-united front work. The Department of Mainland Operations focuses its work on gathering intelligence and PRC studies. It also coordinates with other government agencies to dispatch secret agents to the mainland for establishing intelligence networks within the PRC.[11] It publishes its own materials and periodicals such as 'The Outlook of the Mainland', 'The Compilation of Communist Bandits Materials', and 'Communist China Studies'.

The Department of Overseas Affairs is mainly in charge of looking after and offering services to overseas KMT members. The department is the KMT's united front organ overseas. The Department of Cultural Affairs is in charge of Taiwan's ideological and anti-communist education at the college level. It compiles its own 'Teaching Materials on Mainland Affairs' as the textbook for the colleges' 'Mainland China Study Course'.[12] This department also examines cultural issues between the two Chinas, such as whether Taiwan and the mainland can proceed with cultural exchanges.[13] In fact, its functions and tasks somewhat overlap with those of the ROC's Government Information Office.

Of the government agencies perhaps the *Li-Hsing* Committee (the full title of this committee was the Committee for Countering Communist Bandits' Economic Offensives) was until recently the most influential and oldest government organization that formulated policy to counter the actions of the PRC. Formed in 1965, it operated until 1988 with the following mission: to stabilize Taiwan's economic base and maintain Taiwan's security; to promote Taiwan's foreign trade; to counter-attack the PRC's economic united front; and to develop overseas trade among the overseas Chinese and win them over to the ROC. According to committee chairman Chou Hung-tao, due to *rapprochement* between the two Chinas in recent years, this organization has shifted its focus to the following areas: to promote indirect trade between Taiwan and the mainland; to relax restrictions on trade between Taiwan and the mainland, the trade between Taiwan and the East European countries, and monitor this activity. In August 1988, Taipei decided to abolish this committee and passed its work to the Workshop for Mainland Affairs.[14] Taipei did not give details of why this committee was disbanded; however, given the fact that the two Chinas' relations are more relaxed, the nature and title of this committee were not suitable for the times.

After the PRC and Britain began negotiations in the early 1980s concerning the question of Hong Kong, the Hong Kong Group was established for managing issues related to Hong Kong. Later in 1987 when Portugal agreed to return Macao to Beijing in 1999, this group was renamed the Hong Kong and Macao Group. The main functions of this group is to monitor Beijing's Hong Kong and Macao policy; to assist Chinese in Hong Kong and Macao to escape PRC rule after the years 1997 and 1999 respectively, and to look after Taipei's interests in these two colonies. In October 1990, this *ad hoc* group was incorporated into the MAC.

The Bureau of Entry and Exit in a sense is the ROC's doorkeeper. It screens all visitors to Taiwan to prevent unwanted characters from entering and, to the extent that it is possible, prevents PRC agents from infiltrating Taiwan.

The Military Intelligence Bureau and the Special Intelligence Office are the two main pillars of the ROC's intelligence operations against the PRC. Both agencies dispatch agents to the mainland and overseas to collect the PRC's confidential documents, to monitor the mainland's broadcasts, and gather sundry information.[15] The Military Intelligence Bureau also engages in analysis of the PRC and publishes a monthly periodical called *Communist Bandit Research* and the *Yearbook on Communist China*.[16]

The General Department of Political Warfare is mainly in charge of the ideological education of the armed forces personnel and psychological warfare against the PRC. It compiles materials called the *Original Sources of Communist China* which is useful for PRC watchers.[17]

The Taiwan Garrison General Headquarters had the authority to censor Taiwan's publications for the purpose of preventing the entry of the PRC's communist ideology into Taiwan during the martial law period. This unit was disbanded in 1992 with the official termination of the Period of Communist Rebellion in Taiwan.

The function of the Investigation Bureau is similar to the USA's FBI, that is, maintaining Taiwan's domestic security. Department Three of this Bureau is mainly responsible for countering infiltration and subversion efforts by the PRC and detecting activities of the PRC's agents in Taiwan. Department Six is in charge of information gathering and research concerning the PRC.[18] The Investigation Bureau also sends its agents overseas and publishes a monthly periodical *Studies on the Communist Party's Problems.*

In order to manage the increasing volume of trade between the two Chinas, the ROC established the Mainland Section within the Board of Foreign Trade in September 1988. This Section's missions are: to control indirect trade between the two Chinas; to set up an advance-alarm system for the two Chinas' trade and monitoring imports from the PRC; to gather business information about the PRC; to conduct research and formulate trade policy between the two Chinas; and to coordinate other government agencies in creating regulations and laws governing Taiwan-Mainland trade.[19]

It is not clear which unit within the Ministry of Foreign Affairs is responsible for handling relations between the two Chinas in the international environment; however, the Department of Information and Cultural Affairs as well as the International Department are reputed to manage the ROC's interest in relations and disputes between the two Chinas in the international arena. The Chung Hwa Travel Service serves as Taipei's unofficial embassy in Hong Kong.

The Mongolian and Tibetan Affairs Commission handles all matters concerning Tibet and Mongolia. In addition to a chairman, a number of members serve as advisers on policy. This Commission has a Mongolian Affairs Department and a Tibetan Affairs Department.[20] The Commission wields little influence in Taiwan as it serves no obvious function, being merely a political symbol. Some Taiwanese Chinese have questioned its necessity and suggested it be abolished.[21]

The Overseas Chinese Affairs Commission is commissioned

to represent the interests of Chinese nationals overseas. It seeks to protect their rights, as well as to promote better relationships between overseas Chinese and their host countries.[22] The main task of this Commission is competing with the PRC's overseas Chinese united front efforts and getting overseas Chinese to support the Taipei government. Whether it actually contributes to strengthening Taiwan's position in its confrontation with the PRC or not has been questioned in Taiwan. Public opinion is in favor of its being abolished or absorbed within the Ministry of Foreign Affairs.[23] As long as the PRC maintains its corresponding organization, however, it is doubtful that Taipei will abolish its own.

Of the mass organizations, the Grand Alliance for China's Reunification Under the Three Principles of the People (hereafter referred to as Alliance) is the best organized of the nongovernmental anti-united front organizations of the ROC. It was formed in 1983 and is currently headed by Mah Soo-lay, the former General-secretary of the KMT. Members of this Alliance are from all walks of life, both within Taiwan and overseas. The main mission of this Alliance is to 'overthrow the Communist regime and reunify China on the basis of Three Principles of the People.'[24] In the past, it has held seminars, conferences, and exhibitions concerning the two China issue, and has promoted its mission in Taiwan and abroad. It has also established a foundation for sponsoring overseas PRC scholars and students. In December 1988, this Alliance arranged for five PRC overseas students to make a trip to the ROC with Beijing's consent, the first of its kind since 1949. In addition, the Alliance produces radio and television programmes aimed at disseminating information about Taiwan's policies on the mainland. It has also set up many overseas associations in the hope of expanding its anti-united front work.[25] At present, this organization has focused its work on the PRC's overseas scholars and students because Taipei regards them as the social elite, who will someday become leaders in guiding Beijing towards the development of Western style democracy.[26] Whether this notion is sound or overly optimistic only time can tell.

The World Anti-Communist League (WACL) and The Asian Pacific Anti-Communist League (APACL) are similar organizations sponsored by the ROC government. APACL was founded in June 1954, while the WACL was started in 1967 by APACL, which then became a regional organization within WACL, the global body.[27] During the height of the Cold War, these two organizations enjoyed prominence in the world-wide anti-Communist movement. Since the 1970s, the evolution of *detente* between East and West has dramatically decreased their clout. Even the 'New Cold War' period of the early 1980s could not restore the importance of these two organizations. At present, in order 'not to offend the USSR and the PRC, many countries have refused to permit these two organizations to hold their annual conference on their territory; some countries even regard the WACL as a "Fascist group". Yet, some "extreme-rightists"—confusingly—referred to the WACL as a "terrorist group".'[28] The continued existence of the WACL and the APACL is due mainly to Taipei's political beliefs. Whether this kind of organization still serves the ROC's national interests, however, needs to be reexamined.

The Red Cross Society of the ROC can trace its origins back to 1904 and was recognized by the International Committee of the Red Cross in 1912. According to its constitution, it 'offers care to the wounded and relief to prisoners of war . . . and help to refugees from mainland China. . . .'[29] In October 1987, Taipei's new mainland policy, that is, allowing its people to visit their relatives on the mainland, has made this society more influential in Taiwan. This organization has been appointed to handle the necessary paperwork for those Taiwanese Chinese who intend to visit the PRC.[30] In March 1988, this society was granted responsibility for forwarding letters to both Taiwanese and mainland Chinese via Hong Kong. Thus, the 39-year-old ban on correspondence between Taiwan and mainland China has been lifted through indirect means.[31]

The Alumni Association of Military Academies of the ROC was founded in June 1988. It is said that the foundation of this association was initiated by the ROC's Ministry of National Defence for the purpose of countering the PRC's united front efforts of Beijing's Alumni Association of Huangpu Military Academy.[32]

The Association for Promotion of Peaceful Reunification was organized in October 1988 by some pro-Taipei American-Chinese scholars in the US. To date, it has about forty members from 35 different universities located in some twenty states of the US. According to its President, Dr. Leng Shao-chuan, the idea of establishing this association derived from a member of Taipei's old guard, Mr. Han Li-wu. This organization seeks to promote the reunification of China on the basis of democracy, freedom, and equity in accord with the ROC's policy.[33]

The Relief Association for Mainland Refugees is in charge of looking after those mainland Chinese who have fled or defected to Taiwan. Since November 1988, this association and its affiliates in Hong Kong, the Free China Relief Association in Hong Kong and Kowloon, and the Hong Kong Service Center, have begun to look after those mainland Chinese now permitted to visit dying relatives and attend their funerals in Taiwan.[34]

The Society for Mainland China Studies was formed on 12 March 1989 by a number of Taiwan's scholars. The main purpose of this society is to provide analysis to the government as a reference for mainland policy; to unite with mainland intellectuals for planning China's future; and to study PRC affairs from the perspective of the Taiwanese Chinese.[35]

The Planning and Research Commission on the Recovery of the Mainland has been grouped within the ROC's National Assembly. The main function of this commission was to research how the mainland should be reconstructed after the ROC has returned to power. Political reality, however, has frustrated this commission for 40 years. The members in this commission come mainly from the Kuomintang old-guard and the commission is moribund. Therefore Taiwan's opposition party members in the Assembly have proposed abolishing this commission and it was abolished in 1990.[36]

In academic circles, perhaps the Institute of International Relations (IIR), the Research Institute for Taiwan's Economy, and the Chung Hwa Economic Research Institute are the three most important think-tanks helping Taipei formulate its mainland policy. Within Taiwan, 'there are three main libraries with communist affairs collections, and the IIR's is the best'.[37] The directors of these institutes maintain a very close working relationship with the relevant government agencies. Liu Tai-yin, former director of the Research Institute for Taiwan's Economy, for example, has a very close and friendly relationship with the ROC's President Lee Teng-hui acting as Lee's private advisor for economic and mainland affairs. Thus, these institutes' research findings can even reach the President of the ROC. Through this and other channels, they play a role as a government think-tank.

   The National Security Bureau is perhaps the most influential and top-ranking intelligence agency in the ROC. It commands all Taiwan's intelligence and security units which counter Beijing's intelligence war against the ROC.[38]

   As can be seen from the above, the ROC maintains its equivalent of the united front against the PRC. The two Chinas still engage in a variety of non-military fronts of competition despite their relations gradually improving since 1979. Taipei has put a lot of political and financial resources into this competition. For example, the 1990 government budget for mainland implementing policy was alone around US$250 million.[39] If both Chinas succeed in securing peaceful relations, they would both be able to divert these funds to other government programmes, such as social welfare and public construction.

# Chapter 9

■

## Relations Between the Two Chinas (1987–Mid-1993)

### Some Changes and New Developments

If it was Beijing that took most of the initiatives in the relations between the two Chinas' during the period 1979–86, Taipei has assumed the lead since 1987. The ROC Government has constantly turned a cold shoulder to Beijing's peaceful overtures, yet Taipei has changed its mainland policy.

Aside from those people-to-people and non-official contacts that occured after 1987 (see Chapter 11), Taipei's mainland policy, by degree, has also changed, most notably in regard to the rhetoric of the 'one China' principle. Taipei no longer regards itself as the sole Chinese government to which succeeds the legitimacy of China. Taipei tends to accept coexistence with Beijing both in the international arena and in relations between Taiwan and the mainland.

Taipei has stated on 30 April 1991 that it no longer treats the PRC as a 'bandit regime' or a 'rebellion group'. The ROC has recognized the PRC as a *de facto* and *de jure* political entity that has governed the Chinese mainland since 1949.[1] Taipei's intentions are obvious. It strives to take the lead to recognize the PRC regime in exchange for Beijing's counter-recognition of the ROC. Taipei has tried hard to persuade Beijing to accept the political reality that although there is only 'one China', in fact there are two Chinese governments for the moment and that China has been divided into two areas since 1949.

Taipei seems to believe that if Beijing were accept its rhetoric and policy, the competition for China's sovereignty and legitimacy since 1949 between the two sides could come to an end. If so, the major stumbling block, Chinese sovereignty, in normalizing the two Chinas' relations would be removed and the reunification of China would become possible.

On 23 February 1991, the National Unification Council instituted and adopted the 'Guidelines for National Unification' (see Appendix 9-1). In this document, Taipei classified the process of China's reunification task into three phases: in the short term, exchange and reciprocity between Taiwan and the Mainland; in the medium term, a phase of mutual trust and cooperation between the two sides of the Taiwan Strait; and for the long term, a phase of consultation leading to the unification of China.[2]

It should be noted that in this guideline Taipei does not clearly indicate when the process of China's reunification will proceed from the current short term phase into the medium term or long term phases. In other words, there is no timetable for implementing this guideline. But, Taipei does set a precondition for the guidelines's proceedings beyond the short term phase. The document states that 'the two sides of the Strait should end the state of hostility and, under the principle of one China, solve all disputes through peaceful means, and furthermore respect—not reject—each other in the international community, so as to move toward a phase of mutual trust and cooperation'.[3] This statement reflects Taipei's fundamental position that if Beijing would renounce the use of force against Taiwan, treat Taipei as an political entity to the PRC, and not interfere with Taipei's development of foreign relations with other countries,[4] Taipei would speed up the pace of proceeding with the task of China's reunification.

On 16 July 1992, the ROC passed the 'Special Regulations on the Legal Relations Between the People of Taiwan and the Mainland' (hereafter referred to as the Special Regulations).[5] From the viewpoint of the ROC, the Special Regulations have legalized and institutionalized the exchanges that have occurred between Taiwan and the mainland since 1987. Dr. Ying-jeou Ma, Vice Chairman of Taipei's Mainland Affairs Council, said that the Special Regulations 'have embodied the spirit of 'one country, two areas' that currently exists on the two sides of the Taiwan Strait. He stressed that 'we have not denied the existence of Communist China as a political entity since May 1991 when our government proclaimed the end of the Period of National Mobilization and the Suppression of the Communist

Rebellion'. Ma predicts that the special regulations will lead the two Chinas' relations into a new era.[6]

## Factors Contributing to the Policy Change

Taipei's policy changes cannot be attributed to a single factor. They are the result of a series of developments within and outside of Taiwan. There have been changes in Taiwan's domestic political situation. Taiwan's rapid economic advances have led to the creation of a huge middle class whose political aspirations were restrained by the KMT before 1986. The resulting tension has caused a series of political confrontations within Taiwan, creating conflict between the ruling KMT party and the Taiwanese Chinese opposition members. More particularly, two scandalous incidents occurred during the second half of 1984, which damaged Taipei's image in the international community, aroused the indignation of the Taiwanese people and overseas Chinese, and plunged the KMT into crisis. They were the murder of Chinese-American writer Henry Liu on 15 October 1984 by agents linked to Taiwan in San Francisco,[7] and the discovery of corruption amongst high ranking public servants of the Taipei No. 10 Credit Co-operative.[8] These scandals provoked widespread dismay and an aura of uncertainty within the ROC. Furthermore, Taipei's do-nothing policy toward Beijing's reunification proposals also made Taiwanese Chinese impatient. They preferred to see their government handling the two China issue more actively and pragmatically (see Chapter 10).

Internationally, Taipei's further diplomatic isolation in the world as a result of the ROC-PRC struggle has created anxiety among the Taiwan Chinese about their country's future. 'More and more young Taiwanese are publicly hinting that perhaps Taiwan should try to end its isolation by abandoning its claim on mainland China and declaring its independence'.[9] This development has put the KMT in a difficult situation. The state of PRC-USA relations in the mid-1980s has also worried the ROC. Beijing-Washington ties seemed to be advancing smoothly after the signing of the 'August 17 Communique' in 1982. Washington's promises to sell military weapons to Beijing during the period of 1983 to 1986 worried Taipei,[10] especially when certain US government officials expressed the hope that the two Chinas should begin contact.[11] To the Taiwanese Chinese this sentiment might have been perceived as a harbinger of abandonment by the USA.

Facing these troubles, the ROC's President Chiang Ching-kuo decided to develop two strategies to tackle the situation and preserve the KMT's rule in Taiwan, namely democratization within Taiwan (this will be discussed in Chapter 12), and normalization of its relations with the PRC. It can be argued that Chiang intended to increase Taipei's leverage against Beijing by using democratization. As an elected government with a mandate to confront Beijing, it can avoid accusations that the KMT's position on the two China issue merely represents old guard mainlanders. Besides, democratization may improve cohesion within Taiwan's society. In the meantime, normalization of relations with the PRC might reduce the hostility of the two Chinas and soften Beijing's position of isolating Taipei internationally, thus granting Taipei some latitude in facing its diplomatic difficulties. An improvement in Taipei's international status would also enhance the KMT's ruling position within the ROC.

President Chiang Ching-kuo's inaugural address in 1984 showed signs of flexibility on democratization and diplomacy. He said that there are certain principles that can be changed but some that must be retained, while managing problems within and outside of Taiwan.[12] Further evidence is given by Chiang's speech at the KMT's Central Standing Committee Meeting on 8 October 1986. He said that

> our country is confronting an extraordinary situation because the affairs of the world are changing. The political situation is changing. The environment is changing. . . . We look around the political environment within and outside of our country. If we want to break through the difficulty and create a new situation for our country, we must undertake the necessary self-examination and analyze our working ideas and our methods.[13]

Since Dr. Lee Teng-hui was sworn in as the Eighth President of the ROC in 1990, Taipei's mainland policy has become more pragmatic. Being a Taiwan-born Chinese, President Lee, unlike the two former presidents Chiang Kai-shek and Chiang Ching-kuo, bears fewer political and historical burdens derived from the entanglement between the KMT and the CCP, and manages the two China issue pragmatically, with a reasonable approach, carefully taking into consideration reality and practicality.

The massacre of June 4, 1989 and the collapse of communism in the East Bloc during the early 1990s have encouraged Taipei. It manifested the failure of Communism. Taipei therefore believes that a sound, positive and aggressive mainland policy may enable Taiwan to exert its influence within the mainland and to peacefully change the communist system in mainland China.

## Implications of the New Policy

Taipei's new mainland policy has many implications. Taipei has declared that it relaxed its mainland policy and allowed its people to visit their mainland relatives mainly for 'humanitarian reasons' and according to 'traditional moral philosophy'.[14] The new policy has not only placated homesick refugee mainlanders in Taiwan but has also benefited those Taiwanese Chinese who actually have no relatives in the mainland but would like to go sightseeing or look for business and investment opportunities on the mainland. The new policy satisfies peoples' demands and contributes to Taiwan's social stability.[15] Allowing Taiwanese Chinese to visit the mainland may reduce to some extent what some consider the 'dangerous growth in "Taiwanese consciousness"',[16] this term being a virtual synonym for Taiwanese independence. The new policy towards the mainland serves to remind the Taiwan Chinese that the term 'China' not only means the island of Taiwan but also the area on the mainland controlled by the PRC. Taipei perhaps believes that by cultivating a 'great China consciousness' within the minds of Taiwan Chinese, its 'one China' principle can remain a viable option. As well, Taipei intends to use its new policy to assure Beijing that Taipei still maintains the one China principle and therefore 'reduce Beijing's unnecessary suspicion and prevent Beijing from taking abrupt action'.[17]

The new mainland policy, however, might also create some contrary results. When Taiwanese Chinese visit the mainland they may believe the differences in living standards and the political and social systems between the two sides too great to surmount, and become favourably inclined toward independence. Last but not least, the new policy manifests Taipei's positive response toward Beijing's appeal for the 'three links' and 'four exchanges' which it initiated in 1979. Once the door of *detente* has been opened neither China can close it again without sound reason. From a long-term perspective, this policy can only lead to more healthy and constructive relations between the two Chinas.

Taipei believes that when the mainland Chinese observe that their Taiwan compatriots who visit the mainland are more wealthy, they might prefer Taiwan's system and pressure Beijing to conduct further reform or even press for the substitution of Taiwan's system for communism in a political counterattack. It still remains to be seen if the ROC's political goals can be realized through this new mainland policy. In any case, this new policy has created another avenue for the two Chinas to handle their relations.

## Beijing's Responses

Since Taipei announced the lifting of its ban on mainland visits in late 1987, Beijing's responses have been positive. Beijing has stated that Taipei's new mainland policy represented a positive development in the two Chinas' relations. Beijing has also issued a number of documents to its agencies regarding how to properly manage the mainland visits of Taiwanese compatriots.[18] Zhao Ziyang, former Secretary General of the CCP, also mentioned four guiding principles to handle the present stage in relations between Taiwan and the mainland: to seek consensus; to erase enmity; to follow in proper sequence and make gradual progress; and to promote reunification.[19]

Despite praising Taipei's policy modifications and the gradually increasing contacts between the two Chinas during this new period, Beijing has continued to criticize Taipei's entrenchment on the Three Nos Policy and its refusal to accept its 'one country, two systems' proposal. Correspondingly, Taipei has complained of Beijing's failure to renounce the use of force against Taiwan, and its continuing policy of isolating the ROC internationally. Because of these differences, the integration process is not progressing as successfully as it might be.

At his first press conference after assuming the presidency in February 1988, the ROC President Lee Teng-hui openly expressed Taipei's dissatisfaction with Beijing's Taiwan policy. He said that Beijing is trying to use the 'one country, two systems' formula to force the ROC into being one of the PRC's local governments. He said that the PRC is trying to chase the ROC into a blind alley, to press the ROC to surrender. He said that 'you (Communist China) should not have this kind of old notion, that is, that I possess the military forces therefore I can bully you and I can force reunification with you.' He warned Beijing that 'I think Taiwan's situation is quite complex; therefore, the more you press, the stronger that resistance will be'.[20] After criticizing Beijing's Taiwan policy, President Lee said that whether the relations between Taiwan and the mainland could be improved depended solely on Beijing's attitude and actions toward Taiwan. He suggested that Beijing renounce the use of force, abolish the 'Four Cardinal Principles', and stop its efforts aimed at the international isolation of Taipei. Then the ROC could consider modifying its three nos policy and assisting Beijing with economic aid.[21] Since that press conference, President Lee has reiterated other suggestions on several different occasions;[22] however, Beijing's responses have disappointed Taipei.

Therefore, President Lee has reminded the Taiwan Chinese that it would be wishful thinking to consider themselves able to coexist peacefully with the mainland. The relations between Taiwan and the mainland are still characterized as relations between the 'enemy and us'. Therefore, he emphasized, 'contacts between the two sides of Taiwan Strait are not a fervent and fantastic longing but a very serious matter'.[23] Taipei has decided to proceed with the exchanges and contacts between Taiwan and the mainland according to the following principles: (1) personal contact only and no government-to-government contact; (2) only indirect contacts through a third party and no direct contacts; (3) only one-way contact from Taiwan to the PRC and no two-way contacts; (4) gradually increasing contacts and not rapidly expanding contacts; and (5) national security has first priority as contacts should not endanger the ROC's security.[24]

These principles guiding exchanges have caused Beijing

concern. Kuo Xiangzhi, an associate researcher of the Institute of Taiwan, at the Chinese Academy of Social Sciences in Beijing, has said that Taipei's action is not in line with a policy of solving the China issue. He criticized Taipei's new mainland policy for creating a situation of 'separation without divorce, coexistence without talk'. He said that Taipei began exchanges with the mainland in 1987 motivated to sell its 'Taiwan experience' model to the mainland, to accumulate negotiation capital, to bargain with the CCP, and therefore to achieve a condition that favors Taiwan's position in the resolution of the two China issue.[25] Another researcher, Li Jiaquan, also said that Taipei's 'gradual contact' approach can be interpreted as 'indefinitely postponing direct dialogue and consultation between the two sides of the motherland'. He criticized Taipei's current mainland policy as being merely a series of 'tactical retreats so they can dig in for further refusals.'[26]

Moreover, when Taipei put forward a number of new ideas mentioned in previous chapters, such as 'one country, two areas' and 'two equal political entities', Beijing's responses have been uniformly negative. Beijing even gibed Taipei status as the 'Republic of China' including legislation when Taipei passed the 'Special Regulations' on 16 July 1992. Beijing stated that the legitimacy of the ROC no longer existed after the founding of the PRC on 1 October 1949.

In contrast to Taipei's cautious attitude, Beijing seems eager to resolve the two China issue. Analyzing Beijing's policy toward Taiwan since 1979, a clear picture can be briefly sketched with reunification following three steps: (1) three links and four exchanges between the two side of the Taiwan Straits; (2) the two Chinas proceed to direct negotiations; and (3) reunification of China according to the formula of 'one country, two systems'. As of the publication of this book, Beijing had not positively answered Taipei's proposals but has repeatedly encouraged Taipei to sit down to direct talks. Beijing hinted to Taipei that in direct discussions between Taipei and Beijing all matters concerning the two sides of the Taiwan Strait would be negotiable.[27] Taipei has made no response so far regarding Beijing's hint.

Despite the above-mentioned obstacles that have been hindering the process of the two Chinas' integration, the prospects of improved relations between the two Chinas is still promising. Both Taipei and Beijing have recognized that the exchanges currently occurring between the two side of the Taiwan Straits are constructive developments. Taipei has indicated that it will not retreat from its new mainland policy, despite the fact that Beijing's responses to its proposals have been lukewarm at best.[28] In the meantime, Beijing has also praised Taipei for having 'undeniably played a role in this overall improvement in relations'.[29] On its part, Taipei seems to believe that only by continuing exchanges with the mainland can the 'Taiwan experience' have an impact on the mainland's economic and political reforms. It is still too early to say whether or not relations between the two Chinas will be completely normalized in the future. Only the passage of time can provide the answer to this question.

Despite the entrenchment of each side's political position, people-to-people contacts between the two China's have increased by leaps and bounds. As a result, some administrative problems ensuing from these contacts have concerned both Chinese government and their peoples. These problems typically involve marriages, inheritances, document verification, crime, investment protection, and so on. Since 1991, therefore, Taipei has repeatedly sent its non-official delegations to Beijing for consultations to resolve difficulties stemming from these problems, as well as trying to promote relations between the two Chinas.

These efforts culminated in the Koo-Wang talks which were held in April 1993.[31] This meeting marked the highest level of 'non-official' contact between the two China's since 1949. Thanks to meticulous care, the meeting was conducted in such a way that both sides appeared equal in every sense of the word. Taipei considered the meeting as one between two private entities, here, the SEF and the ARATS, commissioned by the authorities in the two areas of China to solve problems arising from cross-strait exchanges. Discussion of political issues was banned. Taipei has reiterated that the meeting in its nature and purpose was not a meeting between the KMT and the CCP or between the two Chinese governments.[32] Nevertheless, the Koo-Wang talks marked a big step forward in the relations between the two Chinas. At the very least, the talks indicated that both sides would like to sit and talk with each other to solve their problems. Whether this kind of meeting proves useful in fundamentally improving the relations between the two remains to be seen, especially in light of Beijing's continued intransigence towards Taipei's three pre-conditions (not isolating the ROC internationally, renouncing the use of force against Taiwan and treating the ROC as an equal entity). The issue, in terms of integration theory is whether or not the spill-over or ramification effect postulated would in fact be valid for the Chinese case. This issue, both in practical terms as well as its implications for integration theory is worthy of our close observation.

# Chapter 10

■

## Other Voices in Taiwan and Alternatives to Two Chinas

The previous chapter presented the Republic of China's official position regarding the two China issue. The attitudes of the non-governmental elite and the general public in the ROC in this regard have not been discussed. Donald J. Puchala says that both of the principal schools of integration theory, 'communication' and 'neo-functionalism', emphasize the role that the elites plays during the process of integration because they believe that 'it is the elites who initiate amalgamation, not the masses'.[1]

Ernst B. Haas also points out that integration involves a process of verbal and symbolic communications between crucial elites with mutual expectations and mutual responsiveness between elite communities among the different nations or communities.[2] Therefore, the elite's viewpoints are essential to the process and outcome of integration. Also, in a democratic society, the general public expresses their viewpoints which sometimes are considered by the government while formulating policy. Theoretically, therefore, the non-governmental voices within a country might influence the government's decision-making.

According to Roy C. Macridis,

> in most political regimes the decision makers, generally the officials who hold responsible positions (they issue and execute orders), are part of what may be loosely called the governing elite. The governing elite in general consists of people with greater income or knowledge and skills, or status and political influence, including those who occupy decision-making positions. Industrial leaders, managers, intellectuals, political leaders, religious leaders, representatives of major interests and other groups and associations, doctors, lawyers, engineers—they all make up the elite. The government officials and even the political leaders who make decisions, the

political elite, are only a part of the elite and in some regimes
it is but the tip (not the top) of the elite iceberg'.[3]

Karl W. Deutsch refers to the governing elite as the top five
per cent of a country's adult population, as identified by a
combination of income, occupational status and educational
level, 'who would tell us a good deal about what was and
what was not politically acceptable in that country'.[4]

In the light of the influence of these elite groups' in policy-
making, and government's respect of the general public demands
in a democratic society as a whole, this chapter will therefore focus on the views of the governing elite and the general
public in the ROC concerning the two China issue. Meanwhile,
the discussion of Taiwan independence is covered in Chapter
13. These non-governing elites and the viewpoints of the general public in the ROC to some extent exercise influence on
the political elite that makes the ROC's mainland policy.

## Other Voices in the Republic of China

Other voices in the ROC are beginning to be heard as a result
of a resurgence of political thought and free speech associated with the gradual democratization in Taiwan since the
1980s. Apart from Taipei's proposal for the reunification of
China under the Three Principles of the People (one China:
the ROC) and Beijing's formula for the reunification of China
on the basis of one country, two systems (One China: the
People's Republic of China), the following list outlines the
various other proposals initiated by Taiwanese Chinese either
within or outside Taiwan since 1980:[5]

(1)  One China: the Concept of Multi-System Nations
     1.  The German Model
     2.  The Korean Model
         a.  One China, Two Separate Administrations
         b.  One China, Two Seats
         c.  One China, Two Governments
(2)  One China: the Olympic Games Model
(3)  One China: the Pattern of Federation
(4)  One China: the Pattern of Confederation or Commonwealth
(5)  One China: the Belligerents Model
(6)  The Greater China Economic Circle

At this point, the author would like to briefly introduce these models without commenting on their feasibility, which is beyond the scope of this study. All the main viewpoints and voices, not including Taiwan's independence, concerning the resolution of the two China issue in Taiwan would have been presented.

## Model 1: The Concept of Multi-System Nations

This concept was broached in 1980 by Yung Wei, politics professor of the National Taiwan University and the Chairman of the Research, Development, and Evaluation Commission of the ROC Government's Executive Yuan (Cabinet). He argued in a seminar paper that a survey of literature on divided nations like Germany before 1990, Korea, and China, reveals two basic problems. Firstly, there is the lack of a commonly accepted term which is neutral and precise enough to be used as an effective operational concept for empirical research on divided nations. Secondly, there is a failure in differentiating two separate types of division and accompanying unification processes: those that involve confrontation between communist and non-communist systems and those that do not. He proposed to substitute the term 'multi-system nations' for 'divided states' and 'divided nations' to redress this deficiency. He argued that the new term can clarify the fact that the reality in a so-called 'divided nation' is not the separation of one nation into two or more nations, but the emergence of more than one political system within one nation, either as a result of an imposed international arrangement or as a product of an internal war. More significantly, he posits that the term 'multi-system nation' reflects faithfully the true nature and cause of division, that is, the confrontation and competition between non-communist systems and communist systems within various countries.[6]

Yung Wei compared the two Chinas' relations with those of the erstwhile two Germanies and the two Koreas. He pointed out that the two Germanies have somewhat 'resolved' their problems and reduced their mutual hostilities which has led to: (1) the exchanges of representatives between Berlin and Bonn; (2) dual recognition of the two Germanies by other states; (3) dual representation of both Germanies by the diplomatic corps of other states; (4) membership for both East and West Germany in the United Nations; and (5) direct trade and tourism between the two nations. In the Chinese case, he said, the situation represents the opposite end of the spectrum to the German arrangements. The two Chinas have virtually no interaction at all. In the case of Korea, he argued that the two Koreas fall somewhere between the two Germanies and the two Chinas. Although the two Koreas have not thus far formally recognized each other, a North-South dialogue has been maintained intermittently since July 1972. He indicated that the *detente* between the two Korean governments has led to dual recognition and dual representation of the two Korean governments in a number of countries.[7]

As a high-ranking official in the ROC government, Yung Wei's arguments have drawn much attention within and outside Taiwan. Yung Wei's arguments and Taipei's elastic diplomacy whereby Taipei would do whatever it can to maintain either official or unofficial relations with those countries which have established diplomatic ties with Beijing since the mid-1980s have caused objections from Beijing charging Taipei with trying to create the reality of 'two Chinas' or 'one China, one Taiwan'.[8]

Beijing's objections notwithstanding, Yung Wei's theory has expanded the latitude of Taipei's policy-making and thinking, as his viewpoints have also been accepted by many other Taiwanese Chinese scholars. Professor Michael Ying-mao Kau, the Executive Director of the 21st Century Foundation in Taipei, advocates the concept of a 'multi-system nation' and regards it as the most practical and reasonable solution for handling the two Chinas' relations during the transitional period before they achieve unity in the future. He says that the formula has been widely accepted by the international community and successfully applied to the cases of Korea and Germany; therefore the international status of the ROC and the related problems can also be managed by applying this formula. As for the two Chinese governments concerned, Kau argues that the idea of a 'multi-system nation' does basically correspond to the principle of 'one China' upon which both Taipei and Beijing insist. In terms of this theory, Taiwan should be able to enjoy its own international legal status. For example, Taipei should still be able to exercise its diplomatic power independently and maintain its official ties with other countries without retaining its independence as a separate country. In the meantime, the door for the reunification of Taiwan and the mainland would still remain open. Professor Kau suggests that Taipei not mix the issue of its relations with the mainland and that of the ROC's international status. The former issue should be resolved by the Chinese themselves, while the latter issue is related to the recognition of the ROC by foreign governments in general.[9] Only by maintaining such as a separation can the ROC properly improve its diplomatic relations while at the same time enhance its leverage vis-à-vis the PRC.

The concept of 'multi-system nations' has given rise to two models for resolving Taipei's diplomatic isolation on the one hand, and tackling the relations between Taiwan and the mainland on the other. The first to be examined is the German model.

## The German Model

When both Germanies concluded their Treaty on the Basis of Relations Between the Federal Republic of Germany and the German Democratic Republic in 1972, the 'German Model' for multi-system nations was established. Under this model both Berlin and Bonn mutually recognized each side's independent sovereignty within their domain while internationally they practiced the principle of dual recognition and had the equal right to participate in international activities.[10] As a result of this treaty, the two Germanies at that time became two independent political entities despite the fact that Bonn then maintained that Germany was in a condition of 'one nation, two states'. At the same time, East Berlin had developed another theory that Germany was under the condition of 'two nations, two states'.[11]

A Taiwanese-Canadian scholar, Hsiao Hsin-yi, suggested that the two Chinas should copy the German model to manage their problems. He presciently argued that despite the two Germanies becoming two states, the possibility still existed for them to incorporate in the future.[12] In 1987, two ROC legislators Yu Ching and Chu Kao-cheng DPP members who obtained their Ph.D. degrees from West Germany, also requested Taipei to consider the German model.[13]

## The Korean Model

Generally speaking, the 'Korean model' can be described as a model of 'one country, two governments, two seats'. Both North and South Korea accept the principle of dual recognition from third countries and dual representation in a number of international organizations on an equal basis. This model, from the viewpoint of Taiwan scholars, can also serve Taiwan's interests. Inspired by this model, three variations have been put forward.

(1) One China, Two Separate Administrations. Professor Shen Chun-shan, Dean of the Faculty of Science, Chin-hua University, put forward his idea in 1987, saying that the ROC should employ this model to counter the PRC's proposal of 'one country, two systems'. Under this arrangement, he says, both Taipei and Beijing could still maintain the 'one China' principle in the same way as Korea so that they could enjoy sovereign rights jointly. Furthermore, Taiwan and the mainland should administer their respective territories separately and compete with each other peacefully and equally for the time being. He concludes that time would decide which system is more suitable for the development of a reunified China in the future.[14]

(2) One China, Two Seats. Professor Winston L. Y. Yang, a Chinese-American scholar, advocates this approach suggesting that before the achievement of reunification, the two Chinas should still maintain the 'one China' principle while both Taipei and Beijing would have the equal right to seats in international organizations on the basis of 'peaceful coexistence and competition'.[15]

(3) One China, Two Governments. Legislator Lin Yi-hsiang of the KMT put forward this idea in April 1989, and urged Taipei to change its outdated mainland policy once described as 'Han and Thief cannot coexist' to one of peaceful coexistence with Beijing until the time is ripe for China's reunification.[16] The specific outcome of this idea would be the ROC's release from the self imposed confinement of anti-communist ideology in favour of pragmatism in its policy towards Beijing and in the field of foreign affairs. This idea could also imply Taipei's recognition, on a reciprocal basis, of the Beijing government and of the PRC's *de facto* control of the mainland. If so, it might to some extent imply the withdrawal of Taipei's long-time position towards the two China issue, that is, there

is one China, the ROC. The implementation of the 'one country, two governments' idea could produce the following benefits: bring the hostility of the two sides to an end; retain the principle of the reunification of China; assist Taipei's return to international society; and reduce the two Chinas' military expenditures, which could then be used in constructing the two Chinas' modernization programmes.[17] On 8 May 1989, President Lee Teng-hui during an interview with Japan's *Yomiuri Shimbun*, told Japanese correspondents that the idea of 'one country, two governments' was proposed by the legislators but that it did not represent the government's policy. He said, however, that Foreign Minister Lien Chan regards this idea worthy of further study. Lee emphasized that the ROC still insists on the principle of 'one China'; he added, however, 'any idea that will contribute to an expansion of latitude in Taipei's foreign relations, we will study'.[18]

## Model 2: One China—the Olympic Games Model

After a long process of negotiations between Taipei, Beijing and the International Olympic Committee (IOC), Taipei decided to participate in the 1984 Los Angeles Games under the name of 'Chinese Taipei' while Beijing retained its official title 'the People's Republic of China'. This arrangement has been set up as a precedent to allow both Taipei and Beijing to participate in non-governmental international organizations. Professor Weng Sung-jan of the Chinese University of Hong Kong suggested in 1985 that both Chinas could apply this model for conducting their international relations. Nevertheless, unlike the German and the Korean models, the 'Olympic Model' has the disadvantage that the PRC can still keep its national identity as an international legal entity while the ROC becomes a 'local' team without an official status in international affairs.[19]

## Model 3: One China—the Pattern of Federation

One commonly accepted definition of a federal state is 'a state composed of political subdivisions that have certain governmental powers of their own, or in which certain powers are shared between the central or national government and the subdivisions. From the international point of view, however, the whole is considered a single independent state, and the foreign relations for the whole are generally carried on by the central government'.[20] It has been suggested that the mainland, Taiwan, Macau and Hong Kong could form a 'Federal Republic of China,' a 'United States of China,' or other similar federated systems.[21] On 13 June 1988, Hsu Cho-yun, a Chinese-American scholar, told the ROC's legislators during the testimony session that China is too huge to govern effectively, therefore both Taipei and Beijing should consider the adoption of a federal system for a reunified China.[22]

In December 1991, the Chinese Socialist Democratic Party, during the campaign of the National Assembly elections, put forward the idea of establishing 'The Federal Republic of China' as a solution for the two China issue. This party argued that it is impossible for Taiwan to reunify the mainland for the moment; Taiwan, however, does not want to be 'liberated' by the PRC. This party therefore suggested that the resolution of the two China issue should wait until the two Chinas have fully realized democratization. After that, the 'Federal Republic of China' can be founded on the basis of a federation model and implement a socialist democratic system.[23]

## Model 4: One China—the Pattern of Confederation or Commonwealth

A 'confederation' is typically defined as a 'group of states which, while maintaining their separate independence and entities, combine in the joint exercise of certain governmental functions, often defence and foreign relations'.[24] A confederation differs from a federal state in that countries in a confederation retain full sovereignty. In addition, decisions may be made by unanimity or majority vote, but no state can be forced to accept a majority decision. Further, a confederation lacks the powers to make and enforce laws, its decision-making authority is only as extensive as the consensus developed within the association, whereas in a federal state, political authority is constitutionally divided between a central and regional units of government. Therefore, confederation can be considered as a 'halfway house between independent state action and the establishment of a federal system'.[25]

The term 'commonwealth' usually means the voluntary association of independent states that were once parts of the British Empire. The essence of this commonwealth system is cooperation engendered through consultations among members. No formal treaty ties or permanent institutions exist, except for a secretariat. It is a unique political system in that its members freely cooperate and assist each other without specific binding agreements or commitments. In addition, members are free to leave the commonwealth at any time.[26]

Both systems of confederation and commonwealth share one similarity—members can retain full sovereignty and independent status. The main proponents of these models are Mei Ko-wang, the former Principal of Tunghai University in Taiwan, Professor Hungdah Chiu, Maryland University, USA, and Fei Hsi-ping, at the time a Legislator. They proposed to create a loose organization such as a 'Confederation of Greater China',[27] or 'the Greater China Commonwealth',[28] or other symbolic organizations under which there would be no central government and both Taipei and the mainland (some proposals would also include Hong Kong and Singapore) will possess their own sovereignty and independent diplomatic and defence powers. They argue that if Beijing abolished its communist system, its economic condition would supposedly catch up with Taiwan within fifty years. Should that day come, the two Chinas could naturally be incorporated together. When such a confederation of China is established, Taiwan could assist the mainland to realize its modernization programs.[29]

## Model 5: One China—the Belligerents Model

According to conventional international law there are three types of international personalities: the states, the belligerents, and insurgents. The DPP legislator Chu Kao-cheng put forward this model in November 1988 and suggested that both Taipei and Beijing both mutually recognize each other as the two 'belligerent groups' so that the ROC can promote its status as an international judicial person and break through Taiwan's diplomatic difficulties. Chu pointed out that the

ROC's isolation in the international community is not only caused by the ROC's foreign policy *per se* but also by the hostility between the two Chinas. Taipei should therefore talk directly with Beijing to work out the two China issue and 'compel' Beijing to recognize the *de facto* condition of 'belligerence' between Taiwan and the mainland, and that the two China issue is an issue resulting from the civil war. If Beijing opposes this idea, he says, Taiwan could counter that it would not exclude the possibility of proclaiming its independence as a form of leverage against Beijing.[30]

## Model 6: The Greater China Economic Circle

Chiu Chuan-huan, Senior Advisor to the ROC president, proposed this model in January 1992. He argues that the time for world economic competition and cooperation has arrived during the post-cold war period. Chinese people, including those on the mainland, Taiwan and Hong Kong, should ride the developing trend of the world and form a Greater China Economic Circle to promote the mutual benefits across the Taiwan Strait. Chiu adds that due to the huge differences in political ideologies and living standards between the two sides of the Taiwan Strait, political reunification of the Mainland and Taiwan for the moment is impracticable.

Many obstacles notwithstanding, the two Chinas could start from conducting the tasks of economic cooperation and economic integration which may eventually contribute to political integration of the two Chinas in the future, he suggests. Chiu stresses, however, that there are some preconditions before the two Chinas undertake economic cooperation. Beijing should recognize Taipei as a political entity and as its counterpart, respect the ROC's political status, and not interfere with Taipei's development of foreign relations on the basis of the 'one China' principle.[31]

The above-mentioned models have some obvious similarities. They all to some extent support the 'one China' principle upon which both Chinas insist. They all posit that the current division of China is merely a temporary and transitional situation; therefore they believe that China will be reunified in the future when the time is ripe. However, during the transitional period there should be some kind of arrangement for the two Chinas to coexist peacefully on the basis of equal rights and equal status both in the international community as well as in their mutual relations. They all advocate the necessity of normalizing relations between the two Chinas through indirect or direct contacts and exchanges which will contribute to mutual understanding and the establishment of a consensus between the two Chinas finally leading to the unity of China. As a whole, these models all aim at solving Taipei's international status problem on the one hand and normalizing the two Chinas' relations on the other.

## Public Opinion in the ROC

In Western countries, to some extent there has been a correlation between a government's policy-making and public opinion. Theories of democracy generally maintain that national administrators respond to aggregate citizen preferences. Democracy is to a large extent usually identified 'with political equality, popular sovereignty, and rule by majorities'.[32] Therefore, in this part of the discussion, the author cites some opinion polls to serve as a rough indicator of the attitude of the Taiwan Chinese toward the two China issue since 1987.[33] Due to press censorship and the limitations in the political environment, there is no opinion poll before 1987 in Taiwan that was conducted publicly and permitted to release the results.

In mid-1987, when the ROC government announced that it would relax its mainland policy and allow its citizens to visit relatives in the mainland, Taiwan's media began to conduct a number of public polls. On 9 September, 1987, Taipei's *United Daily News* conducted a telephone survey in Taiwan and found that 73.7 per cent of those polled reported they knew of the government's decision to allow Taiwan Chinese to visit the mainland, while 26.3 per cent responded 'no idea' about this decision.

This figure indicated that most Taiwan Chinese are concerned about and pay attention to Taipei's mainland policy-decisions. When asked whether they approved of this policy or not, 45.4 per cent responded 'yes' while 9.1 per cent said 'no'. Interestingly, forty per cent of the persons sampled in this poll responded 'no comment' about this policy while 5.5 per cent approved.

Since most of the Taiwanese Chinese have no relatives in the mainland, this policy is not so relevant to them. This poll also showed that only 16.6 per cent of the sample have relatives in the mainland while the majority of the persons said they had 'no' relatives in the mainland, thus this policy has little impact on the general public. The questionnaire therefore required more questions: (a) If you have relatives in the mainland, would you go to see them? About 46.2 per cent said yes while 37.9 per cent said no and 12.9 per cent were undecided. (b) If you do not have relatives, would you favor travel to the mainland? About 47.7 per cent said yes while 40.9 per cent responded no, and the rest of the sample persons were undecided or had no idea.[34] This poll revealed that in mid-1987 some Taiwan Chinese still maintained a wait-and-see attitude toward Taipei's mainland policy. Perhaps they were not sure whether Taipei was serious in its policy change after nearly four decades of a closed-door policy towards the mainland.

However, a March 1988 telephone survey conducted by *The Independence Evening Post* in the Taipei metropolitan area found large differences from the results of the previous one. Table 10-1 shows part of this questionnaire and the results.[35]

This survey found that 76.8 per cent of the sample approved the ROC government's visiting-relatives policy compared to 45.4 per cent in the previous poll. This shows that most of the polled citizens favoured the increase of people-to-people exchanges and contacts between Taiwan and the mainland. Also, only between 13.1 per cent to 23.1 per cent of the polled persons think that exchanges and contacts between the two Chinas will endanger the ROC's security. This results indicate that Taiwanese people perceive the mainland as less of a threat to Taiwan's security.

**Table 10-1** A Survey on Taipei Citizens' Opinions Concerning the Relations Between Taiwan and the Mainland

Question 1. Do you approve of the lifting of the ban on travel to the mainland?
Yes 76.8%;  No 10%;  Other respondents 13.2%
Question 2. Do you approve of mainland Chinese visiting relatives in Taiwan?
Yes 45.6%;  No 25.6%;  Other respondents 28.8%

**Table 10-1** (Cont.)

Question 3.  Do you approve of our athletes attending sports events in the mainland?
Yes 67.6%;       No 8.1%;       Other respondents 24.3%

Question 4.  Do you approve of the mainland's athletes attending our sport events?
Yes 72.5%;       No 7.1%;       Other respondents 20.4%

Question 5.  Do you approve of our scholars attending academic activities in the mainland?
Yes 65.2%;       No 9.1%;       Other respondents 25.7%

Question 6.  Do you approve of the mainland's scholars attending our academic activities?
Yes 70.5%;       No 8.0%;       Other respondents 21.5%

Question 7.  If necessary, do you approve of our journalists covering news stories in the mainland?
Yes 74.5%;       No 5.2%;       Other respondents 20.3%

Question 8.  If necessary, do you approve of the mainland's journalists covering news stories in Taiwan?
Yes 61.7%;       No 13.7%;       Other respondents 24.6%

Question 9.  Do you think that the lifting of the ban on visiting relatives and on travel between the two sides of Taiwan Strait will endanger Taiwan's security?
Yes 23.1%;       No 36.9%;       Partially 24.8%
No idea 15.2%

Question 10.  Do you think that the implementation of sports exchanges between Taiwan and the mainland will endanger Taiwan's security?
Yes 13.7%;       No 54.1%;       Partially 11.4%
No idea 20.8%

Question 11.  Do you think that the implementation of academic exchanges between Taiwan and the mainland will endanger Taiwan's security?
Yes 13.1%;       No 53%;       Partially 10.2%
No idea 23.7%

Question 12.  Do you think that the lifting of the ban on journalists will endanger Taiwan's security?
Yes 20.2%;       No 47.7%;       Partially 14.1%
No idea 18%

*Source*: *The Independence Evening Post*, 14 March 1988, p. 3.

On 12 April 1988, Taipei's *China Times Express* conducted another telephone survey in the Taipei metropolitan area and found that thirty-three per cent of the sample responded that they 'agreed strongly' or 'agreed' with the idea of direct trade with the PRC. This idea contravenes Taipei's official policy at present. Twenty-nine per cent 'disagreed strongly' or 'disagreed' with this idea and 38 per cent were not sure or offered 'no comment'. When asked if they approved mail exchanges between Taiwan and the mainland, 53 per cent favoured this idea, while 11 per cent were against, while 36 per cent said 'not sure' or no comment. In a query regarding approval of Taiwan's sports team attending the 11th Beijing Asian Games in 1990, 60 per cent of the sample said yes while only 8 per cent responded no.[36]

Response to this poll indicates the cautious attitude of the Taiwan Chinese toward the idea of direct trade with the mainland because of the sense of risk in proceeding with direct trade with the mainland. The other contributing factor could be the Taiwanese people's waiting for a clearer official trade policy toward the mainland. This poll also reveals that most of the Taiwan Chinese prefer to proceed with mail and sport exchanges with the mainland.

In order to further understand the Taiwanese people's opinions concerning the mainland, the *United Evening News* in April 1988 conducted a series of island-wide telephone surveys which focused on business people, academics and the general public. The first poll surveyed the executives of 477 manufacturers in Taiwan to explore their opinions concerning the conduct of business with the mainland (Table 10-2).

**Table 10-2** A Survey of Taiwanese Manufacturers' Opinions Concerning the Conduct of Business with the Mainland

Question 1: The mainland is a potentially huge market with a large population. Its economic development has begun to accelerate, therefore, we should not give up the mainland market. Do you agree with this viewpoint?
(1) Agree strongly 21%       (2) Agree 41%
(3) Disagree 21%             (4) Disagree strongly 1%
(5) No comment 25%

Question 2: People say that the reason why Communist China permits Taiwan's businesspeople to do business in

**Table 10-2** (Cont.)

the mainland is mainly for the purpose of conducting united front work. Do you agree with this viewpoint?
(1) Agree strongly 5%      (2) Agree 30%
(3) Disagree 23%           (4) Disagree strongly 2%
(5) No comment 40%

Question 3: Some people say that the New Taiwan Dollar is appreciating constantly while Taiwan's labor costs are also getting higher and higher; therefore, only by investment in the mainland can Taiwan's economy further develop and improve. Do you agree with this viewpoint?
(1) Agree strongly 3%      (2) Agree 22%
(3) Disagree 45%           (4) Disagree strongly 4%
(5) No comment 26%

Question 4: People say that Communist China changes its policy frequently, therefore, the risk is too high to do business with the mainland. Do you agree with this viewpoint?
(1) Agree strongly 27%     (2) Agree 42%
(3) Disagree 11%           (4) Disagree strongly 1%
(5) No comment 19%

Question 5: People say that with the mainland's abundant resources and Taiwan's production and management skills, the economy of both Taiwan and the mainland can strongly develop. Do you agree with this viewpoint?
(1) Agree strongly 16%     (2) Agree 46%
(3) Disagree 12%           (4) Disagree strongly 1%
(5) No comment 25%

Question 6: People say that Taiwan's economy would soon be controlled completely by the mainland if we lift the direct trade ban with the mainland. Do you agree with this viewpoint?
(1) Agree strongly 5%      (2) Agree 28%
(3) Disagree 34%           (4) Disagree strongly 6%
(5) No comment 27%

Question 7: If the government lifted the direct investment ban, would you invest and establish your firm in the mainland?
(1) Yes 12%                (2) No 41%
(3) Depends on             (4) Have not considered
    the situation 32%          this issue yet 11%
(5) No comment 4%

**Table 10-2** (Cont.)

Question 8: If the government lifted the direct trade ban, will you conduct business directly with the mainland?
(1) Yes 42%              (2) No 26%
(3) Depends on the       (4) Have not considered
     situation 24%             this issue yet 6%
(5) No comment 2%

Questions citied here are part of this poll's questionnaire.

*Source: The United Evening News*, 3 May 1988, p. 11.

The results of this poll show the conflicting attitudes of Taiwanese business people towards doing business with the mainland. Sixty-two per cent of the sample believed that combining the mainland's resources and Taiwan's management skills could improve and promote the economic development of the two Chinas. They also however, suspected Beijing's sincerity and distrusted the mainland's economic policies. Sixty-nine per cent regarded trade with the mainland as too risky, while less than 50 per cent responded positively to the idea of direct trade with or investment in the mainland if the ROC government permits. Nevertheless, this poll also revealed the great interest of the Taiwanese business community in the mainland market. Sixty-two per cent of the respondents said that Taiwan should not give up the mainland market.

The second poll was aimed at academic circles in Taiwan. It surveyed 319 university professors and found that academics in the ROC strongly favored the increase of academic exchanges between the two Chinas. Table 10-3 is compiled from part of the telephone survey questionnaire.

This poll has shown that the majority of scholars in this survey would like to see a significant relaxation of relations between Taiwan and the mainland. About seventy per cent of the surveyed persons believed that the increase of cultural and academic exchanges would contribute to the reduction of hostility and tension across the Taiwan Strait. The scholars in Taiwan, however, are not sure about the future development of the two Chinas' relations. Opinions in this regard are mostly 'keeping the status quo' and 'difficult to predict'.

**Table 10-3** A Survey of the Academic Circles' Opinions Concerning Academic Exchanges Between Taiwan and the Mainland

Question 1: Do you think that the scholars on both sides of the Taiwan Strait should proceed with academic cooperation?

(1) Yes 41.1%  (2) Yes, but selectively 30.1%
(3) No 6%  (4) Others 22.8%

Question 2: Do you approve of both sides' scholars attending each other's academic seminars?

(1) Yes 72.6%  (2) Yes, if the seminar was held by academic groups 13.8%
(3) No 3.1%  (4) No comment 10,5%

Question 3: Do you approve of the import of the mainland's academic periodicals?

(1) Yes 53.3%  (2) Yes, but selectively 37.9%
(3) No 0.9%  (4) No comment 7.9%

Question 4: Do you approve of the import of movies, video cassettes, and music tapes from the mainland?

(1) Yes 20.7%  (2) Yes, but selectively 61.8%
(3) No 4.7%  (4) No comment 12.8%

Question 5: Do you approve of the establishment of a special institution for handling the issues concerning relations between Taiwan and the mainland?

(1) Yes 75.5%  (2) No 4.1%
(3) No comment 20.4%

Question 6: Do you believe that the increase of cultural and academic exchanges would reduce tension and hostility across the Taiwan Straits?

(1) Yes 47%  (2) A little help 23.2%
(3) Not at all 8.9%  (4) Not sure 15.8%
(5) No comment 5.1%

Question 7: Do you think that the increase of cultural and academic exchanges between Taiwan and the mainland would contribute to the disappearance of the consciousness of Taiwan independence?

(1) Yes 22%  (2) Possible 25.2%
(3) No 7.9%  (4) Depends on the situation 14.5%

**Table 10-3** (Cont.)

(5) No correlations between cultural and academic exchanges and independence consciousness 11.9%

(6) I have not considered this 18.5%

Question 8: Could you please predict the possible developments of the relations between Taiwan and the mainland in the future 10 years?

(1) They will increase the exchanges but still maintain the status quo 42.9%

(2) It is very difficult to predict 41.3%

(3) Taiwan will reunify with the mainland on the basis of the Three Principles of the People 2.5%

(4) They will achieve unity through negotiations 1.3%

(5) They will establish a 'Confederation of China' 0.9%

(6) Communist China will take over Taiwan by force 0.3%

(7) The Communist regime will collapse automatically 0%

(8) Taiwan will declare itself as a new and independent country 0%

(9) Others 10.8%

*Source: The United Evening News, 4 May 1988, p. 11.*

The third poll (Table 10-4) surveyed 1,100 members of the general public in Taiwan concerning their attitudes towards the resolution of the two China issue in this poll.

This poll shows that 56.3 per cent of surveyed persons advocate the reunification of China. They are confused, however, about the future development of relations between the two Chinas. Unlike academics, about 10.5 per cent of these people support the idea of Taiwan's independence.

**Table 10-4** A Survey on the General Public's Opinion Concerning the Future of China

Question 1: Some people argue that we can break through the current diplomatic difficulties only through a declaration

**Table 10-4** (Cont.)

of independence for Taiwan, which would attract many
countries' recognition. Do you agree?
(1) Agree strongly 1%    (2) Agree 12%
(3) Disagree 41%    (4) Disagree strongly 9%
(5) No idea about this    (6) No comment 7%
issue 30%

Question 2: Some people say that only through achievement
of China's reunification can both Taiwan and the mainland have a bright future. Do you agree?
(1) Agree strongly 11%    (2) Agree 35%
(3) Disagree 17%    (4) Disagree strongly 1%
(5) No idea about this    (6) No comment 12%
issue 24%

Question 3: Some people argue that the difference between
Taiwan and the mainland is too great for reunification.
Do you agree with this?
(1) Agree strongly 2%    (2) Agree 18%
(3) Disagree 39%    (4) Disagree strongly 3%
(5) No comment 13%    (6) No idea 25%

Question 4: Do you approve of Taiwan's independence?
(1) Approve 10.5%    (2) Disapprove 61.6%
(3) No idea 22.6%    (4) Depends on the
situation 3.5%
(5) No comment 1.8%

Question 5: Do you approve of the reunification of China?
(1) Approve 56.3%    (2) Disapprove 5.6%
(3) No idea 20.4%    (4) Depends on the
situation 6.5%
(5) No comment 1.2%

Question 6: Will the relations between Taiwan and the mainland become more hostile or more friendly during the
next ten years or will the status quo be maintained?
(1) More friendly 36.1%    (2) More hostile 2.2%
(3) The maintenance of    (4) Not sure 11.7%
the status quo 17.7%
(5) No idea 24.5%    (6) No comment 0.7%

*Source*: *The United Evening News*, 7 May 1988, p. 11.

The three polls shown above have roughly indicated the attitude of the Taiwan Chinese concerning the two China issue and how to handle the relations between Taiwan and the mainland. It seems that public opinion in Taiwan favors a more normal relationship between Taiwan and the mainland accomplished through various exchanges and contacts.

During the period from June 1989 to November 1991, a number of institutions in Taiwan have further conducted a series of polls aimed at understanding Taiwan people's expectations concerning the future relations of the two Chinas. Table 10-5 has compiled these polls together and found that Taiwan people's expectations toward the future relations between Taiwan and the mainland have fluctuated from time to time. Different institutions conducting the polls have usually obtained different results especially concerning the question of 'reunification'. This divergence can be attributed to the difference of the sample questions that each institution has designed for its questionnaires.

Roughly speaking, Table 10-5 indicates that the percentage of Taiwan people's expectations about the issue of Taiwan's independence is low. According to this table most people have expressed uncertainty in their expectations concerning the evolution of relations between Taiwan and the mainland. They either expect the two Chinas' relations to be a maintenance of the status quo or have a wait-and-see attitude. They seem to prefer procrastination as a strategy to handle the current relations across the Taiwan Strait. It should be noted that a considerable percentage of the sample responds non-commitally 'No idea', 'No comment', 'Do not know', or 'Refuse to answer'. A refined study of these respondents' attitude concerning the two China issue is necessary because their position might eventually influence the balance between the factions of pro-unification and pro-independence in Taiwan.

## Conclusion

The ROC government has produced a series of policy reforms concerning both Taiwan's domestic politics and Taiwan's relations with the mainland. These reforms include lifting martial law, removing bans on political parties and abolishing

**Table 10-5:** Taiwan People's Expectations Toward the Relations Between Taiwan and the Mainland   (Unit:%)

| Poll Questions \ Poll Time | June 1989 | June 1990 | Jan. 1991 | Feb. 1991 | April 1991 | May 1991 | June 1991 | Aug. 1991 | Sep. 1991 | Oct. 1991 | Oct. 1991 | Nov. 1991 | Nov. 1991 | Nov. 1991 |
|---|---|---|---|---|---|---|---|---|---|---|---|---|---|---|
| Immediate Negotiations | — | — | — | — | 6.6 | — | — | — | 4.3 | — | — | 1.8 | — | — |
| Reunification | 20.5 | 64.6 | 31.3 | 69.0 | 0.2 | 65.0 | 62.5 | 51.0 | — | 36.1 | 40.0 | — | 22.6 | 24.1 |
| Taiwan Independence | 2.1 | 10.6 | 3.6 | 8.0 | 6.4 | 10.0 | 12.3 | 6.0 | 4.1 | 4.5 | 3.0 | 3.8 | 5.3 | 4.1 |
| Maintaince of the status quo | 20.7 | 4.6 | 21.4 | 3.0 | — | 4.0 | 4.5 | 5.0 | — | 43.4 | 20.7 | 24.7 | 52.0 | 47.5 |
| Wait-and-see | 36.8 | 3.5 | 23.6 | 2.0 | 0.1 | 2.0 | 4.2 | 7.0 | — | — | — | — | — | — |
| Maintaince of the status quo, while waiting til the time is ripe to discuss the issue of reunification | — | — | — | — | 82.0 | — | — | — | 57.5 | — | — | 18.6 | 24.3 | 21.0 |
| Others/No idea/ No Comment/Do Not Know/Refused to Answer | 19.7 | 16.7 | 20.1 | 16.0 | 4.7 | 19.0 | 26.0 | 31.0 | 34.0 | 16.0 | 36.3 | 18.6 | 21.0 | 24.3 |
| Poll Institutions | R.D.E.C., ROC 1 | The United Daily News | M.A.C., ROC 2 | The United Daily News | M.A.C., ROC | The United Daily News | The China Times | The United Daily News | M.A.C., ROC | The China Times | The United Daily News | M.A.C., ROC Eepress | The China Times | The China Times |

1. Abbreviation of the Research, Development and Evaluation Commission, Executive Yuan, R.O.C.
2. Abbreviation of the Mainland Affairs Council, Executive Yuan, R.O.C.

*Sources*: Quoted from Huang, Kuen-hui, *The Mainland Policy and the Two Sides' Relations*. Taipei: The Mainland Affairs Council, Executive Yuan, January 1992, p. 43. Huang is the Chairman of the MAC.

newspaper censorship, as well as permitting the visitation of relatives across the Taiwan Strait. Although Taipei's modifications of its mainland policy were considered humanitarian, they were essentially a breakthrough step in facilitating the establishment of relations between the two Chinas after 40 years of virtual separation.

Nevertheless, political factors still remain the main element hampering the normalization of relations between the two

Chinas. Members of the elite in the ROC has put forward a number of models aimed at solving the difficulty of Taipei's international status on the one hand, and trying to lead the relations of Taiwan and the mainland to a more sound and peaceful course on the other. The PRC, however, regards these models as contravening its long-time 'one China' position. Beijing suspects that the ulterior intention of these models are aimed at creating a situation of two Chinas. In the meantime, the ROC government also maintains a reserved attitude toward some of those models proposed by the Taiwanese people, partly because those models also violate Taipei's one China principle. The other reason for this ambivalence is Taipei's understanding that without concessions on the part of Beijing these models would be difficult to implement.[37]

Despite the continuation of a confrontational situation across the Taiwan Strait, the majority of the Taiwan Chinese still favor the increase of exchanges and contacts between Taiwan and the mainland. Taiwan people seem to prefer to adopt a strategy of delay as a means to manage the current relations between Taiwan and the mainland and to understand that only time can solve the two China issue. While waiting for a solution, they would like to promote mutual understanding with their compatriots in the mainland. Whether this public opinion will influence Taipei's mainland policy and its foreign policy has become a key point in deciding the future course of development in the two Chinas' relations.

# Prospects for Integration and Disintegration

# Chapter 11

∎

## Contacts Between the Two Chinas

Reviewing Beijing's reunification proposals and repeated calls for implementing its three links (postal service, transportation, and trade) and 'four exchanges' (academic, cultural, athletic, and technological) between the two sides of the Taiwan Strait, the author would argue that Beijing seems to realize the importance of embarking on non-political contacts with Taiwan as currently the best approach to promote mutual understanding and reduce hostility between the two Chinas.

Before 1986, Taipei had never explicitly accepted Beijing's appeals; however, in practice, some links and exchanges had existed between Taiwan and the mainland. Since Taipei's modification of its mainland policy in 1987, these contacts and exchanges have increased dramatically. Thus far, the Republic of China (ROC) has retained the principles of its Three Nos policy towards the People's Republic of China (PRC). In international activities, the ROC abides by the major tenets of 'anti-communism and national restoration to take a "no concession and no avoidance" or "Two Nos" position' in dealing with the PRC.[1] In a nutshell, the ROC would allow its citizens to sit with, to talk to, to compete against, or to contact the PRC's people on any international occasion.

In this chapter, the author will, through case studies and communicational approaches, review and analyze a range of contacts which have occurred between the two sides since 1979. Five cases have been chosen for this purpose: (1) people-to-people contacts; (2) trade relations; (3) the Olympic Games Model; (4) the case of the Asian Development Bank; (5) the two airlines talks between the two Chinas. These cases have been selected because they all have important implications for evaluating relations between the two Chinas and predicting future developments.

## Case 1: People-to-People Contacts

Although the 'Three Nos' policy is currently in effect, viola-
tions of this policy have already occurred, which were ignored
prior to 1986. As Professor Shen Chun-san pointed out, a considerable gap exists between what the two Chinese governments say and what they do; in practice, both Taipei and
Beijing are quite flexible in dealing with each other.[2] Shaw
Yu-ming, a former spokesman of the ROC Government, has
said in 1985 that 'Taipei has repeatedly attempted to exercise
flexibility within a fixed posture of one China. . . . So long as
it is a non-governmental gathering, the ROC is willing to bend
over backwards to join'.[3] The modification of Taipei's mainland policy starting 1987 has to some degree resolved the
issue of contacts between the two sides. Some questions, however, still remain regarding the ROC's position toward the
mainland. How flexible the ROC will be in dealing with the
PRC as long as the Three Nos policy remains in effect, and
how exactly to discriminate between the principles of the
Three Nos and the Two Nos, remain to be answered. The following case studies will help elucidate these points.

### Fishermen Reception Stations

For many centuries, Chinese fishermen have been fishing on
the Taiwan Strait and in the waters of the continental shelf.
Fishing on these immense waters is sometimes difficult because
of unforeseen natural disasters such as stormy weather, typhoons,
and the like. Therefore, being a fisherman is seen as the most
risky job in Chinese society. It is an undeniable fact that, following the reduction of tension, the two sides of the Taiwan
Strait have been helping each others' fishermen from time to
time, despite the fact that these two Chinas were technically
still at war. In general, such assistance was rendered for humanitarian reasons, and both sides kept these contacts in low
profile.

In May 1973, the PRC reported a rescue for the first time—
that of twelve Taiwan Chinese fishermen—and stated that 'during their stay in Fujian, they were warmly treated by local
authorities and people'.[4] After the PRC's proposal for 'three links'
and 'four exchanges' in January 1979, Beijing accelerated its

friendly gestures toward Taiwan's fishermen. At least fourteen Taiwan Fishermen Reception Stations, located mainly in the provinces of Zhejiang, Fujian, and Guangdong, have been established and publicly promoted by the PRC since 1979.[5] It is unknown how many of Taiwan's fishermen have stayed in these stations; however, according to Beijing's reports, more than one thousand fishermen and 130 fishing boats were accommodated by Fujian's reception station in 1979.[6] In 1981, 3,000 Taiwanese fishermen and 400 fishing boats sought shelter in these stations.[7] According to Beijing, the original purpose of the reception centers for Taiwanese Chinese fishermen was simply to provide havens in stormy weather, for when boats needed repairs, and facilities for those who were curious to visit. Later, the scope of these services was expanded to other fields: such as sightseeing, travel, looking for relatives, medical treatment and trade.[8]

Officially, Taipei bans its fishermen from staying in the mainland harbors; however, in practice Taipei ignores these contacts as long as the fishermen have no political motivation. In the meantime, Taiwan also renders similar services to mainlanders. Mainland Compatriots Reception Centers have been established in Quemoy and Mazu islands, located offshore to the mainland but still part of the ROC. These centers offer water, food, machine-repairs, medical services, and so on. A major incident occurred in March 1980, when the Taiwan's Seamen Association invited 17 mainland seamen, who worked on a West German freighter which had called at Keelung harbor, to tour Taipei city. It was the first such visit by mainland Chinese to Taiwan. The ROC's explanation for this action was mainly to show Taiwanese Chinese's fraternal love to their mainland compatriots.[9] Beijing was excited by this and said that 'it was a good thing because it helped enhance mutual understanding between the people on the mainland and Taiwan. . . . We hope that there will be more contacts of this kind in the future'.[10]

However, Beijing's hopes were set back in August 1981, when 27 fishermen were sentenced to prison terms from five months to one year by the ROC government for trading with the mainland Chinese in the Taiwan Strait.[11] A number of factors could have accounted for Taipei's behavior: the fishermen had in fact broken the law which prohibited the conducting of any direct business with the mainland; Taipei resented

Beijing's exertion of power on Washington in an attempt to prevent the sale of new American jet fighters to the ROC; and ROC Air Force Major Huang Che-cheng defected to the mainland with an F-5E fighter on 13 August 1981. All of these factors alarmed Taipei, causing distrust about Beijing's intentions, and directly or indirectly fostering a sense of insecurity within Kuomintang (KMT) power circles, thus leading to a more cautious attitude toward the Chinese Communist Party (CCP). Even after this case, however, Taiwan's fishing boats still continued to seek shelter in mainland ports for emergencies and other purposes.

Before 1986, the exchange pattern between the two Chinas' fishermen was primarily one in which Taiwan's fishermen took shelter in the mainland. Mainland fishermen rarely called on Taiwan's harbors, but instead primarily stopped by the islands of Quemoy and Mazu. This situation, however, changed after 1987 when Taipei lifted martial law and relaxed the restrictions of contacts between the two sides of the Taiwan Straits. Ever since, the PRC's fishermen and fishing boats have been constantly visiting Taiwan's harbors and coastal areas (mainly the north-east part of Taiwan) in groups without obtaining any prior permission from the ROC government.

This situation has alarmed Taipei. According to the ROC's Ministry of National Defense, during 1988, at least 5,200 of mainland China's fishing boats illegally intruded into Taiwan's territorial waters. Taipei stated that the mainland fishermen's actions 'have created serious security problems for Taiwan'.[12] What was noted as worse than the mainland fishermen's intrusion into Taiwan's waters was their illegal entry into Taiwan in groups. According to captured mainland fishermen, the principal reasons why they steal into Taiwan is to seek work opportunities in Taiwan. However, Taipei is convinced that this must involve some kind of plot organized by Beijing.[13] In order to contain this 'dangerous' situation, Taipei has begun to disperse, detain, arrest, and quarantine mainland fishing boats that wander into Taiwan's waters. In addition, the ROC has begun to fortify its coastal security defence to prevent these intrusions.[14]

In fact, the illegal entry of the mainland Chinese and the fishing boats has developed into a sensitive problem for Taipei. Politically, the ROC still claims its sovereignty over the mainland and mainlanders; therefore, the mainland fishermen are still technically the ROC's citizens. If so, how can one government stop its people from moving from place to place within the country. Taipei seems to have no legal ground to punish these mainland fishermen. In reality, however, the two Chinas are officially still at war. It is possible—even likely—that some of these mainland fishermen are the agents of Beijing, spying on or testing Taiwan's coastal defense systems. This would explain why Taipei always arrests and then releases the mainland fishermen after investigating them, supplying them with food, fuel, and water. According to Taipei, during the period from September 1989 to the end of 1992, for example, 742 mainland fishing boats were detained or quarantined; 21,475 mainland fishermen had been detained and interrogated. In addition, more than 20,000 mainland fishermen have illegally entered Taiwan.[15] If both Chinas do not cooperate to solve this problem immediately, the illegal intrusion of the mainland fishing boats and fishermen into the ROC territory would become an added source of tension in the Taiwan Strait.

## Visiting Relatives and Travelling

On 1 January 1979, the USA shifted its diplomatic recognition from Taipei to Beijing. To show its rising self-confidence, on the same day the ROC allowed its people to travel abroad freely for the first time since 1949.[16] There were many reasons for this decision: Taiwan had enough foreign exchange reserves (US$6 billion in 1978) to allow its people to spend abroad; it allowed the people to demonstrate the country's confidence; it offset the disadvantages of diplomatic isolation; and it represented Taipei's decision to open the door for those who had relatives on the mainland to meet with them in neutral countries (mainly in Hong Kong).

In Asia, Taiwan is second to Japan in terms of tourism generating foreign exchange reserves.[17] Some of the Taiwanese Chinese quietly visited the mainland by way of Hong Kong. In the early 1980s, this action was a violation of the ROC's official policy, and one would be charged with engaging in 'communicating with the bandits' in mainland China. Worrying that this trend might increase and Beijing would take advantage of this situation in its 'united front' strategy, Taipei stopped issuing visas for those who chose Hong Kong as their first or only destination.[18] In other words, the ROC still encouraged its people to go abroad, but Hong Kong was temporarily excluded, mainly for political reasons. This ban was lifted in July 1987.

Taipei's policy prior to 1987 did not seem to be effective. There were between 5,000 and 10,000 Taiwan Chinese touring the mainland each year before 1986.[19] One leading magazine in Taipei even explicitly described how to arrange a mainland trip and what kind of treatment to expect if you are a Taiwan compatriot, reporting that 'holding the ROC passport to travel the mainland has become an open secret'.[20] This magazine went on to report that, before 1986, several hundred Taiwan Chinese had visited the mainland each year, mainly by travelling through Hong Kong, Tokyo, and New York. Most of these people were elderly expatriate mainlanders who have been separated from their relatives for 37 years. It also says that Chinese fom Taiwan could enjoy privileges such as duty free purchases, 50 per cent discount on the cost of hotel accommodations, meals, special services, and so on during their sojourn on the mainland.

As mentioned earlier, however, visiting the mainland before 1986 violated the law of the ROC. According to extant regulations, those who have been to the mainland would have their passport rescinded; moreover, if someone is found guilty of working for the PRC after returning from the mainland, they would be sentenced to prison.[21] But, an old Chinese saying has proven apropos: 'the force of evil always manages to beat the force of law'; Beijing and some Chinese from Taiwan have managed to circumvent Taipei's policy. According to this magazine article, after checking the travellers' ROC passports and the Hong Kong Entry Permits, the PRC's travel agent in Hong Kong would issue Taiwan Compatriot Identity Cards to the Taiwan Chinese, which would function as visas to enter the mainland. By so doing, there would be no record on ROC passports, and no one will know that the travellers have been on the mainland. Despite the absence of records on the passport, Taiwan has still managed to monitor entry into the mainland. One source reported that there are many Taiwan agents in each transit station, collecting information or comparing notes with the transit governments and using materials, such as 'passenger flight lists, mainland's local newspaper reports,

and other tourists remarks', which might enable Taipei to identify who has visited the mainland.[22]

With the lifting of the ban on visiting relatives in November
1987, Chinese from Taiwan have flocked to the mainland.
Under the rules set by the ROC government, anyone, other
than a person in active military police, or civil service, can
travel to the mainland once a year for the purpose of 'visiting relatives'. (This restriction was later lifted.) If the relative
in question is dying or seriously sick, the allotment of trips
to the mainland can be increased.[23] All such trips are to be
made through an intermediate point, such as Hong Kong, and
are to last no longer than three months. Those who want to
visit relatives in the mainland must apply and receive government permission, otherwise they will be forbidden to leave
Taiwan for two years after their return from the mainland.[24]
But Taipei has turned a blind eye to those Taiwanese Chinese
who have no relatives on the mainland, but who still travel to
do business, which in fact is prohibited by the ROC government.

According to the PRC, over 450,000 Chinese from Taiwan
have visited the mainland in 1988 for various reasons such
as visiting relatives, travel, and business.[25] According to a
source from Hong Kong's travel agencies, at least one hundred groups per day (altogether about 1,300 people) of Chinese
from Taiwan entered the mainland via Hong Kong in March
1988. Among these groups, only about 20–30 (altogether about
300 people) were truly visiting relatives; the rest of the groups
were sightseeing, as they had no relatives in the mainland.[26]
By February 1992, at the least, over three million Taiwan people had visited the mainland, according to Beijing.[27] These
facts have revealed that, although Taipei has not lifted the
travel and business bans, Taiwanese Chinese have already
begun to initiate such activities in the mainland under the
guise of 'visiting relatives'.

In the meantime, Taipei has also agreed, effective as of 9
November 1988, to issue entry permits—with some conditions
attached—to mainland Chinese for family reunion, visiting
dying relatives, or attending family members' funerals in
Taiwan.[28] It seems likely that Taiwan will continue to allow
more mainlanders to come to Taiwan if Taipei finds that such
a policy of relaxation does not endanger to its security and
that the relations between the two Chinas improves steadily
in the future.

It is superfluous to say how ardent Beijing is to encourage such visits, since the guarantee of 'freedom of entry and exit' that the PRC issued in 1979.[29] The PRC hopes that such contacts will reduce suspicion and hasten reunification between the two sides. Beijing has instructed its responsible agencies to manage carefully the affairs relevant to the interest of the Taiwan compatriots under the guidelines of the 'three priorities' policy: (Taiwan compatriots should be received first, served first, and provided with the best quality service).[30]

Aside from the political implications, Taipei policy to allow people to visit the mainland has brought many economic benefits to the mainland. For instance, residents of Taiwan returning to the mainland usually bring an abundance of gifts for their less fortunate brethren. These gifts include cameras, two-door refrigerators, color television sets, automatic washing machines, personal computers, and so on, which are in heavy demand on the mainland as components of the so-called '10 big consumer items' in the mainland.[31] According to Taipei, since the lifting of the travel ban, Taiwanese Chinese have spent at least US$100 million per month in the mainland.[32] Hence, since 1987 the ROC has in effect initiated economic aid to the PRC. The Council for Economic Planning and Development, the ROC Cabinet's economic think-tank, stated in its research report that the spending of the Taiwan Chinese in the mainland might increase further when the Taiwanese Chinese expand their activities in the mainland from merely visiting relatives, to fields of travelling and investment. The Council stated that the ROC government should keep an eye on this developing situation and evaluate its possible impact on Taiwan's finance and economy.[33]

The lifting of the travel ban to the mainland has also created some problems for the ROC government. For example, Taipei has complained that there have been intensified PRC efforts to infiltrate Taiwan since the visits began, a more lax vigilance on Taiwan against PRC intrusion, an increased exchange of capital and technology across the Taiwan Strait, and requests by mainlanders to visit relatives in Taiwan.[34] Nevertheless, Taipei is content to maintain its 'visiting relatives' policy, at least from a political standpoint. ROC government officials asserted that 'the lifting of the travel ban will have the side effect of putting Taiwan on the political offensive against Beijing for the first time in decades'.[35] Shaw Yu-ming, a former spokesperson for the ROC Government, said that 'for so long they've been trying to push us around, we now want to call the shots. We are going to show that we don't fear them any more. The battle between the two sides now is over the hearts and minds of the people. If we allow our people to go to the mainland, they can bring tidings of democracy and freedom to the mainland'.[36] Taipei's optimism does not appear to be unfounded, judging from comments made by Chinese from Taiwan who have been to the mainland. For example, Yeh Ming-zong, a businessman, said that the mainland 'is at the stage of development that Taiwan reached 20 or 30 years ago'. 'On the mainland, the food is bad and the clothes are shabby', added Tu Shu-rong, an insurance company employee in Taipei. Another Taiwan visitor said that 'for so many years, everyone (in the mainland) ate from the same big pot and didn't work hard. On Taiwan, everyone worked very diligently. We competed, and we earned a lot of money'.[37]

In November 1988, the ROC's Bureau of Entry and Exit conducted a survey of those 5,170 people who had visited mainland relatives between 2 November 1987 and 2 November 1988; 45.2 per cent of those surveyed said 'they could not get accustomed to life in the mainland', while 38.23 per cent indicated that 'they felt life (in the mainland) was very inconvenient'. Although Taipei only allows its citizens to stay in the mainland three months each visit, in fact, 85.23 per cent of those surveyed stayed in the mainland less than one month.[38] The Interior Minister Wu Poh-hsiung said that the biggest benefit of lifting travel bans to the mainland has been to let the Taiwanese Chinese understand that the mainland is 'really poor and backward' in its standard of living, and that Taiwan indeed offers 'progress and prosperity'.[39]

Contacts between sports people, academics, and students have increased dramatically between the two sides after 1991. Taipei has permitted all of its public servants, except those high-ranking government officials in charge of administrative affairs, to visit the mainland. Meanwhile, scholars from the two Chinas also frequently cooperated in organizing academic seminars to discuss Dr. Sun Yat-sen or economic affairs that concern both sides of the Taiwan Strait. It is expected that people-to-people contacts will steadily increase in the future across the Taiwan Strait if the two Chinas' relations remain warm.

## Other Contacts

Contacts between sports people, academics, and students have also gradually increased between the two sides since 1979. In February 1984, the ROC's former Prime Minister, Sun Yun-suan, formally announced that Taiwan and mainland Chinese could meet as long as group meetings and contacts were non-political and both parties are given equal status.[40] In fact, before this announcement, a few individual scientists from the both sides had met, unintentionally or on purpose, at international scholarly conventions. In April 1982, a conference, sponsored by the Association for Asian Studies of the US, brought the two Chinas' scholars under the same roof for the first time since 1949, where they took the opportunity to discuss the Hsin-Hai Revolution of 1911. Significantly, each delegation was headed by a ranking party member, and as one Western participant said, 'it was a historic occasion and the beginning of an academic dialogue'.[41]

Another major meeting between academics of the two sides occurred in September 1988 when Taiwan's delegates, including personnel of Academia Sinica (the ROC's highest academic institution under the direction of the ROC Presidential Office) attended the 22nd Annual Conference of the International Council of Scientific Unions (ICSU) in Beijing. Originally, Taipei rejected attending this meeting for fear of violating the 'no official contact' policy. However, a compromise was reached after Academia Sinica President Wu Ta-you warned that the ROC's highest academic institution risked losing its membership in the prestigious ICSU if it boycotted the meeting. It was decided that Taiwan's scientists could attend as representatives of a 'private group' called 'the Academy Located in Taipei', the name under which Academia Sinica holds membership in ICSU in order to differentiate it from the Beijing delegation.[42] This meeting represented the first case in which representatives of the two Chinas were allowed to sit together in an official international academic meeting held on the mainland. Taipei, however, maintains that this meeting was not official and was 'no contravention of the "three nos" policy'.[43]

Student contacts between the two sides of the Taiwan Strait in other countries have also increased since 1979. The US is the biggest destination for students from both sides. Notably, 93 per cent of the ROC's students who go abroad study in the

US.[44] During the 1987–8 academic year, according to the New York-based Institute of International Education, there were 180,500 students from Asia studying in American universities. The largest delegation was from the ROC, about 26,668 students, whereas, the PRC, with 25,200 students, was second to the ROC. It is believed that the PRC students in the US will outnumber the ROC's in the near future, and the US would continue to be the most important meeting ground for students from the two Chinas.

Apparently, students from both sides help each other, exchange reading newspapers, magazines, viewpoints, and sometimes even live in the same flat. These occurrences are no longer news but commonplace. Of course, it is too early to expect that the students have overcome all differences, especially the political ones, within this short time period. However, it can be hoped that the US and other advanced countries' political systems, cultures, philosophies, and ideas can provide a common ground for the students, with different ideological and social backgrounds, which is conductive to realizing ways of solving the reunification task.

Since December 1988, in order to help the mainland students understand Taiwan's situation and developments, Taipei has begun to invite the PRC's students who study abroad (mainly in the US) to visit Taiwan.[45] This programme has received Beijing's approval.[46] Knowing that most of the PRC students face financial difficulties, Taipei's 'Grand Alliance for China's Reunification Under the Three Principles of the People' has raised US$1 million from Taiwan's businesspeople for a scholarship foundation to aid overseas mainland students.[47] Taipei seems to believe that making an 'investment' in the PRC's students (the PRC's social elites and the possible heirs to the Beijing regime in the future) will be conducive to the realization of its ideal of reunifying of China under its terms— democracy, freedom and the well-being of the people.

Cultural exchanges have also gradually increased between the two sides. Publications, films, and television programmes published and produced by the PRC hve been allowed into Taiwan since 28 July 1988, with the stipulation that those materials pose no threat to the ROC's national security.[48] Most Taiwanese Chinese are, in fact, curious about the mainland. For example, when the film, *The Last Emperor* (the first film made on the mainland permitted to be shown in Taiwan), premiered in Taipei in April 1988, more than 20,000 Taipei citizens crowded into the four movie houses where the Oscar-winning film was being shown.[49] In addition, Taiwan's artists have held many art exhibitions on the mainland. In addition, since 1987 journalists from Taiwan have covered news stories from the mainland without obtaining Taipei's consent.[50] All of these activities have been conducted under the guise of visiting relatives on the mainland. On 18 April 1989, however, Taipei decreed formally that its journalists and movie makers can cover news stories and shoot movies on the mainland. This permit allows them to stay in the PRC no more than six months at a time.[51] On 10 June 1989, Taipei further lifted the ban on telecommunication services between the two sides, while mail exchanges were also officially relaxed.[52]

## Case 2: Growth of Entrepot Trade

What is the motivation for integration among communities? Karl Deutsch believes that joint rewards or group interests are the prime factors. However, he also points out that integration can result in mutual deprivations or penalties. He argues that therefore, 'rewards must come before the penalties, and rewards must be strong and frequent enough to initiate the habit'.[53] Along these lines, if the ROC and its people were invited to talk without any explicit reward, according to Deutsch's general theory, the PRC's reunification scheme would be less successful than if Beijing could devise a way in which Taipei could first share interests and only later be penalized (if we presume that reunification represents a penalty to Taiwan). Trade relations between the two sides seems to be an area which Beijing can use as such an incentive to Taiwan.

### The Evolution of Beijing's Policy

The trade between the two sides started as an exchange between fishermen of merchandise and other things such as yellow-fish, watches and silver coins, which finally evolved into indirect trade relations. From Beijing's viewpoint, trade with Taipei promotes the image of contact between the two governments, and could serve as 'a means of leverage or lure for Taiwan to eventually accept its reunification offer'.[54] Mainly for political reasons, therefore, the PRC fully supports trade with the ROC. An internal document issued by the United Front Work Department of the CCP in May 1985 revealed Beijing's plan. It said that 'Under the shrinking situation of the international market and the upsurge of protectionism in the United States and Western European countries, we can definitely, step by step, lead Taiwan's industries to further rely on our market as long as we adopt well-organized and well-guided measures. Continuing to develop these efforts would effectively lead us to control the operation of Taiwan's economy that would speed up the reunification of the motherland'.[55]

In order to entice Taiwan's businessmen, Beijing announced in April 1980 that Taiwan's products would be duty-free as 'inter-provincial material exchanges'; in addition, Taiwan's ships which are 'nationality ships' would not be levied tontax.[56] This most-favoured-status policy toward Taiwan had shortcomings as some other countries, through false labelling and other means, took advantage of this tariff relaxation. As a result, Beijing cancelled this duty-free policy.[57]

On 1 May 1981, Beijing announced another approach to court its antagonist: 'Taiwan imports, by whatever channel, are still considered domestic products and thus exempt from custom tariffs. Instead, they are charged a lower adjustment tax which the mainland uses to regulate inter-provinicial trade'.[58]

It is evident that the mainland's huge market and Beijing's most-favoured-status policy are tempting bait, attractive to Taiwan's businesspeople. As a result, some private and indirect trade has been initiated since 1979. To the average businessperson in Taiwan, the interest in trade with the mainland, although it might be a 'sugar-coated poison' (as the government of the ROC has described it), would be more important than anti-communist ideology. Beijing's ultimate goal is direct rather than indirect trade. The significance of the former will be greater than the latter both politically and economically.

In order to achieve this goal, in May 1985, the PRC announced that Taiwan's products will be completely duty-free if the businesspeople of Taiwan could satisfy the following four conditions: they must directly contact the mainland's institutions that are in charge of Taiwan trade affairs; they must show copies of the businesspeople's identity card, business register certification, import-export permission certification, and some documents that prove the businesspeoples' positions in their companies; and ships must travel directly from Taiwan to mainland harbors.[59] The purpose of this policy, aside from political objectives, is to ensure that the products imported are genuinely from Taiwan and the businesspeople are truly Taiwan compatriots.

After Taipei's lifting of the travel ban in 1987, more and more Taiwan businesspeople have gone to the mainland to search for trade and investment opportunities. The amount of indirect trade between the two sides and investment by Taiwan Chinese in the mainland has increased exponentially. In order to cope with this new situation, on 6 July 1988, the PRC announced new rules and principles comprising a set of regulations designed to encourage Taiwanese Chinese to invest on the mainland. Yuan Mu, spokesman for the PRC's State Council, stated that 'no matter whether publicly or collectively owned, big or small, or run by individuals, companies from Taiwan will all receive the same treatment (as foreign-funded companies) when they come to the mainland to invest, and their legitimate rights and interests will be protected along with their safety and freedom to come and go'.[60] Yuan said Chinese from Taiwan can start up private companies, or participate in joint ventures or co-operative enterprises; engage in offset trade; supply materials for processing; purchase enterprise shares and bonds; buy land-use rights, and so on. Again, Beijing casts a political light on this new policy, stating that the mainland's trade policies towards Taiwan 'are aimed at promoting the peaceful reunification of the motherland according to the principle of 'one country, two systems'.[61]

## Taipei's Response

Taipei is faced with somewhat of a dilemma in trying to manage this issue. The ROC's economic development relies highly on its export-oriented foreign trade; therefore, any trade opportunities are welcomed by Taipei. Taipei's apprehension, however, is primarily political. Taipei officials fear that Beijing will let its industries and businesspeople become overly dependent on the mainland, and then use trade as a means to blackmail Taiwan for political ends. The former ROC's Premier Yu Kuo-hua made this point explicit, saying that 'we can not rely on enemy's milk to feed our babies'.[62] A poignant example took place in 1985, when the PRC suddenly cancelled a US$2 million order for motor scooters from Taiwan's Paijifa Industrial; the company nearly instantly went bankrupt.[63] Furthermore, the PRC unilaterally treats the ROC's products as 'inter-provincial material exchanges' levying some symbolic tax, underscoring their view that Taiwan is one of the PRC's provinces or districts. If Taipei officially accepted this gesture, Taiwan will essentially admit to being such a province of the PRC.

Nevertheless, decision-making cannot escape from reality. Beijing's peaceful overtures, and the growing public pressure from within Taiwan, has forced Taipei to adjust its trade policy. In March 1984, Taipei announced that, for the first time since 1949, the ban would be lifted on the imports of 1,157 agriculture commodities from Hong Kong and Macao, which were potentially mainland goods, and stated that the government would continue to ban the import of mainland products.[64] Although this statement seems contradictory, Taipei could not make a plain statement at that time for fear of repercussions.

On 4 July 1985, the ROC announced three principles to govern trading with the PRC: no direct trade would be permitted between the two sides; businessmen were prohibited from contacting the mainland; and the government would no longer prevent entrepot trade.[65] Entrepot trade with the mainland, thus, has been officially permissible since 1985. It should be noted, however, that Taipei's permission to trade with Beijing is only one-way, that is, Taiwan can export but not import.

Taipei's decision was based on the three following considerations: Taipei had to prevent itself from falling into Beijing's political trap. It could not ignore the trade issue forever when there were potential advantages to Taiwan; for example, the mainland market could serve as one more outlet for Taiwan's industrial products, and a source of more foreign currency reserves. It is difficult, technically speaking, to prevent entrepot trade. Any third party can easily resell Taiwan's products to the mainland—in which case Taipei would be powerless to stop such transactions.

Despite the ROC government's policy of no direct trade with the mainland, public opinion in Taiwan favors widening the scope of permissible dealings with the mainland. Many argue that mutual benefits might result from trade between the two Chinas. The mainland can offer its abundant natural resources such as oil, coal, uranium, and so on, as well as cheap labour and a vast market. For its part, Taiwan 'has good intermediate-level technology, large amounts of idle capital, cheap manu-factured products that are most appropriate for the mainland's less-developed industrial base, and managerial know-how'.[66] *International Business Week* predicted that a new Asian eco-nomic superpower is looming—meaning Greater China—which includes the economies of the PRC, Taiwan, and Hong Kong. It reported that 'blending Chinese scientific and military research, raw materials, and labor with Taiwanese money and marketing skills and Hong Kong's financial and communica-tions conduits will catapult Greater China into a position right behind Japan as Asia's next economic superpower, displacing South Korea'.[67]

In January 1992, the Conference for Greater China Economic Mutual Assistance System, sponsored by the PRC, the ROC, and Hong Kong's non-official institutions, was held in Hong Kong. Experts and scholars from these three places attended this conference and were trying to form an institution that would be analogous to the concept of the Greater China Economic System. However, political reasons have prevented this idea from becoming reality.[68]

From the standpoint of trade profit and nationalism, the prospect of a 'Greater China' economy will, to some extent, entice some Taiwanese Chinese to advocate closer economic cooperation between Taiwan and the mainland. Furthermore, Taiwan businesspeople, who fear losing export orders to other Asian competitors, who are able to import low-priced raw materials from the PRC, have also constantly complained about Taipei's trade policy toward the mainland. Taiwan business-people are apparently tired of being handicapped by Taiwan's labour shortage, which has caused wages to double in recent years; a more than 40 per cent appreciation of the New Taiwan Dollar since 1986; and the US government's pressure to nar-row the trade imbalance presently favourable to Taiwan, between the ROC and the US. Taiwanese Chinese need new markets and workers. The mainland, which shares the same language and tradition with Taiwan, has therefore become the first pre-ference for trade and investment among Taiwan business-people.

Taipei also recognizes the importance of the mainland mar-ket to its survival. According to an ROC Board of Foreign Trade research report, the lifting of direct trade bans with the mainland would promote Taiwan's competitiveness with other newly industrialized Asian countries.[69] Taipei, however, has harbored a constant concern that Taiwan's economy would become overly dependent on the mainland which could thus create a vested interest in Taiwan which could be leveraged by Beijing, to try to accommodate Beijing's interests.[70] Indeed, Taipei's mentality toward trade with the mainland could be considered to be as ambivalent as Shakespeare's famous line of Hamlet: *To be, or not to be.* Hence, one Chinese-American scholar has described the mainland's market and raw materials as 'a fatal attraction' to the ROC.[71]

But the relaxation of Taiwan's mainland policy since 1987 has buttressed the growing commercial ties between the two Chinas. In July 1988, Taipei decided, during the KMT's 13th Party Congress session, to allow imports of raw materials from mainland China through third party countries as part of the ROC's new liberalization policies.[72] Vincent C. Siew, then Director-general of the Board of Foreign Trade, said that 'we expect entrepot trade with the mainland because of growing imports'.[73] In the meantime, Taipei has decided to stop calling products from the mainland 'bandit goods' or referring to the mainland as 'bandit territory'. Taipei now refers to mainland imports as 'products from the Chinese mainland', or 'products from Communist China', for the first time since 1949.[74] This is a big step forward in improving the two Chinas relations. In June 1989, in order to prevent sophisticated products from being exported to the PRC, Taipei formally relaxed its trade policy from permitting only entrepot trade to also allowing indirect trade with the mainland. Taipei said that this would make it easier for Taipei to control the export destination of Taiwan products.[75]

In a nutshell, Taipei's trade and economic policy toward the PRC thus far can be summarized in three points: prohibition of direct trade and investment between Taiwan and the mainland; no interference with entrepot or indirect trade; and gradual relaxation of the imports of mainland's raw materials. These points do not mean that Taipei is to bar direct trade with the mainland forever. Direct trade between the two sides is possible if the two Chinas' relations can be further improved in the future. A harbinger of direct trade is founded in Article 35 of the Special Regulations on the Legal Relations Between the People of Taiwan and the Mainland instituted in mid-1992 by the ROC. Article 35 states that, in principle, the conduct of direct trade with the mainland is prohibited and restricted, except those transactions that have the permission of the Executive Yuan (the ROC's cabinet).[76]

## The Present Situation with Entrepot Trade

By 1991, entrepot trade between the two Chinas jumped from US$77.76 million in 1979 to US$5.39 billion (See Table 5-1). The mainland's purchases from Taiwan include textile machinery, telecommunications equipment, petrochemicals, television sets, motorcycles, and so on. For its part, Taiwan buys textile items, raw materials, Chinese herbal medicines and so on from the mainland. In 1992, the ROC is the fifth largest trade partner (after the USA, Japan, Hong Kong, and Germany) of the PRC, while the PRC is the ROC's fifth largest trade partner (after the USA, Japan, Hong Kong, and Germany).[77] According to the ROC's Board of Foreign Trade, if the two sides were allowed to trade freely and directly, the value of trade between Taiwan and the mainland could reach US$40 billion per annum.[78]

**Table 11-1:** Entrepot Trade Between the Two Chinas 1979–1991

| Year | Total Amount of the Trade | From the ROC to the PRC | Growth Rate % Over Previous Year | From the PRC to the ROC | Growth Rate % Over Previous Year |
|---|---|---|---|---|---|
| 1979 | 77.76 | 21.47 | — | 56.29 | — |
| 1980 | 311.18 | 234.97 | 994.41 | 76.21 | 35.39 |
| 1981 | 459.33 | 384.15 | 63.49 | 75.18 | −1.35 |
| 1982 | 278.47 | 194.45 | −49.38 | 84.02 | 11.76 |
| 1983 | 247.69 | 157.84 | −18.83 | 89.85 | 6.94 |
| 1984 | 553.20 | 425.45 | 169.55 | 127.75 | 42.18 |
| 1985 | 1,102.73 | 986.83 | 131.95 | 115.90 | −9.28 |
| 1986 | 955.55 | 811.33 | −17.78 | 144.22 | 24.43 |
| 1987 | 1,515.47 | 1,226.53 | 51.18 | 288.94 | 100.35 |
| 1988 | 2,720.91 | 2,242.22 | 82.81 | 478.69 | 65.67 |
| 1989 | 3,483.39 | 2,896.49 | 29.18 | 586.90 | 22.61 |
| 1990 | 4,043.62 | 3,278.26 | 13.18 | 765.36 | 30.41 |
| 1991 | 5,393.11 | 4,667.15 | 42.36 | 1,125.95 | 47.11 |

Unit: Million US Dollars
*Source*: Board of Foreign Trade, Ministry of Economic Affairs, ROC.

In spite of the ban on direct trade and investment, these activities have occurred and continue to increase between the two Chinas. According to a survey report made by Taipei's Board of Foreign Trade, the value of direct trade in 1987 exceeded US$100 million. The PRC's Fujian province facing Taiwan is the hub of mainland-Taiwan direct trade, and Fujian authorities have designated 11 ports to handle these trade transactions. At present, at least six shipping routes have been privately operated between the two sides, mainly to deliver foods from the mainland to Taiwan.[79] In the ROC, there is a popular expression within business circles concerning the two sides' trade. Businesspeople claim that, 'in the past three decades Taiwan's economy has relied on the USA; however, Taiwan's economy will depend on the mainland from now on for the next three decades'.[80]

The direct trade is primarily conducted at night by fishermen from Taiwan. The PRC's 'official trading companies are being set up as well. Transactions involve a combination of New Taiwan, Hong Kong and US dollars, and barter and credit sales are also common'.[81] Aside from direct trade, Taiwan has so far indirectly invested roughly US$5.5 billion in the mainland as of 1992, making it the fourth biggest foreign investor in the PRC after Hong Kong (US$24.8 billion), US (US$4.4 billion), and Japan (US$3.3 billion).[82] At this moment, Taiwan's businesspeople busily shuttle between the two sides looking for trade and investment opportunities. Dr, Chen Li-an, the ROC's former Minister of Economic Affairs, even admitted the failure of efforts to persuade Taiwanese Chinese not to do business with the mainland.[83]

## Implications

The ROC's economy depends heavily on foreign trade, which has grown from US$303 million in 1952 to over US$130 billion in 1991. Beijing seems to be convinced that 'economic imperatives will drive the Taiwan economy into greater interdependence with the mainland. These imperatives include perceived problems with the economic transition in Taiwan, considerations of comparative advantage (Taiwan-manufactured goods and technology for mainland raw materials), as well as the increasing spectre of protectionism in the West which is forcing Taiwan firms to seek out alternative markets'.[84] If so, would Beijing employ economic pressures as a political lever against Taipei in the future? Could such pressure of Beijing succeed?

In reality, these questions involve too many difficult unpredictable variables to answer them at this moment. Nevertheless, to some extent, studying the market interdependence between Taiwan and the mainland can help predict the answers to these questions. At present, the percentage of entrepot trade in Taiwan's is a trivial proportion of the ROC's yearly foreign trade. For example, during the period from 1978 to 1991, the percentage of entrepot exports from Taiwan to the mainland was consistently less than 4 per cent of Taiwan's annual total export trade, while the percentage of entrepot imports from the mainland to Taiwan was less than 2 per cent of Taiwan's yearly total import amount.[85] These figures indicate that at this stage the economic interdependence between the two sides is not so close, thus, the mainland market is not essential to Taiwan's economic survival.

What, however, if the two sides' trade increases to the point that would enable Beijing to launch an economic war against Taiwan? According to the author's interviews with Taiwanese businesspersons, the possibility and capability of Beijing launching an economic war are, respectively, low and limited. The market replacement ability would be a factor preventing Beijing from doing so. The mainland market is hardly indispensable to Taiwan, which would still sell the overwhelming majority of its products to and buy raw materials from other countries. Taiwan's businesspeople have already taken measures to avoid risks and damages in conducting trade and investment activities with the mainland. For example, most Taiwanese Chinese's investment in the mainland thus far has been in short-term, low-cost, and labour-intensive, industries. In addition, the general attitude of Taiwan businesspeople to mainland trade and investment is cautious and prudent. The increase of economic ties between Taiwan and the mainland also increases the PRC's economic dependence on Taiwan. An economic war would harm both Taiwan and the mainland. The worst result of any economic blackmail triggered by Beijing would be damage to the gradually improving relations between the two sides, that would thus hamper the integration process of the two Chinas. The PRC is unlikely to overlook this potiential damage in evaluating options.

## Case 3: The Model of the Olympic Games

The 1984 Olympic Games was the first time since 1949 that the two sides demonstrated their flexibility towards each other on the sporting field. The admission of the PRC into the UN in 1971 had effectively isolated the ROC in international society. In the meantime, Beijing has made every effort to expel Taipei from international organizations. The ROC has finally realized that 'if it forces its friends to choose between Taipei and Peking as China's sole representative, some may opt for Peking'.[86] Therefore, when Beijing was trying to squeeze Taipei out of the Olympic Games during the 1970s, the ROC realized that the time to compromise had come, if it did not want to be further isolated from the world by the PRC.

### Historical Background

Early in 1954, the International Olympic Committee (IOC) recognized Taipei's China National Amateur Athletic Federation as the China Olympic Committee. In the meantime, the IOC also recognized the legal status of Beijing's All-China Athletic Federation, therefore hoping that the two Chinas could co-exist within the IOC (according to the IOC rule, only one national committee was permitted to represent a country). However, the PRC insisted that it was the only China and refused to cooperate alongside the ROC in the IOC; thus, a 'two-China' problem was also created within the Olympic arena. In protest against the IOC's recognition of Taipei and what it considered as 'the so-called "two Chinas" scheme', Beijing announced in 1958 that 'it would no longer recognize the International Olympic Committee and severed relations with it'.[87] Beijing also withdrew from nine international sports federations in protest against their respective 'two-Chinas' policies. Following these actions, Beijing had no contact with the IOC until 1975.

In 1975, the PRC's All-China Sports Federation believed that the international situation was ripe for its return to the IOC. Its officials therefore, decided to reapply for IOC membership on the condition that it was 'the sole legitimate national sports organization governing sports on the entire territory of China (including Taiwan Province)', and that the ROC was to be expelled from the IOC.[88] Beijing failed to get sufficient support for these proposals and was not admitted.

In 1979, Beijing, using the name of the Chinese Olympic Committee, again applied for membership and tried to replace Taipei within the IOC. This time the IOC in its convention at Montevideo passed, with 36 votes for and 28 against, the 'China Issue Resolution' under which (a) it recognized both Taipei and Beijing as IOC members; (b) the name, display flag, constitution, and anthem that the two Chinas would use in the Olympic games would be discussed as soon as possible after this meeting.[89] This resolution was based on the reality that both Taipei and Beijing had their own jurisdiction and the admission of the PRC should not be detrimental to the ROC within the Olympic movement.

Knowing that if the ROC should still insist that it represented the whole of China, the ROC would likely be excluded from the IOC, Taipei's delegation announced shortly after the meeting that it would accept this resolution and not oppose Beijing's admission to the IOC as long as the ROC's membership remained intact and the question of name, flag, and anthem were treated on an equal footing.[90] Beijing regarded this resolution as displaying an attitude of favouring 'two Chinas' and refused to accept it. The PRC insisted that Beijing's Olympic Committee had to be recognized as the sole legitimate Chinese organization within the IOC. Furthermore, the PRC remonstrated that the IOC should forbid the ROC to use its official name, national flag and anthem in future games.

Under pressure from the PRC, the IOC during an executive committee meeting in Puerto Rico in June 1979, decided to confirm that the National Olympic Committee of the PRC was to be designated the 'Chinese Olympic Committee', using the official flag and anthem of the PRC; in the meantime, the ROC's Olympic committee would be named the 'Chinese Taipei Olympic Committee' and its anthem and flag was required to be different from those presently used and approved by the executive committee of the IOC. This decision was submitted to the eighty-nine IOC members for a postal vote on October 26, 1979. A month later, the whole membership of the IOC, with 62 votes for and 17 against, two ballots spoiled, and eight members not returning their ballot papers, approved the so-called 'Nagoya Resolution'.[91]

To Beijing, the Nagoya Resolution marked a great victory.

To Taipei, the worst thing was its new name—Chinese Taipei Olympic Committee—which denoted Taipei's localization under Beijing's 'Chinese Olympic Committee' should the ROC accept it. Meanwhile, the demand that Taipei use a new Olympic emblem and a new flag was considered an insult. Beijing may have hoped that these terms would not be acceptable to Taipei with the result that the latter might withdraw from the IOC as the PRC did in 1958.

Taipei's discontent and anger were as expected.[92] But, it decided to stay within the IOC. After two years of litigation and bickering with the IOC, Taipei finally reached an agreement with the IOC in March 1981 which guaranteed that the accord would entitle the ROC 'to participate in future Olympic games. . . like every National Olympic Committee with the same status and the same rights'.[93] The ROC did agree to change the name, flag, and anthem used in the games. In the summer of 1984, the athletes from the two sides of the Taiwan Strait appeared together for the first time since 1949. In the summer of 1988 and 1992, the two sides' athletes again met in Seoul and Barcelona respectively.

## Implications

Will the Olympic case become a model for the two Chinas to manage their future relations? What is the ROC's attitude regarding the potential of this model? According to Chu Fu-sung, the former Minister of Foreign Affairs of the ROC, the Olympic Formula is a measure applicable only to non-governmental international organizations and activities.[94] Another political observer in Taipei, Lee Lien, made the following comments: the Olympic model 'is an expedient the ROC adopted in one isolated case, which is significantly different from China Taipei. . . . The term Chinese Taipei. . . means that an Olympic delegation was formed by the Chinese who regard Taipei as their capital or political entity'.[95] These two men emphasized exactly the same point: the 'Olympic Formula' only applies to unofficial occasions. This position, however, was soon challenged in the Asian Development Bank (ADB), which will be discussed in the next case.

Before doing that, the author would like to express some thoughts on the Olympic case: (a) the Olympic model is a product of *realpolitik*. It has also demonstrated the possible flexibility of the two sides toward each other. In this case, the ROC merely loses 'face', while the substance of controlled co-existence continued. Although the government of the ROC has reiterated the limitation of the Olympic model, some Taiwanese Chinese have begun to urge Taipei to apply this model for Taiwan to regain for membership in other international organizations. For example, in November 1991, the third Asia Pacific Economic Cooperation meeting, an official and ministerial-level conference, was held in Seoul. The ROC, under the name of 'Chinese Taipei', was admitted to the conference simultaneously with the PRC.[96] In fact, the IOC formula has enormously influenced the decisions made by other international sporting organizations. Under the title of 'Chinese Taipei', the ROC has regained membership in 28 international sporting organizations. In addition, Taipei was re-admitted into the Asian Games on 25 September 1986 following a break of 13 years.

This model is instructive to the ROC on how to avoid further isolation in the world. To Taipei, facing the challenge of retaining membership in the IOC became more important than retaining a name. During the 1984, 1988 and 1992 Olympic Games, the ROC demonstrated it was a full and independent member over which the PRC had no control in spite of Taipei's participation under the new name, flag, and anthem. The ROC's 'one country, two names (the ROC/Chinese Taipei), two flags' (one official and one for the Olympic games) has set a precedent in the history of international sporting politics.

Although the Olympic model has resolved the two Chinas' stalemate and allows the two sides to compete together on international sporting occasions, until 1987 the ROC still prohibited its teams from attending any international tournaments that were held in the PRC. However, since 1987, Taipei's implementation of a new and flexible mainland policy has finally led Taipei to announce that Taiwan athletes, on the basis of the Olympic formula, may participate in competition within the PRC if the mainland tournaments are staged by international, non-governmental groups in which the ROC holds membership.[97]

However, just when the above problem was resolved, another immediately arose. This time the Chinese translation of the term of 'Chinese Taipei' has triggered another semantic dispute between the two Chinas. Taipei insists that the term of

'Chinese Taipei' should be translated as 'Chung-Hua Taipei' / 中華台北 (the ROC's spelling) or 'Zhonghua Taibei' / 中華台北 (the PRC's spelling). It should be noted that both Chinas' transliteration and character systems are used in this explanation. Both of these terms mean a sport team formed by the Chinese people (including the mainland Chinese) who identify Taipei as the location of their country's capital. Phonetically, 'Chung-Hua Taipei' or 'Zhonghua Taibei' is more similar to the pronunciation Republic of China—'Chung-Hua Min Kuo' / 中華民國 or 'Zhonghua Minguo' / 中華民國. Politically, Taipei seems to believe that the translation of 'Chung-Hua Taipei' or 'Zhonghua Taibei' is more meaningful to the ROC because the sports team named 'Chung-Hua Taipei' or 'Zhonghua Taibei' is sent by the country called 'Chung-Hua Ming Kuo' or 'Zhonghua Mingguo' which has nothing to do with the PRC.

However, Beijing insists that the Chinese translation of 'Chinese Taipei' should be 'Zhongguo Taibei' / 中國台北 or 'Chung-kuo Taipei' / 中國台北 which implies Taipei's subjection to its rule since internationally most countries officially recognize the People's Republic of China as 'China /Zhongguo' / 中國. Beijing might think that if the Chinese translation of 'Chinese Taipei' becomes 'Chung-Hua Taipei' or 'Zhonghua Taibei', rather than 'Zhongguo Taibei' or 'Chung-Kuo Taipei', the political effect of Beijing's victory in the IOC in 1979 over the name dispute with Taipei would be diminished.

Taipei has made its stance clear that if Beijing still insists on its position, Taiwan's athletes would not be allowed to participate in competitions held in the mainland. In April 1989, both Chinas finally reached a compromise, Beijing agreeing to accept Taipei's term 'Chung-hua Taipei' / 中華台北 or 'Zhonghua Taibei' / 中華台北 in exchange for Taipei's promise to call the mainland's sports team as 'China /Zhongguo' / 中國, or Chung-kuo /中國, if the mainland's sports teams were invited to attend international tournaments held in the ROC in the future.[98] The conclusion of this agreement further revealed the two Chinas' flexibility in handling non-official matters. It also paved the way for sporting exchanges between the two sides in the future. In mid-April 1989, the ROC's gymnastic team attended the Asian Gymnastic Tournament held in Beijing, the first time since 1949 that athletes from Taiwan attended a sporting event on the mainland.

## Case 4: Asian Development Bank (ADB)

On 25 October 1971, the twenty-sixth session of the General Assembly of the UN adopted the draft resolution proposed by Albania, with 76 votes for, 35 against, and 17 abstentions, which recognized the PRC as the only Chinese government.[99] As a result, 'a symbol of legitimacy accorded to the ROC' during the first 26 years of the UN's history had 'come to an end'.[100]

According to Resolution 396 (V) of the General Assembly dated 14 December 1950, other departments of the UN were required to follow the General Assembly's resolution regarding recognition and representation of the PRC. Therefore, the ROC had lost its membership not only to the UN, but also to the UN's sixteen specialized agencies. Meanwhile, the PRC, as the self-proclaimed successor of the ROC, has been accepted by one associated agency of the UN and fifteen specialized UN agencies, the one exception being the General Agreement on Tariffs and Trade.[101] Furthermore, under Beijing's pressure, most other inter-governmental international organizations had no choice but to choose Beijing rather than Taipei to chair the China seat. At present, the Asian Development Bank (ADB) is the most important inter-governmental organization to which the ROC still belongs. However, the dispute over the name of the ROC once again emerged in 1983.

### Background of the Asian Development Bank Dispute

In April 1980, when the ROC was forced to leave the International Monetary Fund (IMF), Yu Kuo-hua, then Governor of the Central Bank of the ROC, said that it was less harmful from a financial and economic viewpoint for the ROC to withdraw from the IMF than to remain. He conceded, however, that 'the loss of the seat would inevitably further isolate Taiwan from the international community and prevent the island from obtaining certain economic information and consultation restricted to IMF members'.[102] In May that year, the ROC was forced to leave the IMF's sister organization, the World Bank.[103] Given that the ROC relies heavily on international economic activities, continuing to play an active role as a member in an organization like the ADB became increasingly important,

especially after its withdrawal from the world's two most important financial organizations, the IMF and the World Bank.
Moreover, retaining membership in the ADB also became politically significant because of Beijing's continued attempts to completely isolate Taipei from inter-governmental organizations.

The ADB was founded in 1966. The ROC was one of the
founding members under the name the Republic of China,
with its *de facto* territories at that time, Taiwan and the
Pescadores. Prior to 1985, the ADB has 46 member states including the US, Japan, and France. In February 1983 when Taipei
learned that Beijing was about to apply for membership in
the ADB and try to expel Taipei, the ROC made a preemptive
announcement:[104]

(1) The ROC is a founding member of the ADB and has
always faithfully carried out its duties; therefore, there is
absolutely no so-called question of China representation
rights or the qualification of the ROC for membership;
(2) There is no provision in the ADB's constitution regarding the expulsion of a member state;
(3) Agreement 36 of the ADB particularly prohibits politics
from interferring in its policy and decisions;
(4) The ADB is not a specialized agency of the United Nations;
therefore, the latter's resolutions do not apply to the ADB
or to the so-called membership problem;
(5) The budget that the ROC submitted to the ADB in 1966
was based on its effective jurisdiction territory and population, Taiwan and the Pescadores, as well as the per capita
income, tax revenue, and exports of these territories. This
condition of admission was totally different from the cases
of the United Nations and its agencies.

Taipei was optimistic about retaining its membership within
the ADB for the following reasons: (1) the ADB was a regional
organization and 'the pattern used for the IMF or the World
Bank, involving matters of existing representation, cannot be
used'.[105] (2) Taipei in the ADB, unlike its position within the
UN, was only speaking for Taiwan, not the whole of China.
Therefore, if the PRC wanted to join the ADB, it should be
regarded as a new country seeking its own membership in the
bank, with its application having no bearing on other member states. (3) Two influential member states, the US and Japan,
supported Taipei's continued membership in the bank.

According to the regulations of the ADB, any country

applying for membership has to obtain a two-thirds majority vote of the Board of Governors of the ADB and three-quarters majority of voting members before becoming a new member. Ballot rights are proportionately distributed to members based on the percentage of their contribution to the founding budget; therefore, countries such as the US and Japan who submitted the majority of the budget in 1966 would have a decisive influence on the outcome of this issue.[106]

In 1983, the PRC officially applied for ADB membership demanding, as expected, that the ROC should be expelled for the following reasons: the PRC is the sole legal government of China; therefore, the ROC has no right to a seat in the ADB, and the ROC is 'no longer a member of the UN or any of its specialized agencies', therefore, Taipei is not qualified to be a member of the bank.[107] Beijing's position was opposed by some member states, particularly the US.[108] In November 1983, both the US Senate and House of Representatives passed an appropriations bill for 1984 that authorized the US government to provide financial support to international financial organizations such as the ADB. This bill was accompanied by a proviso that Taiwan should be allowed to remain in the ADB as a regular member. Moreover, regardless of how the ADB handled the PRC's application case, the status of the ROC in the ADB should not be changed.[109] The bill might have technically implied that if Taiwan's membership status in the bank were changed, this could lead to the termination of US financial support to the ADB specified in this legislation.

In May 1985, the 18th annual meeting of the Board of Governors of the ADB was held in Bangkok. This time Beijing changed its position: the PRC should be seated in the ADB as the sole representative of China; the ROC could stay in the ADB under the new name of 'Taiwan, China' or 'Taipei, China'. Moreover, the PRC stated that it had already reached an understanding with the ADB regarding this problem (see Appendix 11-1). Various factors could explain why Beijing changed its course. First of all, there was no legal precedent basis for expulsion of a member state from the bank. To the ADB, retaining a member state like the ROC that had already started making contributions to the bank before the PRC joined and held an excellent credit record was an asset. In addition, the US and some members made it a condition of admitting the PRC that Beijing drop its demand to expel Taipei. Under these circumstances, the PRC had no choice but to compromise. Furthermore, the PRC deliberately intended to copy the non-official Olympic model in the ADB; by so doing, it could achieve the following purposes: show its sincerity about peaceful reunification with Taiwan; if Taipei accepted, to embarrass the ROC, since Taipei had proclaimed that the Olympic version was limited to non-governmental organizations; Taipei might not accept this arrangement and hence withdraw from the bank, and then Beijing would naturally occupy the China seat; and Beijing hoped that the door for the two sides 'to communicate and stay together would not close, or push Taiwan towards seeking independence'.[110]

This time the ROC seemed to face 'the lesser of two evils—isolation or reduced status'.[111] The ROC's main worry was to retain its name. Taipei in reality had already silently discarded its 'you-enter-I-leave' foreign policy since accepting the Olympic model and was therefore willing to co-exist with the PRC as long as it could keep its name intact. Beijing, however, only wanted to co-exist with Taipei, subject to the latter's changing its name. Since Beijing was unable to take over the ROC by force at the moment, and the possibility of reunification was still uncertain, the best way for Beijing to subjugate its antagonist has been through diplomacy. Through the Olympic and the ADB models, the PRC, has at least nominally downgraded the ROC's status both in inter-governmental and non-governmental organizations.

Despite the US's sympathy with the ROC's position, Washington cannot contravene its official policy that 'recognizes the Government of the People's Republic of China as the sole legal government of China'.[112] Meanwhile, knowing that Taipei might be uncompromising about the 'name' issue, President Ronald Reagan sent his close associate, William Clark, a former national security adviser, to Taipei to persuade the ROC to accept the new name and hoped that the ROC would consider staying in the ADB.[113]

On 10 March 1986, the PRC was formally admitted to the Bank. Chen Muhua, the president of the people's bank of the PRC, said that 'in accordance with the understanding we reached with the bank, the Taiwan authorities shall remain in the ADB under the designation of 'Taipei, China'.[114] The ROC's lack of enthusiasm was predictable as can be seen in the following announcement:

The ADB's decision is not only detrimental to the rights and status of the ROC but also violates the Bank's Charter which states that "decisions of the bank should be relevant only to economic affairs and not be affected by politics. . . . This decision will ruin the reputation of the bank as a non-political international financial institution. The ROC has asked the ADB to reconsider this case in the hope that a just and equitable solution will be reached.[115]

It is evident that the ADB decision is another product of *realpolitik*. However, to the ROC it was a case of 'whether Taipei could adjust its policies to take account of current realities and seek a formula to allow it to maintain a formal role in international affairs'.[116] It has also inevitably brought internal discord to the island. Older, conservative party leaders have argued that 'Taiwan should have nothing to do with the Communists'.[117] The main concern of these people appears to be Beijing's attempt to 'localize' Taipei's status. If 'Taipei, China' were from now on to be accepted on any official occasion, the ROC could merely be lumped with 'Shanghai, China', 'Beijing, China', or 'Hong Kong, China', creating the impression the ROC was a local government subordinate to the central government of the PRC.[118]

In the meantime, younger, more moderate leaders, worried that Taiwan's international standing could suffer a serious blow if it withdrew from the ADB'[119] have been urging a more pragmatic policy. In April 1986, for example, thirty members of the national legislature, most of them KMT members, issued an appeal for the government to adopt extraordinary measures to maintain the ROC's membership in the ADB.[120]

## The ADB's 21st Annual Meeting at Manila

Again, Taipei's apprehension regarding the ADB case remains political. The designation of 'Taipei, China' seems even worse than the IOC model of 'Chinese Taipei'. This designation clearly signifies Taipei's subjection to PRC rule. Nevertheless, Taipei acknowledged reality and stated that it would continue its contribution to the ADB, fulfill its commitments and 'carry out its duty as a member of the ADB'.[121] After a two year boycott of ADB activities (1986 and 1987), the ROC decided to send delegates to attend the ADB's 21st annual meeting at Manila in April 1988.

In order to protest the ADB's decision, Taipei's delegates took some 'small actions' during the meeting sessions, such as covering up the designation on the badges issued by the ADB, wearing badges depicting the 'national flag of the Republic of China', and placing a plate reading 'under protest' alongside the desk-plate reading 'Taipei, China'.[122] Chi-cheng Chang, the head of the ROC delegation, also made the following statement:[123]

**Statement by ADB Governor Dr. Chi-cheng Chang**
I reiterate my protest against the redesignation of my country in the ADB as 'Taipei, China'. Such arbitrary redesignation has never been accepted by my Government. The official designation of my country is contained in the signed copy of the Charter of the ADB and in the instrument of ratification duly deposited by my government in 1966. There has been no change in the status of my country in the ADB since that time. While we will continue to make constructive contributions to the purpose of the Bank, the participation of my delegation in ADB activities does not imply in any way that we have accepted the blatantly unfair redesignation of my country referred to above.

Meanwhile, Beijing criticized Taipei's protest actions, and blamed the ADB for failing to take timely rectifying measures to prevent Taipei's inappropriate behavior (see Appendix 11-2). As an intermediary, the ADB felt the need to state its position. R. D. Pacheco, Chief Information Officer of the ADB, issued the following statement:[124]

The Bank has complied with and continues to abide by the understanding between the Asian Development Bank and the People's Republic of China. The administrative arrangements made by the ADB Secretariat are in accordance with the understanding. The Chairman of the Board of Governors has requested the Governor for Taipei, China not to tamper with the arrangements.

## The ADB's 22nd Annual Meeting at Beijing

In May 1989, Beijing was selected for and took charge of the ADB's 22nd Annual Meeting. Again, Taipei faced a difficulty: attendance of or absence from the Beijing meeting. After long consideration, the ROC finally sent Finance Minister Dr. Shirley

W. Y. Kuo to attend the meeting. It was the first time since 1949 that an ROC official has appeared and met PRC officials on the mainland. During the opening ceremony, Dr. Kuo and other Taiwan delegates stood with other countries' delegates in salute to both the PRC President and the PRC's national anthem. In the meantime, Dr. Kuo again made a symbolic protest against the ADB's redesignation of its name in the Bank. All developments and actions have aroused the interest and concern of China watchers everywhere. What do these developments and actions mean to both Taipei's foreign policy and the two Chinas' relations?

According to Taipei, the decision to attend this meeting in Beijing does not signify that the ROC is changing its long positions of anti-communism and the 'one China' principle. Rather, Taipei has said, the ROC has the obligation as a member state of the Bank to attend the ADB's annual meeting even though it was held in Beijing. Taipei stressed that Dr. Kuo's role in the ADB meeting at Beijing was that of an ADB governor rather than as a ROC finance minister. Therefore, Taipei has claimed that it was merely sending delegates to the PRC for this international conference, and that this despatch of representatives had nothing to do with Taipei's mainland policy or any other political implications.[125]

Obviously, Taipei has tried to play down the political significance of its decision to attend the Beijing meeting. Notwithstanding, this decision has many political implications for relations between the two sides, as well as for Taipei's foreign relations. It would seem to indicate a pragmatic resolution on the part of Taipei to expand the scope of its foreign relations, regardless of the 'name' problem, in response to gradual international isolation. It would also mean the further *detente* of the two Chinas' relations. Meanwhile, Beijing appeared well satisfied with Taipei's attendance of this meeting. According to an anonymous senior Xinhua News Agency official in Hong Kong, the PRC positively welcomed Kuo's visiting the mainland. The officer said that if more high-ranking officials, like Dr. Kuo, visited from Taipei, the better Taipei's decision-makers could understand today's PRC and make more sound and realistic policies towards the PRC.[126]

The decision to attend the Beijing meeting also satisfied the Taiwanese Chinese who have different attitudes and positions toward the two China issue. Those who advocate the eventual

reunification of Taiwan and the mainland, the *Tong pai*, believed
that the ADB meeting drew the two sides closer; meanwhile,
those who advocated the positions of Taiwan independence
or two Chinas argued that the Beijing meeting in reality was
Taipei's practice and demonstration of a two Chinas or 'one
China, one Taiwan' policy. Apparently, these people have interpreted Taipei's decision to attend the Beijing meeting in terms
of their own political beliefs and ideas.

Taipei's decision, the author would argue, however, has pre-
faced the ROC's present and future strategies and endeavors
from now on to impress upon the international society that
the ROC (or Taiwan; or Taipei, China; or Chinese Taipei, or
an entity using other names) is another Chinese nation, independent from the PRC at this moment. Taipei seems to have
intentionally left to Beijing the problematic speculations generated by its attendance.

## Implications

The ROC has been constantly trying to remind other member
states that it is a sovereign state having nothing to do with
the PRC. Both the Manila and the Beijing meetings however,
have shown Taipei's inability to change the *fait accompli* of
the understanding reached between the Bank and the PRC.
But, it seems that there is no overall gain or loss. Accepting
the ADB model of the ROC does not mean that Taipei is truly
subject to the PRC, either nominally or practically, as long as
Taipei's membership is not subordinated. If the PRC is prevented from extending its jurisdiction over the ROC and from
taking *de facto* control of Taiwan, any proclamation that 'Taipei,
China' is subject to Beijing is merely wishful thinking.

Furthermore, membership in the ADB or any other kind of
international organization would be conductive to Taipei's connections with other countries, increasing its visibility in the
international arena. On the other hand, isolation could have
led to the eventual loss of the ROC's independence, and thus
would have been counterproductive. In addition, some people
in Taiwan believe that the ADB case can theoretically serve
as a model for the ROC returning to other inter-governmental
organizations.[127] From this perspective accepting this model
could change this issue from a defensive to an offensive
strategic advance.

## Case 5: The Two Airlines Talks

On 3 May 1986, a Boeing 747 cargo plane from the ROC's China Airlines (CAL) was hijacked to the PRC by its own pilot, Wang Hsi-chueh. It became a sensational incident because it ultimately led to the first formal talks between the two Chinas since 1949.

It should be noted, however, that it is not an entirely new phenomenon that the two sides 'exchange' military aircraft as a result of air force defections (Table 11-2). All of the previous cases, except the cargo plane, were military defections. According to precedent, neither side of the Taiwan Strait would return the defected pilots and aircraft because the two parties were technically still at war and trying to exploit every opportunity for political propaganda. This time, however, the case of the hijacked cargo plane proceeded differently. Beijing sent a telegram to Taipei saying that the PRC would like to return the plane, crew members, and the cargo; but, officials asked that Taiwan 'send a representative to Beijing as soon as possible to discuss [these] matters'.[128] The main reason for the mainland making such a prompt gesture was to use this incident as 'the first step towards eventual political discussions with Taiwan'.[129]

CAL said, however, that it would abide by the government's policy and not initiate contact with the mainland. Instead, CAL suggested that Hong Kong-based Cathay Pacific Airways and Lloyds of London (CAL's insurance agent) could act on CAL's behalf as intermediaries in negotiations with Beijing over the return of the plane and the two crew members.[130] In the meantime, Taipei agreed that 'the plane incident would be handled solely by CAL through the third party, while there would be no government intervention'.[131]

Beijing, as expected, refused to negotiate with any third party and insisted that 'matters between the Chinese should be resolved by the Chinese'.[132] At the same time, knowing that Taipei would be reluctant to negotiate if the PRC insisted that both sides were to meet on the mainland, Beijing sent another telegram to Taipei on May 11:

> As we indicated earlier, the talk between China Airlines and the Civil Aviation Administration of China is purely business talk that has nothing to do with politics. . . . Therefore,

**Table 11-2:** Airplane Defections Between The Two Chinas
(1977–1991)

| Date | Type of Aircraft | Pilot's Name | Destination |
|---|---|---|---|
| 1977–7–7 | MiG-19 | Fan Yuan-yen | ROC |
| 1981–8–13 | F-5E | Huang Ze-chen | PRC |
| 1982–10–16 | MiG-19 | Wu Jung-ken | ROC |
| 1983–4–23 | U-6A | Lee Da-wei | PRC |
| 1983–8–7 | MiG-21 | Sun Tien-chin | ROC |
| 1983–11–14 | MiG-17 | Wang Hsueh-cheng | ROC |
| 1985–8–24 | IL-28 | Hsiao Tien-jun | ROC |
| 1986–2–21 | MiG-19 | Chen Pao-chung | ROC |
| 1986–5–3 | Boeing 747 | Wang Xi-chueh | PRC |
| 1987–11–19 | MiG-19 | Cheng Tsai-tien | ROC |
| 1989–2–11 | F-5E | Lin It-sien | PRC |

*Note*: (a) This table does not include the three incidents where two
PRC civilian aircraft were hijacked by the mainland Chinese
to the ROC in 1983 (through South Korea) and 1988 respectively; and one Taiwanese civilian aircraft which was unsuc-
cessfully hijacked by a Taiwan Chinese to the PRC in 1988.
(b) Some of the defectors flew to South Korea first and were
later received by the ROC government.
*Source*: Author

we hope that your company (CAL) can send your representatives to talk with us rather than through a third party.
If you feel that it is inconvenient for you to come to Beijing,
you can assign another suitable place for a meeting. . . . It
will not be our responsibility for the delay in returning the
plane and the crew if your company still insists on no contact with us regarding this matter.[133]

On the one hand, this cable message clearly revealed Beijing's
strategy of employing the 'carrot and stick' approach; on the
other hand, it shows the reasoning and flexibility of Beijing.
If Taipei rejected discussions, then Taipei, not Beijing, would
be blamed for not taking measures to resolve this problem.
The ROC faced a dilemma in this situation. As one leading
newspaper in Taipei pointed out:

Communist China's 'united front' plot in this incident is
evident. They refused to talk with a third party for the

> purpose of pressing our CAL to talk to them directly in the hope of creating an image and precedent of direct contacts between the two sides of the Taiwan Strait. . . . If CAL did so, it will contravene our government's 'three nos' policy because people will know that. . . it must be with the consent of our government.[134]

Taipei understood that Beijing had the upper hand in this incident because both plane and crew members were stranded on the mainland. However, from a humanitarian point of view, Taipei had an obligation and responsibility to bring back the two crew who wished to go home. In addition, abandoning an expensive plane without any effort to retrieve it might provide a reason for taxpayers to condemn the government as careless and irresponsible, despite any recovery of costs from the airline's insurance company. The most important thing was how the KMT could show its credibility and capability to its people in this incident after suffering the series of setbacks in its struggle with the PRC since the 1970s. Given these considerations, the ROC decided this time to change its course.

On 13 May 1986, CAL unexpectedly informed the CAAC, through Hong Kong's Cathay Pacific Airways, of its willingness to meet in Hong Kong to discuss the problem. Simultaneously, CAL declared that its decision was based on 'humanitarian considerations'. Furthermore, this was CAL's own decision, having no connection at all with the government; the talks between CAL and the CAAC would be 'purely a business-related matter'. In reality, this meeting was unnecessary. According to international protocol, CAAC should return the crew, plane, and cargoes unconditionally; any excuse that delayed the return of the crew and items was unacceptable.[135]

From May 17 to May 20, 1986, Taiwan's CAL and the mainland's CAAC met in Hong Kong, and reached an agreement after four rounds of talks, regarding the details of how to return the plane, its crew, and cargoes to Taiwan. On May 23, the plane, cargo and crew were finally released to Taiwan, and this incident was brought to conclusion.[136]

## Implications

Since the 1950s, both Chinas have continuously enticed the other party's military and civilian personnel to defect with the promise of money, promotion, and medals, to achieve political objectives. As an old Chinese saying puts it, 'generous rewards rouse one to heroism'; therefore, it would be useful to treat the CAL incident as an usual defection case. In the past, the defector who flew to Taiwan would be hailed as an 'anti-communism freedom-seeker' and rewarded with gold (the quantity of gold reward depends on which type of aircraft the PRC's defectors delivered to Taipei. The gold quantity ranges from 500 taels of gold to 8,000 taels of gold for different type of aircraft. (1 tael is equivalent to 1.33 ounces). The freedom seeker would also be promoted, and awarded a medal.[137] For instance, when Taiwan's air force pilot Huang Tze-cheng defected to the mainland in August 1981, he received a reward equivalent to US$360,000 and a commission as a deputy commander in one of the PRC's Air Force academies.[138] This time the leading player in the CAL incident, Wang Hsi-chueh, has been promoted from a pilot to Deputy-Director and Vice-General Chief of pilots in the Beijing Civil Aviation Administration Bureau of the CAAC.[139] Of course, from a humanitarian point of view, these defectors have a choice in the matter; however, exploiting these events for political ends and accepting the rewards offered oppose the true meaning of humanitarianism. As Liao Kuang-sheng has pointed out, under this lasting situation of civil war, 'good or bad, right or wrong have been confounded'; he added that 'the political value has stretched the standard of law, and influenced social morality and ethical concepts. This is the biggest puzzlement of the Chinese people between the two sides of the Taiwan Strait'.[140]

Beijing's attempt to manipulate the CAL hijacking incident to achieve political, united-front ends is evident. For example, after the two Chinas reached an agreement, Beijing promptly announced that the two airlines talks have shown that 'there is no problem that cannot be resolved between us countrymen and brothers'.[141] Taipei, however, immediately countered that the talks 'do not hold any political portents and have nothing to do with the set policy' of the ROC. 'Any wider interpretation or speculation (regarding these talks) is completely unwarranted'.[142] In order to show its resolve, the KMT Central Committee issued an internal document which pointed out that the 'three nos policy was, is, and will not be changed'.[143]

The repercussions of the CAL case were profound. An editorial in a major Taiwan newspaper stated that 'we believe that [these talks] have intensified our people's demands and expectations regarding the flexible employment of the "three nos" policy', then proceeded to raise three sensitive questions:[144]

> Can this precedent be applied to similar cases hereafter? Like CAL, there are many private organizations in our country; what is the limitation of contacts of these organizations with their counterparts in the mainland? It is understandable that CAL's talks with the CAAC were based on humanitarian grounds; however, there are numerous areas of such humanitarian concerns such as split families, broken marriages, and the death and birth of relatives existing between the two sides of the Taiwan Strait. How will the government tackle these kinds of problems in the future.

Clearly, the CAL case had the effect of reinforcing Taipei's modification of its mainland policy in 1987. This case changed the Taipei leaders' traditional perception that dealing with the CCP would always be wrong and that Taipei would be at a disadvantage in such dealings. Moreover, the CAL case has established a precedent of both sides to follow should similar problems arise. It also helped to foster a consensus between the two Chinas on how to treat future defection incidents. For example, on 12 May 1988 a CAAC Boeing 737 was hijacked to Taiwan by two mainland passengers. With the experience of handling the CAL case behind it, Taipei sophisticatedly handled this incident without requiring Beijing's attention.[145] In addition, both Chinas have subsequently implemented new policies which reduce the chances of defections happening again. In August 1988, Beijing took the initiative and announced that it had abolished its reward system for defectors from Taiwan. In September 1988, Taipei also announced a policy to reduce the amount of gold paid to the PRC's air defectors.[146] In May 1991, Taipei announced its intention to abolish its reward system.[147] Furthermore, the CAL case was clearly 'a victory for younger Nationalist Chinese officials who have been advocating a policy of greater flexibility in dealing with Peking',[148] which could become essential in handling today's relations between Taiwan and the mainland.

## Conclusion

The author would like to use an old Chinese proverb as a commentary for this chapter: when the time is right the ripe melon will fall off the vine. Its basic spirit is somewhat analogous to that of integration, which emphasizes that the process of the integration between communities is slow, similar to the growth of a melon. As contacts and transactions increase between two sides, the attitudes and beliefs of the people that would contribute to the integration may also evolve convergently. The completion of this amalgamation will be as natural as the ripe melon falling off the vine. The author believes this analogy applies to the China issue.

Despite the ROC's nominal stand-off on the proposals of 'three links and four exchanges' by the mainland, people-to-people, academic, sports and trade contacts between the two Chinas had already begun before 1986 and have rapidly expanded since 1987. It is natural that all of these transactions or contacts can help to reduce enmity, create a peaceful atmosphere in the Taiwan Strait and satisfy the mutual curiosity and understanding of the peoples of the ROC and the PRC.

However, these contacts are mere trickles thus far in terms of their scope, extent, and frequency. If the goal of reunification is a big river, the author can imagine that 'countless trickles will be needed to group that big river'.[149] Hence, there is still a long way to go for reunification to become reality. In the meantime, adverse effects could also emerge from these contacts. The two sides might for the foreseeable future find that the gap between them, in life-style, ideology, living standards, and philosophy, is too large. They (especially Taiwan) might prefer to go it alone rather than together. In other words, the two Chinas might come closer together because they do not understand each other and ultimately separate because they understand each other more clearly. Although this possibility is unlikely, in the light of the political reality, it should not be excluded.

The Olympic and the ADB models, from Taipei's point of view, provide two examples of measures that can be adopted to prevent the ROC from being isolated internationally. Some have argued that these two models were merely expedient measures to ensure that the ROC will not become an 'Asian orphan with dignity and self-respect'.[150] The author would argue that so far neither Taipei nor Beijing have fundamentally changed their policies toward each other, especially in regard to touchy political problems, and in spite of the many non-political contacts as well as the more flexible attitudes that have been demonstrated during the past 10 years. The ROC's flexibility 'essentially represents either simple acceptance of realities in a limited sphere, or actions considered advantageous' to itself.[151] The PRC's flexibility aims at a final incorporation of Taiwan by peaceful means through those gradual contacts and exchanges.

The two airlines' talks represented the zenith in relations between the two sides as the discussions were the first of their kind since 1949. However, the author would argue that it was the logical climax of the two governments' policy modifications and domestic developments which enabled them to compromise with each other. The fact that these talks have occurred have spurred a further decrease in tension over the Taiwan Strait. It would be premature, however, to overestimate the significance of the airlines case in relation to the issue of reunification. The author would rather contend that the ROC 'is trying out a more pragmatic approach towards the substantive independence it enjoys in Taiwan that might prove better suited to establishing a more open, mutually beneficial relationship with the mainland and, at the same time, might be more congenial to rising demands at home for faster democratization of the political structure'.[152]

In short, the two Chinas' flexibility and modification in policies and actions is so far limited to non-political areas, and the most sensitive question, that is, the political one, is still unresolved. It seems that the ROC is willing to compromise with the PRC if both are represented as autonomous bodies. As long as Beijing continues to insist on regarding Taipei as one of its local governments, the author thinks that the final resolution of the China issue will remain elusive. Nevertheless, future contacts in a variety of endeavours should have positive effects for normalizing relations between the two sides of the Taiwan Strait.

# Chapter 12

∎

## National Integration of the Republic of China

Like many other developing countries, the Republic of China on Taiwan faces the problem of national integration. Amitai Etzioni describes national integration as 'the ability of a unit or system to maintain itself in the face of internal and external challenges'.[1] Howard Wriggins talks of national integration as a bringing together 'of the disparate parts of a society into a more integrated whole, or to make out of many small societies a closer approximation of one nation'.[2] Myron Weiner describes national integration as 'the integration of diverse and discrete cultural loyalties and the development of a sense of nationality; . . . of political units into a common political process; . . . of the rules and the ruled; . . . of the citizen into a common political process; of individuals into organizations for purposive activities'.[3] Scholars in this field generally agree that national integration focuses on what makes a system cohesive through peaceful means. Successful integration leads to the development of a strong country. Without integration a country would be weak or collapse.

What is the current situation regarding the political integration of the ROC? Is the ROC cohesive enough to face challenges from within and without Taiwan, especially from the PRC? Is the ROC's economic growth compatible with its political development and national integration? There are few questions more central to understanding the thinking of Taiwan's Chinese at present. To explore these questions, some case studies concerning certain important political issues currently existing in the ROC are to be examined in this chapter. Examining these cases may suggest the course of the ROC political development and the impact of this development on the two Chinas' relations.

## Political Problems of the ROC

The first political problem confronting the ROC at this moment is how to maintain a balance between its anachronistic 'old state' political system and the 'new society' of Taiwan. In other words, the transplanted ROC government system needs an overhaul to fit itself into Taiwan's present reality. Political reforms that reflect the fact that the ROC currently is in Taiwan rather than in the mainland are essential.

As mentioned in Chapter 4, in order to cope with the external threat from the PRC and internal opposition by the Taiwanese, the ruling KMT in Taiwan had enforced authoritarian rule in Taiwan prior to 1990. Citing national security as the reason, the ROC government proclaimed martial law in Taiwan and declared that Taiwan was placed under a Period of National Mobilization and the Suppression of the Communist Rebellion (Suppression Period). Under these circumstances, the ROC government in Taiwan exhibited a number of features:[4]

(a) One-party rule: Although Taiwan has two small opposition parties, the Democratic Socialist Party and the Youth Party (both are transplanted from the mainland in 1949), they have no real power and do not constitute a credible opposition.[5] In 1986, the strongest and mainly Taiwanese-based opposition party, the Democratic Progressive Party (DPP), was founded. Since then, the DPP, to some extent, has played the role as a real opposition. Even so, the DPP's power and influence still can not yet compare with the KMT's.

(b) The KMT prohibited the formation of any political opposition prior to 1986 for fear of opposition forces challenging its rule in Taiwan.

(c) Under martial law provisions, the Chinese in Taiwan were not allowed to say, to write, and to publish things that violated the government's policy or orders. Mail was censored. Freedom of assembly and of association were also controlled by the government. The constitutional rights of the people in this regard, to some extent, were impaired.

(d) In order to maintain itself as a government representing the whole of China, the ROC government has retained on Taiwan a two-tiered government structure that has both national and local (provincial and subprovincial) units. The national-level institutions set major policy and, prior to 1987, were dominated by the expatriate mainlanders; the local offices, with limited powers and functions, were staffed primarily by the Taiwanese.

(e) In order to maintain the ROC's legitimacy as a 'central government' of the whole of China, the majority of members of the ROC's three chambers of the national parliament—the Legislative Yuan (lawmaking body), the National Assembly (this body that elects the ROC president), and the Control Yuan (the ROC's supreme watchdog body)—prior to 1991, have never been changed. Most of these members were originally mainly elected in 1947 on the mainland; these three chambers have remained central representative institutions with a predominance of members originally hailing from the mainland. Members of these chambers have received no direct mandate from the Taiwan Chinese.

(f) The ruling elites of the ROC government lack the consent of the Taiwanese Chinese. The first-generation of mainlanders who followed Chiang Kai-shek to Taiwan were naturally the rulers. However, 'the new breed of KMT mandarins, trained and intellectually moulded by first-generation hardliners . . . have risen through the party bureaucracy without facing any serious popular elections. In fact, few top KMT leaders have ever contested popular elections'.[6]

(g) In order to enable the President to cope with any imminent danger to the security of the nation during the period of 'Suppression of the Communist Rebellion,' the ruling KMT promulgated the Temporary Provisions which were appended to its constitution in May 1948. These provisions effectively give the ROC president more power than is consistent with the ROC's constitution. For example, the provisions offer legal grounds for the presidency to become a tenured position for life without being subject to the two-term restriction prescribed in Article 47 of the ROC's constitution.[7] Furthermore, the premier is the chief executive of the ROC government according to the constitution and is responsible to the Legislative Yuan. However, the Temporary Provisions have supplanted this. The President has now become a supra-executive without any supervision from the parliament, leaving the Premier with administrative responsibility but without real political power.[8]

These are the main features of the KMT's authoritarian government in Taiwan over the past forty-two years. These features, generally speaking, violate principles of liberal democracy

—such as a multi-party system, the guarantee of human rights, the right to vote in the selection of public officers, a popular electoral system and so on.[9]

Since 1986, some democratization has occurred in the ROC, and some authoritarian features have gradually disappeared: the lifting of martial law in 1987, the formal end of the ban on opposition parties in 1989 (although the DPP was actually founded in 1986, from the viewpoint of the ROC government it was formally illegal until Taipei's Legislative Yuan passed the Civil Organization Law in January 1989), and the end of the Suppression Period in April 1991. Nevertheless, the ROC's authoritarian rule, that is, 'a combination of repression, sophisticated controls, limited tolerance of free expression and positive leadership',[10] has still fallen short of real democracy. How to make up this shortfall and practise the democratic and constitutional politics referred to in the 1947 constitution has become the main challenge of the ROC government.

The second political problem that currently confronts the ROC derives directly from the social and economic changes of Taiwan's modernization. Karl W. Deutsch has argued that modern economic development speeds the process of social change, and means a more politicized society in general.[11] As social mobilization thrusts more and more Taiwan Chinese into political life, the ruling KMT faces the problem of satisfying the people's demands for political participation. Along the same lines Samuel P. Huntington pointed out the causal relationship between political development and social and economic changes. He said that

> Social and economic change—urbanization, increases in literacy and education, industrialization, mass media expansion—extend political consciousness, multiply political demands, broaden political participation. These changes undermine traditional sources of political authority and traditional political institutions; they enormously complicate the problems of creating new bases of political association and new political institutions combining legitimacy and effectiveness.[12]

Huntington further indicated that the primary political problem in Third World countries is 'the lag in the development of political institutions behind social and economic change',[13] which causes political instability and disorder. The ROC also faces this problem. In 1988 alone, Taiwan had on average 4 mass demonstrations per day, including the most bloody farmers' revolt in its history on 20 May 1988. Of these demonstrations, 61.6 per cent were directly related to politics.[14] This figure reveals, to some extent, the Taiwan people's dissatisfaction with the ROC's pace of political development.

## Stability Or Instability: The Republic of China in Taiwan

Harry Eckstein describes a stable democracy as one 'which has demonstrated considerable staying power, a capacity to endure, without great or frequent changes in pattern'.[15] Edmund A. Aunger also argues that political stability 'refers to the ability of a system's political institutions to endure without abrupt modification. . . . There is thus a continuity over time in the major institutions of the state'.[16] He suggests four criteria which must be considered in any evaluation of political stability: constitutional durability, political legitimacy, governmental efficacy, and civil order.[17] These four criteria will be applied here in examining the ROC in Taiwan's political situation.

### A. Constitutional Durability

Ted R. Gurr and M. McClelland define constitutional durability as 'the length of time a polity endures without abrupt, major change in the pattern of authority relations among its basic elements'.[18] Two basic issues, in the case of the ROC, have been selected here and discussed: (1) a cabinet or a presidential system for the ROC government (2) parliamentary reform. These two issues concern the future development of Taiwan's political institutionalization. They are also the main factors that cause confrontations within the KMT and between the ruling KMT and the opposition.

### Cabinet System or Presidential System?

The following articles of the ROC's constitution reveal certain characteristics of the cabinet system of the ROC government. Article 53 states that the Executive Yuan, that is, the Cabinet shall be 'the highest administrative organ' of the ROC. Article

55 prescribes that the president, that is the premier of the Executive Yuan 'shall be nominated and, with the consent of the Legislative Yuan, that is, the Parliament, appointed by the president of the ROC. Article 56 states that the vice president, that is, the vice premier of the Executive Yuan, ministers and chairmen of commissions, and ministers without portfolio shall be appointed by the President of the ROC 'upon the recommendation of the president of the Executive Yuan'.[19] Besides these articles, the premier and president must under the constitution both countersign all laws passed by the Legislative Yuan. This indicates that the ROC premier 'holds and assumes the administrative power and responsibilities'.[20] Further, the Executive Yuan has the duty to present a statement of its administrative policies and a report on its administration to the Legislative Yuan, while the legislators shall have the right to question the premier and his ministers and chairmen of commissions during the sessions. In other words, there is a checks-and-balances relationship between the Executive Yuan and the Legislative Yuan of the kind found in Western democracies.

The ROC President's administrative power, however, has been expanded, up until 1991, under the Temporary Provisions Effective During the Period of Mobilization for Suppression of the Communist Rebellion.[21] Under the Temporary Provisions, the president becomes the most powerful administrator of the ROC rather than the premier. According to the Provisions, the president is authorized to establish any organs for making major policy decisions; to make adjustments in the administrative and personnel organs of the government, and so on, without being subject to the restrictions of the constitution and the supervision of the Legislative Yuan.[22] As well, the president and vice president may be reelected without being subject to the two-term restriction. All of these violate the spirit of the constitution. Therefore, many scholars in Taiwan have urged the ROC government to abolish or modify the 'Temporary Provisions' and comply with the constitution, which is the main foundation for implementing and practising democratic and constitutional politics.[23]

## Parliamentary Reform

Parliamentary reform is another important issue causing confrontation and rifts within the KMT and between the ruling

KMT and the opposition parties particularly the DPP, between the government and the people, and between the mainlanders and the Taiwanese. Since the ROC has continued to proclaim itself the sole legitimate Chinese government, political institutions established in the mainland in 1947 are all maintained in Taiwan. Members of the three chambers of the national parliament, through a 1954 interpretation of the Constitution by the ROC's Supreme Court, have lifetime tenure.[24] This fact has incurred the most criticism from the Taiwanese Chinese, especially the opposition parties, since the 1970s when the Taiwanese Chinese gradually perceived that the slogan of 'recover the mainland' could not be easily achieved in the near future.

In 1947, parliament members came from every province in China including Taiwan province. Allocation of parliamentary seats for each province (except for the Control Yuan) were based on the population of each province. Taiwan, because of its small population, claimed few seats. However, when the ROC government moved to Taiwan in 1949, this situation became unfair to the Taiwanese Chinese. In order to placate the Taiwan Chinese and to resolve the problem of the decrease of members, mainly because of natural deaths, of the mainlander-dominated parliament, 'supplementary seats' were created for Taiwanese Chinese so that more Taiwanese Chinese delegates could be elected to the parliament. Elections have been held for this purpose many times since 1969 under The Statute for Elections and By-Elections of National Level Elective Officials in the Free Areas.[25] The situation of membership in the three chambers of parliament in 1988 is shown in Table 12-1.

Although these supplementary elections have pumped some new blood into the parliament, the situation is still far from satisfactory to the Taiwanese Chinese. The percentage of Taiwan-elected members in the parliament is merely 14 per cent of the total number of deputies now serving in the parliament. In other words, only 14 per cent (183 seats) of these deputies have obtained a mandate directly from the Taiwan Chinese. The majority of deputies (1,093 seats) were mainly elected in the mainland in 1947 and 37 seats were selected by the President from overseas Chinese. Many aging deputies are not only negligent in their duty, mainly because of poor health, but also live abroad. Despite this fact, the ROC government

| Table 12-1 Membership of the Parliament February 1988 | | | |
|---|---|---|---|
| Name of Chamber | National Assembly | Legislative Yuan | Control Yuan |
| Number of Members under Constitution | 3,045 | 773 | 223 |
| Number elected on the mainland | 2,961 | 760 | 180 |
| Number who came to Taiwan* | 1,576 | 470 | 104 |
| Of those still serving | 850 | 216 | 36 |
| Supplementary Seats  A. Elected in Taiwan | 84 | 77 | 22 |
| Supplementary Seats  B. Selected by the President | 0 | 27 | 10 |
| Total number of delegated serving | 934 | 312 | 67 |
| Average age ot those mainlander deputies serving | 76.68 | 80.42 | 81.75 |
| Average age of those Taiwan-elected deputies | 47.3 | 49.6 | 56.16 |

* Some mainland deputies did not follow the ROC government to Taiwan in 1949.
Sources: The author compiled these figures from the following materials:
(a) The Republic of China, Taipei: Hilit Publishing Company, April 1988.
(b) The Independence Morning Post, 4 February 1988, p. 2.
(c) China Times, 4 December 1987, p. 2.

still pays them an allowance of about US$40,000 per person yearly and allows them various privileges.[26]

Due to physical infirmity, some aging deputies were unable to perform properly during parliamentary sessions, and some were too weak even to attend these sessions. As a result, parliamentary sessions are sometimes forced to adjourn because they lack a quorum of deputies to legally convene a meeting.[27]

This situation, and the unreasonable structure of the parliament, have become the main cause of political strife in Taiwan in recent years. Not only the opposition parties but also young members of the KMT all have pushed for parliamentary reform as soon as possible.[28] They have branded the parliament as the '10,000-years parliament'[29] and the life-time deputies as the 'old thieves'.[30]

Aware of the importance of parliamentary reform to Taiwan's political stability, the ruling KMT announced on 12 May 1986 that it would conduct a comprehensive study of the six main political issues currently troubling the ROC. Parliamentary reform is one of these six issues, the other five issues being the formation of new parties, self-government at district levels, laws and regulations concerning national security, social trends, and the central task of the KMT.[31]

After this announcement, the ruling KMT took four steps to produce parliamentary reform: (a) Deceased members of the National Assembly would no longer be replaced by the defeated candidates in the 1947 general elections held on the mainland. (b) The KMT proposed to institute a retirement plan to pension off aging deputies whereby each deputy would receive a NT$3.7 million (US$142,307) severance payment. (c) The KMT proposed to increase supplementary seats for the Taiwan Chinese rather than to reelect the existing parliament members. (d) The seats representing provinces in the mainland will not be elected until the mainland is 'recovered' from the Communists.

The ruling KMT was then prepared to adopt a policy of 'gradually rejuvenating the parliament and strengthening its function by simultaneously retiring senior parliamentarians and injecting new blood into the parliament by electing new members' in Taiwan.[32] The retirement plan was to be voluntary rather than compulsory, and the aging deputies would not have to leave the parliament until they died. The KMT was not prepared to have a complete new election for all of the parliamentary members in 1989. By so doing, the KMT believed that the claim that the ROC represented the will of the whole Chinese people would be maintained for several years more. Even if the aging mainlander deputies were all gone, some mainland representatives would be selected or elected from Taiwan's mainlanders, that is, the expatriate mainlanders and their offspring so that the parliament could still be said to be representing the whole of China, rather than Taiwan province only. The aging deputies have especially insisted on this point because they argue that if there were no 'mainland representatives'—even a symbolic number—in the parliament, it would have meant the independence of Taiwan, which they do not want.

The ruling KMT's plan has, as expected, met with objections from some Taiwanese Chinese, especially the DPP. They have insisted on immediate elections for all parliamentary positions claiming that a national parliament without the people's mandate is illegal, which removes the government's authority and legitimacy.[33] They believed that the '10,000-year parliament' should not be resolved by time but by the KMT's sincerely carrying out parliamentary reform. They have appealed to the KMT to identify itself with Taiwan rather than the already lost mainland. They have opposed both the idea of maintaining symbolic seats for Taiwan's mainlanders and selecting overseas Chinese as deputies, because the former might have disrupted the harmonious relations which have gradually formed between the expatriate mainlanders and the Taiwanese; and have considered it nonsensical to select other countries' citizens to speak for the Taiwan Chinese.[34]

According to the author's observations in Taiwan during 1989, there is a consensus among most of the Taiwanese Chinese that parliamentary reform is necessary. However, it is the scope of this reform that becomes the source of argument between conservative and liberal groups and troubles the ruling KMT. A reformed parliament, comprising only Taiwan Chinese, might favor Taiwan independence. For example, the opponents of parliamentary reform argued that the reform was unconstitutional, could aid and abet Taiwan independence sentiments and might lead people to guess that the ROC government had ceased its long held position of recovering the mainland from the communists and intended to stay in Taiwan forever.[35] If so, implementing reform might cause concern in the PRC and rekindle tensions across the Taiwan Strait. However, if the reformed parliament is to represent all the Chinese, the old guard argues, then who should speak for the mainland Chinese? How should they be elected and under what terms?

On 26 January 1989, the KMT-dominated Legislative Yuan, after a number of conflicts between the members of the KMT and the DDP, passed the Law Concerning the Voluntary Retirement of the First Term Senior Parliament Members. The KMT indicated that by gradually increasing Taiwan-elected

**Table 12-2** The Proposed Seats In the Reformed Parliament February 1989

| Name of Chambers | | National Assembly | Legislative Yuan | Control Yuan |
|---|---|---|---|---|
| Of those mainland-electing deputies still serving | | 850 | 216 | 36 |
| Comparison between the numbers of old and new seats* | Elected from Taiwan area | 84 (375) | 73 (121) | 22 (44) |
| | Selected from Overseas Chinese | 0 (0) | 27 (29) | 10 (10) |

* The additional supplementary seats in Taiwan are will be effective from the 1989 election. Figures in the parentheses are the number of a seats after the proposed reformation.
*Source: China Times*, 23 February 1989, p. 1.

deputies and voluntarily retiring the senior deputies, the members of the Legislative Yuan will be completely reelected within four years (six years for the Control Yuan and around ten years for the National Assembly).[36] In the meantime, the KMT has decided to increase the number of supplementary seats allocated Taiwan Province (see Table 12-2).

The ruling KMT's plan does not meet with the agreement of some Taiwanese Chinese, especially the opposition DPP. The DPP demands a completely new election for all seats in the parliament and that there should be no so-called 'mainlander representatives', even a symbolic number, and calls for the abolition of overseas Chinese deputies. In other words, the DPP simply wants a parliament that reflects today's political reality of the ROC in Taiwan and their wish that the ROC in Taiwan should be ruled by the inhabitants of Taiwan.

## National Affairs Conference (1990): a Sign of Compromise

In the past four decades, the constitution of the ROC has been used as a nation-building principle in Taiwan. However, the spirit of this mainland-instituted constitution, due to the extraordinary situation of the ROC, has been distorted under the period of 'Suppression of the Communists'. But the fact that the ROC government has so far failed to recover the mainland from the communist forces means the constitution needs to be modified to correspond with the current political situation in Taiwan and regain its true spirit and principle. Different viewpoints in this regard exist within Taiwan. These viewpoints have become a sensitive political issue and a major point of confrontation within the KMT itself and between the ruling KMT and some Taiwan Chinese.

By early 1990, this deeply-rooted discontent about Taiwan's politics had reached the point of brinkmanship. President Lee Teng-hui faced two unexpected challenges in his 1990 election bid. The one was from the conservatives, who felt that the pace of political reform had been too rapid and sought to protect their position from further erosion. The conservatives raised a counterticket to challenge Lee's prestige in the KMT,[37] a situation without precedent in the KMT's history prior to 1987. This event shook Taiwan's politics profoundly at that time and was described as the confrontation between the 'Mainstream Faction' (pro-Lee) and 'Non-mainstream Faction' (anti-Lee).

The other challenge came from a more liberal constituency, that is, the opposition. In response to the conservatives' bid for power as well as for pressing further reforms, in March 1990, an estimated 10,000 students and adults staged a sit-in at Taipei's Chiang Kai-shek Memorial Park, demanding the abolition of the Temporary Provisions, the direct election of the president by the people, the dissolution of the National Assembly, a timetable on Taiwan's political reforms, and a national affairs conference to discuss Taiwan's political future including the amendment of the constitution.

On March 21 1990, Lee was elected president with the new mandate from the National Assembly. President Lee immediately undertook some measures to further implement political reforms. He restored nearly 30 dissidents' political rights, a bold action from the viewpoints of the conservatives. In June, the Council of Grand Justices, which is responsible for interpreting the Constitution, ruled that all old guard in the three parliamentary bodies would have to retire by 31 December 1991. This rule has paved the way for completely democratic elections of the ROC's representative institutions. To some extent, it also means the end of the remnants of the ROC on the mainland and the real beginning of the representative ROC government on Taiwan. The ROC has transformed from 'China's ROC' to 'Taiwan's ROC'.

In July, the National Affairs Conference (NAC) was convened in accordance with President Lee's promise to the student demonstrators. Representatives of this conference were from all walks of life regardless of their political stands. Many political issues, such as whether to amend the Constitution or write a new one, whether the National Assembly should be abolished or not, and whether to hold direct elections for the offices of president, governor of Taiwan, and the mayors of the island's two largest cities, Taipei and Kaohsiung, were discussed during the sessions of the conference. The NAC, although posessing no statutory powers, served to 'defuse resentments within the population and also strengthened President Lee's ability to implement reform measures'.[38] The most important result of the meeting of the NAC, the author would argue, was the beginning of accelerating the pace of Taiwan's democratization.

## The First Stage of Constitutional Amendment

After long bickering, the KMT leadership in 1991 decided to amend the Constitution in two stages. The first stage of constitutional amendments mainly aimed to provide the legal basis for a total renewal of the three central representative institutions of the ROC Government. After new delegates of the National Assembly (a Constitution formulating and presidential electing body) were elected in Taiwan in the end of 1991 according to the above-mentioned new legal basis, they would proceed to the second stage of constitutional amendments for the major revision of the Constitution which that Assembly was scheduled to debate in the Spring of 1992.

On 8 April 1991, the 539 remaining delegates of the old National Assembly convened to debate the first stage's constitutional amendments. On 22 April, the National Assembly approved a constitutional amendment providing for a total renewal of the National Assembly at the end of 1991,[39] the Legislative Yuan at the end of 1992, and the Control Yuan in early 1993. The new National Assembly has 327 members, a considerable cut in the number of members in comparison with the number under the original Constitution. The Legislative

Yuan and the Control Yuan have also been pared; the former cut from 773 members to 161 while the latter was pruned from 223 members to 29 (see Table 12-3). The membership of the parliament after these constitutional amendments has reflected the pragmatism of the ROC government that has accepted the reality that its governing territories were restricted only to Taiwan and some other small islands and no longer includes the mainland.

**Table 12-3:** Membership of the Parliament after Constitutional Amendment

| Name of Chambers | National Assembly | Legislative Yuan | Control Yuan |
|---|---|---|---|
| Breakdown of Each Chamber's Delegates<br>A. Delegates of Taiwan Chinese* | 221 | 119 | 29 |
| B. Delegates of Taiwan Aborigines** | 6 | 6 | 0 |
| C. Delegates of Overseas Chinese | 20 | 6 | 2 |
| D. Nationwide Representatives*** | 80 | 30 | 5 |
| Total Number of Members | 327 | 161 | 52 |

*Source: The Constitution of the Republic of China.*
  * Delegates of Taiwan Chinese include those elected from Kinmen and Matzu, Fukien Province.
 ** Taiwan aborigines are descendants of Austronesians who lived in southern China in the Neolithic Age. At present, the total population of Taiwan aborigines is 330.000.
*** The 'Nationwide' and 'Overseas Chinese' representatives will be elected from party seats according to the proportional representation rule. The representation of these delegates was a result of a compromise between the conservatives (mainly the old guard) and the reformers.

On 30 April 1991, President Lee further proceeded along with his democratization programmes. He formally declared the end of the so-called 'Period of National Mobilization and the Suppression of the Communist Rebellion' originally proclaimed in 1948. Moreover, President Lee abolished the so-called 'Temporary Provisions' for the 'Suppression' Period', thus he relinquished extraordinary presidential powers and returned to the full provisions of the original Constitution. With these actions, the first stage of constitutional amendments therefore has been completed.

## The Second Stage of Constitutional Amendment

At midnight on 21 December 1991, the election results of the new National Assembly were announced. The ruling KMT won 71.17 per cent of the vote and 254 seats in the National Assembly, while the main opposition DPP captured 23.94 per cent and 66 seats. The candidates of other small parties, the National Democratic Non-Partisan Alliance (2.27 per cent and three seats), the China Social Democratic Party (2.18 per cent and no seats), and independent candidates (0.44 per cent and two seats), shared the rest of the votes and seats.[40] Thus, the election was a landslide victory for the KMT and a severe blow to the DPP. The results of this election consolidated the KMT's position in Taiwan. To some extent, it was construed as a new mandate from the Taiwan people to the KMT to lead the task of the second stage of constitutional amendments.

Starting from 1992, the ROC's politics has entered into a new era. The elderly mainland-elected representatives of the three chambers were all retired by the end of 1991 according to the ruling of the Council of Grand Justices. Parliamentary reform has been peacefully completed. In March 1992, the newly elected representatives of the National Assembly were convened for an extraordinary session to debate how to proceed with major revisions to the Constitution.

During the second stage of the constitutional amendment process, the Taiwan-elected representatives enacted another eight additional clauses appended to the original constitution. Amendment Article 12 stipulated that the ROC's president and vice-president would be directly elected by Chinese on Taiwan and the term of the presidency would be cut from six years to four years effective from 1996 for the ninth term president.

This presidential election reform is the most important result of this stage of constitutional amendment. At the same time, the National Assembly was granted the authority to confirm the appointment of higher-ranking government officials selected by the president. The new presidential election procedure heralds the further Taiwanization of the ROC while the island's democratization would also become perfected.

## B. Political Legitimacy

Seymour M. Lipset has written that the stability of any given democracy depends 'not only on economic development but also upon the effectiveness and the legitimacy of its political system. . . . Legitimacy involves the capacity of the system to engender and maintain the belief that the existing political institutions are the most appropriate ones for the society'.[41] Dankwart A. Rustow has pointed out two prerequisites for political stability: the legitimacy of the political institutions and the legitimacy of the rulers. If the people perceive the political institutions and the rulers as legitimate, the foundation for political stability is ensured.[42] Dennis Pirages argues that if the government, although nominally controlling the territory, can not receive a considerable degree of 'citizen loyalties,' the crises of civil disorder and riot can frequently threaten the country's development and function.[43] How can political legitimacy be measured? Edmund A. Aunger suggested observing a nation's 'negative indicators, that is, by looking for manifestations of illegitimacy, such as organized opposition to a state's constitution, or severe government repression in response to such opposition'.[44]

The Taiwan independence movement, advocated by some Taiwanese Chinese both within and outside Taiwan, could be seen, at least from the viewpoint of the ROC government, as a manifestation of illegitimacy under Aunger's definition. This movement has been challenging the legitimacy of the ROC and questioning the legitimacy of its rulers. It has always had the intention of building a 'new country' in Taiwan and has been engendering a national identity problem in the ROC. This has become another political challenge to the ruling KMT. Since the Taiwan independence movement is so important, its discussion warrants a separate chapter. The author therefore leaves this part of the discussion to Chapter 13 so that

the impact and significance of the Taiwan independence movement on Taiwan's politics and the two Chinas' relations can
be analyzed comprehensively.

## C. Government Efficacy

A further component of political stability is the extent to
which a government can make and carry out prompt and relevant decisions in response to political challenges. Dell G.
Hitchner and Carol Levine point to the 'ineffectiveness of
leadership' as one of the several elements constituting an
obstacle to the Third World's modernization (the other elements include the inadequacy of economic development, the
difficulty of utilizing technology, and the weight of traditional-
ism.[45] Operational measurement of efficacy is not an easy task,
particularly 'because of the difficulty in evaluating the
"relevant decision" and "political challenges" which define
efficacy'.[46] For want of a better method, public opinion in
Taiwan and related materials will be used to help in the
discussions and analyses in this section.

### Comments by the ROC Watchers

The ROC's economic development has been excellent compared with many other Third World countries. As John F.
Copper has said 'in terms of economic growth, Taiwan has
come close to accomplishing in two-plus decades what Western
Europe and the United Stated accomplished in 200 years. It
has also experienced rapid political development'.[47] Lucian
W. Pye has similarly written that the ROC in Taiwan has
'developed into an increasingly complex polity and has a
social system that is not far behind its well-organized and
advanced economy'.[48] Thomas B. Gold also has praised the
ROC government for having made 'miraculous progress at
rapid growth, structural change, improved livelihood, and
political democratization'.[49]

    Jurgen Domes describes the ROC's political system as a
'development-oriented authoritarian system' under which the
KMT does not try to regulate every aspect of social and personal life. As well, the political monopoly of the KMT is based
on the principle of progress towards a developed industrial
mass society, and does not attempt to preserve a traditional

social structure as in preservation-oriented authoritarian systems, he said. Further, the pluralizing factors in Taiwan are mainly provided by functional groups based on divergent interests of political and administrative sub-systems. Finally, he writes that the parameters of political competition in the ROC slowly tend to widen, 'as elements of differentiation are cautiously articulated'.[50] Jurgen Domes's comments, to some extent, indicate the fact that a quasi-democratic political system is in fact existing and operating in the KMT's authoritarian government.

Edwin A. Winckler observes that Taiwan is beginning a systemic transition from 'hard' to 'soft' authoritarianism. 'Hard' authoritarianism on Taiwan has meant mainlander-technocratic rule under a one-man dictatorship. 'Soft' authoritarianism would imply joint mainlander-Taiwanese technocratic rule under a collective party leadership; while the dominance of the 'ruling party' would still be guaranteed.[51]

All of these comments were made by ROC watchers before 1986. In fact, the ROC's political reforms which had started in 1976–77 and have intensified since 1986, have gradually transformed Taiwan's politics from 'a development-authoritarian dictatorship to a pluralistic representative system'.[52]

The above comments made by ROC watchers have, to some extent, confirmed that the ruling KMT's efforts and achievements in the past years, not to only develop the economy but also to practise democratic politics, has succeeded. However, to march further towards a democratic political system is essential to make the ROC the good model (as the ROC sees itself) for the PRC to imitate. Antonio Chiang, the publisher of *The Journalist* in Taipei, shortly after this time, said that the ruling KMT had always wished to export the so-called 'Taiwan Experience' to mainland China. However, he also mentioned that many problems remain in Taiwan's political system. 'We are still under the period of suppression of the "Communist Rebellion". [This period was officially terminated on April 30, 1991.] We still do not have political leaders elected directly by the people. . . . Therefore, to whom should we promote and sell our "experience"?'[53] Chao Chun-shan, Dean of the Faculty of East Asian Studies, National Chengchi University, also indicated that in terms of economic development the 'Taiwan Experience' could perhaps serve as a model for mainland China. However, if the 'experience' means political democratization, he said, 'we still have a long way to go'.[54]

## The Kuomintang in the 1980s

The KMT by nature was a Leninist-style political party with the following traditional characteristics: selective membership recruitment; a revolutionary and nationalist ideology; a centralized decision-making structure under a Central Committee; a policy-making Central Standing Committee and a policy-implementing secretariat with administration, intelligence, and propaganda departments; control of the army through a political cadre system; maintenance of a youth league; and leadership over the policies and personnel of the state apparatus.[55] By December 1991, the KMT had a total membership of 2,356,042, of which 69.63 per cent of members are aged below 40.[56] This statistic could mean that almost 70 per cent of the KMT members were recruited in Taiwan since 1949; 65 per cent of the KMT members were in fact native Taiwanese.[57] Since President Lee Teng-hui, a native Taiwanese, has been elected as the KMT's new chairman after the death of the previous chairman Chiang Ching-kuo, a mainlander, the ruling KMT has in fact already been gradually transformed from 'China's KMT' to 'Taiwan's KMT'.[58] Therefore, to still regard the present KMT as identical to the one that existed four decades ago in mainland China, that is, mainlander-dominated, would be a mistaken perception.

The KMT touches the lives of the people in many ways. The leadership relies on the party's intricate network of connections with mass organizations throughout the country as an important means of indoctrinating and influencing people and winning sufficient support to enable them to go on governing effectively.[59] The achievement of Taiwan's economy should in part be ascribed to a strong one-party political system prior to 1987 which 'appears to meet certain functional needs for a society in the early to middle phases of modernization'.[60] Under the KMT's government, the ROC had a strong leadership with 'highly efficient technocrats'[61] and a well-trained civil service which enabled Taiwan to develop its economy rapidly and share the fruits of this development among all of the Chinese in Taiwan.

However, this does not mean that the KMT is perfect. The

party faces many problems including corruption and the abuse of political power by its officials, as well as a fall in party discipline. The one-party system has generally 'facilitated the perpetuation of privileges of a particular segment of the population'.[62] When this situation persists for a long time, the principle of equity in a society is injured and the privileged class is no longer tolerated by the general public. This is especially so as Taiwan is gradually becoming more and more pluralistic and democratic in the 1980s.

As well, the one-party system, without the checks-and-balances of organized opposition groups, has corrupted some of the KMT's leaders and elites. The financial scandals of the Tenth Credit Cooperative in 1985[63] and the Rong-hsin Garden Project in 1989, and the murder case of a Chinese-American writer Henry Liu[64] in 1985 revealed that KMT officials were abusing political power and enjoying too many political privileges. Some of the KMT's candidates have also used bribery to win elections, including the KMT's election for the members of the Central Committee.[65] Bribery has become a common feature in every election in Taiwan. All of these facts show the deterioration of the KMT's discipline. Wu Chun-tsai, Director of the KMT's Evaluation and Discipline Commission, has confirmed these corrupt activities.[66]

Aside from problems within the KMT, the party's inability to respond to those problems resulting from Taiwan's modernization, such as the demand for popular political participation, has caused further deterioration of the KMT's image and credibility. More and more Taiwanese Chinese 'are dissatisfied with the performance of government officials'.[67] Ma Ying-jeou, the former Chairman of the Research, Development and Evaluation Commission (a Cabinet level organization), has admitted this but explains, 'the increasing degree of dissatisfaction shows that the society in Taiwan is pluralistic. It is not necessarily due to an inefficient administration'.[68] Ma's argument does not explain why more and more of the younger generation in Taiwan now do not want to join the KMT. According to Chuang Huai-yi, Director of the Youth Department, Central Committee of the KMT, only 10 per cent of the university students in Taiwan are interested in joining the KMT, compared with the 50 per cent enrollment rate in previous years.[69] This latest figure indicates how much the KMT's prestige and attraction in the ROC has decreased.

## Chiang Ching-kuo: The Reformer of the KMT

Facing these problems in and outside of the KMT, the ex-Chairman and President of the ROC Chiang Ching-kuo felt the need to reform the KMT to prevent the party's prestige and influence in Taiwan from decreasing further. According to an informed report, Chiang himself was the main initiator of such reforms. It is said that Chiang 'was heartbroken, disappointed, and extremely disillusioned'[70] when he was told of the scandal of the Tenth Credit Cooperative and the murder case of Henry Liu. This mood contributed to the far-reaching decision by Chiang in early 1986 to conduct a series of political reforms, including the reform of the KMT itself. Chiang even believed in 'the creation of new parties as the only way to purify Taiwan politics'.[71] Chiang, old and infirm in 1986, decided to establish a sound and institutionalized political system for the ROC after his era and sought to secure a place in history as an enlightened political leader,[72] much as Deng might be seen to be attempting on the mainland.

Aside from Chiang's initiative, external influences were also important in stimulating the KMT's political reform. King-yuh Chang, former Director of the Institute of International Relations in Taipei, indicated that the views of the US 'are given a great deal of attention [regarding the ROC's political reform] because of the security, political and economic ties' between Washington and Taipei.[73]

Popular perception of Mr. Chiang's merits as an effective leader was confirmed by a telephone survey after his death in January 1988. When the polled people were asked 'between Messrs. Chiang Ching-kuo and Chiang Kai-shek who do you think has made a greater contribution to Taiwan's progress and development?' 40.2 per cent of the sampled persons regarded Mr. Chiang Ching-kuo as having made a greater contribution than his father Mr. Chiang Kai-shek (only 9.4 per cent). 44.2 per cent responded 'no major difference', and 0.8 per cent said 'no contribution at all'; while 3.8 per cent indicated that 'there is no comparison'.[74]

## Civil Order

Civil order is the final component of political stability. It means 'the absence of collective resorts to violence'.[75] Violence 'as a means of bringing about political change is a symptom of malfunction within a political system. It implies a lack of political legitimacy and governmental efficacy'.[76]

## Modernization: The Main Cause of Civil Disorder in Taiwan

Taiwan's civil order has deteriorated in recent years. The frequency of resorting to individual and collective violence to solve political issues in Taiwan has gradually increased. Even in the Legislative Yuan and at the level of city councils, there has been physical violence when legislators and the council members of both the KMT and the DPP have confronted each other over a political bill or other issues. Mass street demonstrations were held on average four times a day during 1988. The reasons for such demonstrations could range from political issues to problems that related to the interests of the general public. Violence has become common at these activities. The author ascribes this phenomenon of civil disorder in Taiwan to the rapid modernization of the ROC in the past decades.

According to William Kornhauser, the degree of social and political instability is related to the rate of modernization. 'The rapid influx of large numbers of people into newly developing urban areas invites mass movements'. He said that when 'industrialization occurred rapidly, introducing sharp discontinuities between the pre-industrial and industrial situation, more rather than less extremist working-class movements emerged'.[77] The overall picture which emerges of an unstable country is:

> one exposed to modernity; disrupted socially from the traditional patterns of life; confronted with pressures to change their ways, economically, socially and politically; bombarded with new and 'better' ways of producing economic goods and services; and frustrated by the modernization process of change, generally, and the failure of their government to satisfy their ever-rising expectations, particularly.[78]

Samuel P. Huntington also pointed out that

> the relationship between social mobilization and political instability seems reasonably direct. Urbanization, increase in literacy, education, and media exposure all give rise to enhanced aspirations and expectations which, if unsatisfied, galvanize individuals and groups into politics. In the absence

of strong and adaptable political institutions, such increase in participation means instability and violence.[79]

He observes that the Western countries' modernization rate was slow and spread over several centuries; therefore, these countries could easily deal with one issue or one crisis at a time caused by modernization, because the rate of modernization was so much faster in the Third World, the problems caused by this rapid modernization, such as centralization of authority, national integration, social mobilization, economic development, political participation, social welfare and so on, 'have arisen not sequentially but simultaneously'.[80] This situation is the most recent challenge to most of the governments in developing countries.

## Modernization: No Change Without Cost

The ROC in Taiwan also faces the above-mentioned problems. The Government's administration efficiency could not often match the people's demands and needs, therefore, social disturbance has occurred. In Taiwan, a phrase from Charles Dickens' famous novel *A Tale of Two Cities* has been cited to describe Taiwan's situation:

'It was the best of times, it was the worst of times.'

Modernization, in Taiwan, has meant a reduction in authoritarian rule and the beginning of real democracy. The impact of the political reform brought about by modernization is ubiquitous, even extending its benefits to high school students because of a lifting of the restriction on hair length.[81] To Taiwan's economy, modernization means 'a greater degree of privatization in all sectors of state-controlled industries[82] which range from the gasoline station to banking and airline services. Modernization has also meant the emergence of a more equal society where the members of the privileged class have been reduced, while people's resentment caused by political repression and injustice could be released by the emergence of a fairer political environment. Hence, modernization, including political democratization and economic prosperity, has brought 'the best of times' and 'the spring of hope' to the Taiwan Chinese. 'Tomorrow will be better,' the KMT's slogan in the election campaign, is the picture of future life in the minds of most Taiwanese Chinese.

Modernization also produces many problems, however, and has created many challenges to the ROC government, especially after the lifting of martial law in 1987. The gradual deterioration of civil order in Taiwan has alarmed many Chinese in Taiwan. Lee Huan, then general-secretary of the KMT, publicly stated that 'although Taiwan is thriving and stable at this moment, it still has many potential problems and crises'. He observed that the current civil disorder is mainly caused by rapid social changes in Taiwan, especially after political democratization. He admits that both the people and the government need time to adapt themselves to the new political situation in Taiwan. However, 'if the period of adaptation takes too long, the people's confidence toward the government will be eventually shaken'.[83]

In fact, some Taiwanese Chinese' confidence about Taiwan has been shaken. This can be found from the result of a telephone survey aimed at Taiwan's top 1,000 manufacturing industries and top 300 service industries. In answer to a question 'what is your main concern regarding Taiwan's politics?' 68.2 per cent of the people polled answered that they worried that Taiwan might fall into chaos due to civil disorder (62.4 per cent worry about the strength of the government's resolution to execute its policies; 35.5 per cent are concerned about the isolation of Taiwan internationally; 24.9 per cent are worried about the possibility of a military *coup d'etat*; while only 18 per cent worry about a military invasion by the PRC). When a further question about Taiwan's civil disorder, 'what are you prepared to do?'', was asked. 9.8 per cent of the polled persons indicated their preparedness to emigrate to other countries if Taiwan's situation becomes more unstable; while 35.6 per cent responded 'not sure what to do' and 54.6 per cent said that they will 'remain in Taiwan'.[84] Executives also expressed their disappointment at the ROC government's ineffectiveness in handling the gradually mounting civil disorder which has caused much inconvenience to the business community and ordinary people alike.[85] Chao Yao-tung, the former minister of the ROC's economic affairs, warned that if the mass demonstrations, and the violence caused by these demonstrations, were not curbed, Taiwan's economic development and foreign investment would be hampered.[86]

Except for those problems that directly derive from modernization, the ruling KMT should also take some of the responsibility for the deterioration of Taiwan's civil order. The pace of political reform seems always to be far behind the people's demands. The KMT still hesitates to proceed with reform, partly because of a minority of conservatives whose vested interests are closely connected to the maintenance of the status quo. The opposition parties always claimed that they would not obey 'bad' laws[87] which were 'illegally' instituted by the retired aging deputies. Therefore, violence and defiance of law and order are commonplace in Taiwan's mass demonstrations. The belief that 'The louder your cry out, the more concessions the government will make' has become a motto in Taiwan's street demonstrations.

The ruling KMT, the author would argue, seems to 'tolerate' this situation for the following reasons. Most street movements are related to politics, and must be handled carefully as Taiwan's political system has not been fully democratized. The enforcement of law and order at the current stage would only cause confrontations and tension between the ruling KMT, the opposition groups, and the people. The KMT also does not want to be too repressive because it wants to win elections by a large margin.

## Solutions for Taiwan's Civil Disorder

The cause of civil disorder in Taiwan can be summarized in two elements: first, the syndrome of modernization; and second, the anachronistic political system of the ROC in Taiwan. Modernization gives Taiwan's people new levels of aspirations and wants. The ability of a transitional society like Taiwan to satisfy these new aspirations, however, increases more slowly than the aspirations themselves. Consequently, a gap develops between aspiration and expectations. This gap generates social frustration and dissatisfaction and this in turn causes political instability.[88] These frustrations and dissatisfactions, however, could be removed 'through social and economic mobility if the traditional society is sufficiently "open" to offer opportunities for such mobility'.[89]

Regarding the anachronistic political system, the ruling KMT must show responsiveness to the Taiwanese Chinese' needs and also a capacity to do something about them. The more the KMT delays showing such a responsiveness, the higher a political price the ruling KMT will need to pay. This cost would include the further deterioration of Taiwan's civil order and the loss of the KMT's prestige both within the ROC and around the world. In February 1989, President Lee Teng-hui expressed his concern about Taiwan's civil order and said that the government will enforce law and order to restore the civil order.[90] This message would be welcome to the general public in Taiwan, who would prefer to have a peaceful and harmonious political environment.

If the KMT intends to reduce civil disorder, however, it must know why and how such disorder is generated. In other words, the KMT should increase its efforts to proceed with political reform. If the people's dissatisfaction is gradually reduced as democracy is fully instituted, civil disorder will be reduced accordingly. Perhaps Karl W. Deutsch's comments are useful for the ROC government. He argued that

> Governments are organizations to enforce patterns of behavior, if necessary, by violence. . . . A sufficiently large part of these patterns must be habitually acceptable to a large part of the population, and they must be sufficiently enforceable among the rest. Government must be able, therefore, to count on two probabilities: (1) a significant probability of enforcing their commands; together with (2) a significant probability of finding them voluntarily complied with by their subjects. Finally, governments must have effective social channels to receive and accept information about major changes in the needs and habits of their population, or in the other relevant conditions of their power.[91]

## Conclusions

Four factors—constitutional durability, political legitimacy, governmental efficacy, and civil order—have been employed in this chapter to evaluate the degree of political stability in the ROC in Taiwan. This political stability is a useful indicator of a country's integration status as well. The result of this evaluation shows that the ROC is currently in a transitional period, with some instability which is mainly the result of the ROC's modernization in the past years and the anachronistic political system of the ROC in Taiwan.

It seems that the ruling KMT has already become aware of the dangers incumbent in this situation and has initiated many political reforms to solve these problems especially since President Lee Teng-hui became the KMT's Chairman in 1988. However, the ruling KMT should understand that 'if particular groups have negative orientations toward the government or major government policies, the consequences may radically affect the level of integration'[92] and stability in Taiwan. An unstable Taiwan will reduce the ROC's ability to counter the PRC's threat. Hence, how to establish a basis for mutual confidence, reach a political consensus, and further improve the communications between the ruling KMT and the opposition parties and groups, in particular the DPP, will become essential issues in the development of Taiwan's stability and integration.

Generally speaking, the political situation in the ROC is favourable, mainly for the following reasons. The Taiwan Chinese understand that they share a common destiny, especially when they perceive the threat from the PRC. Therefore, they realize the importance of unity in the face of this threat. The ROC's economic development in the past years have improved Taiwan people's living standards and created a large middle class in Taiwan which to some extent is the main force for Taiwan's stability. The political reforms of recent years have made the domestic politics of the ROC more cohesive. In the future, it is likely that the ROC government, either governed by the KMT, the DPP or a coalition of parties, would have the ability and the strength to meet political challenges and implement political reforms to further improve the ROC's political system and win the support of Taiwan's people. If so, the national strength of the ROC would also develop sufficiently to face possible challenges from the other side of the Taiwan Strait.

# Chapter 13

■

## The Taiwan Independence Movement and Its Prospects

From the previous chapters, it is obvious that the Republic of China Government's basic position concerning the two China issue is integration rather than disintegration. Other voices in Taiwan also argue that the historic and current division of China is merely a temporary and transitional situation; therefore, they believe that China will be reunified in the future.

In contrast to the above-mentioned viewpoints, however, the advocates of self determination for Taiwan or Taiwan independence, who aim for the permanent separation of Taiwan from the mainland, also exist in Taiwan, and have become the major force of disintegration in resolving the two China issue. As a matter of fact, the advocacy of 'Taiwan Independence' has a long history and social and political background. Generally speaking the main opposition party, the Democratic Progressive Party (DPP), is the main advocate of the independence movement, despite ideological infighting within this party concerning how this movement should be developed. Nevertheless, the DPP claims the purpose of this movement is to try to resolve 'Taiwan's future and the problem of Taiwan's international status'.[1] The DPP questions the Kuomintang (KMT) and argues that 'if the People's Republic of China (PRC) opposes both the *de facto* and *de jure* autonomy of Taiwan and still intends to use force against us [in Taiwan], then considered from the viewpoint of the Taiwanese people's happiness, well-being, and interest, what will the Taiwanese people's choice be'?[2]

In October 1991, the DPP held its 5th Party Plenum and formally incorporated the 'Taiwan Independence Clause' in its platform as a campaign slogan to be used during that year's election to the National Assembly. This has made the Taiwan Independence Movement an implicit political issue before 1990, becoming an open issue in Taiwan for the first time since 1949.

This chapter covers how the Taiwan Independence Movement

emerged; what are Taiwan people's attitudes toward the Taiwan Independence Movement; how the DPP practices the Taiwan Independence Movement; and finally what would be the future development of the Taiwan Independence Movement. Through discussions and analyses of this chapter, it is hoped that the reader can have a better understanding about the Taiwan Independence Movement and its implications toward the resolution of the China issue.

## History

The emergence of the Taiwan Independence Movement can be roughly divided into three stages with each stage reflecting the political environment, both within and outside of Taiwan at various times.

The February 28 Incident in 1947 and the misgovernment of the ruling KMT in Taiwan in the late 1940s highlighted the first stage of the Taiwan Independence Movement. Taiwan dissidents escaped overseas after the February 28 Incident. This incident sowed the seeds of discord and hatred between the expatriate mainlanders and the indigenous Taiwanese and became the principal cause of the Taiwan Independence Movement. The main objective of the Taiwan Independence Movement at this stage was to overturn the expatriated KMT regime.

In the second stage, before 1980, the Taiwan Independence Movement was motivated by the KMT's authoritarian rule and the mainlanders' continuous monopoly of political power. The KMT for its part espoused its 'legitimacy theory', that its Parliament represented the whole of China, and refused to hold a complete re-election, instituting martial law and depriving people of their constitutional rights. Dissidents were arrested and persecuted, for example, the cases of Lei Chen[3] and the Formosa Incident.[4] All of these circumstances further upset the indigenous Taiwanese Chinese. The main purpose of the Taiwan Independence Movement at this stage was to promote the democratization of Taiwan in the face of strict KMT rule, and to oppose the PRC's incorporation schemes. Although under the KMT's authoritarian rule the Taiwanese Chinese were restricted from political participation, they did enjoy an improved economic life, a benefit that has relaxed, to some extent, their discontent with the KMT.

After the 1980s, the Taiwan Independence Movement had entered into the third stage. More democratic policies have been introduced by the KMT. Democratization has improved relations between the KMT and dissident Taiwanese Chinese. For example, martial law was lifted in July 1987, and this resulted in the formation of political parties including the DPP. Further, the bans on freedom of the press and speech were also lifted. Before the ban on freedom of the press was lifted in January 1988, Taiwan had 28 newspapers. At present Taiwan has 151 registered newspapers.[5]

The political development of and the changes in and outside Taiwan since 1979 have led both the KMT and the opposition parties to believe that they share a common destiny. Chang Chun-hong, the third term general-secretary of the DPP, defined the meaning of today's Taiwan Independence Movement:

> First, Taiwan independence refers to the demarcation between Mainland China and Taiwan, the latter of which refuses to be ruled by the Communist mainland regime. Secondly, Taiwan independence means the master of Taiwan should be the majority of indigenous Taiwanese. Thirdly, Taiwan independence connotes the democratization of all of Taiwan's politics. Only through democracy can the Taiwanese eventually and eternally become the 'Masters of Taiwan'. And forthly, Taiwan independence means striving for Taiwan's international status, identity, and dignity.[6]

Chang said that both points 1 and 2 have actually been realized. Taiwan in fact is *de facto* independent under KMT rule. In other words, the KMT, like the DPP, in fact does not want Taiwan to be reunified with the mainland. What the KMT has done in past years is to build a KMT-style Taiwan independent state (that is, the so-called 'B-type Taiwan independence').[7]

Furthermore, President Lee Teng-hui is a Taiwanese who has no connection at all with the mainland. The Taiwanese people have already become the masters of Taiwan. Nevertheless, Chang has said that the goals of the Taiwan Independence Movement have not yet been fully realized. The task of democratization in Taiwan needs further improvement and perfecting. The most urgent task is to reintroduce the 'newly packaged' Taiwan with a popularly elected government into international society and to secure the nation's recognition from other countries. Therefore, Chang has argued, if the KMT intends to eliminate the voice of Taiwan independence, it should immediately institute true democracy rather than repress the independence movement. He said that 'only by implementing democracy can Taiwan obtain the world's sympathy and support, and increase the possibility of Taiwan's return to the international community'.[8]

In other words, the current stage sees the Taiwan Independence Movement pushing the KMT to implement democracy in the domestic arena while pursuing Taiwan's return to global society in the international arena. Antonio Chiang, publisher of a liberal and non-KMT-owned weekly magazine called *The Journalist*, pointed out, 'Sure, some (Taiwan) people believe in Taiwan independence, but for most people independence is just a code word for more democracy. Independence is a very vague, ambiguous word. It is not a legal term in Taiwan in any way. There's a psychological and emotional attachment to that term. And a political one, of course'.[9]

The above discussion indicates how the concept and nature of the Taiwan Independence Movement has been transformed since the 1940s. This movement has its merits in that it has stimulated the development of Taiwan's democratic politics. This democratization is vital for the lengthy peaceful reign of the ROC government, and serves as a model to influence the PRC as well. To the KMT, the Taiwan Independence Movement is not a completely disadvantageous entity, despite the fact that the Taiwan Independence Movement has challenged the ROC's legitimacy. For example, the KMT could use the Taiwan Independence Movement as the expression of public opinion and a reason for not incorporating with the mainland. As well, the Taiwan Independence Movement provides a counter to Beijing's isolation strategy. Taipei has so far never explicitly advocated the idea of Taiwanese independence. However, any relaxation of Taipei's policy toward the Taiwan Independence Movement[10] might lead Beijing to worry that Taipei will side with the movement and seek Taiwan's independence. Under this circumstance, Taipei's foreign policy would become far less responsive to Beijing. Taipei can let Beijing understand that if it continues to isolate Taipei internationally, the isolation would generate political problems for the ruling KMT, and might boost the prospects and the power of the Taiwan Independence Movement in Taiwan. This situation would be obviously disadvantageous to both Taipei and Beijing. Hence, both the CCP and the KMT, from this viewpoint, would appear to share a common interest in preventing Taiwan's independence from becoming a reality.

In the meantime, Taipei is in a dilemma over how to handle the Taiwan Independence Movement. The Taiwan Independence Movement can help Taipei to counter, to some extent, Beijing's offensive, but if it were to succeed, then the KMT's government in Taiwan may be threatened. Taipei can not repress the Taiwan Independence Movement too much because of potential political backlash domestically, and concern for human rights internationally. On the other hand, Taipei cannot allow the Taiwan Independence Movement absolute freedom as this might reintroduce tension into the Taiwan Strait. How to secure and how to balance between playing the 'Taiwan Independence Movement card', and at the same time controlling the expansion and development of the Taiwan Independence Movement has become a controversial issue for the ruling KMT.

## Taiwan Independence: A Major Wish?

How many Taiwanese Chinese advocate independence? No official figures from the ROC government are available at the moment to answer this question; some public opinion statistics, however, are available from other sources. Taipei's Foundation for Public Opinion Research conducted a telephone survey in February 1988 to learn how many Taiwanese Chinese support independence. The figures are given in Table 13-1.

**Table 13-1:** A Survey of Opinion about Taiwan Independence

| | |
|---|---|
| (1) Agree strongly | 2.1% |
| (2) Agree | 7.4% |
| (3) Depends on situation | 2.9% |
| (4) Disagree | 40.9% |
| (5) Disagree strongly | 23.9% |
| (6) No comment | 4.8% |
| (7) No idea | 17.3% |
| (8) No answer | 0.7% |

\*   This telephone survey was conducted throughout Taiwan and randomly selected 1,145 Taiwan Chinese, age 20 and above, from the telephone book in February 1988. The sample error is ±2.95%. Survey period: February 4–9, 1988.

*Source: United Evening News*, 11 March 1988, p. 2.

This poll indicated that only 9.5 per cent of the sample 'agree strongly' or 'agree' with the idea of Taiwan independence, while 64.8 per cent 'disagree strongly' or 'disagree'. Those aged between 20 to 34, less educated (high school level only), non-KMT members, and mainly Taiwanese are inclined to support Taiwan's independence. Those sampled who received a higher education (tertiary degree and above) are inclined to oppose Taiwan's independence. Ninety-percent of mainlanders and those who consider themselves exiled mainlanders or KMT members also oppose Taiwan's independence.[12]

This poll revealed that the main advocates of independence remain the native Taiwanese and non-KMT members. This fact corresponds to the historical background of the Taiwan Independence Movement.

In January 1992, Huang Kuen-hui, Chairman of Taipei's Mainland Affairs Council, released a report concerning the ROC Government's mainland China policy and the relations between Taiwan and the mainland. In his report, Huang compiled a table selected from a series of public opinion polls in Taiwan concerning Taiwan people's attitudes toward Taiwan's independence during the period from June 1989 to June 1991.[13] Part of his table's contents have been compiled in Table 13-2.

Table 13-2 has indicated that the percentage of the sampled people with different opinions on Taiwan's independence has varied from time to time. Nevertheless, this table shows that no more than 21 per cent of Taiwan's people agree with Taiwan's independence, while over 60 per cent disagree. In the meantime, Table 13-2 also indicated that on the average, 50 per cent of the sample population believe that the PRC will launch an outright attack on Taiwan if Taiwan proclaims its independence, while 26.4 per cent fall in the category 'impossible'. Strictly speaking, Table 13-2 is not very sophisticated. Some theoretical and methodological problems involving data acquisition techniques that accompany this use of public opinion polls do exist in the table; but it serves as a useful referential index for readers to understand Taiwanese people's attitudes toward Taiwan's independence.

The Taiwanese Chinese are psychologically cautious about politically sensitive topics such as Taiwan's independence, since they are not allowed to freely advocate and promote independence *per se*. According to Article 2 of the National Security Law of the ROC, the right of assembly and association

**Table 13-2:** Taiwan People's Viewpoints Toward Taiwan Independence

| Poll Organization | Poll Time | 1. Taiwan Independence | | 2. Will the PRC Attack Taiwan if Taiwan Proclaims Independence | |
|---|---|---|---|---|---|
| | | Agree | Disgree | Possible | Impossible |
| Foundation for Public Opinion Research | June 1989 Oct. 1989 Dec. 1989 | — 15.8% 8.2% | — — — | 40.5% 53.9% 40.4% | — — — |
| Capital Morning News | July 1989 | 11.9% | — | — | — |
| Graduate School of Sociology, Tung-hai University | November–December 1989 | 6.7% | — | — | — |
| Foundation for Public Opinion Research | June 1990 | 12.5% | 67% | — | — |
| United Daily News | Oct. 1990 | 21% | 57% | — | — |
| Foundation for Development and Research on the Two Sides of the Taiwan Strait | October 1990 | 16.2% | 62.7% | 49.4% | 20.1% |
| Foundation for Public Opinion Research | December 1990 | 12.0% | 61.7% | 50.8% | — |
| Chinese Television Station | March 1991 | — | — | 43.8% | 47.2% |
| China Times | June 1991 | — | — | 50.4% | 23.6% |
| Foundation for Public Opinion Research | June 1991 | 12.7% | 65.3% | 58.4% | 16.7% |

*Source*: Huang Kuen-hui, *Mainland Policy and the Two Sides Relations*, Taipei: The Mainland Affairs Council, January 1992, p. 44.

of the people shall honor the Constitution, accept the indivisibility of Taiwan and Mainland China, and reject communism,[14] thus, the above-mentioned polls may be also psychologically biased against Taiwan's independence. Beijing meanwhile reiterates its threat to use military force against Taiwan if Taiwan proclaimed independence. This threat may serve as another leverage to check the forces advocating Taiwan's independence in Taiwan. Some political observers in Taiwan say a more likely range of support for the cause of Taiwan independence would be from '20 per cent to 30 per cent'.[15] The author would argue, however, if Taiwan's people could completely free themselves from the persecution and/or repression of the National Security Law and the military threat of Beijing; the advocacy for the cause of Taiwan's independence should be at least over 40 per cent.

In May 1993, Taipei's Foundation for Public Opinion Research conducted another poll right after the Koo-Wang talks were held between the two Chinas. This survey found that 23 per cent of the sample advocated Taiwan's independence, the highest percentage to date. Whether even more Taiwanese Chinese will support an independent Taiwan as Taiwan becomes more democratic is a potential development worthy of close attention.

## The Democratic Progressive Party (DPP)

The formation of the DPP is not only the fruit of Taiwan's opposition movement since 1949 but also marks a milestone in the ROC's institution of democratic politics. The DPP is an alliance of the main political dissidents in Taiwan. Its forerunner was the non-partisan opposition group *Tang-wai*. Until 1986, the *Tang-wai* was not a party but a 'loosely knit movement consisting primarily of small personality-based factions absorbed in large part in local issues'.[16] The main supporters of the *Tang-wai* organized a *Tang-wai* Campaign Assistance Corps to coordinate the campaigns of non-KMT candidates throughout Taiwan in the elections held in 1977, 1980, 1981, 1983, and 1985.

The main motive of the *Tang-wai* was the eventual formation of an opposition party in Taiwan. The political situation as recently as the early 1980s, however, was not ripe for such a move, mainly because of the KMT's objections. In order to avert political confrontations with the ruling KMT, the *Tang-wai's* members further expanded their organization, becoming the *Tang-wai* Association of Public Policy Studies (TAPPS, a quasi-political party) in 1984 rather than a formal political party,[17] as such parties were still banned in the ROC because of the continued existence of martial law.

Although the formation of TAPPS was illegal under the law of the ROC, the ruling KMT did not repress or prohibit TAPPS but sent its party officials to negotiate with representatives of TAPPS in order to maintain political stability and harmony.[18]

The KMT's moderate attitude toward TAPPS was a harbinger of political reform in the ROC in that it encouraged the opposition groups to take further action in forming their own parties.

Political conditions became more supportive of such a move in 1986. Some of the KMT's actions enhanced that possibility; for example, as mentioned earlier, the KMT established a 12-member policy group in May of 1986 to look into six major political issues. As well, Chiang Wego, the newly appointed secretary-general of the National Security Council (this institution oversees all the security agencies of the government), said in June 1986 that 'individuals or organizations in the face of conflicts should seek to reach consensus on major issues and allow minor differences to remain'.[19] These actions further revealed the KMT's preparedness to compromise with opposition groups to consider the practise of democratic politics and led the members of TAPPS to believe that the formation of their party would not result in political repression because the KMT would tolerate the move for the sake of political harmony.

On 28 September 1986, at the third session of TAPPS and without virtually any advance notice, members of TAPPS abruptly announced the formation of the DPP.[20] As expected, the ruling KMT did not suppress the new party but stated that 'our policy of exchanging views with non-partisans to safeguard social stability and promote democracy has never changed'.[21] The KMT's concession towards the DPP substantially advanced the cause of democratization in the ROC. In January 1989, the ROC's Legislative Yuan passed the Civic Organization Law[22] which governs the registration of political and social groups. This law also created an institutional framework within which the DPP and other *de facto* opposition groups can coexist and compete with the KMT for the first time in the history of the ROC.

## The DPP and the Taiwan Independence Movement

Like many new parties, the DPP was at first troubled by factional infighting and a shortage of talent. This plagued the party's development and initially reduced its capacity to compete with the KMT. The infighting was due to differing viewpoints concerning the DPP's ideology and its policy toward the KMT and the PRC.[23] There were and still are two main factions in the DPP: the 'Formosa faction' (*Mei-li-tao Pai*) and the 'New Tide Faction' (*Hsin-chao-liu Pai*).

The *Mei-li-tao Pai* is led by Huang Hsin-chieh, the third term chairman of the DPP. This latter faction favors competition with the KMT through the 'parliamentary approach' rather than employing mass or street demonstrations, regarding the latter approach as a failure because it inconveniences the people and incurs the people's displeasure and also causes tensions between the KMT and the DPP. Although the Formosa faction also supports the idea of Taiwan's independence, it hardly openly discusses it. It prefers to promote this idea through the indirect approach of encouraging 'self-determination' by Taiwan's Chinese. In sum, the self determination model of the Formose faction would be intended to resolve the problems of Taiwan's future political development by means of a plebiscite. Taiwan's peoples, thus, would be able to choose their own destiny.

The 'self-determination' model is not a paradigm as such but has been interpreted differently by different groups in the DPP. The New Tide faction openly refers to 'self-determination' as a synonym for 'Taiwan Independence'. Paisy Hsin-i Pen, the editor of an opposition magazine in Taiwan, says that, 'we can't say "independence" here, because we still can be put in jail. So we say 'self-determination'. That means the people in Taiwan have the right to choose their future'.[24] In fact, the rules of the game have changed, as on May 15, 1992 Article 100 of the Criminal Code of the ROC has been amended to legalize the expression as well as the idea of Taiwan independence within the scope of freedom of speech. The New Tide Faction maintains that Taiwan should become a new and independent country. The Formosa Faction, however, prefers to explain the idea of 'self-determination' in terms of democracy. It argues that the practice of 'self-determination' in Taiwan will possibly result in one of the following three outcomes:[25] the maintenance of the *status quo* of the Taiwan Strait if the KMT were to become the elected government; the achievement of reunification according to Beijing's terms if the PRC could persuade the Taiwanese Chinese to do so; or the independence of Taiwan if the Taiwan Chinese choose neither the KMT's nor the CCP's government.

The Formosa faction seems to believe that both the 'parliamentary' and 'self-determination' approaches, being both democratic operations by nature, are more acceptable to the ruling KMT. Hence, this faction's political goals, such as parliamentary reform, would therefore be more easily achieved. As well, the phrase of 'self-determination', compared with the expression 'Taiwan independence', is less provocative to both the KMT and the PRC. As Huang Hsin-chieh put it: 'in Taiwan, something we can always talk about but not have is mainland recovery. Something we always have but never talk about is our independence'.[26] Huang argues that the rhetoric of Taiwan independence could only lead to repression by the KMT and do no good for the realization of Taiwanese independence. Therefore, he argues that what Taiwan needs at this stage is democratization, especially a complete parliamentary re-election. When Taiwan can practise true democracy, the future of Taiwan (independence or reunification) can be decided by Taiwan residents through the means of a referendum. In relations between Taiwan and the mainland, this faction seems more interested in conducting a direct dialogue, on the basis of government to government relations, with the PRC. It also supports further expansion of the exchanges between the two sides of the Taiwan Strait.

Compared with the moderate approaches of the Formosa faction, the New Tide Faction seems to be more radical. It is also well-organized. The faction's main members are idealistic young people. They favor, it seems, 'mass' or 'street' demonstrations rather than the 'parliamentary' approach to politics because they believe that the former is the best way to bring pressure on the KMT to accept their political terms. They criticize the 'parliamentary' approach as being too mild and making too many compromises with the KMT, who, therefore, would not sincerely conduct political reform. They argue that political power should be obtained from struggle and civil disobedience rather than to expect that it would be given automatically by the ruling KMT. This faction strongly advocates the Taiwan Independence Movement and intends to transform the ROC into the 'Republic of Taiwan' with a new constitution, new parliament, and a new national flag and emblem. Yao Chia-wen, the second term chairman of the DPP, pointed out in March 1988—in his paper titled 'The New Political Situation during the Post-Chiang Ching-kuo Era in Taiwan and in the Strait'—that future political development in Taiwan will be a situation in which 'a new government is blueprinted, a new congress is expected, a new constitution is drawn up, and finally a new country grows'.[27] The full text of this paper rendered into the English language, maintaining the authenticity of this document, can be found in Appendix 13-1.

Yao's paper represents, to a large extent, the New Tide faction's political ideology and position towards Taiwan's politics and the PRC. In the meantime, this faction is less enthusiastic about conducting exchanges with the PRC. They suspect that the *rapprochement* between the KMT and the CCP might result in the sellout of the Taiwanese. Therefore, they prefer to maintain the DPP's 'Taiwanese consciousness' and not to communicate with the mainland.

## The Platform of the DPP's Mainland Policy

Despite its support of the eventual independence of Taiwan, the DPP's mainland policy plank of its platform advocates in the short-term the normalization of the relations between Taiwan and the mainland through exchanges and contacts on the basis of peaceful coexistence and competition. On 13 October 1987, the DPP at its Central Standing Committee Meeting passed the resolution entitled 'The Current Stage's Mainland China Policy of the DPP'. It stated that 'the future of Taiwan should be decided by the people of Taiwan'.[28] The important points of this resolution were:

(a) People should be allowed to travel freely between Taiwan and the mainland, to visit relatives, to travel, to look for relatives, and also to freely exchange postal and telecommunication services, and to sweep their ancestors' tombs.

(b) Contacts between individuals in the fields of culture, academic affairs, arts, technology and science, sports and economics should proceed on a basis of equality between Taiwan and mainland China.

(c) Both Taiwan and the mainland should abolish the policy of the use of force against each other. They should stop the infiltration of covert operations' agents within each other's territories, and end hostile political propaganda. By so doing, the relations between Taiwan and the mainland accordingly could be promoted from the stage of peaceful competition to the stage of peaceful negotiation, and mutual recognition. (d) The DPP's mainland policy would be divided into two stages. In the short term, Taiwan and the mainland should conduct the exchanges on an unofficial basis, while in the long term the two sides of the Taiwan Strait should hold political negotiations. Such negotiations, however, could only be held after the completion of Taiwan's parliamentary reform.

In April 1989, the DPP further elaborated on its mainland policy based on the above-mentioned four points.[29]

## The Resolution of 17 April 1988

On 17 April 1988, the DPP passed a resolution during its Plenary Meeting of the Second Party Congress and proclaimed that the DPP would advocate Taiwan's independence if the following four conditions occurred.[30]
(a)  if the KMT unilaterally embarked on talks with the CCP;
(b)  if the KMT betrayed the Taiwan people's interests;
(c)  if the PRC forcefully reunified Taiwan;
(d)  if the KMT does not sincerely attempt to bring about a genuine democracy.

This resolution obviously reflected the DPP's deep mistrust of the KMT. The DPP attempted taking a preemptive action to prevent a 'sell-out' of the Taiwanese by the KMT and the CCP. It was an elastic resolution. This resolution did reveal the DPP's ulterior motive to promote Taiwan independence through means of indirect expression. However, it could be interpreted that the DPP's refused to advocate Taiwan independence if the four 'Ifs' mentioned above did not occur. The reason why the DPP was so indirect about its pro-independence leanings was because of the tense political atmosphere and that situation in Taiwan at this time right after the death of President Chiang Ching-kuo in January 1988.

Those ROC citizens who openly advocate Taiwan independence within or outside of Taiwan can be punished according to the National Security Law and the sedition articles of the Criminal Law code. But this resolution was a big step for those who advocated Taiwan independence because they could openly talk conditionally about Taiwan independence. It also revealed that Taiwan's degree of democratization as evidenced by increased freedom of speech had proceeded to a considerable level. If so, would the DPP try again to challenge the KMT's will in the future under the blessing of democratization? Would the DPP directly and publicly advocate Taiwan independence without the talisman of 'Ifs' mentioned above? These questions are to be addressed in the latter sections of this chapter.

## The Constitution of the 'Republic of Taiwan'

After the 17 April Resolution, the pro-independence activists in Taiwan further expedited the task of realizing Taiwan independence. Several factors have encouraged the tendencies of the Taiwan Independence Movement. Dr. Lee Teng-hui has become the first Taiwan-born President. This event has brought great jubilation to some Taiwanese. The pro-independence activists intended to utilize this Taiwanese consciousness to promote Taiwan independence. As far as the pro-independence activists are concerned, the unification of Germany, the breakup of the Soviet Union, the emergence of independent Baltic states, and Beijing's approval of the admission of the two Koreas to the U.N. have made the unthinkable much more tenable. The biggest factor behind the Taiwan independence surge is the opening up of politics in Taiwan. Most restrictions on free speech and the press have been lifted. The December, 1991 elections for the National Assembly would be the first in which all the seats would be contested by candidates from Taiwan. In Spring 1992, the 3,250 seat National Assembly would re-examine and no doubt revise the 1947 ROC Constitution that defined Taiwan as a part of China. Both the DPP and the pro-independence activists intended to make the December 1991 election a referendum on independence.

In August 1991, the DPP held its People's Conference for the Instituting of a Constitution. During the session of the conference, the meeting delegates passed the constitutional draft for 'the Republic of Taiwan'.[31] In October 1991 during the 5th Party Plenum of the DPP, a clause for the creation of a separate 'Republic of Taiwan' and 'Taiwan independence' was included in the DPP's platform for the December 1991 elections to the National Assembly.[32]

While the DPP was enthusiastically pushing the Taiwan Independence Movement, some American politicians' speeches in 1991 further excited the DPP. James Lilley, the former U.S. ambassador to the PRC, accused Beijing of 'trying to impose its irrational system on more prosperous areas under the guise of 19th century sovereignty concepts'.[33] James A. Baker III, U.S. Secretary of State, called the PRC 'an anachronistic regime' [that] 'has alienated us by lashing out, by seeking to repress an irrepressible spirit'.[34] American President George Bush, in a speech named China, North Korea, and Burma 'the sources of instability in Asia'.[35] Natale Bellochi, Managing Director of the American Institute in Taiwan, pointed out that Taiwan has developed its unique and separate identity in the world and granting Taiwan an international status has become an international issue.[36] He stressed that internationally the legitimacy of Taiwan's political status has become a reality.[37]

## Beijing's Fury

There is no doubt that Beijing has always kept a close eye on the Taiwan Independence Movement. The Taiwan independence clause in the DPP platform has caused Beijing grave concern and inspired infuriation. Yang Shangkun, the President of the PRC at that time, lividly lashed out at the pro-independence activists and at leaders in Taipei who allegedly condoned pro-Taiwan independence activities. Yang and other Beijing leaders implicitly accused Taipei leaders, such as President Lee, of promoting a Taiwan that would remain technically part of the mainland but would never actually reunite in practice. The PRC has chided those foreign countries that urge Taiwan independence activists to split China for their interests and said that they would not take a wait and see attitude concerning Taiwan independence. They proclaimed that 'those who play with fire will be burned to ashes'.[38] This tirade was the most serious accusation that Beijing has made against Taiwan since 1979.

## Taipei's Dilemma

The DPP and Beijing's antagonistic stances have put Taipei into a dilemma. Any punishment meted out on independence activists might create the impression that the KMT was 'kow-towing' to the PRC and would thus anger the DPP and some Taiwanese who have frequently questioned the KMT's position between Taiwan and Communist China.[39] Also, the ROC's image as a democratic country would be damaged internationally if Taipei attempts to crack down on the DPP. At the same time, Taipei could not neglect Beijing. A 'do-nothing policy' could further provoke Beijing and again create tension between the two sides of the Taiwan Strait.

Taipei, nevertheless, is doing well in managing this dilemma. Privately, the KMT leaders redoubled their efforts to persuade the DPP to moderate its position on Taiwan independence.[40] President Lee Teng-hui even invited the DPP leaders for lunch in his mansion, and tried to ease tensions by urging them to mute their pro-Taiwan independence rhetoric for the sake of Taiwan's stability and security. During these discussions, he spoke in the Taiwanese dialect rather than in Mandarin, the official language used by both the ROC and the PRC, to mollify the DPP leaders and told them that 'Taiwan was already a nation with an independent sovereignty'.[41] Openly, President Lee tried to placate Beijing by charging that those who advocated Taiwan independence would be 'criminals in the history of Chinese culture'.[42] Lee said that China should be and would be reunified in the future and the independence activists would be suppressed by law.[43]

## The Setback of the Taiwan Independence Movement

The KMT however did not resort to using the law against Taiwan independence. It decided to leave this issue unresolved until the December 1991 elections which would be a good opportunity to test the Taiwanese people's attitude toward Taiwan's independence. In the early December election campaign period, the KMT's election slogans were 'progress, stability and prosperity'. The KMT told people that Taiwan's independence would bring disaster to Taiwan because the PRC would attack Taiwan, if necessary, to stop any move toward formal independence.

The KMT's strategy apparently paid off. The DPP in the

1991 National Assembly Election, because of its vehemently separatist stance, only acquired 23.94 per cent of votes in the election while the KMT parlayed that dread of uncertainty into a 71.17 per cent landslide at the polls. Noteworthily, even Lin Cho-shui, the leader of the New Tide faction and radical independence activist, failed in the election.[44] There was no doubt that the result of this election was not only a setback of the DPP but also a blow to the Taiwan Independence Movement. In an interview with the New York Times, Hsu Hsin-liang, the Chairman of the DPP, admitted that the 'cause of Taiwan Independence' scared off voters in December's 1991 Nation Assembly Election and led to the failure of the DPP platform.[45]

## The Future of the Taiwan Independence Movement

The implications of the December 1991 elections for the Taiwan Independence Movement are clear. The tide of the Taiwan Independence Movement seems to have abated for the time being. This movement would not disappear completely in Taiwan, it might well take many years, however, to recover its strength from such a heavy setback. The DPP, being the main patron of the Taiwan Independence Movement, also was confronted with the challenge of regeneration from failure in the elections. Logically speaking, the future of the Taiwan Independence Movement would depend on the future development of the DPP. Should the DPP become the ruling party someday in the future, the possibility of realizing Taiwan's independence would obviously increase. The continous objections of the PRC would always remain as the stumbling blocks to Taiwan's independence.

The infighting within the DPP since its founding in 1986 has never ceased. Such conditions seem to dim the DPP's prospects. The infighting reached its climax at the Party's Third Plenary Conference in October 1988 when both the Formosa and New Tide factions vied for the position of party chairperson. Quarrels, personal attacks, and violence occurred often during the conference. Although the Formosa faction won the election, the result almost split the DPP.[46]

Other serious intra-party squabbling recurred during the end of 1991, when both factions vied for the position of party's secretary-general. Annoyed by continual infighting, Huang Hsin-chiah, the former chairman of the DPP and the leader of the Formosa faction, even went so far as to wonder aloud, 'Why do we not split?', then stated emphatically, 'it is good for everyone!'[47] As a matter of fact, some moderate DPP members foresaw that raising the 'independence issue' would hurt the DPP at the polls, but they were more afraid that the radical wing would bolt from the party, if they insisted on holding a softer line. Obviously, the result of 1991 elections would sow further seeds of discord within the DPP. Therefore, the author would argue, maintaining party unity has become the most urgent task of the newly formed DPP agenda. Yet, it would still be no surprise, however, if the DPP were to be divided someday in the future.

The infighting has not only damaged the DPP's image, it being the biggest and the most influential opposition party, but also has hampered its goal of recruiting new members. When the newly formed DPP secured 23 per cent of the vote in the December 1986 Legislative Yuan election, DPP members were justifiably excited. Legislator Yu Ching (DPP) optimistically announced at a rally that the DPP would recruit 100,000 new members per year.[48] However, Yu's predictions have not yet come true. Apart from the 1,200 party founding members in September 1986, by March 1987 the DPP has only recruited around 1,000 additional members.[49] In November 1987, the total membership of the DPP was around 7,000 people.[50] By June 1992, it was reported in the media that the total membership of the DPP was approximately 40,000 people. As well, the level of education of these new members has also been problematic; most of the new members only reaching a high school level. These developments have not only deeply concerned the DPP's leaders[51] but also suggest that although 23 per cent of the vote went to the DPP, many voters still can not identify with the DPP. Perhaps the weak support for the DPP indicates public perception that it is not yet ready to govern.[52] The DPP's lack of talent also reflects on the quality of the DPP's members' questions raised in the Legislative Yuan. Most of the questions asked by DPP members have focused on issues related to politics while other issues, such as environmental protection, social welfare, economy and taxation that concern the general public have been rarely addressed by the DPP's legislators.

The DPP also faced another credibility problem: in January 1989, when the financial scandal of the Rong-hsin Garden Project was uncovered by the media,[53] both the KMT's and the DPP's deputies were found to be involved in corruption and graft. In mid-1992, a vote-buying scandal occured within the DPP prior to the December 1992 Legislative Yuan election. These events damaged the DPP's image as an alternative to the KMT, due to incriminating evidence and *de facto* liabilities.

In December 1992, the ROC scheduled elections for the Legislative Yuan. These elections were to be the first in which all 161 seats would be contested by candidates from Taiwan. This election event was to become another test for the DPP's popularity with the Taiwanese Chinese. If the DPP could secure more than 23.94 per cent of the vote in the 1992 elections, it would be a big blow to the ruling KMT and would increase the DPP's weight in ROC politics. If not, however, the DPP's prospects would only become dimmer and dimmer.

Learning from its failure in the 1991 election, the DPP changed its campaign strategy for the 1992 election. During the 1992 campaign, the DPP muted the rhetoric about Taiwan's independence, choosing instead to focus on criticizing and revealing the KMT's corruption and inefficiency and bribery in politics. The DPP pragmatically discussed public affairs issues that concerned the general public. This strategy paid off, as the DPP captured 31 per cent of the ballots cast and won a total of 51 seats in the legislature, its best performance since its founding in 1986.

The result of the 1992 election clearly manifest that voters in Taiwan are more concerned with public affairs issues than they are with abstract ideologies. The author ascribes the DPP's victory to the following reasons: a shrewd campaign strategy as mentioned above; and a vague feeling that people in Taiwan might reckon that the KMT, like Japan's Liberal Democratic Party in that country, has governed the ROC for too long, and therefore to give the DPP a chance when the time is ripe.

The result of the 1992 election is a clear warning to the KMT that the clout of the opposition is becoming stronger and that the DPP is well on the way to becoming a viable and vigourous opposition. The time has come for the KMT to seriously consider how to meet the challenges created by Taiwan's rapidly developing society.

## Conclusion

The origin and development of the Taiwan Independence Movement in each of the stages reflect the political environment of the times both within and outside of Taiwan. Today, the concept of the Taiwan Independence Movement, to some extent, has become associated with party politics in the ROC, and has become an issue of political competition between the opposition DPP and the ruling KMT rather than a political ideology. Both parties are now vying for political power through democratic means.

In fact, the ROC government by varying degrees realizes that freedom of speech is a very important principle in practicing a democracy that tolerates dissent. It can not suppress the rhetoric of Taiwan independence on the one hand, while proclaiming it rules a democratic country on the other hand. After a series of confrontations and negotiations in late 1991 and early 1992 between the ruling KMT and the DPP, the KMT finally has agreed to amend Article 100 of the Criminal Law which prohibits the freedom of speech pertaining to Taiwan's independence. After amendment of this article, the ROC government has promised not to suppress the rhetoric of Taiwan's independence as long as the independence activists do not actually undertake action, through force, violence, or coercive means, to realize Taiwan's independence. The opposition DPP, although not completely satisfied, has accepted this amendment.[54] This event has marked a milestone in Taiwan's political reforms and further perfects the task of the ROC's democratization. It should contribute to the harmony of Taiwan's politics and stability and, ultimately, the power balance in Asia as well.

What and where are the future prospects for the Taiwan Independence Movement? Perhaps this is the core question that concerns the China-watcher. Before answering this question, some basic developments of the Taiwan Independence Movement may help us to understand this question. Before the 1980s, the advocates of the Taiwan Independence Movement were radically opposed to the ROC government system because they did not have sufficient opportunities to take part in politics. They antagonized the ROC regime, did not identify themselves with the ROC government and in fact tried to replace the ROC by establishing the 'Republic of Taiwan'.

After the 1980s, however, the situation changed. After the implementation of political reforms, the opposition and the independence activists have had fair opportunities to participate in the government and promote their political ideas. If the DPP can defeat the KMT in elections in the future, they would become the ruling party in the ROC. In other words, Taiwan's independence can be realized in the future legally through democratic process and within the ROC government system as it exists today. If so, is there a need for a new 'Republic of Taiwan'? In fact, if the advocates of the Taiwan Independence Movement identify themselves with the ROC rather than picking up a new country name, Taiwan is already *de facto* and *de jure* an independent country.

Therefore, the author would argue that the Taiwan Independence Movement has become less important while Taiwan is gradually democratizing. The more Taiwan becomes a pluralistic society from a political point of view, the less enchanting the Taiwan Independence Movement would become. The result of the December 1991 National Assembly Elections has manifested that most of Taiwan's people want to maintain the status quo of Taiwan. They neither prefer Taiwan independence nor reunification with the mainland. Regarding the December 1992 elections for members of the Legislative Yuan, the author believes that the results are more of a mandate for democratic politics than a vote for Taiwan's independence. Most Taiwanese would like to see the DPP play the role of a watchdog, vigourously scrutinizing the ruling KMT for the short term, while not excluding the possibility of the DPP to run the government in the long term. The ROC on Taiwan has become a democratic country, thus, people can accept the reality of party politics.

# Chapter 14

■

## Some Prospects for the Future and Recommendations

As mentioned at the beginning of this book, the main purpose of this research is to study the two China issue from the viewpoint of Chinese in Taiwan. The study has focused on the following two principal areas:

To survey the policies and strategies of the two Chinese governments toward each other since 1979, and to ascertain whether the current *rapprochement* between the two Chinas will continue in the future and eventually lead to a peaceful resolution of the two China issue.

To study the viewpoints of the Chinese in Taiwan concerning the two China issue and to relate those viewpoints to the development of the ROC's political reforms in recent years. Subsequently, to evaluate the implications of these political reforms for the evolution of future relations between the two Chinas.

In the introduction, this book did not postulate any specific outcome for the resolution of the two China issue such as integration, disintegration, or maintenance of the status quo, in order to avoid supporting a preconceived idea. Rather, this book establishes six factors, which are: the economic and political systems of the Republic of China (ROC) and the People's Republic of China (PRC), Taiwan's public opinion, transactions between the two Chinas, Taiwan's politics, and the Taiwan Independence Movement, each of which could wield a decisive influence on the outcome of the two-China issue. Each of these factors represents an important element in the explanation of the issue's development. These factors are then used to examine relations between Taiwan and mainland China and to forecast the future development of these relations. Some conclusions therefore concerning the future evolution of the two China issue have been drawn from this research.

*The resolution of the two China issue has been and will remain a multidimensional phenomenon which requires multi-dimensional measurement and analysis over a long period of time*. This study has found that the two China issue encompasses the analysis of the emerging multiple areas of politics, economic systems and ideology between the two Chinas. This requires multidimensional and multivariate description and survey. The PRC seems to oversimplify the conditions, factors, and phenomena of the political integration of Taiwan and the mainland. Beijing has merely described only part of the components of the two China issue—such as nationalism, patriotism, common heritage, family reunion, and so on—and ignored the divergent social, economic, and political systems that have developed in the two sides during four decades of separation.

In addition, major conceptual problems, as well as disagreements about the timing and models related to the resolution of the two China issue, remain between the two Chinese governments. This reflects a gap in perceptions of the two China issue between the two sides. Beijing's leaders, to some extent, seem to believe that the two China issue is purely a matter between the CCP and the KMT and can be simply solved once the two sides' leaders meet together. 'A smile at meeting, and enmity is banished', regardless of other relevant factors and conditions. Taipei's leaders, however, see the two China issue more broadly. They regard it as a matter involving China's modernization in politics and economics, ideology, and human rights. The two China issue, from Taipei's viewpoint, can not be solved 'until a major transformation occurs in the mutual understanding between the two sides, and the understanding of the political leadership or elites of one or both sides'.[1]

*The process of China's integration has been and will remain a 'learning process' in which the integration curve has risen and declined and will continue to undulate. Both Chinas have responded, and will respond, to each other's messages, needs, and actions cautiously and adequately and without resort to violence if they consider that proceeding with integration is in their interests.*

Beijing's peaceful approaches have undoubtedly helped to stablize the situation across the Taiwan Strait and have led neither Beijing nor Taipei to see any virtue in fomenting the war hysteria on which they once thrived. The PRC has appealed to the ROC's political elites with the policy of 'one country, two systems' in which Taiwan's right of autonomy would be maintained and the Taiwan people's life style and living standards would remain unchanged. Similarly, the ROC has responded with its own integration model, The Three Principles of the People, and promised the mainland Chinese that new rights and liberties would be given as a result of China's integration under its model, which would bring them more political, social and economic equality and greater material well-being.

The curve of China's integration, as Deutsch has hypothesized, is typical of integrating entities, and has shown ups-and-downs. The most salient example was the 'Massacre of 4 June 1989' in Beijing's Tiananmen Square. The Chinese in Taiwan were shocked by the PRC leaders' brutality in this incident. Hence, the number of Chinese from Taiwan visiting the mainland immediately declined to its lowest point since 1987.[2] Transactions and communications between the two Chinas seem to have stuttered temporarily. In the meantime, the PRC has accused Taipei of anti-Beijing behavior by sending in 'Kuomintang spies' to take part in the student movements.[3] Beijing therefore arrested 13 alleged 'Kuomintang spies' and a Taiwanese journalist who covered the story in the mainland (Subsequently, this journalist was released and expelled from the mainland) as a warning to Taipei.[4] Nevertheless, the 'Massacre of June 4' has probably not hampered integrative activities for too long, at least judging from political leaders' speeches on both sides. On 28 June 1989, Beijing first expressed its wish to continue the contacts and exchanges with Taipei.[5] Taipei responded on 2 August 1989, stating that it will conduct further transactions with the mainland on an 'incremental and solid basis'.[6] This shows that both sides have learned how to mutually respond to each other's messages and feelings during the process of integration. This lesson is important for the future of integrative activities.

*Transactions between the two Chinas, to some extent, have spilled over into the field of politics. It is argued here that the scope, extent, and frequency of transactions between the two sides will further expand and intensify, provided that political actors and interests groups on both sides desire to do so.*

The study of quantitative densities of transactions between the two Chinas has found that the gradual increase of transactions and communications between the two Chinas since

1987 should contribute, to some extent, to political *rapprochement*. Contacts and exchanges, starting from noncontroversial and simple problems, have fostered a more friendly political atmosphere across the Taiwan Strait. This resulted in Taipei's agreement to send, for the first time since 1949, its Finance Minister, Dr. Shirley W. Y. Kuo to attend the 22nd Annual Meeting of the Asian Development Bank held at Beijing in May 1989 and the Koo-Wang talks in April 1993. As transactions increase between the two sides, the attitudes, beliefs, and expectations of the political elites and people that could contribute to political integration may convergently evolve.

*The gradual increase of communications between Taiwan and the mainland will not result in political integration across the Taiwan Strait if the socio-economic and political conditions of the two Chinas remain unbalanced.*

This analysis has found that there are currently four main obstacles to China's integration. Beijing's 'one country, two systems' proposal intends to subordinate Taipei. This is currently unacceptable to the ROC. Similarly, Beijing does not want to accept Taipei's integration model, that is, reunification of China under the Three Principles of the People. Beijing's failure to exclude the possibility of the use of force against the ROC, and its strategy of isolating the ROC internationally, have constantly offended the Taiwanese Chinese people, devaluing Beijing's efforts to court the Taiwanese Chinese, and causing the Taiwanese Chinese to be suspicious about Beijing's sincerity concerning the peaceful resolution of the two China issue. The gap in living standards, and the differences between the political, ideological, and economic systems of the two Chinas also hamper the process of integration. Chinese from Taiwan, after a visit to the mainland, might find that the gap is too large between the two sides and might prefer to adopt the course of maintaining a status quo situation over a long period of time or disintegration rather than integration. The Taiwan Independence Movement will remain a variable factor to the integration of China especially when both Taipei and Beijing stumble seriously.

*No clear correlation so far exists between the Taiwanese Chinese' attitudes towards and behavior concerning transactions and the process of China's political integration. The assessment of the Taiwan people's attitudes towards political integration should be based not only on transactions data but also on the perceptions, expectations, and political commitments of the Taiwanese Chinese and their political leaders.*

During the course of the author's study, the author has found that the communication approach can serve, to some extent, as a useful model for evaluating the integrative process of the two Chinas. Applying this approach to transactions across the Taiwan Strait, however, has not revealed whether the formation of consensus and political integration is correlated with a simple motivation for more individual contact. The phenomenon of 'mainland fever' is currently widespread in Taiwan. However, analysis of transaction perceptions and behavior of Taiwanese Chinese can not show whether Taiwan's people are motivated by utilitarian reasons such as making money and travelling to the mainland, or by the desire for political integration with the PRC when they conduct transactions with the mainland. The transactions really do no more than reflect the phenomena of the transactions themselves—though, to a very limited extent, they might help us assess certain probabilities for the extent of the process of integration.

Furthermore, it is difficult to predict the role of non-transactional factors such as government policy and the instrumental motives of political elites, in the future process of China's integration by using the communication approach. Neo-functionalism provides another perspective from which to examine this problem. This study reveals the importance of the Taiwanese leaders' commitments to China's integration course. Before 1987, political leaders in Taipei were less enthusiastic about Beijing's appeals for integration, for fear that integration according to Beijing's patterns might lead to a loss of national control. After 1987, many factors (see Chapter 6) have contributed to Taipei's decisions to participate in the integration process. Among the factors, the former President Chiang Ching-kuo's permission to improve communication between Taiwan and the mainland is perhaps the most important in determining what role the ROC would play in efforts towards China's political integration.

*Political developments in recent years have added a new variable to the assessment of the integration process, especially the emerging force advocating Taiwan's disintegration from the mainland. This force, nevertheless, will be modified or checked as long as it sees benefits in abiding by the current transaction and communication patterns.*

No clear correlation so far exists between the advocacy of transactions and political reunification between Taiwan and China as expressed by Taiwanese Chinese. Whether those Chinese who advocate transactions also support reunification needs further research.

The ROC is currently in a period of transition in its policies concerning relations between Taiwan, the mainland and the international community. This transition is caused by the perception of the Taiwanese Chinese that the old policy supported by the old guard can not ensure the survival of the ROC. Without new policies, the ROC will be unable to escape from the difficulties presented by the PRC's united front strategy and international isolation.

After the completion of parliamentary reform, with the old generation fading away and thus reducing resistance to the emergence of new policies, the Chinese in Taiwan might be able to reach a consensus on political integration. A new 'consciousness of the ROC in Taiwan' instead of 'the ROC in the mainland' would almost certainly be demonstrated through the reformed parliament. Such a policy would redefine the two Chinas' relations from the 'domestic' level (Taiwan and the mainland) to the international level (the ROC and the PRC); from the current non-recognition to *de facto* recognition and eventually to the *de jure* recognition of the PRC. Taipei may also request Beijing's recognition in return.

In the meantime, the ROC might seek to return to the international community and to secure other countries' recognition under a different name, such as 'Chinese Taipei' (the Olympic model), 'Taipei, China' (the Asian Development Bank model) or a similar one that can advertise the fact of the ROC's separation from the PRC and yet allow the ROC to remain on a par with the PRC internationally.

Meanwhile, the Taiwanese might not choose independence if the following three conditions are fulfilled: the KMT fulfills its promise concerning political reform in Taiwan, the KMT is able to break through international isolation, and there is normalization of the two Chinas' relations. In regard to the second and the third conditions, Beijing, of course, could exert influence to help to realize or to block the ROC's goal. In this regard, Beijing would have three policy options.

Beijing could insist on the current 'one country, two systems' policy, continue its military threat to limit Taipei's freedom of action, and attempt to block Taipei's access to international society. From the viewpoint of the Taiwan Chinese, this policy is hostile and, if implemented, would continue to foster resentment in Taiwan and increase support for Taiwan's independence, a development that the PRC does not want. Under these conditions, it is difficult to expect that the two Chinas' relations will be completely normalized.

Beijing could accept the 'two Chinas' model and co-exist with Taipei internationally on an equal-footing. The possibility of Beijing's adopting this option seems unlikely at the moment in light of Beijing's ability to counter Taipei internationally. This option also violates the PRC's long-time 'one China' principle.

Beijing could adopt the 'ADB model' or the 'Olympic model' to co-exist with Taipei. Beijing remains the sole legal Chinese government and possesses the main sovereignty of China while Taipei using the designation 'Chinese Taipei', shares part of that legality and sovereignty. This model has also been employed in the Asia-Pacific Economic Cooperation group and in the General Agreement on Tariffs and Trade (GATT). Under this option, the ROC could rejoin the international community and peacefully co-exist with Beijing under the 'one China' principle. This option would partially reduce the resentment of the Taiwanese Chinese at being isolated internationally and may prevent a declaration of Taiwanese independence. It could also help Beijing to avoid the political dilemma it would face over the situation of Taiwanese independence. If Beijing does not take action to prevent independence, it would not only lose prestige internationally but could also cause a political crisis within the PRC. However, if Beijing takes action, possibly employing military force, it would pay a costly price, both politically and economically, to regain Taiwan. Option 3 seems the most likely to be selected by Taipei and Beijing to manage their relations in the short term while retaining the hope of reunification in the longer term.

## Recommendations

According to Dun Li, of the 3,107 years of recorded Chinese history, 1,144 years, or 36.82 per cent, were years of the country's division.[7] Thus, the current separation of Taiwan and the mainland covers an insignificant span in Chinese history. Moreover, during years of division, a multi-state situation was often the case. Therefore, to both ancient and modern Chinese people, 'the existence of multiple political systems has not meant the discontinuity of "one China"; these multiple states still exist within the same cultural sphere of Chinese civilization'.[8]

In fact, the separation of Taiwan and the mainland in the past four decades has enabled the ROC in Taiwan to create the largest advance, in terms of material and spiritual benefits for the Chinese people, in the history of China. Undeniably, this achievement should be at least partially ascribed to the competition between the two Chinas that resulted from the separation. But Chinese history has always been one of union and division and one should not exclude the possibility that the two sides of the Taiwan Strait will be integrated sometime in the very long term, especially as the mainland gradually becomes a democratic society and attains better living standards.

In fact, the two China issue is by nature an issue about the modernization of China. Since Chinese students first put forward the slogans of 'democracy and science' in the May Fourth Movement in Beijing in 1919, the Chinese people have been trying to secure these two things for the purpose of national construction. Unfortunately, these slogans have so far been unrealized in the PRC; Beijing's students again shouted for 'democracy and science' in their ill-fated protest against the PRC government's corruption and authoritarian communist rule in mid-1989.

'Democracy and science', however, have been gradually and partially realized in Taiwan in recent years. It is believed that the big differences in terms of living standards, political and economic systems between the two sides of the Taiwan Strait at the moment are the main obstacles to reunification of the two Chinas. The author argues that if the PRC had the same kind of living standards and the same kind of democratic system as Western countries, the two China issue would become much easier to solve. The Taiwanese Chinese would have no excuse for refusing Beijing's offer. In light of this reality, the PRC government should ask itself why the Taiwanese Chinese do not presently favor reunification. The PRC should further expand its economic reforms, improve the mainland people's life, and undertake political reform before it again tries to court Taiwan. The ROC in the meantime needs to further improve its political system so that Taiwan can become a better model for the mainland and the developing countries of this world.

Technically speaking, the nature of the two Chinas' relations remains hostile despite the transactions and communications that have occurred in recent years. How to establish mutual trust and mutual respect between the two sides has become the first priority for the continuance and strengthening of China's integrative process. Here, the author again utilizes Deutsch's idea of a 'security community' as a guideline for both Chinas to manage their relations. The two Chinas can implement a peaceful 'no-war' condition across the Taiwan Strait on the basis of the 'one China' principle but with the reality of 'two equal and independent governments' so that the integrative process between the two sides can proceed smoothly or in other words, establishing a 'pluralistic security community' in the Taiwan Strait region. The two Chinas should seek to finalize the integration course leading to reunification, provided that all the obstacles such as the gap of living standards and the difference of political systems that hamper the process of China's integration are removed and thus establish an 'amalgamated security community'.

If the above suggestion is acceptable to both Chinas, the two Chinas should establish an adequate and non-official supranational organization or institution across the Taiwan Strait so that the transactional and communicational load between the two sides can be properly expedited. The best location for such a organization is in Hong Kong. Through this organization, the two Chinas can not only directly channel their ideas, needs, and messages, but also systematise their relations. Of course, establishing such a 'security community' needs consistent implemention of an integration policy endorsed by both Chinas and implemented over a long period of time. Chinese on both sides of the Taiwan Strait should work together with patience and understanding to foster a viable environment for the progress of China's integration.

Notwithstanding, the author would argue that the Chinese in Taiwan have, as a basic human right, the right to choose their own destiny and future. From the viewpoint of total national strength, Taiwan would be able to declare its independence if this was the ROC government's intention and the Taiwanese Chinese' decision made through the democratic process. Some world rankings concerning Taiwan in Table 14-1 support the notion that the ROC could have already become an autonomous sovereign state.

Table 14-1 indicates that, in terms of its land area, population, military power and economic capability, the ROC in Taiwan can be ranked as an upper middle echelon country. For the majority of countries in the United Nations to have no official ties with the ROC and for the ROC to be expelled from most international organizations therefore seems unreasonable. The cause of this situation should be partly ascribed to the ROC's insistence on contending with the PRC for political legitimacy and sovereignty over of the whole of China. Other countries have had no choice but to establish official ties with Beijing as it is the larger political power. Should the ROC modify its foreign policy and seek recognition from the international community as representing Taiwan only, it would likely be recognized because of its good record in developing both its economy and political system in recent years. As one Australian newspaper commented: 'if, however, Taiwan were to renounce its claim over mainland China there would be no sustainable reason for countries such as Australia not to extend diplomatic recognition to Taipei'.[9]

The integration of Taiwan and the mainland seems almost impossible at the moment, especially after the tragedy of the massacre of students in Beijing in June 1989. The brutality of the PRC government has again shaken the Taiwanese people's confidence in the communist party and in reunification. Until the PRC can prove that it is a democratic country following accepted civilized norms, the Taiwanese Chinese will not accept political integration with the mainland.

This book has revealed some suggestive trends for the prospects of a resolution of the two China issue. It is intended, however, that the results of this preliminary assessment be tested against other sources of information concerning the six factors examined and reinforced by follow-on research. Future research and analyses in this regard can still employ the neo-functionalist approach to focus on the following topics. Will the PRC's leaders change the present Taiwan policy in the post-Deng era? Will the ROC's leaders or the Taiwanese Chinese opt for the disintegration alternative and openly declare Taiwan's

**Table 14-1:** The World Rankings of the ROC on Taiwan

| Type of Rankings | Rank of Taiwan in the World | Number of Countries Evaluated | Period Covered |
|---|---|---|---|
| Total Land Area | Lower middle 122 | 188 | 1982 |
| Population | Upper middle 41 | 187 | 1981 |
| Most Powerful Nations[1] | Upper middle 12 | 77 | 1980 |
| Most Powerful Military Nations[2] | Top 10 | 50 | 1980 |
| Economic Capability Assessment[3] | Lower middle 41 | 70 | 1980 |

1. Total power = critical mass + economic capability + military capability (national strategy + national will).
2. Equivalent units of combat capability = manpower × coefficient average (consisting of four elements: manpower quality, weapon effectiveness, infrastructure and logistical and organizational quality).
3. Total = GNP + energy + critical minerals + industrial production + food + world trade.

*Source:* Thomas Kurian, (ed.), *The New Book of World Rankings*, New York: Facts on File, Inc., 1984.

separation from the mainland after the completion of Taiwan's parliamentary reform? If declared separation comes to pass, what will Beijing's response be? If not, will Beijing accept Taipei's demand for equal status in the international community? What are the attitudes of the younger generations on both sides concerning the two China issue? Do they perceive the issue differently from their parents? If they do, what does this mean for the resolution of the two China issue? If not, why not?

In addition, transaction flows of the communication approach will remain a useful indicator of the level of China's integration. Will the transactions between the two sides spill quickly over into the political fields? If so, under what conditions? What quantitative densities of transactions are needed for such a spill-over to take place? In future research, however, the influence of the international situation as well as the military dimension should not be ignored. Answers to these questions mentioned above will offer further insight into the eventual resolution of the China issue.

# Notes to the Introduction

1. 'Deng Xiaoping's Comments on the Reunification of the Mainland and Taiwan', *Renmin Ribao*; 30 July 1983, p. 1 (in Chinese). See also 'Message to Compatriots in Taiwan', *Beijing Review*, 5 January 1979, p. 16.

2. Yu-ming Shaw, 'Taiwan: A View From Taipei,' *Foreign Affairs*, 63,5, Summer 1985: 1053–4.

3. 'The Ruling Party Remains the Revolutionary Democratic Party', *United Daily News*, 16 June 1988, p. 1 (in Chinese).

4. 'Dr. Sun Yat-sen's Will', *The Three Principles of the People*, Taipei: China Publishing Co., 1981, p. v.

5. Wang Gungwu, *China and the World Since 1949: The Impact of Independence, Modernity and Revolution*, London: The MacMillan Press, 1977, p. 23.

6. 'Dr. Sun Yat-sen's Will', see note 4 above. See also 'Peng Zhen's Speech at the Beijing Meeting: Commemorating Dr. Sun's 120th Birthday', *BR*, 17 November 1986, pp. 21–4.

7. *Central Daily News (International Edition)*, *CDN(IE)*, 24 July 1986, p. 1; and 5 March 1986, p. 1 (in Chinese).

8. 'Deng Xiaoping on China's Reunification', *BR*, 8 August 1983, p. 5.

9. Deng Xiaoping, 'Uphold the Four Cardinal Principles (30 March 1979)', *Selected Works of Deng Xiaoping (1975–1982)*, Beijing: People's Publishing House, 1983, pp. 153–4 (in Chinese). For the sake of expediting economic development, Deng Xiaoping, since 1992, has changed his attitude toward capitalism, moreover, he has persuaded other leaders to study features from capitalism which would benefit China's economic development. See *The Nineties*, April 1992, p. 50 (in Chinese).

10. Many students of politics are still unclear about exactly 'what is communism?' A clear definition of communism can be found in K. Marx & F. Engels, *The German Ideology—Part One*, London: Lawrence & Wishart, 1970), p. 54. During an interview on 2 September 1986 with Mike Wallace from Columbia Broadcasting System of the US, Deng Xiaoping also defined communism. He said that 'during the "Cultural Revolution" there was a view that poor communism was preferable to rich capitalism. . . . I criticized that view. . . . I refuted that view. . . . According to Marxism, communist society is based on an abundance of material wealth. Only when there is an abundance of material wealth, can the principle of a communist society, i.e. "from each according to his ability and to each according to his need", be practiced'. See 'Deng On Issues of World Interest,' *BR*, 22 September 1986, p. 6.

11. Yu-ming Shaw, 'The Republic of China's Response To International Developments', *Issues & Studies*, July 1985: 27.

   12. Ambassador John H. Holdridge, the then Assistant Secretary for East Asian and Pacific Affairs of the Department of State, USA, used these words before the U.S. Congress House of Representatives Foreign Affairs Committee on 16 July 1981; see *Department of State Bulletin*, 81, 2055, October 1981: 38.

   13. For the entire text of the address, see *CDN(IE)*, 21 May 1990, p. 2.

   14. The principal literature of integration theory includes the following: Ernst B. Haas, 'The Study of Regional Integration: Reflections on the Joy and Anguish of Pre-theorizing', *International Organization*, XXIV, 4, Autumn 1970; Joseph Frankel, *Contemporary International Theory and the Behavior of States*, Oxford: Oxford University Press, 1973; Paul Taylor, 'The Functionalist Approach to the Problem of International Order: A Defence', *Political Studies*, XVI, 3, 1968; James E. Dougherty and Robert L. Pfaltzgraff, Jr., *Contending Theories of International Relations: A Comprehensive Survey*, 2nd Ed., New York: Harper & Row, Publishers, 1981; David Mitrany, *A Working Peace System*, Chicago: Quadrangle Books, 1966; A. J. R. Groom and Paul Taylor, 'Functionalism and International Relations', in Groom and Taylor, (eds.), *Theory and Practice in International Relations: Functionalism*, New York: Crane, Russak, 1975; Karl W. Deutsch et al., *Political Community and the North Atlantic Area: International Organization In the Light of Historical Experience*, Princeton, N.J.: Princeton University Press, 1957; Donald J. Puchala, *International Politics Today*, New York: Dodd & Mead, 1971; Donald J. Puchala, 'International Transactions and Regional Integration', *International Organization*, 24, 4, Autumn 1970; Ernst B. Haas, *The Uniting of Europe: Political, Social, and Economic Forces 1950–1957*, Stanford: Stanford University Press, 1958; Amitai Etzioni, *Political Unification: A Comparative Study of Leaders and Forces*, New York: Holt, Rinehart and Winston, 1965; Joseph S. Nye, *Pan-Africanism and East African Integration*, Cambridge, Mass.: Harvard University Press, 1965; Leon N. Lindberg, *The Political Dynamics of European Economic Integration*, Stanford: Stanford University Press, 1963; Leon N. Lindberg, 'Political Integration As A Multidimensional Phenomenon Requiring Multivariate Measurement', *International Organization*, XXIV, 4, Autumn 1970; Philip E. Jacob and Henry Teune, 'The Integration Process: Guidelines for Analysis of the Bases of Political Community', in Philip E. Jacob and James V. Toscano, (eds.), *The Integration of Political Communities*, Philadelphia: J. B. Lippincott Co., 1964; Charles Pentland, *International Theory and European Integration*, London: Faber and Faber, 1973; James A. Caporaso and Alan L. Pelowski, 'Economic and Political Integration in Europe: A Time-Series Quasi-Experimental Analysis', *American Political Science Review*, 65, 2, June 1975; Johan Galtung, 'A Structural Theory of Integration', *Journal of Peace Research*, 5, 4, 1968; Fred M. Hayward, 'Continuities and Discontinuities Between Studies of National and International Political Integration: Some

Implications for Future Research Efforts', *International Organization*, 24, 4, Autumn 1970; Karl W. Deutsch, *Nationalism and Social Communication*, Cambridge, Mass.: M.I.T. Press, 1953; Karl W. Deutsch, 'The Impact of Communications Upon International Relations Theory', in Abdul Said (ed.), *Theory of International Relations: The Crisis of Relevance*, Englewood Cliffs, N.J.: Prentice-Hall, 1968; Karl W. Deutsch, *The Analysis of International Relations*, Englewood Cliffs, N.J.: Prentice-Hall, 1988; Robert W. Cobb and Charles Elder, *International Community: A Regional and Global Study*, New York: Holt, Rinehart and Winston, 1970; William E. Fisher, 'An Analysis of the Deutsch Sociocausal Paradigm of Political Integration', *International Organization*, XXIII, 2, Spring 1969; Ernst B. Haas, *Beyond the Nation-State: Functionalism and International Organization*, Stanford: Stanford University Press, 1964; Philippe C. Schmitter, 'Three Neo-Functional Hypotheses About International Integration', *International Organization*, XXIII, 1, Winter 1969; Joseph S. Nye, *Peace in Parts: Integration and Conflict in Regional Organization*, Boston: Little, Brown, 1971; Leon N. Lindberg and Stuart A. Scheingold, *Europe's Would-Be Policy: Patterns of Change in the European Community*, Englewood Cliffs, N.J.: Prentice-Hall, 1970; Ernst B. Haas, Mary Pat Williams, and Don Babai, *Scientists and World Order: The Uses of Technical Knowledge in International Organizations*, Berkeley: University of California Press, 1977; Joseph S. Nye, 'Comparative Regional Integration: Concept and Measurement', *International Organization*, XXII, 4, Autumn 1968; Henry R. Nau, 'From Integration to Interdependence: Gains, Losses, and Continuing Gaps', *International Organization*, 33, 1, Winter 1979; Ernst B. Haas, 'Turbulent Fields and the Theory of Regional Integration', *International Organization*, 30, 2, Spring 1976.

15. Ernst B. Haas, 'The Study of Regional Integration', see note 14 above; p. 623.

16. The main works of the communication theorists include the following: Karl W. Deutsch, *Nationalism and Social Communication*, Cambridge, Mass.: M.I.T. Press, 1953; Karl W. Deutsch, *Political Community and the North Atlantic Area*, see note 14 above; Karl W. Deutsch, 'Communication Theory and Political Integration', in Philip E. Jacob and James V. Toscano, (eds.), *The Integration of Political Communities*, see note 14 above; Karl W. Deutsch, 'The Impact of Communications Upon International Relations Theory', in Abdul Said, (ed.), *Theory of International Relations: The Crisis of Relevance* see note 14 above; Karl W. Deutsch, *The Analysis of International Relations*, see note 14 above; Robert W. Cobb and Charles Elder, *International Community: A Regional and Global Study*, see note 14 above; Donald J. Puchala, 'International Transactions and Regional Integration', see note 14 above; pp. 732–763; William E. Fisher, 'An Analysis of the Deutsch Sociocausal Paradigm of Political Integration', see note 14 above; pp. 254–290.

17. Karl W. Deutsch, *The Analysis of International Relations*, see note 14 above; p. 271.

18. See note 17 above, pp. 271–272.

19. See note 17 above, pp. 273–274.

20. See note 17 above, pp. 281.

21. See note 17 above, p. 275.

22. See note 17 above, p. 279.

23. See note 17 above, p. 279.

24. The main works of the neo-functionalist school include: Ernst B. Haas, *The Uniting of Europe*, see note 14 above; Ernst B. Haas, *Beyond the Nation-State: Functionalism and International Organization*: Philippe C. Schmitter, 'Three Neo-Functional Hypotheses About International Integration', *International Organization*, Joseph S. Nye, *Peace in Parts: Integration and Conflict in Regional Organization*, pp. 161–166; Leon N. Lindberg and Stuart A. Scheingold, *Europe's Would-Be Policy: Patterns of Change in the European Community*; Ernst B. Haas, Mary Pat Williams, and Don Babai, *Scientists and World Order: The Uses of Technical Knowledge in International Organizations*; Joseph S. Nye, 'Comparative Regional Integration: Concept and Measurement', *International Organization*, pp. 855–880; Henry R. Nau, 'From Integration to Interdependence: Gains, Losses, and Continuing Gaps', *International Organization*, pp. 119–147; Ernst B. Haas, 'Turbulent Fields and the Theory of Regional Integration', *International Organization*, pp. 173–212.

25. Ernst B. Haas, 'The Study of Regional Integration', p. 627.

26. Ernst B. Haas, *The Uniting of Europe*, pp. 283–298.

27. Ernst B. Haas, *Beyond the Nation State*, p. 38.

28. Ernst B. Haas, 'The Uniting of Europe and the Uniting of Latin America', *Journal of Common Market Studies*, V, June 1967: p. 324.

29. Ernst B. Haas, *The Uniting of Europe*, p. 285.

30. Ernst B. Haas, 'The Study of Regional Integration', p. 627.

31. Ronald Inglehart, 'An End to European Integration?' *American Political Science Review*, LXI, 1, March 1967, pp. 91–105.

32. Philippe C. Schmitter, p. 105.

33. For details, see Amitai Etzioni, *Political Unification*, pp. 138–183.

34. Joseph S. Nye, *Peace in Parts*, p. 93.

35. Ernst B. Haas, 'The Study of Regional Integration', pp. 628–629.

36. Donald J. Puchala, 'Integration and Disintegration in Franco-German Relations, 1954–1965', *International Organization*, p. 220.

37. Ernst B. Haas, 'The Study of Regional Integration', p. 628.

38. See Joseph S. Nye, *Peace in Parts*.

39. See Bruce M. Russett, *International Regions and the International System: A Study in Political Ecology*, Chicago: Rand McNally, 1967.

40. Ernst B. Haas, The Uniting of Europe, p. xxxvi.

41. Fred M. Hayward, 'Continuities and Discontinuities', p. 934.

# Notes to Chapter 1

1. Ernst B. Haas, 'The Study of Regional Integration: Reflections on the Joy and Anguish of Pretheorizing,' *International Organizations*, 24, 4, Autumn (1970): 608. See also Karl W. Deutsch, *Political Community at the International Level: Problems of Definition and Measurement*, Garden City, N.Y.: Doubleday & Co., 1954, pp. 42–5.

2. Leon N. Lindberg, 'Political Integration As a Multidimensional Phenomenon Requiring Multidimensional Measurement', *International Organization*, 24, 4, Autumn (1970): 649.

3. For those who are interested in the two Chinas' relations during the period of 1949–78, see the following materials: *The Collected Documents Concerning the Liberation of Taiwan (1949–1971)*, Hong Kong: The Institute of Contemporary China Studies, 1972 (in Chinese); Ramon H. Myers (ed.), *Two Chinese States*, Stanford, Ca.: Hoover International Studies, 1979; Hungdah Chiu (ed.), *China and the Taiwan Issue*, New York: Praeger, 1979; William R. Kintner and John F. Copper, *A Matter of Two Chinas*, Philadelphia: Foreign Policy Research Institute, 1979; Yung-Hwan Jo (ed.), *Taiwan's Future*, Hong Kong: Union Research Institute, 1974; Hungdah Chiu and Shao-chuan Leng, (eds.), *China: Seventy Years After the 1911 Hsin-Hai Revolution*, Charlottesville, Virginia: University Press of Virginia, 1984; Ralph N. Clough, *Island China*, Cambridge, Mass: Harvard University Press, 1978.

4. 'Message to Compatriots in Taiwan', *BR*, January 5, 1979, pp. 16–17.

5. 'Shelling of Jinmen and Other Islands Stopped,' *BR*, 5 January 1979, p. 4. Beijing also reduced its troops in the Fujian area and shifted them to the Sino-Vietnamese and Sino-Soviet borders; see Jay Mathews, 'China Seen Shifting Troops Away From Taiwan,' *The Washington Post*, 2 January 1979, p. A9.

6. 'Ye Jianying On Policy for Peaceful Reunification (September 30, 1981)', *BR*, 3 February 1986, p. 24.

7. This is the Fourth Constitution of the PRC since its founding in 1949. The first one was adopted in September 1954; the second one in 1975; and the third one in March 1978. Each constitution reflects the background of the PRC's power struggles and political transformation during that time.

8. *The Constitution of the People's Republic of China*, Beijing: Foreign Languages Press, 1983, p. 27.

9. 'Deng Xiaoping on China's Reunification', *RMRB*, 30 July 1983, p. 1 (in Chinese).

10. See Note 9 above.

11. Deng Xiaoping, *Building Socialism With Special Chinese Charac-*

*teristics*, Beijing: People's Publishing House, 1985, pp. 17–19, 29–33, 40,141 (in Chinese).

12. Deng Xiaoping, 'The Speech of Deng Xiaoping on the Third Conference of the Central Advisory Committee of the Chinese Communist Party', *RMRB*, 1 January 1985, p. 1.

13. C. L. Chiou, 'Dilemmas in China's Reunification Policy Toward Taiwan', *Asian Survey*, 26, 4, April (1986): 469.

14. For details, see *The Joint Declaration of the People's Republic of China and the United Kingdom of Great Britain and Northern Ireland Concerning the Hong Kong Issue*, Beijing: Foreign Languages Press, 1984, pp. 3–6.

15. *RMRB*, 1 January 1985, p. 1.

16. Li Jiaquan, 'Formula for China's Reunification', *BR*, 3 February, 1986, pp. 19–20.

17. Deng Xiaoping, 'Building Socialism With Chinese Characteristics', *Fundamental Issues In Present-Day China*, Beijing: Foreign Languages Press, 1987, p. 53.

18. Li Jiaquan, 'Formula for China's Reunification', p. 19.

19. Kuo Jui-hua, *On the Theory and Practice of Communist China's Policy of 'One Country, Two Systems'*, an unpublished M.A. thesis of the Institute of the Mainland China Affairs, Chinese Culture University, Taipei, Taiwan, R.O.C., 1988, p. 25 (in Chinese).

20. Joanne Jaw-ling Chang, *United States-China Normalization: An Evaluation of Foreign Policy Decision Making*, Occasional Papers / Reprint Series in Contemporary Asian Studies, No. 4—1986 (75), School of Law, University of Maryland, U.S.A., p. 79.

21. James C. Hsiung, 'The Uneasy Tranquility Across the Taiwan Strait', a paper presented at the Conference on 'Major Current Issues in East Asia', at St. John's University, USA, 25–6 October, 1985, p. 11.

22. Shaw Yu-ming, 'Taiwan: A View From Taipei', *Foreign Affairs*, 63, 5, Summer (1985): 1054.

23. James C. Hsiung, 'The Uneasy Tranquility Accross the Taiwan Strait', p. 11.

24. Thomas J. Bellows, 'Normalization: A Taiwan Perspective', *Asian Affairs*, 6, July/August (1979): 339–358.

25. Karl W. Deutsch, *The Analysis of International Relations*, p. 197.

26. *RMRB*, 1 February 1979, p. 1.

27. *RMRB*, 1 March 1979, p. 1.

28. *Wen Wei Po*, 20 October 1979, p. 2 (in Chinese). See also Fox Butterfield, 'Peking Says Taiwan Can Keep Autonomy Under Unification', *New York Times*, 10 January 1979, p. A1.

29. *Ta Kung Po*, 21 May, 1980, p. 2 (in Chinese).

30. C. L. Chiou, 'Dilemma in China's Reunification', p. 470.

31. *Ta Kung Po*, 1 October 1981, p. 1.

32. See 'Message to Compatriots in Taiwan', *BR*, 5 January 1979, p. 17.

33. See Jon Nordheimer, 'Reagan Says U.S. Must Continue Its Support of Taiwan Regime', *New York Times*, 14 February 1976, p. 22; and Howell Raines, 'Reagan, Conceding Misstatements, Abandons Plan on Taiwan Office', *New York Times*, 26 August 1980, pp. A1 and B7.

34. 'Joint Communique of the United States and the People's Republic of China, 17 August 1982', *Weekly Compilation of Presidential Documents*, 23 August 1982, pp. 1039–1040. See also 'China, US Issue Joint Communique', *BR*, 23 August 1982, pp. 14–5.

35. For details, see John H. Holdridge's speech before the House Foreign Affairs Committee on 18 August 1982, 'US-China Joint Communique', *Department of State Bulletin*, October (1982): 19–22.

36. *RMRB*, 2 September 1982, p. 2.

37. *RMRB*, 5 June 1983, p. 1.

38. *RMRB*, 19 June 1983, p. 1.

39. Deng Xiaoping, 'More on "One Country, Two Systems"', *BR*, 6 April 1987, p. 22.

40. Li Jiaquan, see note 16 above, p. 19.

41. Deng Xiaoping, 'More on "One Country, Two Systems"', BR, 6 April 1987, p. 22.

42. James C. Hsiung, 'The Hong Kong Settlement: Effects on Taiwan and Prospects for Peking's Reunification Bid', *Asian Affairs*, Summer (1985): 48.

43. The following sources have been used to help analyze this policy: *The Joint Declaration of the People's Republic of China and the United Kingdom of Great Britain and Northern Ireland Concerning the Hong Kong Issue*, Beijing: Foreign Languages Press, 1984; Deng Xiaoping, *Building Socialism With Chinese Characteristics*, pp. 22–32, 40 and 55; *RMRB*, 5 June 1983, p. 1; *RMRB*, 5 August 1983, p. 1; *RMRB*, 19 December 1984, p. 1; *RMRB*, 1 January 1985, p. 1; Chen Linsheng, 'A New Undertaking of Socialist Practice in Our Country— A Preliminary Discussion on "One Country, Two Systems"', *Social Science Monthly*, (Shanghai), No. 11, 15 November (1984): 37 (in Chinese); 'A Significant Concept—Comrade Deng Xiaoping on "One Country, Two Systems"', *Outlook Weekly (Overseas Edition)*, No. 42, 15 October 1984, p. 8 (in Chinese); hereafter *OW(OE)*; 'Deng Yingchao's Talks With Reporters from Hong Kong and Macao', *Wen Wei Po*, March 30, 1985, p. 2 (in Chinese); Yao Iping, '"One Country, Two Systems" Is the Best Model for Peaceful Reunification of China', *Taishin Magazine* (The Voice of Taiwan), June 1986, pp. 3–5 (in Chinese); Guan Mengiue, 'The Issue of "Two Systems In One Nation" and the Expansion of the Patriotic United Front', *Jilin University Journal Bimonthly* (Social Science Edition), No. 4, 1985, p. 2 (in Chinese); Fei Muolong's comments on the seminar held by Hong Kong's Wen Wei Po concerning the Sino-British 'Joint Declaration',

*Wen Wei Po*, 29 September 1984, p. 2; Huan Xiang, 'The Formation Background of "One Country, Two Systems"', *Wen Wei Po*, 29 September 1984, p. 15; Qian Jingrui's speech on the 'Seminar Concerning the Economic and Social Developments Strategy and the Economic Reform in Hangchow', *Wen Wei Po*, 18 July 1984, p. 2; Qian Jaju, 'Will China Change Its Nature—On the Issue of "One Country, Two Systems"', *Jin Po Monthly*, No. 90, January 1985, p. 55 (in Chinese); Tian Zhili, 'A Summary of the Symposium on the Theory of International Relations', *Political Science Bimonthly* (Shanghai), No. 6, 1987, p. 57 (in Chinese); Din Li, 'From the Trend of World Economic Development to See the Important Strategic Decision-Making of "One Country, Two Systems"', *Journal of Henan University* (Social Science Edition), No. 3, 1986, pp. 10–15 (in Chinese); Deng Cao, '"One Country, Two Systems" and the Patriotic United Front', *Kuanming Ribao*, 4 March 1985, p. 3 (in Chinese).

44. 'Top Leaders Vow Taiwan Flexibility', *BR*, 25 March 1985, p. 7.

45. C. L. Chiou, 'Dilemma in China's Reunification', p. 470.

# Notes to Chapter 2

1. John Stuart Mill, 'Representative Government, 1861, reprinted in part in Alfred Zimmern,' *Modern Political Doctrines*, London: Oxford University Press, 1939, p. 206.

2. Message to Compatriots in Taiwan', *BR*, 5 January 1979, p. 16.

3. For example, see *Reunification of the Motherland Is Everybody's Responsibility*, Beijing: Beijing Publishing House, 1985 (in Chinese).

4. Huan Xiang, 'On Sino-U.S. Relations' *Foreign Affairs*, 60:1, Fall (1981): 48.

5. See Zhao Quansheng, 'An Analysis of Unification—The PRC Perspective', *Asian Survey*, 23, 10, October (1983): 1098–99. The other three reasons are: (a) the ROC challenges the PRC's sovereignty and attracts mainland dissidents, hence, the ROC by its very existence causes trouble for the Beijing government; (b) the separation of the two Chinas is symbolic of the interference by Western nations in the PRC's domestic politics; (c) the PRC is worried that after Taiwan's ageing ruling group passes from power, Taiwan might seek independence.

6. See *BR*, 19 October 1981, p. 15 and 20; 30 January 1984, pp. 21–3; 17 November 1986, p. 21; and others.

7. Sun Yat-sen, *The Three Principles of the People*, pp. 5, 6, and 17–18.

8. *Selected Works of Mao Tse-dong: Volume V*, Peking: Foreign Languages Press, 1977, p. 15.

9. Herbert S. Yee, 'China's Reunification Offensive and Taiwan's Policy Options', *The World Today*, January (1982): 33.

10. Dan C. Sanford, *The Future Association of Taiwan With The People's Republic of China*, Berkeley: University of California, 1981, p. 49.

11. 'Denouncing Kuomintang Congress', *BR*, 20 April 1981, p. 6.

12. For reference, see Graham T. Allison, *Essence of Decision*, Boston: Little, Brown and Company, 1971, pp. 1–33, 162, 168, and 171. See also Glenn H. Snyder and Paul Diesing, *Conflict Among Nations*, Princeton: Princeton University Press, 1977, pp. 348–9; Charles W. Kegley, Jr. and Eugene R. Wittkopf, *American Foreign Policy*, New York: St. Martin's Press, 1982, pp. 270–93, 493, 520; John D. Steinbruner, *The Cybernetic Theory of Decision* Princeton: Princeton University Press, 1974, p. 14; Michael P. Sullivan, *International Relations: Theories and Evidence* Englewood Cliffs, N.J.: Prentice-Hall, 1976, p. 272; Joseph Frankel, *Contemporary International Theory and the Behavior of States*, pp. 65–72.

13. James E. Dougherty and Robert L. Pfaltzgraff, Jr., *Contending Theories of International Relations*, p. 474.

14. 'Message to Compatriots in Taiwan', *BR*, 5 January 1979, p. 17.

15. 'Deng Xiaoping on China's Reunification', *RMRB*, 30 July 1983, p. 1.

16. John K. Fairbank's comment in Richard Moorsteen and Morton Abramowitz, *Remaking China Policy*, Cambridge, Mass.: Harvard University Press, 1971, pp. xiii–xiv.

17. Richard H. Solomon, 'East Asia and the Great Power Coalitions', *Foreign Affairs*, 60, 3, Special copy (1981): 694.

18. Chen Yun, 'Reunification on the Basis of One National Title and One Capital', *Cheng Ming*, August 1986, in 'The Little Supplement', p. 1 (in Chinese).

19. 'Liao Chengzhi's Letter to Chiang Ching-kuo', *RMRB*, 25 July 1982, p. 1.

20. 'Hu Yaobang's speech at the Beijing Rally in Commemoration of 70th Anniversary of 1911 Revolution', *BR*, 19 October 1981, pp. 14–21.

21. 'Message to Compatriots in Taiwan', see note 14 above, p. 17. Similar rhetoric can be found in 'Work Together to Invigorate China', *The Taiwan Issue: Its History and Resolution*, Beijing: Beijing Review, 1987, p. 110. Ironically, when Chiang Kai-shek died in 1975 the PRC reprimanded him as the 'common enemy of the Chinese people whose hands were stained with the blood of the revolutionary people of China', see 'Peking Calls Chiang "Traitor"', *New York Times*, 7 April 1975, p. 34.

22. 'Chiang Kai-shek's Hometown', *BR*, 13 October 1986, p. 24.

23. Frank S. T. Hsiao and Lawrence R. Sullivan, 'The Politics of Reunification: Beijing's Initiative on Taiwan,' *Asian Survey*, 20, 8, August (1980): 800–01.

24. Mao Tse-tung, 'Introducing the Communist', *Selected Works of Mao Tse-tung, Volume II*, pp. 285–300.

25. Mao Tse-tung, 'The Question of Independence and Initiative Within the United Front', and 'Introducing the Communist', see note 24 above, pp. 213–16 and 285–305.

26. *A Comprehensive Glossary of Chinese Communist Terminology*, Taipei: The Institute of International Relations, 1978, p. 332.

27. *The Dictionary of Political Economy*, Hong Kong: Chao Young Publishing House, October 1975, pp. 255–56.

28. Mao Tse-tung, 'Introducing the Communist', see note 24 above, pp. 285–93.

29. See *A Comprehensive Glossary of Chinese Communist Terminology*, p. 637; and the editorial, 'Chairman Mao's Theory of the Differentiation of the Three Worlds Is a Major Contribution to Marxism-Leninism', *RMRB*, 1 November 1977, p. 1.

30. 'United Front in the New Period', *BR*, 12 October 1979, p. 3.

31. An Zhiguo, 'Wider Co-operation With Non-Communists', *BR*, 29 December 1986, p. 4.

32. Li Zhiping, 'A Brief Remark About the Characteristics of the Patriotic United Front in the New Stage', *Jilin University Journal Bimonthly* (Social Science Edition), No. 5, 1985, pp. 58 and 60 (in Chinese).

33. Chen Li-shen, 'On the Strategy of Communist China's United Front', *Mainland China*, June 1986, p. 17 (in Chinese).

34. He does not elaborate on how he calculated this figure; therefore, the accuracy of this data is questionable. See Xu Xianzhang, 'On the Mission of the New Period's United Front', *Journal of the Northwestern Teachers College*, No. 2, (1985): 29 (in Chinese).

35. Peng Zhen, 'Speech at the Meeting Commemorating Dr. Sun Yat-sen's 120th Birthday', *RMRB*, 13 November 1986, p. 4.

36. *World Development Report 1981*, Washington, D.C.: The World Bank, August 1981, p. 134.

37. 'Hold High the Banner of Mao Zedong's Thought and Adhere to the Principle of Seeking Truth From Facts, 16 September 1978', *Selected Work of Deng Xiaoping 1975–82*, Beijing: Foreign Languages Press, 1984, p. 143.

38. See note 37 above.

39. See Jay Mathews, 'Deng Pledges China to Match Taiwan's Thriving Economy', *The Washington Post*, 11 March 1980, p. A14.

40. Deng Xiaoping, 'We Must Continue to Build Socialism and Eliminate Poverty, 26 April 1987', *Fundamental Issues In Present-Day China*, Beijing: Foreign Languages Press, 1987, pp. 177–8.

41. For details, see Wang Huijiong, 'China's Prospects for the Year 2000', *BR*, 4 November 1985, pp. 18–20.

42. For those who are interested in this aspect see Chu-yuan Cheng, 'China's Economy: New Strategies and Dilemmas', *Current History*,

87,530, September (1988): 253–56, 281, 302–04. See also Chu-yuan Cheng, 'Economic Reform in Mainland China: Consequences and Prospects', a paper presented at the 15th Sino-American Conference on Mainland China, organized by the Institute of International Relations (IIR), Taipei, June 8–12, 1986; and Jan S. Prybyla, 'Baogan Daohu: The Other Side', a paper presented at the 14th Sino-American Conference on Mainland China, organized by Ohio State University, Columbus, Ohio, USA, June 10–14, 1985.

43. *RMRB*, 20 April 1985, p. 1.

44. Deng Xiaoping, 'Speech at the Third Plenary Session of the Central Advisoty Commission of the Communist Party of China, 22 October 1984', *Fundamental Issues In Present-Day China*, p. 76.

45. See note 44 above, pp. 76–7.

46. For details, see 'An Interview With Mr. Hu Yaobang', *Pai Hsing Semi-Monthly*, 1 June 1985, pp. 5–7 (in Chinese).

47. All of these points are Beijing's position of long standing towards the two China issue and have been reiterated by the PRC since then on many different occasions since 1949. A clear explanation of these points could be found in the Shanghai Communique signed by the PRC and the USA on 28 February 1972 during U.S. President Richard M. Nixon's visit to the PRC. See 'Text of Joint Communique', *Department of State Bulletin*, 20 March (1972): 435–38.

48. Robert W. Barnett, 'China and Taiwan: The Economic Issues', *Foreign Affairs*, 50, 3, April (1972): 453.

49. Chiu Hung-dah and Jen Hsiao-chi (eds.), *A Study on the PRC's Negotiation Strategy*, Taipei: United Daily News Service, 1987, pp. 149–53.

50. Mao Tsetung, 'Things Are Beginning To Change', *Selected Works of Mao Tsetung, Volume V*, p. 445.

51. *Foreign Relations and Diplomatic Administration*, Taipei: Ministry of Foreign Affairs, December 1992, p. 30 (in Chinese).

52. 'Exchanges of Official Nature With Taiwan Opposed', *BR*, 29 March 1982, p. 7.

53. 'Note on Taiwan's Issuance of Visas', *BR*, 18 July 1983, p. 9.

54. In 1981, the Dutch Government sold two submarines to Taipei which incurred Beijing's dissatisfaction and its retaliation as Beijing reduced PRC-Dutch diplomatic relations to charge d'affairs level. See 'China Asks for Lower-Level Sino-Dutch Diplomatic Relations', *BR*, 26 January 1981, p. 9; and Yu Pang, 'Dutch Government's Bad Decision', *BR*, 2 March 1981, p. 22; 'China Recalls Ambassador to the Netherlands', *BR*, 9 March 1981, pp. 8–9.

55. Li Shenzhi and Zi Zongyun, 'Taiwan In the Next Decade', *Taiwan Studies Quarterly*, No. 1, 1988, pp. 3–4 (in Chinese).

56. See note 55 above, p. 5.

57. *A Study of the Possibility of the Chinese Communist Using Force Against Taiwan*, Taipei: Government Information Office, ROC,

1986, pp. 1–17 (in Chinese). See also Fox Butterfield, 'Peking Says Taiwan Can Keep Autonomy Under Unification', *New York Times*, 10 January 1979, p. A8; *Foreign Broadcasting Information Service, Daily Report: China*, 11 October 1984, pp. D1–2; 'Deng's Pledge for Hong Kong—But A Warning for Taiwan', *South China Morning Post*, 22 June 1986, p. 1; Chen Dengcai, 'The Peaceful Reunification of Mainland and Taiwan', *OW(OE)*, 27 June 1988, p. 8.

58. Ralph N. Clough, *Island China*, Cambridge, Mass.: Harvard University Press, 1978, pp. 30–1.

59. Yao Yiping and Liu Yuan, 'Taiwan: Prospects for Reunification', *BR*, 17 March 1986, p. 15.

60. Chen Bin, 'On the "New Idea" of Tackling the China Issue', *OW(OE)*, May 16, 1988, p. 7; see also Li Shenzhi and Zi Zongyun, 'Taiwan In the Next Decade', p. 8.

61. *China Times*, 18 April 1988, p. 2 (in Chinese).

62. Chen Fang-ming, 'The New Direction of the PRC's Taiwan Policy', *Democratic Progressive News*, No. 11, 27 May 1988, p. 19.

63. Huan Guocang, 'Taiwan: A View From Beijing', *Foreign Affairs*, Summer (1985): 1065–69.

64. Huan Guocang, 'Beijing Readjusts Its Taiwan Policy', *The Nineties*, 1 June 1985, p. 6 (in Chinese).

65. Lu Keng, 'An Interview With Mr. Hu Yaobang', *Pai Hsing Semi-Monthly*, 1 June 1985, p. 6 (in Chinese).

# Notes to Chapter 3

1. Fu Keng, 'Xi Zhongxun's Speech on the United Front Works Conference', *RMRB*, 4 December 1986, p. 4.

2. *Wen Wei Po*, 3 July 1993, p. 1 (in Chinese).

3. *United Daily News*, 6 July 1993, p. 1.

4. *China Directory 1992*, Tokyo: Radiopress, Inc., 1992, p. 27 and 140.

5. Li Ding, Deputy Head of the CCP's United Front Work Department, made such a comment to Taiwan's journalists in 1988, see *The Independence Morning Post*, 2 August 1988, p. 2.

6. Wang was quite active while in charge of Taiwan affairs during 1982; many overseas Chinese who went back to the mainland were received by Wang. See *RMRB*, 11 July 1982, p. 4; 29 August 1982, p. 4; and 11 September 1982, p. 4.

7. See *RMRB*, 6 February 1983, p. 4. See also *The Dictionary of Contemporary Chinese History*, Beijing: China International Broadcasting Publishing House, December 1987, p. 286 (in Chinese).

8. *China Directory 1992*, p. 1.

9. See Leo Suryadinata, *China and The ASEAN States: The Ethnic*

*Chinese Dimension*, Singapore: Singapore University Press, 1985, esp. Chapter 4 (in Chinese).

10. *China Directory 1992*, p. 139.

11. See *RMRB* (Overseas Edition), 2 February 1989, p. 1 (in Chinese).

12. See 'Mutual Benefit, Mutual Complement: Taiwan Businessmen's Investment in Mainland', *OW(OE)*, No. 37, 12 September 1988, pp. 21–2.

13. See 'Chen Wenyu's Comments Concerning the Establishment of A Stable Economic and Trade Relations Between the Two Sides of the Taiwan Strait', *OW(OE)*, No. 37, 12 September 1988, pp. 21–2.

14. Nan Ming, 'Six Thousand Brains Study Taiwan', *The Journalist*, No. 77, 4 September 1988, p. 65 (in Chinese).

15. *China Directory 1992*, p. 40.

16. Yi Hua, 'On the PRC's United Front Activities', *Mainland China*, June (1986): 24 (in Chinese).

17. *The Dictionary of Contemporary Chinese History*, p. 126.

18. Lu Wang-tai, 'Too Many Drawbacks Receiving Taiwan Compatriots: The Documents of the PRC Reveals the Scandals', *Cheng Ming*, March 1988, p. 19 (in Chinese).

19. See note 18 above, p. 22.

20. Han Wuyian, 'An Interview With the Chairman of the Committee for the Reunification of the Motherland,' *OW(OE)*, No. 33, 15 August 1988, pp. 5–6.

21. 'The Working Group for Reunification of the Motherland of the CPPCC is Founded,' *RMRB*, 30 September 1983, p. 4.

22. Han Wuyian, see note 20 above, pp. 5–6.

23. See *China Directory 1992*, pp. 181–86. See also Tan Fanzhi, (ed.), *The Dictionary of the Party's United Front Work*, Beijing: China Outlook Publishing House, 1988, p. 59 (in Chinese).

24. *The Dictionary of Contemporary Chinese History*, p. 117.

25. Editorial, 'Congratulations on the Foundation of the All-China Federation of Taiwan Compatriots', *RMRB*, 30 December 1981, p. 4; see also *RMRB*, 28 December 1981, p. 1 and 4; and *RMRB*, 17 July 1981, p. 4.

26. 'Introducing Taiwanese Associations on the Motherland,' *Jinji Ribao*, 16 November 1987, p. 3 (in Chinese).

27. See reports from *RMRB*, 29 December 1982, p. 4; 6 February 1983, p. 4; 22 July 1983, p. 4; 7 March 1985, p. 1; 4 June 1985, p. 3.

28. *China Directory 1992*, p. 245.

29. *Jinji Ribao*, 16 November 1987, p. 3; see also *RMRB*, 5 November 1981, p. 4.

30. Cheng Mu-hsing, 'The Mainland's Taiwan Watchers Are Watching Taiwan Everyday—The PRC's Taiwan Research Institutes', *The Journalist*, No. 78, 11 September 1988, pp. 45–6 (in Chinese). See also Chang Jindao, 'The Seminar of Taiwan Fellow-Students Association', *OW(OE)*, No. 35, 29 August 1988, pp. 697–98.

31. *The Dictionary of Contemporary Chinese History*, pp. 697–98.

32. Yu Hsien-ta, 'The Military Heads Convene the Huangpu Alumni and Students', *The Journalist*, No. 68, 3 July 1988, pp. 10–13.

33. See Si Shi, 'We Want to Go Back to Taiwan', *OW(OE)*, 31 October 1988, pp. 21–22.

34. For details, see Chang Jingdao, 'The Formation of the Association for Peaceful Reunification of China', *OW(OE)*, 3 October 1988, pp. 21–2. See also Nang Fang-su, 'The Mainland Formed the Association for Peaceful Reunification of China', *The Journalist*, September 26 October 2, 1988, pp. 16–18.

35. See Lee Chieh, 'The CCP Welcomes Hu Chiu-yuan,' *The Journalist*, September 26–October 2, 1988, p. 21.

36. *A Handbook for Taiwan Compatriots*, Beijing: China Construction Publishing House, 1987, p. 48 (in Chinese).

37. *China Times Express*, 17 October 1991, p. 1 (in Chinese).

38. Yang Jingling, 'On Taiwan Studies,' *Fujian Journal*, January 1987, pp. 60–1 (in Chinese).

39. See note 38 above, p. 61.

40. Terry Cheng, 'Think-tank Institute Studies Taiwan Links', *South China Morning Post*, 2 December 1987, p. 5.

41. Nan Ming, 'Six Thousand Brains Study Taiwan', p. 65.

42. 'The Mainland Studies Taiwan's Law', *Wen Wei Po*, 15 December 1988, p. 1.

43. See note 42 above.

44. 'Some Important Regulations Concerning the Contacts Between Our People and Taiwan's People', *A Note For Citizens Going Abroad*, Guangzhou: Liaison Office of Guangdong People's Government, July 1985, pp. 26–7 (in Chinese).

45. Karl W. Deutsch, *The Analysis of International Relations*, p. 200.

# Notes to Chapter 4

1. *Central Daily News*, 2 January 1950, p. 1 (in Chinese), hereafter *CDN*.

2. *CDN*, 11 October 1951, p. 1.

3. *A Brief Introduction of the Republic of China*, Taipei: Government Information Office, 1987, p. 2 (in Chinese).

4. *Q & A About the Republic of China*, Taipei: Kwang Hwa Publishing Company, September 1987, p. 13.

5. See Note 4 above, pp. 3 and 14.

6. At that time, most of the Taiwanese Chinese came from south China, and some had arrived as early as the Third Century A.D. It was not until the Sui Dynasty (581–618), however, that immigrants

from the Chinese mainland reached sizable numbers. The very first settlers were aborigines from Southeast Asia who were pushed into the mountains by subsequent waves of Chinese migrants. Immigration from the mainland continued until the Japanese occupation in 1895 and was resumed in 1945 when the Japanese departed. See *Q & A About the ROC*, Note 4 above, p. 21.

[7.] Joseph Frankel, 'Taiwan—The Most Stable Part of China?' *The World Today*, May (1976): 199.

[8.] For an example, see Thomas B. Gold, *State and Society in the Taiwan Miracle*, Armonk, N. Y.: M. E. Sharpe, 1986. See also Shirley W. Y. Kuo, Gustav Ranis, and John C. H. Fei, *The Taiwan Success Story: Rapid Growth With Improved Distribution in the Republic of China, 1952–1979*, Boulder Colo.: Westview Press, Inc., 1981; and James C. Hsiung (ed.), *Contemporary Republic of China: The Taiwan Experience 1950–1980* (New York: Praeger Publisher, 1981), especially Section 3, pp. 119–174; Walter Galenson (ed.), *Economic Growth and Structural Change in Taiwan*, Ithaca: Cornell University Press, 1979; K. T. Li, *The Experience of Dynamic Economic Growth on Taiwan*, Taipei: Meiya, 1976; Yuan-li Wu, *Becoming an Industrialized Nation: ROC's Development on Taiwan*, New York: Praeger, 1985; A. James Gregor, Maria Hsia Chang, and Andrew B. Zimmerman, *Ideology and Development: Sun Yat-sen and the Economic History of Taiwan*, Berkeley: Institute of East Asian Studies, 1981.

[9.] 'Tomorrow Will Be Better? Fredrick Chien's Comments', *The Independence Morning Post*, 12 September 1988, p. 2 (in Chinese). Hereafter *IMP*.

[10.] Wang Huijiong, 'China's Prospects for the Year 2000', *Beijing Review*, 4 November 1985, p. 19. Hereafter *BR*.

[11.] Deng Xiaoping, 'Build Socialism With Chinese Characteristics, 30 June 1984', *Fundamental Issues In Present-Day China*, p. 55.

[12.] *Economic Development 1991, Taiwan, Republic of China*, Taipei: Ministry of Economic Affairs, 1991, pp. 4 and 29.

[13.] See *IMP*. Note 9 above.

[14.] *The ROC Joins the UN*, a pamphlet issued by the ROC Foreign Ministry, May 1993.

[15.] *CT*, 20 January 1993, p. 11 (in Chinese).

[16.] 'ROC Now Almost Freed From Debts', Free China Journal, 27 February 1989, p. 8. Hereafter FCJ.

[17.] Yuan-li Wu, 'Income Distribution in the Process of Economic Growth in Taiwan', in James C. Hsiung (ed.), *Contemporary Republic of China: The Taiwan Experience 1950–1980*, p. 162.

[18.] Shirley W. Y. Kuo, Gustav Ranis, and John C. H. Fei, *The Taiwan Success Story*, pp. 33–5.

[19.] 'ROC Family Incomes Up', *FCJ*, 21 July 1988, p. 2.

[20.] The ROC Government has already taken measures, such as strengthening vocational training, launching more employment

assistance programs, and expanding the social welfare system, to prevent the income gap from further widening. See China Times, 29
August 1988, p. 1. Hereafter CT. However, whether these measures
are to be effective remains to be seen.

21 See President Lee's speech on 9 October 1988 for a celebration
of the ROC's 77th anniversary, *Commercial Times*, 10 October 1988,
p. 1 (in Chinese).

22. Jurgen Domes, 'Political Differentiation in Taiwan: Group
Formation Within the Ruling Party and the Opposition Circle 1979–80',
*Asian Survey*, XXI; 10, October (1981): 1011.

23. Wilbur W. White, *White's Political Dictionary*, Cleveland, Ohio:
World Publishing Company, 1947, p. 26.

24. Roy C. Macridis, *Modern Political Regimes: Patterns and Institutions*, Boston: Little, Brown & Company, 1986, pp. 212–3.

25. After World War Two, Taiwan was returned to the ROC from
Japan. On 27 February 1947, a (mainlander) policeman, while checking for smuggled cigarettes, had a row with a cigarette vendor woman
and abruptly gunned down a (Taiwanese) bystander. This incident
stirred up latent discontent of the native Taiwanese about the KMT's
suppressive rule at that time. A public demonstration resulted from
this incident the next day in Taipei and similar demonstrations spread
quickly throughout the rest of Taiwan. Approximately 10,000 to
30,000 Taiwanese Chinese were killed by KMT troops from the mainland stationed in Taiwan. This unfortunate incident has sown hatred
between the mainland refugees and the Taiwanese since then and
has hampered the process of integration within Taiwan's society.
After forty years, the memory of this unhappy incident has gradually faded from popular consciousness. Nevertheless, some Taiwanese
still use this incident as a reason to oppose the KMT's rule in Taiwan.
It is also still the bane of Taiwan's political cohesion. See *The Dictionary of Contemporary Chinese History*, Beijing: China International
Broadcasting Publishing House, December 1987, p. 286 (in Chinese);
Wei Ming, *Taiwan's February 28 Incident*, Hong Kong: The Seventies
Magazine House, 1975 (in Chinese). See also *Youth Daily News*, 20
March 1985, p. 2 (in Chinese).

26. Ambrose Yeo-chi King, 'The New Era of the Political Modernization
in Taiwan', CT, August 14–16, 1979, p. 2.

27. 'Will the Good Chiang Did Live After Him?' *The Economist*, 16
January 1988, p. 21.

28. The *United Daily News*, 7 February 1988, p. 2 (in Chinese).

29. Peng Huai-eng, *The Analysis of the Republic of China's Political
System*, Taipei: Times Cultural Publishing Company, 1987, p. 468 (in
Chinese).

30. The PRC has always inserted the One China principle and a
clause to the effect that 'Taiwan is a part of the PRC' in any communique when it established diplomatic relations with other countries.

For examples, see the documents related to the PRC's establishment of diplomatic relations with Australia, New Zealand, Japan and the USA. *BR*, 29 December 1972, p. 3; 6 October 1972, p. 12; 22 December 1978, p. 8. Beijing has also repeatedly emphasized that both sides of the Taiwan Straits stand in the same boat regarding the two China issue and have praised the Taiwan authorities for having 'always taken a firm stand on one China and having been opposed to an independent Taiwan.' See 'Message to Compatriots in Taiwan,' *BR*, 5 January 1979, p. 17.

31. James C. Hsiung, 'The Tranquility Across the Taiwan Strait', a paper presented at the Conference on Major Current Issues in East Asia, at St. John's University, New York City, New York USA. October 25–6, 1985, p. 2.

32. During the past forty years, the ROC has never renounced the idea that someday it will return to the mainland, or at least reunify with the PRC according to its conditions. In his address to the nation on the ROC's national day 10 October 1988, President Lee Teng-hui again stressed the belief that China must be reunified under the 'Three Principles of the People'; see 'President Lee Teng-hui's Double Ten Day Speech', *Commercial Times*, 10 October 1988, p. 1.

33. Hungdah Chiu, 'To Promote Taipei As the Economic and Trade Center of East Asia; To Peacefully Reunify the Two Sides of the Taiwan Straits', *China Times*, 29 July 1988, p. 2.

# Notes to Chapter 5

1. *The Washington Post*, 12 January 1979, p. A29.
2. *New York Times*, 3 October 1981, p. 5.
3. Editorial, 'The Way To Unification', *China News*, 26 September 1981, p. 2.
4. See *The Compilation of the Reference Materials Regarding Counter-Attacking Communist Bandits' United Front*, Taipei: Department of Mainland China Affairs, Central Committee of the Kuomintang, 30 June 1987, p. 34 (in Chinese).
5. See Note 4 above, p. 51.
6. See *CDN(IE)*, 4 August 1988, p. 1 (in Chinese).
7. *China Times Express*, March 23, 1991, p. 2 (in Chinese).
8. For example, see Zhou Zheng, 'For China's Prosperity and Reunification', *BR*, 21 September 1981, pp. 24–8; 'Hu Yaobang's speech at Beijing Rally in Commemoration of 70th Anniversary of 1911 Revolution', BR, 19 October 1981, p. 20; Li Wen, 'A Review of CPC-KMT Co-operation', BR, 17 March 1986, pp. 18–21; and Yang Yuanhu, 'Cooperation and Mutual Benefit: Reunification of the Motherland', *OW(OE)* No. 28, 11 July 1988, p. 3 (in Chinese).

⁹· Yin Ching-yao, 'The Bitter Struggle Between the KMT and the CCP', *Asian Survey*, XXI, 6, June (1981): 622–31.

¹⁰· Warren Kuo, *The History of the Chinese Communist Party, Book One*, Taipei: Institute of International Relations, September 1969, p. 100 (in Chinese).

¹¹· Wang Yuan, *Communist China's Power Struggle and Policy Struggle*, Taipei: School of East Asia Studies, National Chengchi University, 1982, pp. 36–40 (in Chinese).

¹²· See Note 9 above, Yin Ching-yao, p. 626.

¹³· Chiang Kai-shek, *Soviet Russia in China*, London: George G. Harrap & Co., 1957, pp. 104 and 126.

¹⁴· Du Jian, et al., *A Brief History of the People's Liberation Army*, Beijing: Soldier Publishing House, 1982, pp. 38, 44, 49 and 55 (in Chinese).

¹⁵· See Note 13 above, p. 55.

¹⁶· Thomas B. Gold, 'The Status Quo Is Not Static: Mainland-Taiwan Relations', *Asian Survey*, XXVII, 3, March (1987): 302.

¹⁷· See Jerome Alan Cohen and Hungdah Chiu, *People's China and International Law: A Documentary Study, Vol. 1*, Princeton, N.J.: Princeton University Press, 1974, pp. 391–3. See also 'The Peaceful Liberation of Tibet', *Peking Review*, 5 May 1959, pp. 17–18.

¹⁸· 'On The Policies for Our Work In Tibet—Directive of the Central Committee of the Communist Party of China', *Selected Works of Mao Tsetung, Volume V*, Peking: Foreign Language Press, 1977, p. 74.

¹⁹· See 'Tragedy of Tibet Provides Objective Lesson for ROC, President Chiang Warns', *FCJ*, 19 December 1982, p. 1. Some scholars might disagree with this point, however, it merely reflects Taipei's official viewpoint.

²⁰· 'Opposing Arms Sales and Offering Military Technologies to Taiwan', *RMRB*, 20 March 1986, p. 1.

²¹· Chen I-mei, 'An Interview With Dr. Yang Li-yu,' *IMP*, 15 August 1988, p. 2.

²²· 'Special Report: The PRC's United Front Toward Taiwan,' *China Spring*, No. 28, October 1985, pp. 11–15 (in Chinese).

²³· Huang Shih-chung, 'An Interview With Dr. King C. Chen', *China Spring*, No. 29, November 1985, p. 23.

²⁴· C. L. Chiou, 'Asian Countries' Political Culture,' *The Seventies*, November (1983): 70.

²⁵· See *The Compilation of the Reference Materials Regarding Counter-Attacking Communist Bandits' United Front*, pp. 17–18 and throughout.

²⁶· Ying Tao, 'The "Two China" Hoax', *BR*, 11 March 1958, p. 7.

²⁷· See Zhuang Qubing, Zhang Hongzeng, and Pan Tongwen, 'On the US "Taiwan Relations Act"', *China & the World*, Beijing: Beijing Review Foreign Affairs Series, 1982, pp. 82–3.

28. For example, see Nathaniel B. Thayer, 'China: The Formosa Question', in Gregory Henderson, Richard Ned Lebow, John G. Stoessinger (eds.), *Divided Nations In A Divided World*, New York: David Mckay Company, Inc., 1974, pp. 99–125 and 434–5. See also Ray E. Johnson, 'Alternative Frameworks for Assessing the International Status of Multi-System Nations: Germany, Korea, China / Taiwan,' *The Journal of East Asian Affairs* 11, 1, Spring/Summer 1982: 90–123.

29. James C. Hsiung, 'The Uneasy Tranquility Across the Taiwan Strait,' see Chapter 4, Note 31 above, p. 10.

30. Gregory Henderson, et al., *Divided Nations In A Divided World*, p. 436.

31. See Note 29 above.

32. Ralph N. Clough, 'Taiwan's International Status', in Hungdah Chiu and Robert Downen (eds.), *Multi-System Nations and International Law: The International Status of Germany, Korea and China*, Baltimore: University of Maryland School of Law, Occasional Papers/Reprints Series in Contemporary Asian Studies, No. 8-1981(45), p. 141.

33. Chen Chang-wen, 'Participation In the International Community But also Maintenance of Basic National Policy', a paper presented to the Conference on Meeting the Challenge organized by the *China Times* in Taipei, June 1–3, 1988, p. 6 (in Chinese).

34. David S. Chou, 'International Status of the Republic of China', a paper presented to the 'Conference on Some Inquiries of International Law and Affairs', organized by the Institute of Asia and the World in Taipei, 30 August 1986, p. 4.

35. John F. Copper, 'Taiwan In 1986: Back on Top Again', *Asian Survey*, XXVII, I, January 1987: 85.

36. See Frederic L. Kirgis, Jr., *International Organizations In Their Legal Setting*, St. Paul, Minn.: West Publishing Co., 1977), p. 89; see also James Crawford, *The Creation of States In International Law*, London: Oxford University Press, 1979, p. 36.

37. Chi-di Chen, 'On Its Own—the Republic of China,' *Asian Affairs*, Fall 1983: 61.

38. David S. Chou, see note 34 above, p. 2.

39. Chi-di Chen, 'On Its Own', p. 62. See also Hungdah Chiu, 'The International Legal Status of the Republic of China', *CDN(IE)*, 17 April 1980, p. 1.

40. John F. Copper, 'The International Status of Taiwan: A Multilevel Perspective,' manuscript, p. 9; cited in David S. Chou, 'International Status', p. 3. Similar viewpoints were also expressed by von Glahn, see Gerhard von Glahn, *Law Among Nations: An Introduction to Public International Law*, New York: MacMillan Publishing Co., 1981, pp. 68–9.

41. *Taiwan, Hearings Before Senate Committee on Foreign Relations, 96th Congress, 1st Session, on Bill S. 245, February 5, 6, 7, 8, 21, and 22, 1979*, Washington, D.C.: U.S. Government Printing Office,

1979, p. 148. See also Louis Henkin, Richard C. Pugh, Oscar Schachter, Hans Smit, *International Law, Cases and Materials*, St Paul, Minn.: West Publishing Co., 1980, pp. 207–8.

42. James Crawford, see Note 36 above, pp. 142–3.

43. See Note 36 above, pp. 146, 151, and 152.

44. James C. Hsiung, see Note 27 above and Chapter 4, Note 31, 'The Uneasy Tranquility Across the Taiwan Strait', p. 10.

45. David S. Chou, see Note 32 above, 'International Status', p. 9.

46. Aleth Manin, 'Divided Nations and International Law: The Case of Taiwan', in Chiu and Downen (eds.), Law, see Note 32 above, pp. 160–6.

47. Yu-ming Shaw, 'Taiwan: A View From Taipei,' *Foreign Affairs*, Summer 1985: 1050.

48. See the joint communiques on the establishment of diplomatic relations between the PRC and Belgium and Peru, *Peking Review*, 29 October 1971, p. 4; and November 1971, p. 5.

49. See the 'Joint Communique' between the PRC and the Philippines, *Peking Review*, 13 June 1975, p. 8.

50. For examples, see the communiques of the establishment of diplomatic relations between the PRC and the UK, the USA, Australia, and New Zealand, *Peking Review*, 17 March 1972, p. 3; 29 December 1972, p. 3; 22 December 1978, p. 8.

51. For example, see the communique of establishment of diplomatic relations between the PRC and Japan, *Peking Review*, 6 October 1972, p. 12. See also 'China and the Netherlands Raise Level of Diplomatic Relations', *Peking Review*, 26 May 1972, p. 20.

52. See Ming-min Peng's testimony on *United States-China Relations 11 Years After the Shanghai Communique*, during a hearing before the Subcommittee on Asian and Pacific Affairs of the Committee on Foreign Affairs, House of Representatives, 98th Congress, 1st Session, 28 February 1983, Washington, D.C.: U.S. Government Printing Office, 1979, p. 92.

53. See *Peking Review*, 19 November 1971, p. 4; 20 October 1972, p. 4; and 18 August 1978, p. 3.

54. James C. Hsiung, 'The Uneasy Tranquility Across the Taiwan Strait', p. 10.

55. See Ming-min Peng's testimony, Note 49 above, p. 92.

56. *China's Reunification: Is the 'Nine-Point Proposal' A Feasible Solution?* Taipei: China Mainland Affairs Research Center, 1982, p. 17 (in Chinese).

57. See Note 54 above, p. 14.

58. An Zhiguo, 'Notes From the Editors: Hong Kong and Taiwan', BR, 26 December 1983, p. 4.

59. 'Major Firm To Quit Hong Kong', *Financial Review*, 12 August 1988, p. 47.

60. See An-chia Wu, '"One Country, Two Systems": A Model for

Taiwan?', *Issues & Studies*, July 1985: 58; John P. Burns, 'The Process of Assimilation of Hong Kong (1997) and Implications for Taiwan', *AEI Foreign Policy and Defense Review*, 6, 3, 1986: 24; James C. Hsiung, 'The Hong Kong Settlement: Effects on Taiwan and Prospects for Peking's Reunification Bid', *Asian Affairs*, Summer 1985: 56. See also Weng Sung-jan, 'On "One Country, Two Systems"', *The Nineties*, December 1985: 36 (in Chinese); and Liao Kuang-shen, 'How To Break Through the Stalemate Situation Between the Two Sides of the Taiwan Strait', *Cheng Ming*, April 1988: 13 (in Chinese).

61. Li Yi, 'Taiwan's Latest Policies Concerning Mainland China and Hong Kong', *The Nineties*, April 1988: 44. Taipei maintains that Beijing did not keep its promises to Hong Kong regarding Hong Kong's political system, implementing democracy, and a direct election in Hong Kong in 1988 as promised principally in the Sino-British Declaration. Originally, Hong Kong prepared to proceed with direct vote in 1988, however, under PRC pressure, the Hong Kong government agreed to postpone the direct vote until 1991. Beijing's interference in this matter has eroded confidence of Hong Kong people in the PRC. For an example, see Fan Su, 'A Bleak Election for the Legislative Council', *The Nineties*, September 1988: 62–3; see also Melinda Liu, 'Hong Kong Needs Autonomy With Legal Guarantee', *Cheng Ming*, September 1988: 64–5. According to Weng Sung-jan, political science professor of Hong Kong Chinese University, Hong Kong, people have started to emigrate in waves to other countries in order to escape Beijing's rule after 1997. He said that over 20,000 Hong Kong people had already left Hong Kong during the period 1982–5. The figures for 1986 and 1987 climbed even higher and reached 40,000 people and 53,000 respectively. He predicted that Hong Kong's emigration tide will keep going until 1997; see *China Times*, 2 September 1988, p. 3.

62. Weng Sung-jan, 'From the Hong Kong Experience Toward A Way to Realize the Solutions of Reunification, Self-Determination, and "One Country, Two Systems"', *Ming Pao Monthly*, November 1987, p. 37 (in Chinese).

63. Yang Jiagi, the former director of the Institute of Political Science, at the Chinese Academy of Social Sciences in Beijing, writes that 'one country, two systems' is a 'brand new' and 'scientific' creation of Deng Xiaoping and is an 'unprecedented' idea in the history of mankind; see Yan Jiagi, 'The Scientific Meaning of "One Country, Two Systems" and Its Characteristics', *Hongchi* (Red Flag), 16 March 1986: 18–20 (in Chinese).

64. Xu Jiatun, the former Director of the PRC's Xinhua News Agency's Hong Kong office, went so far as to declare that 'capitalism is one of the greatest achievements of mankind.' See 'No News Is Good News For HK's China News Agency', *Financial Review*, 12 August 1988, p. 47.

65. Tsao Po-I, 'The Contribution of the Reunification of China Under the Three Principles of the People Toward the Free World', *CDN(IE)*, 10 May 1986, p. 1.

66. Chien-min Chao, '"One Country, Two Systems": A Theoretical Analysis', *Asian Affairs*, Summer 1987: 112.

67. Yu-ming Shaw, See Note 47 above, p. 1056.

68. Christopher S. Wren, 'Rise of A New Generation In China and Taiwan Dims Hopes of Reunification', *New York Times*, 21 February 1984, p. A6. One of Taipei's evening papers opined that 'if all the mainland Chinese spit saliva on us, we Taiwan Chinese would be sunk'; see Editorial, 'The Three Nos Policy Means No Surrender', *The Great China Evening News*, 9 March 1987, p. 2.

69. Karl W. Deutsch, 'Communication Theory and Political Integration', in Karl W. Deutsch (ed.), *The Integration of Political Communities*, p. 70.

70. See Note 66 above, p. 71. See also Bruce M. Russet, *Power and Community in World Politics*, San Francisco: W. H. Freeman and Company, 1974, pp. 329–31.

71. Tillman Durdin, 'The View From Taiwan', *Asian Affairs*, 8,1, September/October 1980: 5.

72. Christopher S. Wren, 'A New Generation', see Note 67 above, p. A6.

73. Parris Chang, 'Taiwan In 1982: Diplomatic Setback Abroad and Demands for Reforms at Home', *Asian Survey*, XXIII, 1, January 1983: 41.

74. Yu-ming Shaw, 'Taiwan: A View From Taipei', see Note 44 above, p. 1054. See also An-chia Wu, '"One Country, Two Systems"': A Model For Taiwan?' See Note 57 above, p. 55. Wu said that the ROC has no reason to accept Beijing's overture to negotiations, otherwise, it will immediately face the problem of a challenge to its legally constituted authority; social instability in Taiwan; a possible military adventure by the PRC; and economic problems. Hong Kong writer Chi Hsin also expressed a similar views, see Chi Hsin, 'Taiwan's Dilemma Under The Hong Kong Model', *The Nineties*, May 1985: 53.

75. See Note 65 above, Christopher S. Wren, 'A New Generation', p. A6.

## Notes to Chapter 6

1. Herbert S. Yee, 'China's Reunification Offensive and Taiwan's Policy Options', *The World Today*, January 1982: 36.

2. See *The Compilation of the Reference Materials Regarding Counter-Attacking Communist Bandits' United Front*, p. 14.

3. *CDN*, 29 March 1981, p. 1.

4. For example, one of Taiwan's legislators in March 1988 questioned Premier Yu Kuo-hua regarding the definition of the 'Three Principles of the People' and its relationship to the resolution of the two China issue; see *China Times*, March 26 1988, p. 2. For those who are interested in and intend to know more about the policy of reunification of China under the Three Principles see *The Road for China's Reunification*, Taipei: Central Daily News, 1981 (in Chinese).

5. Sun Yat-sen, *The Three Principles of the People*, Taipei: China Publishing Company, 1981, pp. 56 and 133.

6. See *The Compilation of the Reference Materials*. See also Chiang Ching-kuo, *China's Reunification and World Peace*, Taipei: China Publishing House, November 1986 (in Chinese); and President Lee Teng-hui's speech on 9 October 1988, the eve of the ROC's National Day, *Commercial Times*, 10 October 1988, p. 1.

7. Sun Yat-sen, *The Three Principles*, see Note 5 above, p. 1.

8. 'Taiwan Won't Budge: Chiang', *South China Morning Post*, 11 October 1985, p. 10.

9. *China Times*, 1 October 1987, p. 2.

10. Deng confessed that 'in today's world, our country is counted as poor. Even within the third world, China still rates as relatively underdeveloped.' He said that the CCP should promote 'the growth of the productive forces' and improve 'the material and cultural life of the people.' Otherwise, he said, 'how can we talk about the superiority of the socialist system? We should ponder the question: What have we really done for the people?' For details, see Deng's address to the Standing Committee of the Jilin Provincial Committee of the CCP on 16 September 1978, 'Hold High The Banner of Mao Zedong Thought and Adhere to the Principle of Seeking Truth From Facts', *Selected Works of Deng Xiaoping 1975–82*, Beijing: Foreign Languages Press, 1984, p. 143.

11. See ROC Premier Sun Yun-chuan's speech on 10 June 1982, before a group of American scholars who participated in the 11th Sino-American Conference on Mainland China Affairs; *CDN (IE)*, 11 June 1982, p. 2.

12. See ROC President Lee Teng-hui's remarks at the press conference on 22 February 1988; *CDN*, 23 February 1988, pp. 1–2.

13. Deng Xiaoping, 'Uphold the Four Cardinal Principles', *Selected Works of Deng Xiaoping 1975–82*, pp. 172–86.

14. *The Constitution of the People's Republic of China*, Beijing: Foreign Languages Press, 1983, p. 5.

15. The ROC also has its 'four firm and unchangeable principles.' They are: (1) The system of the State of the ROC, as established under Article 1 of the Constitution, founded on the Three Principles of the People, shall be a democratic republic of the people, to be governed by the people, and for the people. (2) the overall goals of the ROC,

namely anti-Communism and national recovery, will never be changed.
(3) The ROC will always remain with the democratic bloc and its
dedication to upholding righteousness and justice and safeguarding
the peace and security of the world will never be changed. (4) The
resolute stand of the ROC in never compromising with the Chinese
Communist rebel group will never be changed. See *Republic of China:
A Reference Book*, Taipei: United Pacific International, Inc., July 1983,
p. 293.

16. See *The Constitution of the People's Republic of China*, Note
14 above, p. 27. See also *Sino-British Joint Declaration on the Question
of Hong Kong*, Beijing: Foreign Languages Press, 1984, pp. 36–7.

17. See *Sino-British Joint Declaration*, Note 14 above, p. 35.

18. 'They Wish To Wipe Us Out', *FCJ*, 27 October 1988, p. 1.

19. Bei Bei, 'Why We Oppose the "Four Cardinal Principles"',
*CDN(IE)*, 19 October 1988, p. 2. The author of this article is a
visiting scholar from the PRC to the USA, Bei Bei is his pseudonym.

20. Deng Xiaoping, 'Uphold the Four Cardinal Principles', p. 178.

21. Lee Wen-lang, 'The Multi-Diplomacy Principle and Our Country's
Situation in the World', *China Times*, 1 September 1988, p. 2.

22. Chiang Kai-shih, 'The Self-Determination of Taiwan's Inhabitants
and Taiwan's Return To the World Arena—An Interview With Dr.
Peng Ming-min', in Wu Li-hui (ed.), *Self-Determination and Independence*, Kaohsiung: New Taiwan Books Series 5, n. d., pp. 251–6.

23. '"Multiple Recognition" Policy Proposed For ROC', *FCJ*, 28
March 1988, p. 1.

24. For examples, see *The Independence Morning Post*, 14 April
1988, p. 5; *China Times*, 23 March 1988, p. 2; *Central Daily News*,
6 April 1988, p. 3.

25. Lu Bing, 'On Taiwan Authority's Efforts to "Break Through" in
Foreign Relations', *OW(OE)*, No. 32, 8 August 1988, pp. 5–6.

26. Lee Wen-lang, see Note 21 above.

27. Richard M. Nixon, 'Asia After Vietnam', *Foreign Affairs*, October
1967: 121.

28. See the late ROC President Chiang Ching-kuo's talks on 12
January 1981, during the opening ceremony of a military conference
in Taipei; *CDN*, 13 January 1981, p. 1, and *CDN*, 29 November, 1978,
p. 1. In fact, the USSR's Foreign Minister Andrei A. Gromyko in
1972 had already ruled out the possibility that the USSR would
change 'its policy towards Nationalist China to counter Communist
China', see 'Gromyko Advises Nations on China', *New York Times*,
29 January 1972, p. 7.

29. *CDN(IE)*, 15 March 1986, p. 1.

30. Yu-ming Shaw, 'Taiwan: A View From Taipei', p. 1056.

31. See President Lee Teng-hui's comments in an interview with
South Korea's Hankbook Ilbo in August 1988, *CDN(IE)*, 2 August
1988, p. 1.

32. Editorial, 'On Mainland Policy After the 13th KMT Party Congress', *China Times*, 16 July 1988, p. 3.

# Notes to Chapter 7

1. The author defines the ROC's 'victory' as follows: the ROC's economic achievements in Taiwan serve as a development model for the PRC to imitate and prod the PRC to change and reform; a reunified China is not merely based on Beijing's terms but also Taipei's, which would include freedom, democracy, and prosperity; a reunified China is without any trace of communism. If these three conditions can be achieved, from the author's viewpoint, it really does not matter which 'China' (Beijing or Taipei) represents the reunified China in the world.

2. Donald Shapiro, 'Taiwan Ties Survival To Economic Gains', *New York Times*, 21 August 1972, p. 43.

3. See Note 2 above.

4. 'Interview With Reader's Digest: Lee Says Road Back Still Long', *FCJ*, 31 October 1988, p. 2.

5. A CCP classified document obtained by the Military Intelligence Bureau, Ministry of National Defense of the ROC, as yet unpublished.

6. Ding Li, 'From the Development Trend of the World Economy to See the Great Strategy of "One Country, Two System"', *Henan University Journal Bimonthly* (Social Science Edition), 31 May 1986: 11–12 (in Chinese).

7. 'Deng On Issues of World Interest', *BR*, 22 September 1986, p. 5.

8. Seymour M. Lipset, *Political Man: The Social Bases of Politics*, Baltimore: The Johns Hopkins University Press, 1981, p. 31.

9. See Note 8 above, p. 64.

10. Samuel P. Huntington, *Political Order in Changing Societies*, New Haven: Yale University Press, 1977, pp. 33–4.

11. See Note 10 above, p. 34.

12. In fact, the causal factors of democracy remain controversial topics in the study of social modernization theory. Contemporary writers, such as Lerner, Almond and Verba, argue that besides the economy, education, media, culture, and personality are also essential factors for the process of democratic development. Arat argues that 'it is clear that democracy is not a one-way ladder that countries climb as their economy and social structures develop.' See Zehra F. Arat, 'Democracy and Economic Development: Modern-ization Theory Revisited', *Comparative Politics*, 21, 2, October 1988: 33.

[13.] Chalmers Johnson, 'The PRC's Strategy Toward Taiwan on the Reunification Issue', *China Spring*, November 1985: 76 (in Chinese).

[14.] John F. Copper, 'Taiwan In 1986: Back On Top Again', *Asian Survey*, 27, 1, January 1987: 91.

[15.] Editorial, 'Promising Changes In Taiwan', *New York Times*, 9 December 1986, p. A34.

[16.] See Premier Yu Kuo-hua's comments; *CDN(IE)*, 20 August 1986, p. 1.

[17.] 'Taiwan's Future', *Asian Wall Street Journal*, 16 December 1986, p. 8.

[18.] Dean Acheson, *Present at the Creation*, New York: Norton, 1969, p. 61.

[19.] K. J. Holsti, *International Politics: A Framework for Analysis*, Englewood Cliffs, N.J.: Prentice-Hall, Inc., 1977, p. 309.

[20.] Clare Hollingworth, 'More Talk of "One Country: Two Systems"', *Pacific Defense Reporter*, December 1988–January 1989, p. 60.

[21.] Paul Mann, 'Taiwanese Arms Accord Clears F-5E Production', *Aviation Week & Space Technology*, 23 August 1982, p. 21. Similar viewpoints also can be found in Martin L. Lasater, *Taiwan: Facing Mounting Threats*, Washington, D.C.: The Heritage Foundation, 1984.

[22.] Li Shenzhi and Zi Zongyun, 'Taiwan In the Next Decade', *Taiwan Studies Quarterly*, No. 1, 1988: 3–4 (in Chinese).

[23.] Huan Kuocang, 'The Present and the Future Relations Between the Two Sides of the Taiwan Strait', *China Tribune*, 26, 5, 10 June 1988: 61 (in Chinese).

[24.] Edmund Lee, 'Beijing's Balancing Act', *Foreign Policy*, Summer 1983: 45. Edmund Lee is this scholar's pseudonym.

[25.] Dick Wilson, 'Hands Across the Straits', *Asia Pacific Community*, Fall 1980, p. 38. See also Brian Crozier, 'The Art of Survival', *National Review*, 6 December 1974, p. 1402; and Robert A. Scalapino, 'China and Northeast Asia', in Betty Neville (ed.), *The China Factor: Sino-American Relations and the Global Scene* (Englewood Cliffs, New Jersey: Prentice-Hall, Inc., 1981), pp. 204–5.

[26.] A document secured by the Military Intelligence Bureau, Ministry of National Defense, R.O.C., it was included in *The Analysis of the Current Mainland China Situation*, Taipei: The General Political Warfare Department, Ministry of National Defense, 30 April 1986, p. 413 (in Chinese).

[27.] Christopher S. Wren, 'Rise of A New Generation in China and Taiwan Dims Hopes of Reunification', *New York Times*, 21 February 1984, p. A6.

[28.] See *Commercial Times*, 7 June 1989, p. 3.

[29.] For details, see Ray S. Cline, 'World Power Assessment', in Thomas Kurian (ed.), *The New Book of World Rankings*, New York: Facts on File, Inc., 1984, pp. 79–81.

[30.] See *China Times*, 11 April 1989, p. 2.

[31] Jun-yen Wu, 'Will Cheng Wei-yuan Repel the Invader?' *The Journalist*, April 17–23, 1989, pp. 38–9 (in Chinese).

[32] See Lael Morgan, 'Alaska's Far-out Islands: The Aleutians', *National Geographic*, 164, 3, September 1983: 345.

[33] Parris H. Chang, 'The Assessment of the PRC's Use of the Force in the Taiwan Straits', *Central Daily News*, 30 May 1988, p. 2.

[34] See Yu-hua Chang, 'A Rugged Road of the Development of Our Country's Nuclear Arms', *The Independence Morning Post*, 9 March 1988, p. 5. See also Stephen Engelberg, 'Taipei Halts Work on Secret Plant to Make Nuclear Bomb Ingredient', *New York Times*, 23 March 1988, pp. A1 and A15.

[35] Stephen Engelberg, see Note 34 above, p. A1.

[36] Yu-hua Chang, 'A Rugged Read', see Note 34 above, p. 5.

[37] See 'Taiwan: Don't You Shove Me Around', *The Economist*, 2 April 1988, p. 24.

[38] Dan C. Sanford, *The Future Association of Taiwan With the People's Republic of China*, Berkeley, Ca.: University of California, 1981, p. 3.

[39] Ralph N. Clough, *Island China*, Cambridge, Mass.: Harvard University Press, 1978, pp. 116–8.

[40] David G. Muller, Jr., *China As A Maritime Power*, Boulder, Colo.: Westview Press, 1983, p. 230.

[41] K. J. Holsti, *International Politics*, see Note 19 above, p. 308.

[42] See *CDN(IE)*, 31 May 1989, p. 1.

[43] *The Military Balance 1988–1989*, London: The International Institute for Strategic Studies, 1988, pp. 224–7. The ROC's defence expenditure has been maintained at a high percentage of government spending in the past decades.

[44] Ibid., p. 178; and *The Military Balance 1978–1979*, p. 60.

[45] 'ROC's Own AAM 'Sword' Successfully Test-Fired', *FCJ*, 26 May 1986, p. 1.

[46] See *China Times*, 19 March 1988, p. 2.

[47] See 'Thumbs Up For ROC Fighter!', *FCJ*, 15 December 1988, p. 1; 'Made-in-Taiwan Jet Passes Its Flight Test', *Far Eastern Economic Review*, 8 June 1989, p. 23; *China Times*, 27 December 1988, p. 3; *CDN(IE)*, 14 April 1989, p. 1; and *Asian Security 1988–9*, London: A Wheaton & Co., Ltd., 1988, p. 73.

[48] See Note 45 above, *FCJ*, 26 May 1986, p. 1.

[49] See Chang Kuo-li, 'The Next Generation of Warships Sail to the Legislative Yuan', *China Times Weekly*, No. 538, June 19–25, 1988, pp. 9–13 and 122–26; see also Chao Hu-yuan, 'The Plan for the Next Generation of Warships', *China Times*, 26 February 1988, p. 2; *Central Daily News*, 3 November 1987, p. 2.

[50] *CDN(IE)*, 16 June 1989, p. 2.

[51] *CDN(IE)*, 5 June 1989, p. 7.

[52] *United Daily News*, 18 December 1987, p. 2.

<sup></sup>53. 'ROC Goes Down Under To Thwart Missile Attack', *FCJ*, 1 August 1988, p. 1.

54. See Note 43 above.

55. See *The Compilation of the Reference Materials*, pp. 20–8.

56. For the full English text, see Sun Yun-chuan, 'China Issue and the Reunification of China', *CDN(IE)*, 11 June 1982, p. 2.

57. *CDN(IE)*, 22 September 1988, p. 1.

58. See *China Times*, 30 July 1988, p. 2.

59. See Note 58 above.

## Notes to Chapter 8

1. Hsiao Chang-lo, 'The Mainland Policy of the Kuomintang During the Current Stage' *CDN(IE)*, 13 July 1988, p. 1.

2. See *CDN(IE)*, 6 September 1988, p. 1. See also 'Who's Who In the ROC', *Republic of China 1988: A Reference Book*, Taipei: Hilit Publishing Company, Ltd., 1988, pp. 427–94.

3. See *China Times*, 19 August 1988, p. 1; and *CDN(IE)*, 14 October 1988, p. 1.

4. *FCJ*, 25 February 1991, p. 1.

5. *The Straits Exchange Foundation*, Taipei: SEF, April 1980, p. 4.

6. *The United Daily News*, 3 October 1990, p. 2.

7. An-chia Wu, 'The ROC's Mainland Policy in the 1990s', *Issues & Studies*, 27, 9, September (1991): 5.

8. *CDN(IE)*, 30 August 1988, p. 1.

9. *CDN(IE)*, 31 August 1988, p. 1.

10. *China Times*, 4 July 1991, p. 2.

11. The KMT openly admitted, during the session of The 13th Party Congress held in July 1988, that 50 of the delegates had worked as undercover agents in China; see *CDN(IE)*, 4 July 1988, p. 2, and 6 July 1988, p. 1. Also see 'Taipei Relaxes Bar on Chinese Trade', *The Australian*, 15 July 1988, p. 8.

12. Chiu Chao, 'The So-called "Communist Bandits Studies" Agencies', *The Asian*, 1 October 1984, p. 43.

13. Kuo Hong-chi, 'The Department of Cultural Affairs Wants To Recover the Mainland?' *The Journalist*, No. 87, November 7–13, 1988, p. 80.

14. This information was obtained from the *China Times*, 8 May 1988, p. 3; *The Independence Morning Post*, 20 June 1988, p. 2 and 19 June 1988, p. 2. See also Wu Fu-chen, 'To Unmask *Li Hsing* Committee's Secret Face-Veil', *The Independence Morning Post*, 27 March 1988, p. 5; and 'Anti-Red Group Set To Disband', *FCJ*, 29 August 1988, p. 2.

15. For details in this regard, see the 'Special Report on the Two

Chinas' Intelligence Warfare', *The Journalist*, No. 86, 31 October–6 November 1988, pp. 8, 12–27.

16. Chiu Chao, see Note 12 above, p. 44.

17. See Note 12 above, p. 43.

18. Liu I-deh, 'The Revelation of Intelligence Units' Budget,' *Democratic Progressive News*, No. 8, 6 May 1988, p. 14.

19. *Commercial Times*, 23 September 1988, p. 2.

20. *Republic of China 1988*, p. 129.

21. *CDN(IE)*, 22 November 1988, p. 2.

22. *Republic of China 1988*, p. 129.

23. Hu Yuan-hui, 'News Analysis', *The Independence Evening Post*, 10 October 1987, p. 2. See also *China Times*, 16 October 1987, p. 2.

24. *Newsletter of the Grand Alliance for China's Reunification Under the Three Principles of the People*, No. 29, 25 February 1988, p. 8; and No. 30, 25 April 1988, p. 4 (in Chinese).

25. *CDN(IE)*, 22 October 1988, p. 1.

26. 'Lee Wants Alliance Action', *FCJ*, 27 October 1988, p. 2.

27. *Republic of China 1988*, p. 363.

28. Tung Meng-nan, 'The WACL Becomes An Orphan of the Anti-Communism Movement', *The Journalist*, No. 79, 12–8 September 1988, pp. 38–41. See also Yang Kuei-mei, 'We Only Want Anti-Communism, We Don't Need Facism', *The Journalist*, No. 99, 30 January–5 February 1989, pp. 72–3.

29. *Republic of China 1988*, p. 367.

30. See *Central Daily News*, 16 October 1987, p. 2.

31. 'Mainland Mail Made Easy', *FCJ*, 11 April 1988, p. 3.

32. Yu Hsien-ta, 'The Military Heads Convene the Huangpu Alumni and Students', *The Journalist*, No. 68, 3 July 1988, p. 13.

33. See *CDN(IE)*, 24 October 1988, pp. 1 and 8.

34. See *CDN(IE)*, 4 November 1988, p. 1; and 9 November 1988, p. 1.

35. See *CDN(IE)*, 11 March 1989, p. 1.

36. 'We Shall Not Abolish the Commission for Recovery—Mainland', *CDN(IE)*, 24 December 1988, p. 2.

37. Margaret Scott, 'Everything You Want To Know About China', *Far Eastern Economic Review*, 4 December 1986, p. 46.

38. For example, see *China Times*, 6 January 1988, p. 12. According to this paper, the National Security Bureau, in order to counter Beijing's united front tactics after Taipei's open door policy toward the mainland, has set up a special task force named 'Ching Shan' (Green Mountain) to train Taiwan's security officers for detecting Beijing agents' infiltration and preventing Beijing from conducting united front efforts in Taiwan through the Taiwan Chinese who have visited the mainland.

39. *The Independence Morning Post*, 31 March 1989, p. 5.

# Notes to Chapter 9

1. See President Lee Teng-hui's proclamation on 30 April 1991 regarding the end of the Period of National Mobilization and the Suppression of the Communist Rebellion, *China Times*, 1 May, 1991, pp. 1–2.

2. *Guidelines for National Unification*, Taipei: The Mainland Affairs Council, 1991.

3. See Note 2 above.

4. Lee Teng-hui, 'Opening a New Era for the Chinese People', *China Times*, 21 May 1990, p. 1. See also Premier Hau Pei-tsun's speech in the Legislative Yuan, *The United Daily News*, 22 February 1992, p. 1.

5. For the whole text, see *CDN*, 17 July 1992, p. 4.

6. *The United Daily News*, 17 July 1992, p. 2.

7. For details, see Fox Butterfield, 'Slaying Was Ordered From Taiwan, Lawyer Says', *New York Times*, 5 December 1984, p. A18; see also 'Taiwan Arrests Agents in US Slaying', *New York Times*, 16 January 1985, p. A3; and Steve Lohr, 'Author Is Called Agent for Taiwan', *New York Times*, 26 January 1985, p. 3.

8. See 'Taiwan Official Named', *New York Times*, 22 August 1985, p. D8; and Marvine Howe, 'Domestic Scandals and Trade Fears Leave Taiwan Uncertain', *New York Times*, 27 October 1985, p. 16.

9. Nicholas D. Kristof, 'Taiwan's Risky Refrain: "Self-determination"', *New York Times*, 14 December 1986, p. 14.

10. For example, see John Felton, 'Reagan Plans Pragmatic Pilgrimage to Peking, *Congress Quarterly Weekly Report*, 14 April 1984, p. 864; and Wayne Biddle, 'US Said to Plan to Sell Naval Weapons to China', *New York Times*, 13 January 1985, p. 12.

11. For example, see Nang Fang-shuo, 'Mainland Policy Under the US's Pressure', *The Nineties*, July 1988, pp. 18–21. See also 'Secretary Visits Asia', *Department of State Bulletin*, 87, 2122, May (1987): 11.

12. *CDN(IE)*, 21 May 1984, p. 1.

13. *CDN(IE)*, 9 October 1986, p. 1.

14. *China Times*, 16 October 1987, p. 2.

15. Shou-chung Ting, 'Republic of China's Changing Mainland Policy and Its Implications for the Reunification of China,' a paper presented at the Conference on the Impact of the Pacific Century on Euro-Asian Relations in Taipei, March 1988, p. 4.

16. Huang Kuang-kuo, 'The Taiwan Complex and the China Complex: Confrontation and Resolution,' *China Tribune*, 25, 1, 10 October (1988): 17–18.

17. Shou-chung Ting, see Note 15 above, p. 7.

18. Bao Xing, 'A Pleasant Change of the Two Sides' Relations', *OW(OE)*, 26 October 1987, p. 1.

19. *China Times*, 2 October 1987, p. 1.

20. 'The Text of President Lee's Press Conference,' *Central Daily News*, 23 February 1988, pp. 1–2.

21. See Note 20 above.

22. For example, see *China Times*, 2 April 1988, p. 1; *The Independence Morning Post*, 30 July 1988, p. 1; and *The United Daily News*, 21 May 1990, p. 1.

23. *The Independence Morning Post*, 7 April 1988, p. 1.

24. *The Independence Morning Post*, 19 August 1988, p. 2.

25. Li Tahong, 'Beijing Scholars' Comments on Taiwan Authority's Mainland Policy'. *OW(OE)*, 4 July 1988, p. 6. See also Li Suiwuang, 'On the KMT's 13th Party Congress', *OW(OE)*, 4 July 1988, pp. 21–2.

26. Li Juaquan, 'How Come Taiwan's Policy Changes,' *BR*, February 15–28, 1988, p. 20.

27. *The United Daily News*, 22 July 1992, p. 1.

28. Bao Xing, 'Further Advice for Taiwan Authority', *OW(OE)*, No. 44, 31 October 1988, p. 1. See also Chen Bing, 'On Mr. Chen Li-fu's Proposal', *OW(OE)*, No. 37, 12 September 1988, p. 4. See also *China Times*, 1 July 1992, p. 1.

29. See Premier Yu's comments, *Commercial Times*, 1 January 1989, p. 1. See also *The United Daily News*, 18 July 1992, p. 3.

30. Zhang Fei, 'New Trends in Taiwan', *BR*, January 9–15, 1989, p. 4.

31. The term Koo-Wang refers to Dr. Koo Chan-fu and Wang Dzohan. Dr. Koo, a Taiwanese tycoon, is the chairman of the Chinese National Federation of Industries and the Straits Exchange Foundation as well as a standing committee member of the KMT. Weng is the former mayor of Shanghai and Chairman of Beijing's Association for Relations Across the Strait. Both of them are important political personalities.

32. 'President Lee Stresses Taipei, Peking Equal', FCJ, 7 May 1993, p. 2.

# Notes to Chapter 10

1. Donald J. Puchala, 'Integration and Disintegration In Franco-German Relations, 1954–1965', *International Organization*, 24, 2, Spring (1970): 220.

2. Ernst B. Haas, 'The Study of Regional Integration: Reflections on the Joy and Anguish of Pretheorizing', p. 628.

3. Roy C. Macridis, *Modern Political Regimes: Patterns and Institutions*, p. 5.

4. Karl W. Deutsch, *Politics and Government: How People Decide Their Fate*, Boston, Mass.: Houghton Mifflin Company, 1980, p. 47.

5. Refer to Michael Ying-mao Kau, 'On How to Break Through the

Current Diplomatic Difficulties,' *China Times*, 10 May 1987, p. 2; see also Weng Song-jan, 'From the Hong Kong Experience Toward A Way to Realize Reunification, Self-determination, and "One Country, Two Systems"', *Ming Bao Monthly*, November 1987, p. 37 (in Chinese).

6. See Yung Wei, 'The Unification and Division of Multi-System Nations: A Comparative Analysis of Basic Concepts, Issues, and Approaches', a paper prepared for and delivered at the Symposium on Functional Integration of Divided Nations, Seoul, Republic of Korea, October 6–7, 1980, pp. 2–3. See also Jen Hsiao-chi, 'Yung Wei: Why I Put Forward the Idea of "Dual Recognition"', *Global Views Monthly*; 15 May 1988, pp. 102 and 107–9 (in Chinese).

7. See Yung Wei Note 6 above, pp. 5–7.

8. 'Exchanges of Official Nature With Taiwan Opposed', *BR*, 29 March 1982, p. 7.

9. Michael Ying-mao Kau, 'The Reunification Issue of the Divided Nations,' in Lu Keng (ed.), *Debates Concerning the Issue of China's Reunification*, Hong Kong: Pai-Shing Cultural Company, 1988, pp. 259–293 (in Chinese).

10. See John H. Herz, 'Germany,' in Gregory Henderson, Richard Ned Lebow, and John G. Stoessinger (eds.), *Divided Nations In A Divided World*, New York: David Mckay Company, 1974, pp. 3–42; Berenince Carrol, 'The Partition of Germany: Cold War Compromise', in Thomas E. Hachey (ed.), *The Problem of Partition: Peril to World Peace*, Chicago, Ill.: Rand McNally, 1972; Lawrence L. Whetten, *Germany's Ostpolitik*, London: Oxford University Press, 1971.

11. Gottfried-Karl Kindermann, 'The Case of Germany,' in Hungdah Chiu and Robert Downen (eds.), *Multi-System Nations and International Law: The International Status of Germany, Korea and China*, Baltimore: University of Maryland School of Law, Occasional Papers/Reprints Series in Contemporary Asian Studies, No. 8-1981 (45), pp. 113–116. See also Jurgen Domes' comments about this article, pp. 116–7. Regarding East Germany's idea of 'two nations, two states', See pp. 78–9.

12. Hsiao Hsin-yi, 'The Future Relations Between the Two Chinas', in Wu Li-hui (ed.), *The Future of Taiwan*, Kaohsiung: New Taiwan Book Series 1, no date, p. 273 (in Chinese).

13. See *China Times*, 28 October 1987, p. 1; *United Daily News*, 10 October 1987, p. 2; *Central Daily News*, 26 September 1987, p. 2; and Terry Cheng, 'Taipei Opposition Looks At German Model', *South China Morning Post*, 6 October 1987, p. 19.

14. 'Shen Chun-shan's Comments on the Future Relations Between Taiwan and the Mainland', *The Independence Evening Post*, 5 September 1987, p. 2; and *China Times*, 1 September 1987, p. 2. See also Shen Chun-shan, 'The Peaceful Competition of "One Country, Two Systems": Respecting the Will of 18 Million Taiwan People', *The Seventies*, April 1984, pp. 69–73.

15. See Winston L. Y. Yang and Michael Ying-mao Kau, 'On the Issue of China's Reunification: A Response to the Special Article of the "Outlook Weekly"', *The Nineties*, February 1988, pp. 71–73; Winston L. Y. Yang, 'From "One Country, Two Teams" to "One Country, Two Seats"', *The Nineties*, January 1985, pp. 66–67; and Winston L. Y. Yang and Michael Ying-mao Kau, 'The Key for the Issue of China's Reunification: Another Response to the Special Article of the "Outlook Weekly"', *The Nineties*, November 1988, pp. 86–89.

16. *CDN(IE)*, 9 April 1989, p. 1.

17. See the editorial, *United Daily News*, 10 April 1989, p. 2.

18. *CDN(IE)*, 8 May 1989, p. 1.

19. Weng Song-jan, 'On "One Country, Two systems"', *The Nineties*, December 1985, p. 32.

20. Wilbur W. White, *White's Political Dictionary*, p. 110.

21. Fang Su, 'Lu Li's "Federal States Fever"', *The Nineties*, December 1988, pp. 48–51.

22. See *China Times*, 14 June 1988, p. 2; See also Chang Yu-fa, 'Some Thoughts Regarding the Federation System in China,' *The Independence Morning Post*, 5 April 1988, p. 3.

23. *The China Times*, 19 December 1991, p. 18.

24. Wilbur W. White, *White's Political Dictionary*, p. 69.

25. Jack C. Plano and Roy Olton, *The International Relations Dictionary*, Santa Barbara, Ca.: ABC-Clio, Inc., 1988, p. 307.

26. See Note 25 above, pp. 324–325.

27. Fei Hsi-ping, legislator of the ROC, put forward this idea in 1984 for solving the China issue. Both Taipei and Beijing, however, rebuffed this idea. See *CDN(IE)*, 20 October 1984, p. 1. For those interested in Mr. Fei's idea of 'confederation,' see Ko Li-shih, 'Confederation—the Bridge for the Peaceful Reunification of the Two Chinas: Mr. Fei Hsi-ping's Comments'. *China Spring*, October 1985, pp. 34–36; see also Ting Tin-yu, 'A Feasible Approach to Solve the Two Chinas' Differences: Confederation', *China Times*, 16 June 1988, p. 3; Huang Kuo-kuang, 'The Extent and Limit of the Exchanges Between the Two Sides', *China Tribune*, 25 April 1988, pp. 8–11. Both Ting and Huang are professors of National Taiwan University.

28. For details see Mei Ko-wang, 'A Reunification Model: The Great China Commonwealth', *Global Views Monthly*, 1 February 1988, pp. 118–120.

29. Hungdah Chiu, 'Only the Confederation System Can Achieve the Reunification', in Lu Keng, (ed.), *Debates Concerning The Issue of China's Reunification*, p. 272.

30. *The Independence Morning Post*, 17 November 1988, p. 2.

31. For details, see *The China Times*, 18 January 1992, p. 7.

32. Robert A. Dahl, *A Preface to Democratic Theory*, Chicago: University of Chicago Press, 1956, p. 34.

33. There are some theoretical and methodological problems that

accompany the use of public opinion polls. However, it is outside the scope of this chapter to fully test their propositions. Some polls shown in this discussion are technically not very sophisticated, for example, they do not indicate how the population sample is chosen, the sampling error and so on.

34. The sample in this poll is 816 people. Among them, 79.7 per cent are Taiwanese while 20.3 per cent are mainlanders. See *United Daily News*, 16 October 1987, p. 2. There are four main newspaper groups in the ROC: (a) the China Times Group (*China Times, Commercial Times* and *China Times Express*); (b) the United Daily News Group (*United Daily News, Economic Daily News* and *United Evening News*); (c) the Independence Group (*The Independence Morning Post* and *The Independence Evening Post*); and (d) the KMT's group of newspapers (*Central Daily News, Central Daily News (Overseas Edition), China Daily News* and *Taiwan Daily News*). The United Daily News Group publishes newspapers overseas. Except for the KMT's newspapers, the former three groups are all privately controlled. However, the owners of the China Times and the United Daily News Groups were both former standing committee members of the KMT's central committee; to some extent, these two groups are pro-KMT. Since the lifting of newpaper ban on 1 January 1988, the position of these two groups, pressed by competition from other newspapers, is becoming more liberal and outspoken, especially the China Times Group. The Independence Group is run by the non-KMT people, therefore this group's newspapers always seem to be more independent and objective.

35. The sample in this poll includes 1,158 people. Among them 74.5 per cent are Taiwanese while 25.5 per cent are mainlanders. See *The Independence Evening Post*, 14 March 1988, p. 3.

36. The sample size in this poll includes 443 people. See *China Times Express*, 12 April 1988, p. 3.

37. For example, see *China Times*, 28 October 1987, p. 1.

# Notes to Chapter 11

1. *CDN(IE)*, 4 October 1986, p. 2 (in Chinese).

2. 'An Interview With Professor Shen Chun-san', *China Spring*, November 1985, p. 59 (in Chinese).

3. Shaw Yu-ming, 'Taiwan: A View From Taipei', *Foreign Affairs*, Summer (1985): 1054.

4. *Peking Review*, 11 May 1973, p. 4, and 25 May 1973, p. 4.

5. See the following *RMRB* issues: 30 August 1979, p. 4; 2 November 1979, p. 3; 23 February 1980, p. 4; 24 October 1980, p. 1; 12 November 1980, p. 8; 31 December 1980, p. 1; 19 January 1981, p. 5; 19 June

1981, p. 5; 14 January 1982, p. 1; 23 August 1984, p. 2; 27 December 1984, p. 4. See also Li Chaochen, 'The Now-Peaceful Taiwan Strait', *China Reconstructs*, 35, 10, October (1986): 33–40 (in Chinese). These reception stations are located at: Shipukong, Cengjiamon, Zongmon, Quchiang (Zhejiang Province); Xiapu, Sangsa, Pingtan, Putian, Huian, Zhongwu, Jinjiang, Xiamen, Dongsan Island (Fujian Province); Jiaotzchen (Guangdong Province).

6. *RMRB*, 23 February 1980, p. 4; *NYT*, 10 April 1980, p. A9. See also Julian Baum, 'People-to-People Ties Ease Tensions Between China and Taiwan', *The Christian Science Monitor*, 4 January 1985, p. 9.

7. *RMRB*, 14 January 1982, p. 1.

8. Li Chaochen, see Note 5 above, p. 40.

9. *CDN(IE)*, 27 March 1980, p. 1, and 28 March 1980, p. 3; see also *RMRB*, 5 April 1980, p. 1; and *NYT*, 28 March 1980, p. A6.

10. 'Seamen From the Mainland Visit Taiwan', *BR*, 14 April 1980, p. 4.

11. *CDN(IE)*, 15 August 1981, p. 2; see also *NYT*, 16 August 1981, p. 3. These 27 fishermen were charged with engaging in 'smuggling activities', specifically exchanging Taiwan-made watches for the mainland's silver coins and gold bars in the Taiwan Straits. The Taipei District Court found all of the accused not guilty and said that 'we still claim our sovereignty over the mainland; therefore, there is no boundary between the mainland and Taiwan'. Since there is no boundary between the two sides, the fishermen's trade with their mainland compatriots did not constitute smuggling. However, Major Huang's defection to the mainland on 13 August 1981, triggered the Taiwan High Court's review of this case. On 14 August 1981, the 27 fishermen were sentenced to prison on a charge of trading gold bars, which violated the ROC's General Mobilization Law. Taiwan formerly prohibited private trading of gold in the past; this ban, however, has been lifted since October 1986.

12. *CDN(IE)*, 25 February 1989, p. 2.

13. *China Times*, 11 January 1989, p. 1 (in Chinese). See also *CDN(IE)*, 15 March 1989, p. 2; and 20 April 1989, p. 1. In order to check mainlanders' smuggling into Taiwan, the ROC government has offered a reward of US$1,850 plus 15 days holiday for those coastal defense soldiers and police who catch smuggling mainlanders; see *The Independence Morning Post*, 17 March 1989, p. 6 (in Chinese).

14. See Note 13 above.

15. *China Times*, 9 February 1993, p. 6.

16. Editorial, 'Permitting People to Sightsee Abroad Is A Mark of Stability and Progress', *CDN(IE)*, 3 January 1979, p. 1.

17. *The Free China Journal*, 29 February 1988, p. 3. Hereafter *FCJ*.

18. *CDN(IE)*, 11 March 1982, p. 2.

19. No official reports has been issued by the two sides in this regard before 1986; however, many other publications have made

relevant detailed reports. See Christopher S. Wren, 'China and Taiwan: A Web of Unofficial Contacts', *NYT*, 22 February 1984, p. A4; Daniel Southerland, 'Xiamen Revises Its View of Taiwan', *The Washington Post*, 16 December 1985, p. A22; Carl Goldstein, 'Patience With Threats', *Far Eastern Economic Review*, 24 July 1986, p. 25; 'Taiwan in Transition', *The Economist*, 17 May 1986, p. 31; My figures were obtained from both *The Economist* and the *Far Eastern Economic Review*, hereafter *FEER*.

20. 'How to Visit Your Mainland Relatives', *Times News Weekly*, 29 September 1986, pp. 32–5; and 'A Half-Open-Half-Secret Visit Between the Two Sides', *Times News Weekly*, 23 March 1987, pp. 14–18 (in Chinese).

21. Editorial, 'To Remain Vigilant About the Chinese Communists' United Front Trap', *CDN(IE)*, 6 January 1986, p. 1.

22. 'A Half-Open-Half-Secret Visit Between the Two Sides', See Note 20 above, pp. 14–18.

23. *CDN(IE)*, 22 February 1989, p. 2.

24. 'How to Process the Paper Work in Regard to Visiting Mainland Relatives', *CDN*, 16 October 1987, p. 2. At present, the forbidden period has been shortened to one year.

25. *RMRB (Overseas Edition)*, 9 February 1989, p. 5.

26. *Economic Daily News*, 6 April 1988, p. 6 (in Chinese).

27. *The United Daily News*, 24 February 1992, p. 6.

28. *CDN(IE)*, 23 September 1988, p. 2; and *China Times.* 22 February 1989, p. 2. In the past, a mainland resident has been required to reside at least five years (recently reduced to four years) in a non-communist country before being considered eligible to apply for permanent residence in Taiwan. *The United Daily News*, 23 January 1992, p. 1 (in Chinese).

29. 'Responses to Chairman Ye Jianying's Statement', *BR*, 19 October 1981, p. 7. The magazine of the All-China Federation of Taiwan Compatriots has published, in 1986, a series of articles regarding how to travel in the mainland; see Yang Yenming, 'Do You Want to Visit the Mainland?' *Taishin Magazine (The Voice of Taiwan)*, April 1986, pp. 46–47; May 1986, pp. 42–42; and June 1986, pp. 45–47 (in Chinese).

30. *RMRB(OE)*, 1 March 1988, p. 5.

31. Daniel Southerland, 'Gift-Laden Travelers Flock to Communist Mainland As Taiwan Lifts 38-year Travel Ban', *The Washington Post*, 27 December 1987, pp. A25 and A31. See also *Commercial Times*, 20 March 1988, p. 24 (in Chinese).

32. *CDN(IE)*, 30 July 1988, p. 1.

33. *Economic Daily News*, 16 April 1988, p. 2.

34. See Wang Yuan-jen's comments, *CDN(IE)*, 30 July 1988, p. 1. Wang is the Director of the Bureau of Entry and Exit of the ROC government.

[35.] Daniel Southerland, 'Taiwan to End 38-Year Ban On Travel to Mainland China,' *The Washington Post*, 20 September 1987, p. A1 and A34.

[36.] See Note 35 above.

[37.] See Ann Scott Tyson, 'Taiwanese Make a 40-mile Trip That Spans 40 Years', *The Christian Science Monitor*, 1 December 1987, p. 1. See also Hsin-hsing Wu, 'A Money-Oriented Mainland China', *Commercial Times*, 13 January 1989, p. 6.

[38.] 'Mainland Life Not Taiwan Style', *FCJ*, 7 November 1988, p. 3.

[39.] *CDN*, 9 January 1988, p. 2.

[40.] See *CDN(IE)*, 1 February 1984, p. 1, and *RMRB*, 20 February 1984, p. 4.

[41.] Fox Butterfield, 'Peking Debates Taipei for First Time Since '48', *NYT*, 4 April 1982, p. 26. See also *CDN(IE)*, 2 April 1982, p. 1. and 4 April 1982, p. 1; *RMRB*, 4 April 1982, p. 1 and 7 April 1982, p. 4.

[42.] See *China Times*, 16 August 1988, p. 2 and 17 August 1988, p. 1.

[43.] *The Independence Morning Post*, 19 August 1988, p. 1.

[44.] According to ROC Ministry of Education statistics, 5,979 Taiwan students were approved to study abroad in 1985, among which 5,532 students went to the US, while fewer than 500 students went to European and other countries; see *The Great China Evening News*, 6 November 1986, p. 4.

[45.] According to Taipei, priority will be given to those students with expertise, those who will return to the mainland someday, those who have visas to return to countries where they studying and those holding round-trip plane tickets, see *FCJ*, 22 September 1988, p. 3; and 'Regulations Concerning the Visiting of Experts, Overseas Students and Scholars from the Mainland,' *United Evening News*, 1 December 1988, p. 3.

[46.] See *Yangcheng Wanbao*, 11 December 1988, p. 1 (in Chinese).

[47.] See *CDN(IE)*, 16 March 1989, p. 2.

[48.] 'ROC Opens Up M'land Window', *FCJ*, 4 August 1988, p. 2; and 8 August 1988, p. 2. However, the ROC sets five conditions for mainland materials being allowed admission to Taiwan: (a) the material should not be financed, published, issued or produced by any official mainland Chinese institution or official; (b) it should not contain mainland Chinese Communist propaganda; (c) it should not bear or carry any official mainland Chinese emblem; (d) it should not spread rumors or false news to affect Taiwan's security, to incite people, or spread seditious propaganda; (e) it should not violate existing laws of the ROC on publications, films, broadcasts, television, and related areas.

[49.] See *China Times*, 24 April 1988, p. 10. The author, at that time in Taipei, lined up for two hours to buy a ticket for this film.

50. *RMRB(OE)*, 9 February 1989, p. 5.

51. See *CDN(IE)*, 18 April 1989, p. 1.

52. See *Commercial Times*, 10 June 1989, p. 3.

53. Karl W. Deutsch, 'Communication Theory and Political Integration', in Philip E. Jacob and James V. Toscano (eds.), *The Integration of Political Communities*, New York: J. B. Lippincott Co., 1964, pp. 53–5.

54. 'Taiwan In Transition', *The Economist*, 19 October 1985, p. 38.

55. The CCP's classified unpublished document obtained by the Military Intelligence Bureau of the ROC.

56. 'Trade Between the Mainland and Taiwan Belongs to the Inter-Provinces Material Exchanges', *RMRB*, 5 April 1980, p. 1.

57. Li Chaochen, 'The Now-Peaceful Taiwan Strait', *China Reconstructs*, September 1986, p. 12.

58. See 'Regulations Concerning the Trade Between Taiwan and the Mainland', *Taishin Magazine*, February 1986, p. 11 (in Chinese). Tariff for Taiwan products ranges from 0 per cent to 45 per cent, while tariffs for products from other countries ranges from 50 per cent to 150 per cent. Therefore, Beijing's policy still favors Taiwan.

59. Liang Mien-kuan, 'The Golden Route Between Taiwan-Hong Kong-China', *The Nineties*, May 1985, p. 11 (in Chinese).

60. 'Mainland Invites Taiwan Investors', *BR*, July 18–24, 1988, p. 5. For those who are interested in trade regulations between Taiwan and the mainland, see *The Handbook for Trade Between the Mainland and Taiwan*, Beijing: Modern Publishing House, 1989 (in Chinese).

61. See Note 60 above.

62. See *Youth Daily News*, 5 March 1986, p. 2 (in Chinese).

63. See 'Trade Flows Where No Diplomat Goes', *The Economist*, 22 March 1986, p. 72; and 'Re-exports of Taiwan Foods to China Soar', *South China Morning Post*, 5 January 1985, p. 1; *CDN(IE)*, 19 July 1985, p. 1. The reason why the mainland suddenly cancelled the order was not clear; however, Paijifa's overdependence on the mainland market was the main factor that caused the company's bankruptcy. In fact, however, nothing ventured nothing gained. Risk always accompanies business activities. The case of Paijifa on the one hand indicated the potential instability of mainland trade; while on the other hand., it also revealed the mismanagement of the company.

64. *CDN(IE)*, 8 March 1984, p. 2; *RMRB*, 11 March 1984, p. 4.

65. *CDN(IE)*, 5 July 1986, p. 1.

66. See Carl Goldstein, 'Trade Booms Despite the Ban by Taiwan', *FEER*, 24 July 1986, p. 30; 'The Development Trend of the Two Sides Trade', *Industry and Commerce Monthly*, May (1988); 29–37 (in Chinese); and the editorial, 'Some Suggestions Concerning Our Trade and Economic Relations with the Mainland', *Commercial Times*, 30 May 1988, p. 2.

67. Dori Jones Yang and Dinah Lee, 'Asia's New Fire-Breather: The Rise of Greater China As An Economic Power', *International Business Week*, 19 September 1988, pp. 18–21.

68. For details, see *The United Daily News*, 22 January 1992, p. 2.

69. See *Commercial Times*, 10 October 1988, p. 6.

70. See Chang King-yuh's comments. He is a former spokesman of the ROC government, *FCJ*, 23 December 1985, p. 1.

71. See Wu Yuan-li, 'The Fatal Attraction: Investment in the Mainland', *Commonwealth*, June (1988): 34–36 (in Chinese).

72. 'Mainland Raw Material Imports Cheer Taiwan', *FCJ*, 18 July 1988, p. 8.

73. '"Bandit" Label Dropped', *FCJ*, 18 August 1988, p. 1.

74. See *CDN(IE)*, 17 August 1988, p. 2.

75. See 'Ma Ying-jeou's Comments Concerning the Two Sides' Relations', *CDN(IE)*, 26 June 1989, p. 2.

76. See *CDN(IE)*, 31 January 1989, p. 1.

77. See *China Times*, 11 February 1992, p. 11.

78. See *The Independence Morning Post*, 10 December 1988, p. 6. According to this Bureau's economic analyst, the trade pattern between neighboring states usually has a higher degree of interdependence because of geographical advantages. The analyst said that the degree of interdependence can incorporate as much 30 per cent of one country's total trade amount. Therefore, the analyst infers that the degree of the two Chinas' trade interdependence might reach this level (30 per cent). In 1991, the ROC's total foreign trade amount was over US$130 billion; if so, the total amount of the two Chinas trade should be able to reach US$40 billion in the future if there is no negative factor to hamper the conduct of trade between the two Chinas.

79. See *China Times*, 7 October 1988, p. 2; and Yang Kuei-mei, 'A Secret That Even the Shrimp and Fish Know', *The Journalist*, No. 84, October 17–23, 1988, pp. 42–47.

80. Yang Kuei-mei, See Note 79 above, p. 47.

81. Carolyn Leung, 'China Trade With Seoul and Taipei Soars, Says Report', *South China Morning Post*, 13 October 1987, p. 3.

82. *Two Sides Economic and Statistical Monthly Report*, Taipei: Mainland China Affairs Office, June 1993, p. 47 (in Chinese).

83. See *The Independence Morning Post*, 18 September 1988, p. 6.

84. Denis Fred Simon, 'Taiwan's Political Economy and the Evolving Links Between the PRC, Hong Kong, and Taiwan', *AEI Foreign Policy and Defense Review*, 6, 3, (1986): 48.

85. *China Times*, 11 February 1992, p. 11.

86. 'Coming In From the Cold?' *FEER*, 4 May 1979, p. 24.

87. Wen Wei-ming, 'US "Two Chinas" Scheme in World Sports', *Peking Review*, 3 August 1962, p. 15.

88. 'All-China Sports Federation Reiterates China's Just Stand', *Peking Review*, 9 July 1976, p. 6.

[89.] *CDN(IE)*, 28 November 1979, p. 1 and 24 March 1981, p. 2.

[90.] *CDN(IE)*, 9 April 1979, p. 1; see also *NYT*, 11 May 1979, p. A4.

[91.] *Olympic Review*, No. 145, November 1979, pp. 626–8. See also 'China's Legitimate Seat In IOC Restored', *BR*, 2 November 1979, p. 3; 'The Constitution of the IOC Should Not Be Violated', *CDN(IE)*, 28 October 1979, p. 1.

[92.] See the editorial, 'Protest the Nagoya Resolution That Violates the IOC Constitution', *CDN(IE)*, 28 November 1979, p. 1.

[93.] *Olympic Review*, No. 162, April 1981, p. 211.

[94.] 'Olympic Rule Limited', *FCJ*, 30 September 1984, p. 1.

[95.] Dong Yu-ching, 'Olympic Model Use Limited', *FCJ*, 21 October 1984, p. 1.

[96.] *The United Daily News*, 12 November 1991, p. 2.

[97.] See 'Mainland Door Opened Wider', *FCJ*, 26 September 1988, p. 1.

[98.] See *CDN(IE)*, 3 February 1989, p. 1; and *CDN(IE)*, 7 April 1989, p. 2. See also Bao Xing, 'Welcome Taiwan Compatriots to Beijing', *OW(OE)*, No. 16, 17 April 1989, p. 1.

[99.] 'A Victory for World's People', *Peking Review*, 29 October 1971, p. 6.

[100.] Chen Chi-di, 'On Its Own—The Republic of China', *Asian Affairs*, Fall (1983): 58.

[101.] *The Europe Year Book 1985: A World Survey, Vol. 1, Part 1: International Organizations*, London: Europe Publications Limited, 1985, p. 34. Beijing's customs policy and economic practices at present fail to meet GATT requirements; thus, Beijing has been denied entry into GATT.

[102.] *NYT*, 22 April 1980, p. D6; see also *CDN(IE)*, 19 April 1980, p. 1.

[103.] *NYT*, 16 May 1980, p. D4; see also 'Taiwan—Out But Not Down', *FEER*, 23 May 1980, pp. 64–5.

[104.] Editorial, 'Insistence on the Principle of the Asian Development Bank and Preservation of Our Membership', *CDN(IE)*, 23 February 1983, p. 1.

[105.] 'Taiwan—Out But Not Down', *FEER*, 23 May 1980, p. 65.

[106.] See *CDN(IE)*, 23 February 1983, p. 1 and 7 May 1983, p. 1. The US and Japan were predominant among the other founding countries of the ADB in 1966, in terms of population, tax revenue, exports and other economic indicators. These two countries each submitted US$200 million of the total US$1 billion founding budget.

[107.] 'China Should Become Member of Asian Bank', *BR*, 16 May 1983, p. 4.

[108.] See Note 107 above. See also 'US Stand on Bank Refuted', *BR*, 4 April 1983, p. 8. The US and Japan insisted that Beijing should apply for new membership within the ADB rather than simply expel Taipei and replace their seat; see Byron S. J. Weng, 'Taiwan's International Status Today', *The China Quarterly*, September (1984): 467.

[109.] See Steven R. Weisman, 'President Says US Is Backing Peking Regime', *NYT*, 29 November 1983, p. A1 and A11; see also 'US "Two Chinas" Policy Protested', *BR*, 5 December 1983, p. 10.

[110.] Lee Yi, 'A Subtle Change Before Approaching the ADB Annual Meeting', *The Nineties*, March 1986, p. 43.

[111.] Byron S. J. Weng, 'Taiwan's International Status Today', p. 468.

[112.] 'Joint Communique on the Establishment of Diplomatic Relations', *Department of State Bulletin*, 79, 2022, January (1979): 25.

[113.] Carl Goldstein, 'An Alias To Save A Seat', *FEER*, 23 January 1986, p. 36. See also 'Seminar: The New Direction of the US China Policy', *The Nineties*, March (1986): 57.

[114.] See *Asian Development Bank Annual Report 1985*, Manila: Asian Development Bank, 1986, p. 1.

[115.] *CDN(IE)*, 12 March 1986, p. 1. Regarding the ROC's position, see *CDN(IE)*, 15 March 1986, p. 1; 29 April 1986, p. 1; 2 May 1986, p. 1; 17 October 1986, p. 1.

[116.] Carl Goldstein, 'An Alias To Save A Seat', *FEER*, 23 January 1986, p. 36.

[117.] Lena H. Sun, 'China, Taiwan Banking Relationship Viewed As Positive Step for Rivals', *The Washington Post*, 30 April 1986, p. A15.

[118.] Taipei suggested that it would like to accept the name of 'China, Taipei' if Beijing were to enter a 'China, Beijing', however, the PRC rejected this idea immediately. See *FEER*, 23 January 1986, p. 36.

[119.] See Note 118 above.

[120.] *CDN(IE)*, 29 April 1986, p. 1.

[121.] *CDN(IE)*, 25 April 1986, p. 1. In recent years, Taiwan has become a net contributor rather than a borrower of funds. It is said that Taipei's contribution might be indirectly borrowed by Beijing if both sides work together in the ADB; see 'Growing Economic Ties But No Political Trust', *FEER*, 24 July 1986, p. 24.

[122.] *China Times*, 30 April 1988, p. 2.

[123.] A document that the author obtained from the Central Bank of the ROC.

[124.] See Note 123 above.

[125.] See the announcement of the Government Information Office of the ROC, *China Times*, 10 May 1989, p. 2.

[126.] See *The Independence Morning Post*, 11 May 1989, p. 2.

[127.] See *United Daily News*, 15 April 1988, p. 2.

[128.] 'Taiwan Pilot Returns to Mainland', *BR*, 12 May 1986, p. 9.

[129.] See 'When Dragons Touch', *The Economist*, 17 May 1986, p. 31; see also 'A Jumbo Windfall: Peking Capitalizes on CAL Defection Wanting Direct Talks', *FEER*, 15 May 1986, p. 17; and Daniel Southerland, 'Peking, Taiwan Official Meet', *The Washington Post*, 18 May 1986, p. A26.

[130.] See *CDN(IE)*, 5 May 1986, p. 2; 6 May 1986; 7 May 1986, p. 2.

131. See Chu Deng-kao's talks. Chu is the former Deputy Minister of the Ministry of Communications of the ROC, *CDN(IE)*, 5 May 1986, p. 2; and *RMRB*, 8 May 1986, p. 4.

132. *RMRB*, 7 May 1986, p. 4.

133. *RMRB*, 12 May 1986, p. 1.

134. Editorial, 'How To Tackle It? And Why? The Two Big Problems After the CAL Plane-Loss', *The United Daily News*, 7 May 1986, p. 2.

135. *CDN(IE)*, 14 May 1986, p. 1.

136. See *CDN(IE)*, 21 May 1986, p. 1; and 23 May 1986, p. 1; see also *RMRB*, 21 May 1986, p. 1 and 24 May 1986, p. 1.

137. For example, Chen Pao-chung, formerly in the PRC's Air Force, had been promoted and rewarded with five thousand taels of gold by the government of the ROC after his defection to Taiwan via South Korea in February 1986; see *CDN(IE)*, 18 May 1986, p. 1. According to Taipei, the ROC has awarded about US$2.7 million worth of gold to 13 mainland Chinese defectors in the past 30 years; see 'Fly Now (or Low) Pay Later', *FCJ*, 19 September 1988, p. 2.

138. *NYT*, 24 April 1983, p. A3.

139. *Taishin Magazine*, July 1986, p. 1.

140. Liao Kuan-shen, 'From the CAL Incident Toward a Way To Realize China's Reunification', *Hongkong Economic Journal Monthly*, 10:3, June (1986): 19.

141. 'Talks Over Jet Break Icy Silence', *BR*, 2 June 1986, p. 6.

142. 'Humanitarian Issues vs. Politics', *FCJ*, 26 May 1986, p. 2.

143. 'Our Understanding About the Incident of the CAL Plane', *CDN(IE)*, 31 May 1986, p. 1.

144. *The United Daily News*, 21 May 1986, p. 2; see also Chiu Shui, 'There Are Many Humanitarian Problems Aside From the CAL Case', *Chinese Magazine*, June 1986, p. 6 (in Chinese).

145. See *The Independence Morning Post*, 14 May 1988, p. 1. Taipei quickly arrested these two hijackers and ordered the plane to leave within several hours. In October 1988, these two hijackers were sentenced to prison terms of three and half years because of their action; see *CDN(IE)*, 28 October 1988, p. 2. Taipei's action can serve as a good example for the two Chinas to handle similar incidents and deter hijacking from happening again between the two Chinas.

146. See *China Times*, 15 September 1988, p. 1. New rates of gold rewards for the PRC's military aircraft: (a) Chien-8 fighter or Hung-6 bomber (equivalent to the MiG-23): 8,000 taels (same as the old rate); (b) Chien-7 fighter (MiG-21) 4,000 taels (7,000 taels old rate); (c) Hung-5 light bomber (Ilyushin-28): 3,000 taels (6,000 taels old rate); (d) Chien-6 fighter (MiG-19): 2,000 taels (5,000 taels old rate); (e) Chien-5 fighter (MiG-17): 500 taels (3,000 taels old rate); (f) military helicopter: 300–700 taels (500–1,000 taels old rate); (g) Twin-propeller aircraft: 300–500 taels (500 taels old rate).

147. *China Times*, 2 May 1991, p. 1.
148. *The Washington Post*, 18 May 1986, p. A26.
149. C. L. Chiou, 'Knots, Trickles, Dead Water, and New Opportunities of the China Issue', *China Spring*, February 1986; p. 78.
150. Weng Sung-jan, 'The Development of the Relationship of the Two Sides In the Next Decade', *The Nineties*, February 1986, p. 28.
151. Tillman Durdin, 'The View From Taiwan', *Asian Affairs*, 8, 1, September/October (1980): 3.
152. 'Growing Economic Ties But No Political Trust', *FEER*, 24 July 1986, p. 24.

# Notes to Chapter 12

1. Amitai Etzioni, *Political Unification: A Comparative Study of Leaders and Forces*, New York: Holt, Rinehart and Winston, 1965, p. 330.
2. Howard Wriggins, 'National Integration,' in Myron Weiner (ed.), *Modernization: The Dynamics of Growth*, Washington, D.C.: Voice of America Forum Lectures, 1966, p. 197.
3. Myron Weiner, 'Political Integration and Political Development', *The Annals of the American Academy of Political and Social Science 357*, March (1964): 52–64.
4. Parris H. Chang, 'Evolution of Taiwan's Political Leadership After Chiang Ching-kuo', *AEI Foreign Policy and Defense Review*, 6, 3, (1986): 10–11.
5. Since 1949, the KMT has periodically subsidized these two parties as part of allocating the fee for 'anti-communism propaganda'. In 1988, each party received NT$2,680,000 (US$99,000) from the KMT. See *The Independence Morning Post*, 30 March 1989, p. 5.
6. Shim Jae Hoon, 'Awash In A Sea of Money', *FEER*, 15 September 1988, p. 51.
7. For details, see *Republic of China 1988*, Taipei: Hilit Publishing Company, 1988, p. 117.
8. See Hu Fo's comments in *China Times*, 5 January 1989, p. 2. Hu is a political science professor at National Taiwan University.
9. To define 'democracy' is not an easy task. Like such words as 'progress', 'justice', or 'welfare', it does not call to mind a tangible object or a sharp image. Moreover, it can mean different things to different people. The Communist nations also describe their governments as 'People's Democracies' or 'Socialist' Democracy' and it is not difficult to see that they are imparting to the word 'democracy' a meaning quite different from that held in the Western world, that is, a liberal democracy. Therefore, when liberal democracy is genuinely implemented the five conditions mentioned should be included.

302 NOTES TO PAGES 202 TO 205

See Robert K. Carr, Marver H. Berstein, and Walter F. Murphy, *American Democracy in Theory and Practice*, New York: Holt, Rinehart & Winston, 1963, pp. 30–2. The political reforms in Poland and the Soviet Union (before 1991) in recent years have shown the concept of 'liberal' democracy as an universal concept which to some extent has been accepted by some of the erstwhile communist countries.

[10.] Richard Halloran, 'Signs of Dissent Absent in Taiwan', *New York Times*, 2 May 1976, p. 12. See also Ralph N. Clough, Island China: Cambridge, Mass.: Harvard University Press, 1978, p. 34.

[11.] Karl W. Deutsch, *Nationalism and Its Alternatives*, New York: Alfred A. Knopf, 1969, pp. 21–4.

[12.] Samuel P. Huntington, *Political Order In Changing Societies*, New Haven, Conn.: Yale University Press, 1977, p. 5.

[13.] See Note 12 above.

[14.] See *China Times*, 31 March 1989, p. 2.

[15.] Harry Eckstein, *Division and Cohesion in Democracy: A Study of Norway*, Princeton, N.J.: Princeton University Press, 1966, p. 227.

[16.] Edmund A. Aunger, *In Search of Political Stability: A Comparative Study of New Brunswick and Northern Ireland*, Montreal: McGill-Queen's University Press, 1981, p. 39.

[17.] See Note 16 above, pp. 40–61. See also Ted R. Gurr and M. McClelland, *Political Performance: A Twelve-Nation Study*, Beverly Hills: Sage Publications, 1971, pp. 6 and 71. See also Rod Hague and Martin Harrop, *Comparative Government*, London: The MacMillan Press, 1982, pp. 7–8.

[18.] Ted R. Gurr and M. McClelland, See Note 17 above, p. 11.

[19.] For details, see *Republic of China 1988*, Note 7 above, pp. 510–12.

[20.] Lin Chia-chen, 'Towards the Cabinet System', *Commercial Times*, 28 April 1989, p. 2.

[21.] For details, see *Republic of China 1988*, Note 7 above, pp. 517–8.

[22.] Theoretically speaking, the National Assembly, the presidential electoral body, should function as the watchdog of the President. However, given the fact that this chamber's aging deputies are lacking the people's mandate and are pro-KMT, the President is in fact free from being accountable to the people.

[23.] See *China Times*, 2 June 1988, p. 3; and 12 April 1989, p. 2. See also Hu Fo, 'Reconstruction of the Constitutional Political System and Creation of the New Politics', a paper presented at the Seminar 'Meeting the Challenges and Creation of the New Politics' held in Taipei, Taiwan, ROC during the period of June 1–3, 1988.

[24.] According to the ROC's constitution, the term for members of the Legislative Yuan is 3 years and 6 years for both members of the National Assembly and Control Yuan. The term of the first elected legislators started from 7 May 1948 and should have expired on 7 May 1951. The term for both members of the National Assembly and the Control Yuan accordingly expired in 1954. The ROC at that time retreated to Taiwan, however, and was unable to hold a nationwide election including the mainland for members of the three chambers of the parliament. In order to resolve this political difficulty, the ruling KMT, through an interpretation of the Constitution by the Supreme Court, requested members of the Parliament to continue exercising the popular right until the day that the mainland would be recovered. See Premier Yu Kuo-hua's and Justice Minister, Shih Chi-yang's, answers to the questions raised by DPP members in the Legislative Yuan; *China Times*, 31 October 1987, p. 1.

25. 'Ruling Kuomintang to Study Four Issues', *FCJ*, 19 May 1986, p. 1.

26. *The Independence Evening Post*, 29 October 1987, p. 2.

27. *China Times*, 26 March 1989, p. 2.

28. *China Times*, 25 October 1987, p. 2.

29. Carl Goldstein, 'The Young Turks Use Opposition Street Tactics', *FEER*, 3 September 1987, p. 16. See also *The Independence Morning Post*, 4 February 1988, p. 2.

30. *The Independence Evening Post*, 28 October 1987, p. 2.

31. *Central Daily News*, 13 May 1986, p. 1.

32. 'Parliament Plan OK'd', *FCJ*, 6 February 1989, p. 1.

33. 'Reelection Totally, Otherwise, Confrontation', *The Independence Morning Post*, 6 March 1988, pp. 1–2.

34. See Yao Chia-wen's comments, *The Independence Morning Post*, 4 February 1988, p. 2. Mr. Yao was the two-term chairman of the DPP. See also 'The Supplementary-Elected Legislators Advocate a Total Reelection', *China Times*, 2 November 1987, pp. 1–2; and 'Opposing the Maintenance of the Mainlander Representative System', *China Times*, 2 January 1988, p. 2.

35. 'Aging ROC Parliamentary Members May Be Asked to Give Up Seats', *FCJ*, 8 February 1988, p. 1.

36. See *CDN(IE)*, 27 January 1989, p. 1. See also *China Times*, 27 February 1989, p. 2.

37. This counterticket was headed by the President of the Judicial Yuan Lin Yang-kang, a Taiwan-born politician, with Chiang Wei-kuo, the surviving son of Chiang Kai-shek, as vice-presidential nominee. After considerable negotiation, however, Lin and Chiang withdrew from the race.

38. June Teufel Dreyer, 'Taiwan in 1990: Finetuning the System', *Asian Survey*, XXXI, I January (1991): 60.

39. For the whole text of the amendments, see *Free China Journal*; 2 May 1991, p. 1.

40. *United Daily News*, 22 December 1991, p. 1.

41. Seymour M. Lipset, *Political Man: The Social Bases of Politics* (Baltimore: The Johns Hopkins University Press, 1988), p. 64.

42. Dankwart A. Rustow, *A World of Nations: The Problems of*

*Political Modernization*, Washington, D.C.: Brookings Institution, 1967, p. 157.

43. Dennis Pirages, *Managing Political Conflict*, New York: Praeger Publishers, 1976, p. 52.

44. Edmund A. Aunger, 'In Search of Political Stability', p. 45.

45. Dell G. Hitchner and Carol Levine, *Comparative Government and Politics*, New York: Harper & Row Publishers, 1981, pp. 54–8.

46. Edmund A. Aunger, 'In Search of Political Stability', p. 49.

47. John F. Copper, 'Taiwan: New Challenges to Development', *Current History*, April (1986): 183.

48. Lucian W. Pye, 'Taiwan Developments and Their Implications for US-PRC Relations', *The Rand Publications Series*, N-2138, March (1984): v.

49. Thomas B. Gold, *State And Society In The Taiwan Miracle*, Armonk, N.Y.: M.E. Sharpe, 1986, p. 7.

50. Jurgen Domes, 'Political Differentiation In Taiwan: Group Formation Within the Ruling Party and the Opposition Circles 1979–80', *Asian Survey*, 21, 9, September (1981): 1011.

51. Edwin A. Winckler, 'Institutionalization and Participation on Taiwan: From Hard to Soft Authoritarianism?' *The China Quarterly*, September (1984): 482.

52. Jurgen Domes, 'Taiwan in 1991: Searching for Political Consensus', *Asian Survey*, XXXII, I January (1992): 46.

53. Antonio Chiang, 'When Will the Kite Become A Free Bird?' *The Journalist*, February 6–19, 1989, p. 46.

54. Chao Chun-san, 'Opening for Visiting Relatives—Our Self-examination', *CDN(IE)*, 5 November 1988, p. 1.

55. Yangsun Chou and Andrew J. Nathan, 'Democratizing Transition in Taiwan', *Asian Survey*, 27, 3, March (1987): 227. See also *The Kuomintang: A Brief Introduction 1987–88*, Taipei: Central Committee, the Kuomintang, ROC, 1988.

56. *The Kuomintang*, see Note 55 above.

57. Carl Goldstein, 'Oiling the Old Machine', *FEER*, 3 September 1987, p. 15.

58. Antonio Chiang, 'The "Red Guard" in the Kuomintang', *The Journalist*, December 5–11, 1988, pp. 56–7.

59. Ralph N. Clough, *Island China*, Cambridge, Mass.: Harvard University Press, 1978, p. 51.

60. Samuel P. Huntington, 'Social and Institutional Dynamics of One-Party Systems', in Samuel P. Huntington and Clement H. Moore (eds.), *Authoritarian Politics in Modern Society: The Dynamics of Established One-Party Systems*, New York: Basic Books, 1970, p. 12.

61. Ralph N. Cough, *Island China*, p. 67.

62. Fred M. Hayward, 'Continuities and Discontinuities Between Studies of National and International Political Integration: Some

Implications for Future Research Efforts', *International Organization*, 24, 4, Autumn (1970): 935.

[63.] Due to mismanagement this Cooperative, a big-name savings and loan institution in Taiwan, suddenly collapsed in early 1985. The result of lengthy investigation has shown that at least 15 finance officials were responsible for this scandal, including two former finance ministers, Loh Jen-kang and Hsu Li-deh. Chiang Yen-shih, the then secretary-general of the KMT, also stepped down accepting 'moral responsibility' for this incident.

[64.] Henry Liu, a Chinese-American writer, was murdered in San Francisco by two killers dispatched by Taiwan's Military Intelligence Bureau in 1985. Vice Admiral Wong Hsi-ling, head of this Bureau, was convicted of plotting Liu's death and was given a life sentence, along with the two killers.

[65.] Hsu Chin-yun and Tung Chin-fong, 'Bribery Everywhere', *The Journalist*, July 25–31, 1988, p. 65.

[66.] See *China Times*, 16 August 1988, p. 2.

[67.] 'Official Image Needs Polishing', *FCJ*, 22 August 1988, p. 3.

[68.] 'Ma Says Discontent Shows Pluralism', *FCJ*, 10 October 1988, p. 3.

[69.] See *China Times*, 16 March 1989, p. 2.

[70.] See Jung Fu-tien, 'The Mental Progress of President Chiang's Pushing for Political Reform', *United Daily News*, 30 August 1987, p. 2. See also Carl Goldstein, 'New-look Old Guard', *FEER*, 3 September 1987, p. 17.

[71.] Robert Grieves, 'Chiang Ready to Welcome Opposition', *The Times*, 29 November 1986, p. 8.

[72.] See then Vice President Lee Teng-hui's talks in the article of Jung Fu-tien, 'The Mental Progress of Chiang', p. 2.

[73]. King-yuh Chang, 'Democratization of A Modernizing Society: The Case of the Republic of China,' reprinted from 'Progress in Democracy: The Pacific Basin Experience' presentations at the Ilhae / Carnegie Council Joint Seminar, July 2–3, 1987, Seoul, Republic of Korea.

[74.] This telephone survey was conducted by the independent magazine, *the Journalist*, on January 14 and 15, 1988. The 1,600 persons sampled were randomly selected from Taipei, Taichung, and Kaohsiung, the three biggest cities of Taiwan. For details, see *The Journalist*, January 9–15, 1989, pp. 26–8.

[75.] Harry Eckstein, 'Division and Cohesion in Democracy', p. 32.

[76.] Edmund A. Aunger, 'In Search of Political Stability', p. 55.

[77.] William Kornhauser, *The Politics of Mass Society*, Glencae, Ill.: Free Press, 1959, p. 145.

[78.] Wallace W. Conroe, 'A Cross-National Analysis of the Impact of Modernization Upon Political Stability', unpublished M.A. thesis, San Diego State College, 1965, pp. 65–73, 86–7.

79. Samuel P. Huntington, *Political Order in Changing Societies*, p. 47.

80. See Note 79 above, p. 46. According to Cyril E. Black, the first modernizing nation, England, took 183 years, from 1649 to 1832, to complete its modernization task. The United States, the second modernizing, took 89 years, from 1776 to 1865, to modernize itself. For 13 countries during the Napoleonic period (1789–1815), the average period of modernization was 73 years. But for 21 of the 26 countries which began modernization during the first quarter of the 20th century and had emerged by the 1960s, the average was only 29 years. See Cyril E. Black, *The Dynamics of Modernization*, New York: Harper and Row, 1966, pp. 90–94.

81. Prior to 1986, Taiwan's high school boys were ordered to keep a military short cut of hair, at times, even as bald as that of a monk; while the girls' hair could exceed the end of their ears only by a little. Taipei claimed that this regulation was aimed at maintaining students' discipline, an idea coming from the military command. This regulation, however, did hurt those young students' feelings as they considered it an ugly hairstyle.

82. Shim Jae Hoon, 'Awash In A Sea of Money', *FEER*, 15 September 1988, p. 15.

83. Ti Ying, 'Kuomintang: How to Save the Confidence of Industrialists', *The Commonwealth*, 1 May 1988, p. 60.

84. 1,242 copies of the questionnaire were issued to these executives; however, only 248 executives from business circles completed the questionnaire and returned it to The Commonwealth magazine. From those the total percentage of the result exceeds 100 per cent because of the multiple choice question. See Yao Ming-chia, 'Noise and Disorder: The Confidence Crisis of the Industrialists', *Commonwealth*, 1 May 1988, pp. 44–52. This magazine is run by a private company and has enjoyed general popularity in Taiwan, especially in business circles.

85. See Note 84 above. See also Yi Ping, 'The Spring of Hope? The Winter of Despair?' *Global Views Monthly*, 15 May 1988, pp. 16–19.

86. *Commercial Times*, 22 May 1988, p. 2.

87. See Legislator Yu Ching's (DPP) comments, *China Times*, 25 November 1987, p. 2.

88. These are terms and concepts employed by Karl W. Deutsch. See 'Social Mobilization and Political Development', *American Political Science Review*, September (1961): 493 ff; see also James C. Davies, 'Toward A Theory of Revolution', *American Sociological Review*, February (1962): 5ff; and K. J. Holsti, 'Underdevelopment and the Gap Theory of International Conflict', *American Political Science Review*, September (1975): 827.

89. Samuel P. Huntington, *Political Order In Changing Societies*, p. 54.

90. *CDN(IE)*, 2 February 1989, p. 1.

91. Karl W. Deutsch, *Nationalism and Social Communication: An Inquiry Into the Foundations of Nationality*, Cambridge, Mass.: The M.I.T. Press, 1962, p. 52.

92. Fred M. Hayward, 'Continuities and Discontinuities', See Note 62 above, p. 936.

# Notes to Chapter 13

1. 'The 2nd Party Congress of the DPP Passes Its Resolution', *Democratic Progressive News*, No. 38, November 14–20, 1987: 1 (in Chinese). Hereafter *DPN*.

2. Editorial, 'Between Taiwan and Communist China: Kuomintang! Which Side Will You Be On?' *DPN*, No. 39, November 21–27, 1987: 2.

3. Lei Chen, a liberal mainlander, a KMT member, and a close colleague of Chiang Kai-shek, published the *Free China* magazine to promote democracy and later attempted to organize the China Democratic Party in 1960. These actions resulted in his being imprisoned for many years.

4. In 1979, efforts by a group of Taiwan Chinese (mainly the Taiwanese, associated with the magazine Formosa) to form a new political group to push for political reforms were broken up forcefully by the KMT. Members of that group were sentenced for sedition. All of these members, were released respectively since 1986. Yao Chia-wen and Huang Hsin-chieh, one after another, were elected chairman of the DPP in 1987 and 1988 respectively. As well, some spouses of those imprisoned, such as Chou Ching-yu and Hsu Rong-shu, won elections by an overwhelming margins in 1986 and became legislators in the ROC government.

5. See *CDN(IE)*, 27 April 1989, p. 2. In fact, only 50 newspapers issue their papers periodically, while the rest of the 101 registered newspapers are inactive.

6. Chang Chun-hong, 'On "Taiwan Independence"', *The Independence Morning Post*, 25 April 1988, p. 5.

7. This term ironically has been labelled on the KMT by elements of the Taiwan Independence Movement who argue that, although the KMT has constantly opposed the idea of Taiwan's independence, the KMT is in fact practicing the idea of the independence of Taiwan. These elements within the Taiwan Independence Movement label their movement as the 'A-type' Taiwan independence.

8. Chang Chun-hong, 'On "Taiwan Independence"', see Note 6 above, p. 5.

9. Clyde Haberman, 'Independent Taiwan: Risky Idea May Be Gaining', *New York Times*, 18 January 1988, p. A3.

10. In recent years Taipei's policy towards the Taiwan Independence Movement seems to be less rigid due to the implementation of the political reform. For example, some DPP members have openly promoted the 'new nation movement' and the idea of Taiwan independence in December 1988 on their island-wide campaign tour. The ROC government did not repress this activity. See *China Times*, 26 December 1988, p. 2; and *The Independence Evening Post*, 5 April 1988, p. 1.

11. This foundation is administered by some of the KMT's younger and liberal members. The credibility of this foundation seems fairly well established in Taiwan.

12. *United Evening News*, 11 March 1988, p. 2.

13. Huang Kuen-hui, *Mainland Policy and the Two Sides Relations*, Taipei: The Mainland Affairs Council, January 1992, p. 44.

14. 'National Security Law', *Central Daily News*, 24 June 1987, p. 1. On 15 July 1987, this law was in effect when martial law was lifted. Taipei argued that this law was enacted for protecting the ROC's national security during the Period of Suppression of the Communist Rebellion. Although the Suppression Period was ended in May 1991, the National Security Law remains in effect today.

15. Clyde Haberman, 'Independent Taiwan: Risky Idea May Be Gaining', *New York Times*, 18 January 1988, p. A3.

16. Yangsun Chou and Andrew J. Nathan, 'Democratizing Transition In Taiwan', *Asian Survey*, 27, 3, March (1987): 281.

17. Yu Ching, 'Some Comments On the Formation of TAPPS', *The Independence Evening Post*, 25 April 1986, p. 2. Yu was a legislator (DPP) in the Legislative Yuan.

18. For those interested in the development of Taiwan's politics during this period, see 'Chiang Seeks Political Dialogue', *South China Morning Post*, 9 May 1986, p. 10; 'A Harmonic Communication Between the Party and the Non-party Members', *United Daily News*, 11 May 1986, p. 1; 'Kuomintang Willing to Compromise As Opposition Leaders Flex Muscles', *Hong Kong Standard*, 21 May 1986, p. 22; Terry Cheng, 'Kuomintang Tries to Head Off Showdown', *South China Morning Post*, 28 June 1986, p. 10; Patrick L. Smith, 'Chiang's Agenda for Taiwan: A New Political Course', *International Herald Tribune*, 25 July 1986, p. 1; Carl Goldstein, 'KMT Widens the Gulf', *FEER*, 21 August 1986, pp. 20–1; Daniel Southerland, 'Aging Leader of Taiwan Relaxes Ban on Opponents', *The Washington Post*, 30 May 1986, p. A25; To Yiu-ming, 'Consolidating Forces to "TRAP" Kuomintang', *Hong Kong Standard*, 16 June 1986, p. 7; and *United Daily News*, 24 April 1986, p. 1.

19. Terry Cheng, 'Kuomintang', p. 10.

20. Some TAPPS members objected to this idea of forming the DPP without warning. They were fearful of the KMT's repression because they were violating the party ban. See Hsin-hsin Yang, 'Birth of Party

Startles Ruling Kuomintang', *South China Morning Post*, 30 September 1986, p. 13; and *The Independence Evening Post*, 29 September 1986, p. 2.

21. 'KMT to Talk With New Party', *South China Morning Post*, 2 October 1986, p. 7.

22. For details of this law, see *CDN(IE)*, 21 January 1989, p. 1.

23. Analyses and discussions in this section are mainly based on the following materials: Hsieh Chang-ting, *Democratic Progressive Party*, Taipei: Free Times Books Series 10, n.d.; Wu Li-hui (ed.), *The Self-Determination and Independence*, Kaohsiung, Taiwan: New Taiwan Books Series 5, n.d.; Wu Li-hui (ed.), *The Future of Taiwan*, Kaohsiung, Taiwan: New Taiwan Books Series 1, n.d.; *Taiwan Christian Presbyterian Church Believers Training Handbook*, Tainan, Taiwan: The Headquarters of the Taiwan Christian Presbyterian Church, 1986, pp. 63–64; Lin Jui, 'The Trend of the DPP's Position Concerning Taiwan Independence', *The Nineties*, May 1988, pp. 48–50; Hu A-nan, '63:37—the Climax of the Party's Seminar', *Democratic Progressive News*, 26 March–1 April 1988, pp. 20–21; Kao Tien-sheng, 'The DPP's Infighting', *The Independence Morning Post*, 23 January 1988, p. 2; Ann Scott Tyson, 'Taiwan Opposition Struggles for Unity to Challenge Government', *The Christian Science Monitor*, 24 December 1987, p. 1; Ann Scott Tyson, 'Taiwan's Opposition Party Pushes for Major Political Reforms', *The Christian Science Monitor*, 23 December 1987, pp. 7–9; Kao Tien-sheng, 'DPP's Internal Cohesion Is Improving', *The Independence Evening News*, 11 November 1987, p. 2; 'Infighting Spoils DPP's Birthday', *South China Morning Post*, 25 September 1987, p. 8; Hong Chien-lung, 'An Interview With Yao Chia-wen and Huang Hsin-chieh', *The Independence Morning Post*, 29 October 1988, p. 2; Chu Kao-cheng, 'The KMT Regime Is An Imperial Government', *Democratic Progressive News*, October 31–November 6, 1987, p. 2; Chu Kao-cheng, 'The Development Crisis of the DPP: A Preliminary Criticism of the Hsin-Chao-Liu Line', *CDN(IE)*, 19 June 1989, p. 7; Lincoln Kaye, 'Ideological Infighting: Opposition Split Could Result In Loss of Key Legislator', *FEER*, 6 July 1989, p. 17.

24. Nicholas D. Kristof, 'Taiwan's Risky Refrain: "Self-determination"', *New York Times*, 14 December 1986, p. 14.

25. For example see former Legislator Fei Hsi-ping's question of the government officers in the legislative Yuan, *The Independence Evening Post*, 24 March 1987, p. 2.

26. Shim Jae Hoon, 'Awash In A Sea of Money', *FEER*, 15 September 1988, p. 52.

27. Yao Chia-wen, 'The New Political Situation Post Chiang-Ching-kuo in Taiwan and in the Strait', a paper prepared for the panel of the Association for Asian Studies, USA, March 1983, p. 3.

28. 'The Current Stage of the Mainland China Policy of the DPP', *Democratic Progressive News*, No. 34, October 17–23, 1987, p. 1.

29. See 'The DPP Passes the Draft of Its Mainland Policy', *China Times*, 25 April 1989, p. 2.

30. *China Times*, 18 April 1988, p. 2.

31. *China Times*, 26 August 1991, p. 7.

32. *China Times*, 14 October 1991, p. 2.

33. *China Times*, 19 July 1991, p. 2.

34. James A. Baker, III, 'America in Asia: Emerging Architecture for a Pacific Community', *Foreign Affairs*, Winter 1991/92: 16.

35. *Bush Says US Is 'Deeply Committed' to Asia/Pacific*, Washington, DC.: USA, 13 November 1991, p. 2.

36. *China Times*, 19 July 1991, p. 1.

37. *The Independence Morning Post*, 9 December 1991, p. 1.

38. *China Times*, 10 October 1991, p. 2. See also *RMRB*, 5 October 1991, p. 1; *RMRB*, 7 September 1991, p. 1.

39. Editorial, 'Between Taiwan and Communist China: Kuomintang! Which Side Will You Be On?' *DPN*, No. 39, November 21–27, 1987, p. 2.

40. *The United Daily News*, 8 October 1991, p. 1.

41. *The United Daily News*, 30 September 1991, p. 3.

42. *China Times*, 10 October 1991, p. 1.

43. *The United Daily News*, 16 October 1991, p. 1.

44. *The United Daily News*, 22 December 1991, p. 1.

45. *The New York Times*, 13 April 1991, p. A7.

46. See *The Independence Morning Post*, 31 October 1988, pp. 1–2. See also Lin Cho-shui, 'A Response to Messrs. Huang Hsin-chich and Chang Jung-hong', *The Independence Morning Post*, 29 October 1988, p. 5; and Lin Cheng-chieh, 'On DPP's Political Policy: An Open Letter to DPP's Chairman Yao Chiu-wen', *China Times*, 3 September 1988, p. 2.

47. *China Times*, 20 November 1991, p. 3.

48. See *The Independence Evening Post*, 12 January 1987, p. 2.

49. See Chen Yu-hsin, 'DPP Won the Vote But No Support From the People', *The Independence Evening Post*, 31 March 1987, p. 2.

50. Lin Jing-kun, 'DPP Should Improve Its Policy', *China Times*, 9 November 1987, p. 2.

51. Chen Yu-hsin, 'DPP Won the Vote', see Note 99 above, p. 2.

52. Shim Jae Hoon, 'Awash in a Sea of Money', *FEER*, 15 September 1988, p. 52.

53. *The Journalist*, January 30-February 5, 1989, pp. 28–52.

54. For details, see *China Times*, 16 May 1992, pp. 1–2.

# Notes to Chapter 14

1. Shuhua Chang, *Communications and China's National Integration: An Analysis of People's Daily and Central Daily News on the China Reunification Issue*, Baltimore, Maryland: Occasional Papers/Reprints

Series in Contemporary Asian Studies, School of Law, University of Maryland, 5, (1986): 109.

2. *Central Daily News*, 27 July 1989, p. 2 (in Chinese).

3. *Renmin Ribao* (Overseas Edition), 23 June 1989, pp. 1–2; and 24 June 1989, p. 1 (in Chinese). Hereafter *RMRB (OE)*.

4. *RMRB* (OE), 7 July 1989, p. 1.

5. *RMRB* (OE), 28 June 1989, p. 1; and 29 June 1989, p. 1.

6. *Central Daily News* (International Edition), 4 August 1989, p. 2.

7. Dun Li, *The Ageless Chinese*, New York: Charles Scibner & Sons, 1965, pp. 562–568.

8. Shuhua Chang, 'China's National Integration', p. 7.

9. Editorial, 'Democracy In Taiwan', *The Australian*, 9 December 1986, p. 12.

# Appendix 9-1

## Guidelines for National Unification

### I. Foreword

The Unification of China is meant to bring about a strong and prosperous nation with a long-lasting, bright future for its people; it is the common wish of Chinese people at home and abroad. After an appropriate period of forthright exchange, cooperation, and consultation conducted under the principles of reason, peace, parity, and reciprocity, the two sides of the Taiwan Straits should foster a consensus of democracy, freedom and equal prosperity, and together build a new a unified China. Based on this understanding, the following guidelines have been specifically formulated with the express hope that all Chinese throughout the world will work with one mind toward their fulfillment.

### II. Goal

To establish a democratic, free and equitably prosperous China.

### III. Principles

1. Both the mainland and Taiwan are parts of Chinese territority. Helping to bring about national unification should be the common responsibility of all Chinese people.
    2. The unification of China should be for the welfare of all its people and not be subject to partisan conflict.
    3. China's unification should aim at promoting Chinese culture, safeguarding human dignity, guaranteeing fundamental human rights, and practicing democracy and the rule of law.
    4. The timing and manner of China's unification should first respect the rights and interests of the people in Taiwan, and protect their security and welfare. It should be achieved in gradual phases under the principles of reason, peace, parity, and reciprocity.

# IV. Process

## 1. Short term—A Phase of Exchanges and Reciprocity

(a) To enhance understanding through exchanges between the two sides of the straits and eliminate hostility through reciprocity; and to establish a mutually benign relationship by not endangering each other's security and stability while engaged in exchanges and not denying the other's existence as a political entity while effecting reciprocity.

(b) To establish a procedure for exchanges across the Straits, to draw up regulations for such exchanges, and to establish intermediary organizations to protect people's rights and interests on both sides of the Straits; to gradually ease various restrictions and expand people-to-people contacts to promote the prosperity of both sides.

(c) In order to improve the people's welfare on both sides of the Straits with the ultimate objective of unifiying the nation, economic reform in the mainland should be carried out forthrightly, the free expression of public opinion there should gradually be allowed to develop, and both democracy and the rule of law should be implemented; while in the Taiwan area efforts should be made to accelerate constitutional reform and promote national development to establish a society of equitable prosperity.

(d) The two sides of the Straits should end the state of hostility and, under the principle of one China, solve all disputes through peaceful means, and furthermore respect—not reject—each other in the international community, so as to move toward a phase of mutual trust and cooperation.

## 2. Medium Term—A Phase of Mutual Trust and Cooperation

(a) Both sides of the Straits should establish official communication channels on an equal footing.

(b) Direct postal, transport and commercial links should be allowed, and both sides should jointly develop the southeastern coastal area of the Chinese mainland and then gradually extend this development to other areas of the mainland in order to narrow the gap in living standards between the two sides.

(c) Both sides of the Straits should work together and assist each other in participating in international organizations and activities.

(d) Mutual visits by high-ranking officials on both sides should be promoted to create favorable conditions for consultation and unification.

### 3. Long Term—A Phase of Consultation and Unification

A consultative organization for unification should be established through which both sides, in accordance with the will of the people in both the mainland and Taiwan areas, and while adhering to the goals of democracy, economic freedom, social justice and nationalization of the armed forces, discuss the grand task of unification and map out a constitutional system to establish a democratic, free, and equitably prosperous China.

*Source*: The Mainland Affairs Council, the Republic of China.

# Appendix 11-1

## Memorandum of Understanding Between the People's Republic of China and the Asian Development Bank

As stated in the cable dated 27 March 1985 from Mr. Wu Xueqian, Minister of Foreign Affairs of the People's Republic of China, addressed to Mr. Masao Fujioka, President of the Asian Development Bank (ADB), the Government of the People's Republic of China (PRC) has reiterated its decision to apply for membership in the ADB as the sole legal government of China. In this connection, the Chinese side and the ADB management, in the course of previous consultations, with regard to the administrative arrangements to be made have reached the following understanding:

1. From the date when the PRC is admitted as a member of the ADB and the sole legal representative of China, the authorities in Taiwan will remain in the ADB under the name of 'Taipei, China'. A decision to this effect will be presented to the Board of Directors of the ADB for their consideration in conformity with the spirit mentioned above. There will be no amendment of the ADB Charter which will affect the status of any existing member of the ADB.

2. Upon the PRC's admission into the Bank, the authorities in Taiwan will be referred to as 'Taipei, China' in all documents, papers, materials, statistics and other publications issued by the ADB. Should the designation in the documents, letters, and other publications sent by the authorities in Taiwan to the ADB be inconsistent with this arrangement, the ADB will change the designation to 'Taipei, China' when it circulates such documents, letters, and other publications.

3. In all statements to be made at the ADB's Annual Meetings and all other ADB meetings, should there occur any situation inconsistent with the above-described redesignation, it will be the responsibility of the ADB secretariat to take necessary measures to ensure consistency. The question of nameplate,

desk-plate and delegation badges will be dealt with in line with the above-mentioned arrangement.

4. Upon the PRC's admission, the ADB will display only the flag of the ADB and the national flag of the host country as the occasion demands.

5. ADB members have the right to determine voluntarily the voting constituency which they will join. Upon the PRC admission, however, 'Taipei, China' will be welcome to join the same voting group with the PRC.

*Source*: The Central Bank, Republic of China

# Appendix 11-2

## Statement by the Delegation of the People's Republic of China to the ADB's Twenty-First Annual Meeting

In accordance with the Memorandum of Understanding signed on 26 November 1985 between the People's Republic of China and the Asian Development Bank, which was unanimously approved by the ADB's Board of Directors, the People's Republic of China was admitted as a member of the ADB as the sole legal representative of China, while the Taiwan authorities would remain in the ADB under the name of 'Taipei, China'. This is the kernel and crux of the Memorandum in question. The ADB management, therefore, has an unshrinkable responsibility for ensuring the full and strict implementation of this Memorandum. Taipei, China, as a member of the ADB, is obliged to strictly abide by the unanimous decision of the ADB's Board of Directors.

We have noted that on formal occasions of the current ADB annual meeting, however, not only have the members of the delegation sent by the Taiwan authorities rejected the redesignation of 'Taipei, China' by covering up the designation on the badges issued by the Secretariat of the ADB, moreover, they have even worn badges of the so-called 'national flag of the Republic of China'. This is an open provocative act defying the Memorandum unanimously approved by the Board of Directors of the ADB. Unfortunately, the management of ADB has failed to take timely rectifying measures, allowing the occurrence of 'two Chinas' during the current annual meeting of the ADB. The Chinese delegation hereby expresses its deep regret and reserves the right to make further response.
Manila, Philippines                                       28 April 1988

*Source*: The Central Bank, Republic of China

# Appendix 13-1

## 'The New Political Situation of the Post Chiang Ching-kuo Era in Taiwan and in the Taiwan Strait' By Yao Chia-wen, Chairman of the DPP

### 1. The Old Color in Taiwan Faded Away

The international status of Taiwan and its nature [as a] country have long been discussed and argued. The external legal status and the nature of [the] country [have] affected the internal political arguments and the development of [the] democratic movement significantly in this beautiful Pacific island [of] Taiwan.

Ever since 1971, when the Government of the Republic of China in Taiwan was expelled from the United Nations, Taiwan has been considered as an independent political unit different from the Republic of China before 1949. However, due to the fact that the same Chinese Government and the same Presidents Chiang still ruled this island, Taiwan was [an] immigrant regime. The color of Taiwan was more Chinese than Taiwanese, [more] immigrant than native.

The old color, however, was fading away. But when the Chiangs were president, they acted as a consistent reminder of the Chinese dynast[ies] in Taiwan. The Chinese color implied a controversial political position that Taiwan is a part of China or Taiwan itself is a China.

When Mr. Lee succeeded Chiang [Ching-kuo] as the new President of Taiwan, the political[ly] consistent reminder disappeared, and the color of China disappeared too.

Taiwan, suddenly in one night, after the replacement of the Chiang presidency, [became] a Taiwanese country and its regime a native regime. The reality of the nature of [a] country and [a] regime exposed, the real color of Taiwan appeared.

### 2. The Old Chinese Dynasty

The KMT tried to preserve a Chinese regime in Taiwan, which denied the rights of the native Taiwanese to enjoy the [authoritative] power in the central government. To a government claim[ing] itself as a government of the Big China with its one billion population, 19 million people on Taiwan certainly have no hope to gain control of it. The KMT not only insisted that Taiwan is a part of China, but also claimed sovereignty over mainland China, including Mongolia. They admitted that they lost control temporarily over mainland China and Mongolia, but they insisted they will recover them some time or other in the future. So the situation in Taiwan was declared as 'abnormal' or 'temporary'. Therefore, it is not strange that a congress survived 40 years without general reelection. And two provincial governments, Hsinchiang and Fukien, provinces of the Mainland, opened offices in Taipei and [still] spend millions and millions of dollars from the Taiwan budget. The KMT government has refused to participate in any organization which accepts the Communist Chinese as members, and has refused to use the term 'Taiwan' to designate its own membership. Any one who challenges this 'Image of the Country' condemned or charged as [an advocate of] 'Taiwan Independ-ence', and calling for Taiwan Independence is viewed as an act[or] of sedition.

Now when the Chinese Dynasties [were] over, and the old color was fading away, that country of China became the country of Taiwan. Since the Peace Treaty with Japan in 1951 transferred no sovereignty of Taiwan to any 'China', this country of Taiwan, from the stand-point of international law, has already enjoyed the independence of a country in some respects, now the question of the the 'Independence of Taiwan' appears with another face. The Independence of Taiwan is the reality. Someone may raise the question 'Should Taiwan be annexed to China'? or 'Should we need reunification'? But changing the status of Taiwan requires a positive decision or determination. The people in Taiwan begin to understand that if nothing were decided, and nothing changed, Taiwan should remain as *de facto* independent. The idea shocks but encourages people so much.

## 3. A Native Regime

Although the political and legal structures remain unchanged, after the assumption of a native Taiwanese president, the Government of the Republic of China is now considered more like a native [Taiwanese] regime than an immigrant or a foreign one.

The fundamental national policy [of the KMT Government [of the ROC] is the 'recovery of Mainland China'. Even when the government stops insisting that they want recovery of Mainland China, this is still their political slogan. The term 'country' or 'nation' has been always referred to as the Big China.

'However, as its color changed, the definition of a 'country' or a 'nation' was changing too. Even when the KMT introduced the National Security Law to replace martial law last year, the term 'national' referred to Taiwan more than to the Big China. After 13th January [1988], when Chiang Ching-kuo died, the reference became more clear. Premier Yu even referred to Taiwan as 'a third country' in an international event when he commented on the new relationship between Peking and South Korea.

The area of territory of this country realistically is limited to the island of Taiwan and other small islands, the adjustment of the national policy and government structures will be followed accordingly. It is not strange that after the government decides to return to the conferences of the Asian Development Bank, and considers entry into GATT, even the official name of 'Republic of China' will not be honored.

'The Congressional reform is the most realistic issue among people in Taiwan. As the claim is made that this is the legitimate government of China, the KMT has refused to accept the proposal that all members of the Congress in Taiwan shall be elected by the people in Taiwan, but rather allows those who were elected 40 years ago to remain in their positions to represent the so-called citizens in residing in the mainland. The Taiwanese people in their democratic movements have long used this issue to show the differences between the political stances of the KMT and the Taiwanese people. The KMT now, after Mr. Lee has assumed his office, decided to introduce a retirement plan to allow the renewal of the Congress. Although the opposition parties were not satisfied with this plan, yet the idea of 'a new Congress of Taiwan' is now adopted.

As the immigrant regime becomes a native regime, and the Chinese country becomes a Taiwanese country, the total legal systems and government structures are to be revised. Even those who support the KMT regime have begun to propose many designs for a new government to come. A new government is blueprinted, a new congress is expected, a new constitution is discussed, and finally a new country grows from these reforms. The demand of the Taiwanese for political reforms will be stronger than before.

## 4. The Strait Bridged

The change in the political situation in Taiwan certainly has reshaped the relationship between two sides of the Strait. Mainland China worries that the loss of [the] Chiangs will cut its links with Taiwan, and that a native-born President will eventually show the true face and the status of Taiwan in its international character. The Taiwan government and people share the same views in allowing the Taiwanese to visit the Mainland, but on the other hand resist the demand of reunification with the Communist Chinese regime.

Most people support a policy to open direct trade across the Strait and to set up culture, sports, and scholarly exchanges. The feelings of hostility against the other side seems to have disappeared. The reduction [of] tension between both sides have the new demand and policy of both the government and the people in Taiwan.

Peking consistently insists that they will use military forces in the Strait, if Taiwan declares independence. But the Taiwanese are aware of the fact that their new country of Taiwan need not bother its neighbor by taking such an unnecessary legal action. They feel more at ease than before. Some legislators inside of the KMT Party have even advocated signing a peace treaty with the PRC to establish peaceful co-existence for both sides. Leaders from the opposition parties feel that they will be more satisfied if the KMT can, quoting Chiang Kai-shek's words 'remain resolutely in the democratic world', which also can be translated as retaining the independent status of Taiwan from China, and replacing its old slogan 'to reunite the whole of China under the San-min-chu-yi (The Three Principles of the people)'. The issue of the Taiwan Strait in the future which needs to be decided and openly declared will be no more whether Taiwan should be declared an independent country, but whether Taiwan should be annexed by China. Taiwan can enjoy its sovereignty without making any formal declaration, so that Peking will have sufficient excuse not to use military forces. The appearance of the real status of Taiwan then brings an opportunity for the Strait to establish peace and friendship if the governments of both sides really seek it.

*Source*: DPP legislator Yao Chia-wen provided this article to the author in 1987. Mr Yao's original document was written in English. Words included within brackets have been added by the author to maintain the authentic meaning and improve its readibility.

# Selected Bibliography

## Government Documents

*A Brief Introduction of the Republic of China*, Taipei: Government Information Office, ROC, 1988 (in Chinese).

*A Note for Citizens Going Abroad*, Guangzhou: Liaison Office of Guangdong People's Government, July 1985 (in Chinese).

*Asian Development Bank Annual Report 1985* Manila: Asian Development Bank, 1986.

*The Compilation of the Reference Materials Regarding Counter-Attacking the Communist Bandits' United Front*, Taipei: Department of Mainland China Affairs, Central Committee of the Kuomintang, 30 June 1987 (in Chinese).

*The Constitution of the People's Republic of China*, Beijing: Foreign Languages Press, 1983.

*The Joint Declaration of the People's Republic of China and the United Kingdom of Great Britain and Northern Ireland Concerning the Hong Kong Issue*, Beijing: Foreign Languages Press, 1984.

*Q & A About the Republic of China*, Taipei: Kwang Hwa Publishing Company, September 1987.

## English-language Books

*A Comprehensive Glossary of Chinese Communist Terminology*, Taipei: The Institute of International Relations, 1978.

Ake, Claude, *A Theory of Political Integration*, Homewood, Ill: Dorsey Press, 1967.

*Asian Security 1988–1989*, London: A. Wheaton & Co. Ltd., 1988.

Black, Cyril E., *The Dynamics of Modernization*, New York: Harper and Row, 1966.

Brown, Seyom, *The Crises of Power*, New York: Columbia University Press, 1979.

Carr, Robert K., Bernstein, Marver H., and Murphy, Walter F., *American Democracy In Theory and Practice*, New York: Holt, Rinehart & Winston, 1963.

Chen King C., (ed.), *China and the Third World: A Foreign Policy Reader*, New York: M.E. Sharpe, Inc., 1979.

Cheng Chu-yuan, *Taiwan Model and Mainland's Modernization*, Taipei: United Economic Publishing Company, August 1986.

Chiang Ching-kuo, *China's Reunification and the World Peace*, Taipei: China Publishing House, November 1986.

Chiang Kai-shek, *Soviet Russia in China*, London: George G. Harrap & Co., 1957.

*China Directory 1989*, Tokyo: Radiopress, Inc., November 1988.

Chiu Hungdah, (ed.), *China and the Question of Taiwan*, New York: Praeger, 1973.

Chiu Hungdah, (ed.), *Chinese Yearbook of International Law and Affairs, Volume 5 (1985)*, Taipei: The Chinese Society of International Law—Chinese (Taiwan) Branch of the International Law Association, 1986.

Chiu Hungdah and Downen, Robert, (eds.), *Multi-system Nations and International Law: The International Status of Germany, Korea and China*, Baltimore: University of Maryland School of Law, Occasional Papers/Reprints Series in Contemporary Asian Studies, No. 8-1981 (45).

Chiu Hungdah, (ed.), *China and the Taiwan Issue*, New York: Praeger, 1979.

Chiu Hungdah and Leng Shao-chuan, (eds.), *China: Seventy Years After the 1911 Hsin-Hai Revolution*, Charlottesville, Virginia: University Press of Virginia, 1984.

Chang Shuhua, *Communications and China's National Integration: An Analysis of People's Daily and Central Daily News on the China Reunification Issue*, Baltimore, Maryland: Occasional Papers/Reprints Series in Contemporary Asian Studies, School of Law, University of Maryland, No. 5, 1986 (76).

Clough, Ralph N., *Island China*, Cambridge, Mass.: Harvard University Press, 1978.

Cobb, Robert W., and Elder, Charles, *International Community: A Regional and Global Study*, New York: Holt, Rinehart, and Winston, 1970.

Cohen, Jerome Alan and Chiu Hungdah, *People's China and International Law: A Documentary Study, Vol. 1*, Princeton, N.J.: Princeton University Press, 1974.

Coleman, James S. and Rosberg, Carl G. Jr. (eds.), *Political Parties and National Integration in Tropical Africa*, Berkeley, Ca.: University of California Press, 1964.

Crawford, James, *The Creation of States In International Law*, London: Oxford University Press, 1979.

Dahl, Robert A., *A Preface to Democratic Theory*, Chicago, Ill.: University of Chicago Press, 1956.

Deng Xiaoping, *Fundamental Issues In Present-Day China*, Beijing: Foreign Languages Press, 1987.

Deutsch, Karl W., *The Analysis of International Relations*, Englewood Cliffs, N.J.: Prentice-Hall, Inc., 1988.

Deutsch, Karl W., *Nationalism and Its Alternatives*, New York: Alfred A. Knopf, 1969.

Deutsch, Karl W., *Nationalism and Social Communication: An Inquiry*

*Into the Foundations of Nationality*, Cambridge, Mass.: The M.I.T. Press, 1962.

Deutsch, Karl W. et al., *Political Community and the North Atlantic Area: International Organization in the Light of Historical Experience*, Princeton, N.J.: Princeton University Press, 1957.

Deutsch, Karl W., *Political Community at the International Level: Problems of Definition and Measurement*, Garden City, N.Y.: Doubleday & Co., 1954.

Deutsch, Karl W., *Politics and Government: How People Decide Their Fate*, Boston, Mass.: Houghton Mifflin Company, 1980.

Dougherty, James E. and Pfaltzgraff, Robert L. Jr., *Contending Theories of International Relations*, New York: Harper & Row, 1981.

Downen, Robert L., *The Taiwan Pawn in the China Game: Congress to the Rescue*, Washington, D.C.: Georgetown University, 1979.

Eckstein, Harry, *Division and Cohesion in Democracy: A Study of Norway*, Princeton, N.J.: Princeton University Press, 1966.

Eckstein, Harry, *The Evaluation of Political Performance: Problems and Dimensions*, Beverly Hills: Sage Publications, 1971.

Etzioni, Amitai, *Political Unification: A Comparative Study of Leaders and Forces*, New York: Holt, Rinehart and Winston, 1965.

Frankel, Joseph, *Contemporary International Theory and the Behavior of States*, London: Oxford University Press, 1973.

Galenson, Walter, (ed.), *Economic Growth and Structual Change in Taiwan*, Ithaca: Cornell University Press, 1979.

Glahn, Gerhard von, *Law Among Nations: An Introduction to Public International Law*, New York: MacMillan Publishing Co., 1981.

Gold, Thomas B., *State and Society in the Taiwan Miracle*, Armonk, N.Y.: M.E. Sharpe, 1986.

Gregor, A. James, Chang, Maria Hsia, and Zimmerman, Andrew B., *Ideology and Development: Sun Yat-sen and the Economic History of Taiwan*, Berkeley: Institute of East Asian Studies, 1981.

Groom, A. J. R., and Taylor, Paul, (eds.), *Theory and Practice in International Relations: Functionalism*, New York: Crane, Russak, 1975.

Gurr, Ted R. and McClelland, M., *Political Performance: A Twelve-Nation Study*, Beverly Hills: Sage Publications, 1971.

Hague, Rod and Harrop, Martin, *Comparative Government*, London: The MacMillan Press, 1982.

Haas, Ernst B., *The Uniting of Europe: Political, Social, and Economic Forces 1950–1957*, Stanford: Stanford University Press, 1958.

Haas, Ernst B., *Beyond the Nation-State: Functionalism and International Organization*, Stanford, Ca.: Stanford University Press, 1964.

Haas, Ernst B., Williams, Mary Pat, and Babai, Don., *Scientists and World Order: The Uses of Technical Knowledge in International Organizations*, Berkeley: University of California Press, 1977.

Henderson, Gregory, Lebow, Richard Ned, and Stoessinger, John G. (eds.), *Divided Nations In A Divided World*, New York: David Mckay Company, 1974.

Henkin, Louis, Pugh, Richard C., Schachter, Oscar and Smit, Hans, *International Law, Cases and Materials*, St Paul, Minn.: West Publishing Co., 1980.

Hilsman, Roger, *To Move A Nation: The Politics of Foreign Policy In the Administration of John F. Kennedy*, New York: Delta, 1967.

Hitchner, Dell G., and Levine, Carol, *Comparative Government and Politics*, New York: Harper & Row Publishers, 1981.

Holsti, K. J., *International Politics: A Framework for Analysis*, Englewood Cliffs, N.J.: Prentice-Hall, Inc., 1977.

Hsiung, James C., (ed.), *Contemporary Republic of China: The Taiwan Experience 1950–1980*, New York: Praeger Publisher, 1981.

Huntington, Samuel P., *Political Order In Changing Societies*, New Haven: Yale University Press, 1977.

Huntington, Samuel P. and Moore, Clement H., (eds.), *Authoritarian Politics in Modern Society: The Dynamics of Established One-Party Systems*, New York: Basic Books, 1970.

Iriye, Akira, *Across the Pacific: An Inner History of American-East Asia Relations*, New York: Harcourt, Brace, and World, 1967.

Jacob, Philip E. and Toscano, Janes V. (eds.), *The Integration of Political Communities*, Philadelphia: J. B. Lippincott Co., 1964.

Jo Yung-hwan, (ed.), *Taiwan's Future*, Hong Kong: Union Research Institute, 1974.

Johnson, U. Alexis, (ed.), *China Policy for the Next Decade*, Cambridge, Mass.: Oelgeschlager, Gunn and Hain, 1984.

Kim, Samuel S., (ed.), *China and the World: China Foreign Policy in the Post-Mao Era*, Boulder, Colo.: Westview Press, 1984.

Kintner, William R. and Copper John F., *A Matter of Two Chinas*, Philadelphia: Foreign Policy Research Institute, 1979.

Kirgis, Frederic L. Jr., *International Organizations In Their Legal Setting*, St. Paul, Minn.: West Publishing Co., 1977.

Kissinger, Henry A., *White House Years*, Boston: Little, Brown and Company, 1979.

Kornhauser, William, *The Politics of Mass Society*, Glencae, Ill.: Free Press, 1959.

Kuo, Shirley W. Y., Ranis, Gustav, and Fei, John C. H., *The Taiwan Success Story: Rapid Growth With Improved Distribution in the Republic of China, 1954–1979*, Boulder, Colo.: Westview Press, Inc., 1981.

*The Kuomintang: A Brief Introduction 1987–88*, Taipei: Central Committee, the Kuomintang, ROC, 1988.

Kurian, Thomas, (ed.), *The New Book of World Rankings*, New York: Facts on File, Inc., 1984, pp. 79–81.

Kusnitz, Leonard A., *Public Opinion and Foreign Policy: America's*

*China Policy, 1949–1979*, Westport, Conn.: Greenwood Press, 1984.

Lasater, Martin L., *Taiwan: Facing Mounting Threats*, Washington, D.C.: The Heritage Foundation, 1984.

Li, K. T., *The Experience of Dynamic Economic Growth on Taiwan*, Taipei: Meiya, 1976.

Li, Victor H. (ed.), *The Future of Taiwan: A Difference of Opinion*, New York: M.E. Sharpe, Inc., 1980.

Lindberg, Leon N., *The Political Dynamics of European Economic Integration*, Stanford, Ca.: Stanford University Press, 1963.

Lindberg, Leon N., and Scheingold, Stuart A., *Europe's Would-Be Policy: Patterns of Change in the European Community*, Englewood Cliffs, N.J.: Prentice-Hall, 1970.

Lipset, Seymour M., *Political Man: The Social Bases of Politics*, Baltimore: The Johns Hopkins University Press, 1981.

Macridis, Roy C., *Modern Political Regimes: Patterns and Institutions*, Boston, Mass.: Little, Brown & Company, 1986.

Mao Tse-tung, *Selected Works of Mao Tse-tung, Volume II*, Peking: Foreign Languages Press, 1969.

Mao Tse-tung, *Selected Works of Mao Tse-tung, Volume IV*, Peking: Foreign Languages Press, 1975.

Mao Tse-tung, *Selected Works of Mao Tse-tung, Volume V*, Peking: Foreign Languages Press, 1977.

Marx, K. and Engels, F., *The German Ideology—Part One*, London: Lawrence & Wishart, 1970.

*The Military Balance 1988–1989*, London: The International Institute for Strategic Studies, 1988.

Mitrany, David, *A Working Peace System*, Chicago: Quadrangle Books, 1966.

Muller, David G. Jr., *China As A Maritime Power*, Boulder, Colo.: Westview Press, 1983.

Myers, Ramon H., (ed.), *Two Chinese States*, Stanford, Ca.: Hoover International Studies, 1979.

Neville, Betty, (ed.), *The China Factor: Sino-American Relations and the Global Scene*, Englewood Cliffs, N.J.: Prentice-Hall, Inc., 1981.

Nye, Joseph S., *Pan-Africanism and East African Integration*, Cambridge, Mass.: Harvard University Press, 1965.

Nye, Joseph S., *Peace in Parts: Integration and Conflict in Regional Organization*, Boston: Little, Brown, 1971.

Pentland, Charles, *International Theory and European Integration*, London: Faber and Faber, 1973.

Pirages, Dennis, *Managing Political Conflict*, New York: Praeger Publishers, 1976.

Puchala, Donald J., *International Politics Today*, New York: Dodd & Mead, 1971.

Rankin, Karl Lott, *China Assignment*, Seattle: University of Washington Press, 1964.

*Republic of China: A Reference Book*, Taipei: United Pacific International, Inc., July 1983.

*Republic of China 1988: A Reference Book*, Taipei: Hilit Publishing Company, Ltd., 1988.

Roper, Elmo, *You and Your Leaders: Their Actions and Your Reactions, 1936–1956*, New York: William Morrow and Co., 1957.

Russett, Bruce M., *International Regions and the International System: A Study in Political Ecology*, Chicago: Rand McNally, 1967.

Rustow, Dankwart A., *A World of Nations: The Problems of Political Modernization*, Washington, D.C.: Brookings Institution, 1967.

Said, Abdul, (ed.), *Theory of International Relations: The Crisis of Relevance*, Englewook Cliffs, N.J.: Prentice-Hall, 1968.

Sanford, Dan C., *The Future Association of Taiwan With the People's Republic of China*, Berkeley, Ca.: University of Califormia, 1981.

Shaw, Yu-ming, ed., *Power and Policy in the PRC*, Boulder, Colo.: Westview Press, 1985.

Snyder, Glenn H., and Diesing, Paul, *Conflict Among Nations*, Princeton: Princeton University Press, 1977.

Sullivan, Michael P., *International Relations: Theories and Evidence*, Englewood Cliffs, N.J.: Prentice-Hall, 1976.

Sun, Yat-sen, *The Three Principles of the People*, Taipei: China Publishing Co., 1981.

*The Taiwan Issue: Its History and Resolution*, Beijing: Beijing Review, 1987.

Wang Gungwu, *China and the World Since 1949: The Impact of Independence, Modernity and Revolution*, London: The MacMillan Press, 1977.

Weiner, Myron, (ed.), *Modernization: The Dynamics of Growth*, Washington, D.C.: Voice of America Forum Lectures, 1966.

Whetten, Lawrence L., *Germany's Östpolitik*, London: Oxford University Press, 1971.

White, Wilbur W., *White's Political Dictionary*, Cleveland, Ohio: World Publishing Company, 1947.

Wu Yuan-li, *Becoming An Industrialized Nation: ROC's Development on Taiwan*, New York: Praeger, 1985.

Young, Kenneth T., *Negotiating With the Chinese Communists: The United States Experience, 1953–1967*, New York: McGraw-Hill Book Company, 1968.

Zimmern, Alfred, *Modern Political Doctrines*, London: Oxford University Press, 1939.

Zhuang Qubing, Zhang Hongzeng, and Pan Tongwen, *China & the World*, Beijing: Beijing Review Foreign Affairs Series, 1982.

## Chinese-language Books

*A Handbook for Taiwan Compatriots* (台胞探親手冊), Beijing: China Construction Publishing House, 1987.

*The Analysis of the Current Mainland China Situation* (匪情分析),
   Taipei: The General Political Warfare Department, Ministry of the
   National Defense, 30 April 1986.

Chiu Hung-dah and Jen Hsiao-chi, eds., *A Study on the PRC's
   Negotiation Strategy* (中共談判策略研究), Taipei: United Daily News
   Service, 1987.

*The Collected Documents Concerning the Liberation of Taiwan
   (1949–1971)* (中共關於解放台灣的文件集), Hong Kong: The Institute
   of Contemporary China Studies, 1972.

Deng Xiaoping, *Selected Works of Deng Xiaoping (1975–1982)*
   (鄧小平文選), Beijing: People's Publishing House, 1983.

Deng Xiaoping, *Building Socialism With Special Chinese Characteristics*
   (建設具有中國特色的社會主義), Beijing: People's Publishing House, 1985.

*The Dictionary of Contemporary Chinese History* (當代中國歷史辭典),
   Beijing: China International Broadcasting Publishing House,
   December 1987.

*The Dictionary of Political Economy* (政治經濟學小辭典), Hong Kong:
   Chao Young Publishing House, October 1975.

Du Jian, et al., *A Brief History of the People's Liberation Army*
   (中國人民解放軍簡史), Beijing: Soldiner Publishing House, 1982.

Fu Chi-hsueh, *The History of China Diplomacy* (中國外交史), Taipei:
   Taiwan Commercial Publishing House, 1983.

*The Handbook for Trade Between the Mainland and Taiwan*
   (兩岸貿易手冊), Beijing: The Modern Publishing House, 1989.

Hsieh Chang-ting, *Democratic Progressive Party* (民主進步黨), Taipei:
   Free Times Books Series 10, n.d.

Kuo, Warren, *The History of the Chinese Communist Party, Book One*
   (中共史論・第一冊), Taipei: Institute of International Relations,
   September 1969.

Lu Keng, *Debates Concerning the Issues of China's Reunification*
   (統一問題論戰), Hong Kong: Pai-Shing Cultural Company, 1988.

Peng Huai-eng, *The Analysis of the Republic of China's Political
   System* (中華民國政治體系的分析), Taipei: Times Cultural Publishing
   Company, 1987.

*People's Republic of China Year Book 1984* (中華人民共和國年鑑 1984),
   Beijing: Xinhua Publishing House, 1984.

*Reunification of the Motherland Is Everybody's Responsibility*
   (統一祖國人人有責), Beijing: Beijing Publishing House, 1985.

*The Road for China's Reunification* (中國統一之路), Taipei: Central
   Daily News, 1981.

*Taiwan Christian Presbyterian Church Believers Training Handbook*
   (台灣基督長老教會信徒手冊), Tainan, Taiwan: The Headquarters of
   Taiwan Christian Presbyterian Church, 1986.

Tan Fanzhi, (ed.), *The Dictionary of Party's United Front Work*
   (黨的統戰工作辭典), Beijing: China Outlook Publishing House,
   1988.

Wang Yuan, *Communist China's Power Struggle and Policy Struggle* (中共的權力鬥爭與路線鬥爭), Taipei: School of East Asia Studies, National Chengchi University, 1982.

Wei Ming, *Taiwan's February 28 Incident* (台灣二二八事變), Hong Kong: The Seventies Magazine House, 1975.

Wu Li-hui, (ed.), *The Future of Taiwan* (台灣的未來), Kaohsiung: New Taiwan Books Series 1, n.d.

Wu Li-hui, (ed.), *Self-Determination and Independence* (自決與獨立), Kaohsiung: New Taiwan Books Series 5, n.d.

## English-language Papers

Arat, Zehra F., 'Democracy and Economic Development: Modernization Theory Revisited', *Comparative Politics*, 21, 2, October (1988): 21–34. (USA)

Barnett, Robert W., 'China and Taiwan: The Economic Issues', *Foreign Affairs*, 50, 3, April (1972): 444–458. (USA)

Bellows, Thomas J., 'Normalization: A Taiwan Perspective', *Asian Affairs*, 6, 6, July/August (1979): 339–358. (USA)

Burns, John P., 'The Process of Assimilation of Hong Kong (1997) and Implications for Taiwan', *AEI Foreign Policy and Defense Review*, 6, 3, (1986): 19–25. (USA)

Caporaso, James A. and Pelowski, Alan L., 'Economic and Political Integration in Europe: A Time-Series Quasi-Experimental Analysis', *American Political Science Review*, 65, 2, June (1975): 421–422. (USA)

Chang, Parris H., 'Evolution of Taiwan's Political Leadership After Chiang Ching-kuo', *AEI Foreign Policy and Defense Review*, 6, 3, (1986),: 10–18. (USA)

Chang Parris H., 'Taiwan In 1982: Diplomatic Setback Abroad and Demands for Reforms at Home', *Asian Survey*, XXIII, 1, January (1983): 38–46. (USA)

Chao Chien-min, ' "One Country, Two Systems": A Theoretical Analysis', *Asian Affairs*, Summer (1987):. 107–124. (USA)

Chen Chi-di, 'On Its Own—the Republic of China', *Asian Affairs*, Fall (1983): 54–69. (USA)

Cheng Chu-yuan, 'China's Economy: New Strategies and Dilemmas,' *Current History*, 87,530, September (1988): 253–256, 281, 302–304. (USA)

Cheng Chu-yuan, 'Economic Reform in Mainland China: Consequences and Prospects', a paper presented to the '15th Sino-American Conference on Mainland China', held by the Institute of the International Relations (IIR), Taipei, June 8–12, 1986. (ROC)

Chiou, C. L., 'Dilemmas in China's Reunification Policy Toward Taiwan', *Asian Survey*, 26:4, April (1986): 467–482. (USA)

Chou, David S., 'International Status of the Republic of China', a paper presented at the Conference on Some Issues of International Law and Affairs, held by Institute of Asia and the World, Taipei, Taiwan, R.O.C., 30 August 1986.

Chou, Yangsun and Nathan, Andrew J., 'Democratizing Transition In Taiwan', *Asian Survey*, 27, 3, March (1987): 277–299. (USA)

Copper, John F., 'Taiwan In 1986: Back on Top Again', *Asian Survey*, XXVII, 1, January (1987): 81–91. (USA)

Copper, John F., 'Taiwan: New Challenges to Development', *Current History*, April (1986): 168–171 and 183. (USA)

Crozier, Brian, 'The Art of Survival', *National Review*, 6 December (1974):1401–3. (USA)

Davies, James C., 'Toward A Theory of Revolution', *American Sociological Review*, No. 27:1, February (1962): 5–19. (USA)

Deibel, Terry L., 'A Guide to International Divorce', *Foreign Policy*, Spring (1978): 27–32. (USA)

Deutsch, Karl W., 'Social Mobilization and Political Development', *American Political Science Review*, September (1961): 493–514. (USA)

Domes, Jurgen, 'Political Differentiation in Taiwan: Group Formation Within the Ruling Party and the Opposition Circle 1979–1980', *Asian Survey*, XXI, 10, October (1981): 1011–1028. (USA)

Durdin, Tillman, 'The View From Taiwan', *Asian Affairs*, 8, 1, September/October (1980): 1–5. (USA)

Fairbank, John K., 'China: Time for A Policy', *Atlantic Monthly*, April (1957): 35–39. (USA)

Frankel, Joseph, 'Taiwan—The Most Stable Part of China?' *The World Today*, June (1976): 199–202. (UK)

Galtung, Johan, 'A Structural Theory of Integration', *Journal of Peace Research*, 5, 4, (1968): 377. (USA)

Gold, Thomas B., 'The Status Quo Is Not Static: Mainland-Taiwan Relations', *Asian Survey*, XXVII, 3, March (1987): 300–15. (USA)

Haas, Ernst B., 'The Study of Regional Integration: Reflections on the Joy and Anguish of Pretheorising', *International Organization*, 24, 4, Autumn (1970): 607–646. (USA)

Haas, Ernst B., 'Turbulent Fields and the Theory of Regional Integration,' *Interntaional Organization*, 30, 2, Spring 1976, pp. 173–212. (USA)

Haas, Ernst B., 'The Uniting of Europe and the Uniting of Latin America', *Journal of Common Market Studies*, June (1967): 315–343. (UK)

Hayward, Fred M., 'Continuities and Discontinuities Between Studies of National and International Political Integration: Some Implications for Future Research Efforts', *International Organization*, 24, 4, Autumn (1970): 917–941. (USA)

Hollingworth, Clare, 'More Talk of "One Country: Two Systems"', *Pacific Defense Reporter*, January (1989): 59–60. (Japan)

Holsti, K. J., 'Underdevelopment and the Gap Theory of International Conflict', *American Political Science Review*, No. LXIX, 3, September (1975): 827–839. (USA)

Hsiao, Frank S. T. and Sullivan, Lawrence R., 'The Politics of Reunification: Beijing's Initiative on Taiwan', *Asian Survey*, 20, 8, August (1980): 789–802. (USA)

Hsiung, James C., 'The Hong Kong Settlement: Effects on Taiwan and Prospects for Peking's Reunification Bid', *Asian Affairs*, Summer (1985): 47–58. (USA)

Hsiung, James C., 'The Uneasy Tranquility Across the Taiwan Strait', a paper presented at the Conference on Major Current Issues in East Asia, at St. John's University, New York, USA, October 25–26, 1985. (USA)

Hsiung, James C., 'Reagan's China Policy and the Sino-Soviet Detente', *Asian Affairs*, 11, 2, Summer (1984): 1–11. (USA)

Huan Guocang, 'Taiwan: A View From Beijing', *Foreign Affairs*, 63, 5, Summer (1985): 1064–1080. (USA)

Huan Xiang, 'On Sino-U.S. Relations', *Foreign Affairs*, 60, 1, Fall (1981): 35–53. (USA)

Inglehart, Ronald, 'An End to European Integration?' *American Political Science Review*, LXI, 1, March (1967): 91–105. (USA)

Johnston, Ray E., 'Alternative Frameworks for Assessing the International Status of Multi-System Nations: Germany, Korea, China/Taiwan', *The Journal of East Asian Affairs*, 11, 1, Spring/Summer (1982): 90–123. (South Korea)

Lee, Edmund, 'Beijing's Balancing Act', *Foreign Policy*, Summer (1983): 40–47. (USA)

Lindberg, Leon N., 'Political Integration As A Multidimensional Phenomenon Requiring Multivariate Measurement', *International Organization*, 24, 4, Autumn (1970): 649–731. (USA)

Nau, Henry R., 'From Integration to Interdependence: Gains, Losses, and Continuing Gaps', *International Organization*, 33, 1, Winter (1979): 119–147. (USA)

Neibuhr, Reinhold, 'China and the United Nations,' *Journal of International Affairs*, May (1957): 185–192. (USA)

Nixon, Richard M., 'Asia After Vietnam', *Foreign Affairs*, No. 46:1, October (1967): 111–125. (USA)

Nye, Joseph S., 'Comparative Regional Integration: Concept and Measurement', *International Organization*, XXII, 4, Autumn (1968): 855–880. (USA)

Puchala, Donald J., 'Integration and Disintegration in Franco-German Relations, 1954–1965', *International Organization*, 24, 2, Spring (1970): 183–208. (USA)

Puchala, Donald J., 'International Transactions and Regional Integration', *International Organization*, 24, 4, Autumn (1970): 732–763. (USA)

Pye, Lucian W., 'Taiwan Developments and Their Implications for US-PRC Relations', *The Rand Publications Series*, N–2138, March (1984): 1–132. (USA)

Shaw Yu-ming, 'Taiwan: A View From Taipei', *Foreign Affairs*, 63, 5, Summer (1985): 1055–1063 (USA)

Shaw Yu-ming, 'The Republic of China's Response to International Developments', *Issues & Studies*, 21, 7, July (1985): 12–31. (ROC)

Schmitter, Phillippe C., 'Three Neo-functional Hypotheses About International Integration', *International Organization*, XXIII, 1, Winter (1969): 161–166. (USA)

Simon, Denis Fred, 'Taiwan's Political Economy and the Evolving Links Between the PRC, Hong Kong, and Taiwan', *AEI Foreign Policy and Defense Review*, 6, 3, (1986): 42–50. (USA)

Solomon, Richard H., 'East Asia and the Great Power Coalitions,' *Foreign Affairs*, 60, 3, Special Copy (1981): 686–718. (USA)

Taylor, Paul, 'The Functionalist Approach to the Problem of International Order: A Defence', *Political Studies*, XVI, 3, (1968): 393–410. (UK)

Weiner, Myron, 'Political Integration and Political Development', *The Annals of the American Academy of Political and Social Science 358*, March (1964): 52–64. (USA)

Weng, Byron S. J., 'Taiwan's International Status Today', *The China Quarterly*, No. 99, September (1984): 462–480. (UK)

Wilson, Dick, 'Hands Across the Straits', *Asia Pacific Community*, Fall (1980): 35–50. (Japan)

Winckler, Edwin A., 'Institutionalization and Participation on Taiwan: From Hard to Soft Authoritarianism?' *The China Quarterly*, No. 99, September (1984): 481–499. (UK)

Wu An-chia, '"One Country, Two Systems": A Model for Taiwan?' *Issues & Studies*, No. 21, 7, July (1985): 33–59. (ROC)

Yee, Herbert S., 'China's Reunification Offensive and Taiwan's Policy Options', *The World Today*, January (1982): 33–38. (UK)

Yin Ching-yao, 'The Bitter Struggle Between the KMT and the CCP', *Asian Survey*, XXI, 6, June (1981): 622–631. (USA)

Zhao Quansheng, 'An Analysis of Unification—The PRC Perspective', *Asian Survey*, 23, 10, October (1983): 1095–1113. (USA)

## Chinese-language Papers

Chen Li-shen, 'On the Strategy of Communist China's United Front,' *Mainland China* ( 中國大陸 ), June (1986): 14–17. (ROC)

Chen Linsheng, 'A New Undertaking of Socialist Practice in Our Country—a Preliminary Discussion on "One Country, Two Systems"', *Social Science Monthly* ( 社會科學月刊 ), No. 11, 15 November (1984): 36–8. (PRC)

Din Li, 'From the Trend of World Economic Development to See the Important Strategic Decision-Making of "One Country, Two Systems', *Journal of Henan University* (Social Science Edition), ( 河南大學學報哲學社會科學版 ), No. 3, (1986): 10–15. (PRC)

Guan Mengiue, 'The Issue of "Two Systems In One Nation"' and the Expansion of the Patriotic United Front', *Jilin University Journal*

*Bimonthly* (Social Science Edition) (吉林大學學報哲學社會科學版), No. 4, (1985): 1–4. (PRC)

Li Shenzhi and Zi Zongyun, 'Taiwan In the Next Decade', *Taiwan Studies Quarterly* (台灣研究季刊), No. 1, (1988): 1–5. (PRC)

Li Zhiping, 'A Brief Remark About the Characteristics of the Patriotic United Front in the New Stage', *Jilin University Journal Bimonthly* (Social Science Edition) (吉林大學學報哲學社會科學版), No. 5, (1985): 58 and 60. (PRC)

Liu Sheng-gi, 'The CCP's Responses Toward the KMT's 13th Party Congress', *Mainland China Study* (中國大陸研究), No. 31:2, August (1988): 5–11. (ROC)

Tian Zhili, 'A Summary of the Symposium on the Theory of International Relations', *Political Science Bimonthly* (政治科學雙月刊), No. 6, (1987): 54–60. (PRC)

Wu Hsin-hsing, 'Integration Theory and the Reunification of China,' *Issues & Studies* (問題與研究), April (1989): 73–85. (ROC)

Xu Xianzhang, 'On the Mission of the New Period's United Front', *Journal of the Northwestern Teachers College* (西北師範學院學報), No. 2, (1985): 29. (PRC)

Yang Jiagi, 'The Scientific Meaning of "One Country, Two Systems" and Its Characteristics', *Hongchi* (Red Flag) (紅旗), 16 March (1986): 18–20. (ROC)

Yang Jingling, 'On Taiwan Studies', *Fujian Journal* (福建學刊), January 1987, pp. 60–61. (PRC)

Yi Hua, 'On the PRC's United Front Activities', *Mainland China* (中國大陸), June (1986): 24. (ROC)

## English-language Periodicals

| | |
|---|---|
| *Backgrounder* (Taipei, American Institute in Taiwan) | (USA) |
| *Beijing Review* (Peking Review before 1979) (BR or PR) | (PRC) |
| *China Reconstructs* | (PRC) |
| *The Economist* | (UK) |
| *Far Eastern Economic Review* (FEER) | (HK) |
| *International Business Week* | (USA) |
| *National Geographic* | (USA) |
| *Newsweek* | (USA) |
| *Olympic Review* | |
| *US News & World Report* | (USA) |

## Chinese-language Periodicals

| | | |
|---|---|---|
| *Cheng Ming* | (爭鳴月刊) | (HK) |
| *China Spring* | (中國之春) | (USA) |
| *China Times Weekly* | (時報新聞周刊) | (ROC) |
| *China Tribune* | (中國論壇) | (ROC) |

| | | |
|---|---|---|
| *Chinese Magazine* | ( 中華雜誌 ) | (ROC) |
| *Commonwealth* | ( 天下 ) | (ROC) |
| *Democratic Progressive News* | (民進報周刊) | (ROC) |
| *Global Views Monthly* | ( 遠見 ) | (ROC) |
| *Hong Kong Economic Journal Monthly* | (香港經濟導報) | (HK) |
| *Industry and Commerce Monthly* | ( 工商雜誌 ) | (ROC) |
| *Jin Bao Monthly* | ( 鏡報月刊 ) | (HK) |
| *The Journalist* | ( 新新聞 ) | (ROC) |
| *Ming Bao Monthly* | ( 明報月刊 ) | (HK) |
| *The Nineties (The Seventies* prior to 1980) | ( 九十年代 ) | (HK) |
| *Outlook Weekly, Overseas Edition (OW(OE))* | ( 瞭望，海外版 ) | (PRC) |
| *Pai Shing Semi-Monthly* | (百姓半月刊) | (HK) |
| *Taishin Magazine* | ( 台聲雜誌 ) | (PRC) |
| *Wide Angle* | ( 廣角鏡 ) | (HK) |

## English-language Newspapers

| | |
|---|---|
| *The Age* | (Australia) |
| *The Asian Wall Street Journal* | (HK) |
| *The Australian* | (Australia) |
| *China News* | (ROC) |
| *The Christian Science Monitor* | (USA) |
| *Financial Review* | (Australia) |
| *The Free China Journal* | (ROC) |
| *Hong Kong Standard* | (HK) |
| *International Herald Tribune* | (USA) |
| *The New York Times* | (USA) |
| *South China Morning Post* | (HK) |
| *The Times* | (UK) |
| *The Washington Post* | (USA) |

## Chinese-language Newspapers

| | | |
|---|---|---|
| *Central Daily News* (CDN) | ( 中央日報 ) | (ROC) |
| *Central Daily News, International Edition* (CDN(IE)) | (中央日報，國際版) | (ROC) |
| *China Times* | ( 中國時報 ) | (ROC) |
| *China Times Express* | ( 中時晚報 ) | (ROC) |
| *Commercial Times* | ( 工商時報 ) | (ROC) |
| *Economic Daily News* | ( 經濟日報 ) | (ROC) |
| *The Great China Evening News* | ( 大華晚報 ) | (ROC) |
| *The Independence Morning Post* | ( 自立早報 ) | (ROC) |
| *The Independence Evening Post* | ( 自立晚報 ) | (ROC) |
| *Jinji Ribao* | ( 經濟日報 ) | (PRC) |

| | | |
|---|---|---|
| *Kuanming Ribao* | （光明日報） | (PRC) |
| *Renmin Ribao* (RMRB) | （人民日報） | (PRC) |
| *Renmin Ribao, Overseas Edition* | | |
| (RMRB(OE)) | （人民日報・海外版） | (PRC) |
| *Ta Kung Po* | （大公報） | (HK) |
| *United Daily News* | （聯合報） | (ROC) |
| *Wen Wei Po* | （文匯報） | (HK) |
| *Yangcheng Wanbao* | （羊城晚報） | (PRC) |
| *Youth Daily News* | （青年日報） | (ROC) |

# Index